TRANSATLANTIC CULTURE IN THE LONG NINETEENTH CENTURY

New Approaches to International History

Series Editor: Thomas Zeiler, Professor of American Diplomatic History, University of Colorado Boulder, USA

Series Editorial Board:
Anthony Adamthwaite, University of California at Berkeley (USA)
Kathleen Burk, University College London (UK)
Louis Clerc, University of Turku (Finland)
Petra Goedde, Temple University (USA)
Francine McKenzie, University of Western Ontario (Canada)
Lien-Hang Nguyen, University of Kentucky (USA)
Jason Parker, Texas A&M University (USA)
Glenda Sluga, University of Sydney (Australia)

New Approaches to International History covers international history during the modern period and across the globe. The series incorporates new developments in the field, such as the cultural turn and transnationalism, as well as the classical high politics of state-centric policymaking and diplomatic relations. Written with upper-level undergraduate and postgraduate students in mind, texts in the series provide an accessible overview of international diplomatic and transnational issues, events, and actors.

Published:
Decolonization and the Cold War, edited by Leslie James and Elisabeth Leake (2015)
Cold War Summits, Chris Tudda (2015)
The United Nations in International History, Amy L. Sayward (2017)
Latin American Nationalism, James F. Siekmeier (2017)
The History of United States Cultural Diplomacy, Michael L. Krenn (2017)
International Cooperation in the Early 20th Century, Daniel Gorman (2017)
Women and Gender in International History, Karen Garner (2018)
International Development, Corinna R. Unger (2018)
The Environment and International History, Scott Kaufman (2018)
Scandinavia and the Great Powers in the First World War, Michael Jonas (2019)
Canada and the World since 1867, Asa McKercher (2019)
The First Age of Industrial Globalization, Maartje Abbenhuis and Gordon Morrell (2019)
Europe's Cold War Relations, Federico Romero, Kiran Klaus Patel, Ulrich Krotz (2019)
United States Relations with China and Iran, Osamah F. Khalil (2019)
Public Opinion and Twentieth-Century Diplomacy, Daniel Hucker (2020)
Globalizing the US Presidency, Cyrus Schayegh (2020)
The International LGBT Rights Movement, Laura A. Belmonte (2021)
Global War, Global Catastrophe, Maartje Abbenhuis and Ismee Tames (2021)
America's Road to Empire (2021)
Militarization and the American Century, David Fitzgerald (2022)

American Sport in International History, Daniel M. DuBois (2023)
Rebuilding the Postwar Order, Francine McKenzie (2023)
Soldiers in Peacemaking, Beatrice de Graaf, Frédéric Dessberg, and Thomas Vaisset (2023)
From World War to Postwar, Andrew N. Buchanan (2023)
The Fear of Chinese Power, Jeffrey Crean (2024)
A Diplomatic History of US Immigration during the 20th Century, Benjamin C. Montoya (2024)
Climate Change and International History, Ruth A. Morgan (2024)

Forthcoming:
China and the United States since 1949, Elizabeth Ingles
Sparking the Cold War, John McNay
The United States and the Ends of Empire, Sean T. Byrnes

TRANSATLANTIC CULTURE IN THE LONG NINETEENTH CENTURY

ANGLO-AMERICAN RELATIONS AND INTERTWINED IDENTITIES

Howard LeRoy Malchow

BLOOMSBURY ACADEMIC
LONDON • NEW YORK • OXFORD • NEW DELHI • SYDNEY

BLOOMSBURY ACADEMIC

Bloomsbury Publishing Plc, 50 Bedford Square, London, WC1B 3DP, UK
Bloomsbury Publishing Inc, 1359 Broadway, New York, NY 10018, USA
Bloomsbury Publishing Ireland, 29 Earlsfort Terrace, Dublin 2, D02 AY28, Ireland

BLOOMSBURY, BLOOMSBURY ACADEMIC and the Diana logo are
trademarks of Bloomsbury Publishing Plc

First published in Great Britain 2026

Copyright © Howard LeRoy Malchow, 2026

Howard LeRoy Malchow has asserted his right under the Copyright,
Designs and Patents Act, 1988, to be identified as Author of this work.

Series design by Catherine Wood.
Cover image: Side by side – Britannia! Britain's Day Dec. 7th 1918 / James Montgomery Flagg
from the Library of Congress

All rights reserved. No part of this publication may be: i) reproduced or transmitted in any form, electronic or mechanical, including photocopying, recording or by means of any information storage or retrieval system without prior permission in writing from the publishers; or ii) used or reproduced in any way for the training, development or operation of artificial intelligence (AI) technologies, including generative AI technologies. The rights holders expressly reserve this publication from the text and data mining exception as per Article 4(3) of the Digital Single Market Directive (EU) 2019/790.

Bloomsbury Publishing Plc does not have any control over, or responsibility for, any third-party websites referred to or in this book. All internet addresses given in this book were correct at the time of going to press. The author and publisher regret any inconvenience caused if addresses have changed or sites have ceased to exist, but can accept no responsibility for any such changes.

A catalogue record for this book is available from the British Library.

A catalog record for this book is available from the Library of Congress.

ISBN:	HB:	978-1-3505-6264-6
	PB:	978-1-3505-6263-9
	ePDF:	978-1-3505-6266-0
	eBook:	978-1-3505-6265-3

Series: New Approaches to International History

Typeset by Integra Software Services Pvt. Ltd.
Printed and bound in Great Britain

For product safety related questions please contact productsafety@bloomsbury.com.

To find out more about our authors and books visit www.bloomsbury.com
and sign up for our newsletters.

CONTENTS

List of Figures	viii
Preface	ix

Introduction: The Nineteenth-Century Transatlantic World — 1

1 Divided by a Common Language — 9
  1. A War of Words — 9
  2. Americanisms — 22
  3. Standard English? Coalescence, Coexistence, and Shifting Hegemonies — 38

2 Theatre/Theater — 55
  1. Transatlantic Relations: American Theater and the British — 59
  2. Daggers Drawn — 71
  3. Performing Americanness (and Britishness) — 77
  4. "The Great Wet Way": Theater and the Growth of a Transnational Industry — 84

3 Tableaux of Race — 93
  1. The Performance of Race — 96
  2. Slavery on the Anglo-American Stage from *Uncle Tom's Cabin* to *The Octoroon* — 114
  3. Anglo-American Racial Representation in the Mid- and Late-Victorian Era — 119

4 The Far West: Imagining, Seeing, Performing — 135
  1. Westward Ho! — 135
  2. The American West in Late-Victorian Britain — 155
  3. Cowboy Anglo-Saxonism — 166

5 Transatlantic Birthright: "A Pilgrimage of the Heart" — 175
  1. The American in Britain — 178
  2. American Anglophilia and the Royals — 189
  3. The Boston Forbeses — 198

Summation and Epilogue — 213

Notes — 219
Select Bibliography — 261
Index — 265

FIGURES

1	"Side-by-Side—Britannia" (1918), by James Montgomery Flagg [Library of Congress]	83
2	"Slaves Waiting for Sale" (1861), by Eyre Crowe [Alamy]	122
3	Charles William Wilson, photo *c.* 1860 [Alamy]	145
4	"Visitors to the National Gallery" (*c.* 1874), by James Jacques Joseph Tissot [Alamy]	180
5	Harvard House, Stratford-upon-Avon [Alamy]	187
6	Thomas Carlyle and R. E. Forbes, photo 1872 [National Portrait Gallery, London]	200
7	John Murray Forbes [Alamy]	203

PREFACE

This collection of essays on Anglo-American cultural relations in the long nineteenth century, the product of several years of teaching and writing about transatlantic history, in a sense follows back from an earlier work of mine on post-Second World War Anglo-American popular culture (*Special Relations: The Americanization of Britain?* [Stanford University Press, 2011]). It has been greatly informed by my students and colleagues. Special thanks must be given to Professors John Fyler, Laurence Senelick, James Rice, Kendra Field, Melanie Hall, and Beatrice Forbes Manz, and to Andrea Forbes Schoenfeld from whose close reading of the section on the Forbeses I greatly profited. Also Nate Therien. Among my students whose research has explored aspects of these themes, I am indebted to Charles Driver. As always, the library services at Tufts University have greatly facilitated my research. Special thanks must also go to the librarians at the Massachusetts Historical Society and the British Library.

Tufts University
January, 2025

Please note this book deals in places with language that we rightly find insulting and abusive in the twenty-first century. As a study of Anglo-American discourse that addresses, in part, the language of racism, these terms are only used when they are drawn from and address common nineteenth-century usage.

INTRODUCTION: THE NINETEENTH-CENTURY TRANSATLANTIC WORLD

Anglo-American relations, from the era of the Revolution and early Republic to that of the so-called great rapprochement at the turn of the next century, have been commonly approached through the history of foreign relations and an often tense political relationship that reflects differing national identities—popular-democratic and local on the one hand and imperial-global on the other. By bringing forward cultural rather than political relations and by examining a variety of sites in the transatlantic world, this study deals as much with similarity and hybridity as with difference. While a perceived dissimilarity sometimes became the touchstone of particular national and imperial projects, it may be argued that the American *and* British insistence on heightening national difference was itself at some deeper level a response to greater familiarity within the tightening transatlantic net. This study explores ways in which cultural self-awareness and cultural performance may simultaneously express *both* similarity and difference, affinity and aversion.[1]

"Culture," as used here, is loosely rather than narrowly defined and ranges across both high and low, formal and popular aspects of American and British mutual awareness. An important element in this search is the understanding that culture is more than material things; it also importantly concerns how these things are *read*, that is consumed and integrated into common life, and how readings are *performed*—literally as in the theater and allusively and internally in private, domestic, and public life. Of course, we cannot hope to treat comprehensively the whole of transatlantic social and cultural interrelations for more than a century of thickening mutual perception and misperception. This exploration might rather be regarded, using a somewhat old-fashioned phrase, as "chapters in" rather than a total history of transatlantic exchange, highly selective topics chosen to corroborate and advance the thesis that national narratives (and especially the American narrative of its self-created exceptionalism) need to be reopened and reexamined.

This study is sensitive to and informed by the "transnational turn" in historical scholarship.[2] It may however be objected that, in a nineteenth-century world drawing closer by transportation, communication, commercial exchange and consumerism, capital export, and immigration, we continue here to privilege the *Anglo-American* transatlantic exchange in an era of a much wider transnational *globalization*. Or that, even in the realm of the transatlantic, many institutions—such as that of slavery—might be better pursued within a broader Western hemispheric, European, and African Atlantic world. This book does not propose an alternative to such wider analyses, but rather seeks to highlight and retrieve the *special* importance of Anglo-American cultural exchange in the evolution of both British and American national life.

These chapters assume that influence was almost always a two-way street, a reciprocity that neither of the particular disciplines of American and British studies has much cared to center. It was a commonplace in the nineteenth century that America should be a beacon to the world, and often American Studies seems to deal less with exchange than with explicating the emergence and growth of the essentially American character unbound by the Old World from which it sprang. At the same time, British studies, when looking beyond the insular domestic, has either been prone to regard the export of British culture as simply a part of its imperial presence in the world, or, more recently and with more complexity and sophistication, to dwell on the interweaving of the domestic and the colonial, to draw the colonies and the Raj back into the cultural and social history of the metropolis. "The empire strikes back" mode of analysis privileges imperial social, cultural, and racial relations in the Caribbean, Africa, and east of Suez. It might do more to draw the United States back into the Anglo-world of the nineteenth and early twentieth centuries. America was not merely, by invitation, an informal part of the far-flung dominions which those such as the young Charles Wentworth Dilke included in their itineraries of empire-tourism. It was more directly a daily "presence" that to a degree at least contested or confirmed, and thus helped to shape, domestic cultural, social, and political life and discourse in Britain.

Chapter 1 begins with language itself. American linguistic difference became a preoccupation in both old Britain and the new Republic, especially in the proliferation of dictionaries both in Britain and in America. There was a heightened concern to confirm, explicate, condemn, provide apologia for, or celebrate a peculiarly American vocabulary, grammar, and accent. For the British, this project can be located within a domestic context, well-established by the end of the eighteenth century, of advancing and codifying the polite speech of southern, metropolitan England; Yankee, back-woods-western, and southern dialects were thus not only understood as exotic and peculiarly American by British standards, but also carried some of the same sense of provinciality untutored by "correct" speech that made the regional vocabulary and pronunciation of Lancashire and Yorkshire increasingly unacceptable.

Language leads us to the oral realm of public readings and lectures, the shared theater of political oratory and evangelical crusades, and also to the missionary rhetoric of transatlantic abolitionism, temperance, and feminism, and to the actual world of the stage. Chapter 2 explores transatlantic aspects of nineteenth-century theater—the anglophone universe of playwrights, star actors (and their often excitable publics), actor-managers, impresarios and agents, and troupes that traveled across an ocean that steamships made ever more regularly and conveniently a bridge rather than a barrier. As more generally in economic and political relations, by the end of the century the world of transatlantic theater which had expressed from the days of the early Republic a kind of British cultural hegemony saw signs of a shift from American dependence to American influence and a degree of Americanization of the "business" of organizing what had become a transatlantic theatrical industry.

Chapter 3 addresses the wider issues of a shifting transatlantic discourse about race, in especially the memoirs of British tourists, in the rhetoric of traveling abolitionists whose lectures shared an element of the stagecraft of the theatrical world, and in the *performance* of race in low comedy and minstrelsy. While the slave narratives of the many Black Americans such as Frederick Douglass who crossed the Atlantic on tour are also treated, the focus here is chiefly on the white construction of race. And so to the theater of race in, of course most notably, the many staged versions of Harriet Beecher Stowe's "Uncle Tom's Cabin" or Dion Boucicault's "The Octoroon," an adaptation of Thomas Mayne Reid's novel *The Quadroon*. If the American Civil War deeply divided British opinion, it was also almost universally portrayed and understood as a theater of tragedy. By the era of Reconstruction, however, popular British representation of America quickly abandoned the familiar charge of hypocrisy. This had been the staple of antebellum abolitionists, English monthlies, and visiting Britons such as Dickens. British visitors come to endorse a transcontinental America of westward "prospects" in which Jim Crow America shared with imperial Britain the "problem" of post-abolition race relations. In some ways—in matters especially of race and empire—Britain and America, or at least their financial, commercial, and professional elites, came to share a world-view as never before, to speak, as it were, the same language.

Chapter 4 carries the theme of performance on to a wider stage, examining the romance of British, often aristocratic, hunters, cowboys, and flaneurs in the American West, and, in Britain, the popular dramatizations offered by visiting cowboy entertainments such as, most famously, those organized by "Buffalo Bill" Cody. Fin de siècle adventure fiction, war in South Africa and in Cuba and the Philippines, American (and Australian) anti-Asian immigration movements, tourism, and nostalgia conspired to advance an ideology of Anglo-American "Anglo-Saxonism." In part inspired by this sense of elite affinity, American new wealth built mansions and filled them, as Linda Colley has recently reminded us, with "British and Irish stuff—furniture, paintings, silver, sculpture, entire rooms gutted out of country houses."[3]

The concluding chapter 5 begins with the great wave of American tourism to Britain that marked the late nineteenth and early twentieth centuries, often a search for family heritage or "birthright" that saw nostalgic associations made concrete in the preservation and endowment of Anglo-American memorial sites and institutions. Anglophilia can also be found in the deep regard many in America expressed for the British royal family—if not for the landed British aristocracy. Queen Victoria was popularly admired in America and was widely eulogized in the American press on her passing in 1901. The section concludes with a brief consideration of the extended Forbes family of Milton Hill near Boston and their sense of Anglo-Scottish provenance and reconnection.

Some Sources

The politics of nineteenth-century Anglo-American relations can hardly be said to be neglected. Bradford Perkins' four detailed volumes have long dominated the field of early and late nineteenth-century Anglo-American diplomacy and foreign policy.[4] The key flash-points of transatlantic crisis—the long-smoldering issues of impressment, blockade, and freedom of the seas, the War of 1812, the evolution of the Monroe Doctrine, the American Civil War and the subsequent claims of the *Alabama* arbitration, or the Venezuelan affair have each attracted a continuing and substantial scholarship. Though the older studies generally paid some attention to "public opinion" and the press, and to economic factors, only relatively recently has there been sustained interest in embedding foreign relations more deeply in their social, cultural, and Atlantic-world contexts.

Beyond diplomacy and foreign relations, there has long been interest in the transatlantic character of a host of nineteenth-century political and moral reform movements—often bound together with the history of Anglo-American nonconformity and especially the Society of Friends. The movement to abolish the slave trade and slavery is most prominent in this regard and the subject of an exhaustive historiography, not only because the movement was nurtured by a decades-long Anglo-American cross-traffic but also because it intersects in its personnel, rhetoric, and tactics with other progressive movements—most notably with early- and mid-nineteenth-century feminism and women's suffrage. Though this literature is extensive and of interest to us, it suffered from a certain staleness. The cultural turn of the last generation or so of scholarship opened up fresh connections and interesting applications, with attention now paid to the transatlantic agency of free black people and new approaches to the astounding transatlantic career of Harriet Beecher Stowe's most "mutable book."[5]

Post-modern, post-colonial literary and historical analysis, with its interest in mentalities, beneath-the-text readings, and sub-altern agency, has spoken most directly to European imperialism and the resistance of the colonized. It has, however, not always been a good fit with the nineteenth-century Anglo-American relationship. While most pronounced in American literary studies and on themes of race and imperialism, these approaches have nevertheless had some constructive impact on transatlantic studies in a century where an assertive new Republic remained uncomfortably both within and outside the sphere of British influence. An example is Elisa Tamarkin's impressive work on Anglophilia in the era before the American Civil War.[6] Studies centering Anglo-American cultural and social interrelations however are generally focused within a particular, circumscribed era or topic and remain likely to treat the subject from within an American perspective. They deal more commonly with the American reception of British influence than with the problematic of British reception and consumption of things American—as one might expect in a nineteenth-century world where Britain was regarded as the dominant global power and America as vulnerable to the coercive informal imperialism of British economic and cultural hegemony. A sense and fear of vulnerability behind a brash assertiveness is perhaps a common post-colonial phenomenon. A dominant motif in American studies has often been the combative creation of an "American identity" through what Kariann Yokota has described as the complicated, often contradictory, and incomplete process of "unbecoming British."[7]

Introduction: The Nineteenth-Century Transatlantic World

If much of the historiography of transatlanticism has revolved around issues of American identity and American perception, emulation, transmutation, or rejection of things British, there has long been some interest, not only among historians, in how the British engaged, responded to, filtered, and accepted or rejected the various "lessons" offered by their reading of American politics and culture. British attitudes toward America and American culture after the Revolution is a large field. Much was written in the Tory and Whig monthlies by early-nineteenth-century commentators, most of whom found much to criticize in American politics and in American social character generally. As, however, Britain itself advanced through the various stages of constitutional and social reform in the long nineteenth century, there emerged a scholarly habit, from Bagehot to Bryce, of searching for American precedent and parallel experience. The first historical studies of the influence of American democracy in Britain, often written by American or British scholars of the left, were informed by such comparative approaches. There has remained a continuing historiography of this kind. Rather less has been done with the influence of British liberal thought and practice in America, partly because the central nostrums of liberal Britain, Free Trade and the gold standard, were problematic for American political economy. Nevertheless, many progressive Americans such as the young Woodrow Wilson nursed an Anglophilic regard for the most famous of British liberal statesmen, William Ewart Gladstone.

Of the several themes of transatlantic relations touched upon in this study that have a substantial archival presence and historiography, perhaps the most useful for our purposes is that of Anglo-American tourism, the back and forth of visitors who burdened library and shop shelves on both sides of the Atlantic with perhaps a half-thousand published memoirs of their travels. Mostly these were the journals of British people making, as transport became safer, more regular, and more comfortable, what came to be routine explorations of a still strange if no longer, except in the western wildernesses, exotic American hinterland. As Emily Catherine Bates asked in her own travel memoir of 1887, "what is there left to say on such well-beaten ground? … It is the same old sheep, but we may serve it with a fresh sauce," which she did—in two volumes.[8] There were also, as the century progressed, ever more Americans who traveled to Britain as tourists, some perhaps en route to Paris and Rome, and others in search of a heritage-confirming Mother Country.

The tourist traffic in both directions, as revealed in what became a prominent literary genre of the century, offers an important primary source for this study, as it long has for early- and mid-twentieth-century historians and literary scholars who were prompted often by an imagined "special relationship" of the English-speaking peoples. These earlier studies of British and European visitors were commonly collections of synopses, more descriptive than analytical, that promised to give revealing snapshot impressions of an emerging America by "outsiders."[9] Since the 1970s, however, there has been a suggestive scholarship informed often by the "reading" of such texts[10] for more than empirically useful information. They are, for example, gendered sources (many of the memoirs were written by middle- and upper-class women), and mirrors generally of the mentalities of those who wrote them. Often they may be interesting for what is *not* said, for what they can tell us about the gaze of the tourist-flaneur, and the way they constantly reproduce the expectations and routines of observation within what had become a self-sustaining and self-replicating genre.[11]

An important part, for this study, of the general phenomenon of transatlantic cross-traffic is that of the theatrical world, long accessible through the memoirs and biographies of actors and managers and the contemporary periodical literature of drama criticism. "Theater history" as a familiar, if somewhat self-contained and gossipy genre has been opened up by the application of new approaches by cultural historians who seek to use theatre and common entertainments to amplify our understanding of, for instance, the popular culture of leisure, gender roles and sexuality, or the ideology and politics of race. The substantial literature now available on transatlantic minstrelsy is but a small part of the wealth of scholarship on transatlantic racial representation and racial politics that has appeared in the last twenty years.

Finally, a study such as this profits from, if it does not exactly locate itself within, the fashionable historiographic concept of "the British world," made prominent in the past ten or twenty years largely by British historians of late nineteenth- and early twentieth-century imperial politics, culture, and demography. British world scholarship seeks to supersede much of the older work on the Empire/Commonwealth and Anglo-Saxonism through a more contemporary approach informed by globalization studies and by comparative approaches to the ways of thinking of, especially, far-flung British settler communities, their cultural worlds and their interactions with both other colonials and the mother country.[12] Some such as James Belich would expand the reach of cultural globality beyond the British imperial sphere to an "Anglo-world" or Anglosphere (a.k.a. the English-Speaking Peoples) that draws America into the picture by searching the parallels between settler communities, British and American "Wests," American expansionism and British imperialism, and racial ideologies.[13] But more frequently British-world scholarship views America as substantially "other," as outside the dominion and colonial circle. There is, nevertheless, a large literature on the parallels, contrasts, and mutual influences of British imperialism and American expansionism and on fin de siècle Anglo-American Anglo-Saxonism.

This book attempts to unpack the Anglo-American, transatlantic world from a number of perspectives and by targeting a variety of entry-points and populations over more than a century of shifting contexts on both sides of the ocean. It is an admittedly ambitious project that can, as suggested above, only illuminate in part some sustained themes and some moments of transition. While it is simply not possible to characterize, as so much scholarship of the past has rather casually done, an American or British "character" or "identity" or "ethos"—these societies were much too complex, layered, and various for simple generalization—I hope to reveal something about dominant and minority cultures, and how these were not self-contained "national" phenomena, but, from the backwoods American frontier to rural Yorkshire or the Lancashire mill town, located within a web of transatlantic relations.

The overarching, perhaps looming context of these chapters in Anglo-American relations is of course the slow-coming tectonic shift in global cultural and political

Introduction: The Nineteenth-Century Transatlantic World

hegemony—from an early and mid-nineteenth century of undoubted British ascendancy to the reversal that would make the twentieth century the American century. This coming transposition was for some nineteenth-century Americans a kind of daydream of wishful thinking—hoped for by many and anticipated by some. For others it could only be realized if ironically Americans became more like the British. For many nineteenth-century Britons the long road of imperial decline, a common trope by the end of the century, was bound up with not only the probability of a coming American dominance—to be resisted or fatalistically accepted—but also a more general sense of the mutability of empires. For many others, it was not so much a zero-sum game between an acknowledged and an aspiring global power. A century of thickening familiarity—in many respects, distant America was a better-known world than that just across the English Channel—meant that the more appropriate analogy was more interior and domestic. The rise of America, from this point of view, was rather like the nineteenth-century rise in England of the northern industrialists to prominence from an obscure, provincial, vulgar, and nonconformist past. The railways and the telegraph that had knit together metropolitan and provincial mid-Victorian Britain were precursors to the steamships and undersea cable that performed the same function for the Anglo-American transatlantic, just as the logical extension of Brunel's Great Western Railway from London to Bristol was Brunel's Great Western steamship service, inaugurated in 1838, and his vision that one might buy a ticket from Paddington to New York City.

CHAPTER 1
DIVIDED BY A COMMON LANGUAGE

Their language is the chief impediment in the way of a mutual understanding. That which seems to bind [the English and the Americans] together, serves too often to dissever them.

[Edward Strutt Abdy, *Journal of a Residence and Tour in the United States of America* (1835), I, v]

We have really everything in common with America nowadays, except, of course, language.

[Oscar Wilde, *The Canterville Ghost* (1887)]

England and America—two nations divided by a common language.

[Attributed to G. B. Shaw]

1 A War of Words[1]

A commonplace of British visitors' writing about the early American republic was the extraordinary eagerness of its citizens for the praise of outsiders and a corresponding thin-skinned tetchiness at any perceived criticism of its institutions, its manners, its politics, its popular and literary culture, or the rustic character of "Brother Jonathan's" way of speaking. Such observations, recorded in the burgeoning genre of British tourists' memoirs, had a long life thereafter. They had been circulating for decades by the time Frances Trollope, Dickens, and many others repeated them. The risible contrast between American boastfulness and American inquisitive sensitivity had contributed to the ironic tone of much reviewing of American politics, society, and literature in the new British monthly and quarterly reviews at the beginning of the nineteenth century. The often furious response which such criticism provoked among the avid American readers of these British journals confirmed an extraordinary American sensitivity and conviction that such criticism was aimed expressly at undermining their brave experiment, the work it was even suggested of government propagandists and provocateurs. But, though a narrow anti-Americanism may well have motivated some reviewers, with distance one may locate critiques of American culture, its literature and its language, within a larger, more general undertaking in Britain to affirm *at home* standards, rules, and metropolitan sophistication in the face of domestic utopian enthusiasms and provincial ignorance, vulgarity, and error.

The reviewers of the new monthlies, as arbiters of polite culture, were, that is, part of a much larger and longer project by which "the language of civility" came to be central to English conceptions of the nation. As political and social authority became more centralized, provincial speech came correspondingly to signify not just "uncivil" rudeness and ignorance (as with the local yokels in Shakespeare), but was emblematic of those who were to be ruled and disciplined.[2] Upper-class, landed and metropolitan, and increasingly university-educated English and Scottish elites worked to disparage and displace the variety, color, and earthiness of various, local, and popular cultural heritage—through ritualized codes of polite behavior and, especially, rules of correct, rational grammar, Latinized sentence structure, and drawing-room pronunciation.

Increasingly, educated, cultured local elites looked to London for standards with which to challenge, and abandon to inferior classes, local "difference," especially the rural, provincial languages of historic communities—the dialects of old England. Differences of vocabulary, grammar, and pronunciation were reconfigured as not only obsolete or arcane but ignorant corruptions of the correct standards of a newly national culture. The displacement by the late eighteenth and early nineteenth centuries of these now hardly comprehensible (to polite society) languages downward to the strictly rural farmland of Somerset or the local working classes of Lancashire or Yorkshire served not only to affirm the cultural and political authority of the well-off, the well-educated, and those who would wish to rise into these classes. It also newly fixed the identity and the subordinate character of the local—both rural and newly industrial—classes through their curiosities of dress, their rough manners, and importantly their odd and amusing vocabularies.

In a sense, the campaign to characterize American writing and speech of the early republic as departing significantly from the accepted criteria of the well-bred, civilized speech and writing of their British progenitors can be understood as but a transatlantic element of this century-long distancing and reshaping of the cosmology of polite-society-as-national-society in domestic and imperial Britain. It was a campaign sharpened of course by an era of revolutions and radical reformism. Obsolete, obscure, and odd, marked by verbal and grammatical laziness and a willful repudiation of cultural authority, the "peculiarities" of American language became in the eyes of many arbiters of "proper" English, the voice of the demos contesting that of quality folk. In other words, early nineteenth-century British fascination with American phraseology, grammar, vocabulary, and pronunciation reflects not simply the enchantment of the exotic, nor an Enlightenment and Romantic scheme, following Herder, to understand language difference as national difference, nor even a post-revolution resentful undertaking to put the Americans in their (badly educated) place—though there is at least in the beginning certainly an element of this. It is the other side of the coin of defining a newly *national* Britain through the correct pronunciation, uniformity of vocabulary, and refinement of writing of its now more culturally homogeneous elite. It also served, in a larger context, to advance Britain as a cultural mother country, and—though liberty-loving Britons scorned to have an Academy to police their tongue—its disciplining seniority among English-speaking peoples.

America and the British Monthlies: the Early Republic

In 1918 William Bateman Cairns (1867–1932), a professor of American literature at the University of Wisconsin, published the first of two volumes on British criticism of American writing, 1783–1833.[3] He drew largely from the English and Scottish monthly and quarterly reviews, widely available in the new Republic and followed avidly by many American readers. Most prominent among these were the *Edinburgh* (1802), the *Quarterly* (1809), the *British Review* (1811), and *Blackwoods* (1817). The anonymous critics who wrote for these reviews and others were notorious at the time both for what many Americans took as their condescension and petty faultfinding, and, worse still, for simply ignoring much good American writing. The widespread assumption was fostered that there was a kind of conspiracy among British critics, both Tory and Whig, to defame and belittle American intellectual production, a belittlement that was wholly in tune with the political and diplomatic sourness of Anglo-American relations in the era of the Napoleonic wars generally and especially during and following the "second war of independence," the Anglo-American War of 1812–15. What made these assumptions about the anti-American bias of British writers all the more painful was the pronounced (cultural) Anglophilia, a long-familiar deference to English taste and literary models, of the expanding educated class in the centers of American literary life in Boston, New York, Philadelphia, and Baltimore. Indignation spread via an agitated anti-British American press out to the more general population, quickly becoming part of a larger, and long-lasting, national discourse about what we would call the patronizing cultural imperialism of the mother country. One pained and angry response, by Robert Walsh, published in Philadelphia in 1819 (once a "jealous step-mother," Britain was now "a malevolent scold"[4]), was widely circulated in the States and provoked some response and debate in the British reviews. One of these carried the oft-quoted dismissal of American literary and artistic production by the essayist, critic, Anglican clergyman, and wit Sydney Smith who, as is well-known, posed the infamous question "who reads an American book?"[5]

By the 1820s the anti-American iniquity of the British reviews, especially that of the *Quarterly*, and of the casually slanderous travel genre they both reviewed and promoted, was a familiar, well-worn part of literary and popular discourse in the United States. A satire of 1824, *John Bull in America* (published in both New York—in two editions—and in London), targeted, especially, the *Quarterly's* opinionated mis-information about the "spitting, gouging, drinking, duelling, dirking, swearing, strutting" Americans and the characterization of the "jargon" of American speakers—republican "slang-whangers"—contrasted with the "pure English" of British travelers.[6]

Cairns, from the distance of a century, set out to challenge, or at least to contextualize and diminish, this American representation of the early nineteenth-century war of reviews. He argued that a close analysis showed that the common, every-day reviewing of American works in the majority of British quarterlies, monthlies, and magazine weeklies, even in Francis Jeffrey's *Edinburgh Review*, known for its sharply anti-American politics, did not set out to demean the literary works of the early Republic. The critical standards applied were generally those applied to British authors as well, and American literary production was hardly ignored. American works such as those of Washington Irving were widely available, circulated, read, and reviewed in metropolitan Britain. In fact, after 1815 some journals met what one assumes was their readership's demand by presenting regular sections on American literature, including extracts from American publications. On the whole, Cairns claimed, "British interest in American thought and American writings was considerable … fostered by the prevalent custom of reprinting American works of all sorts in England" and the "great majority of English readers were disposed to be fair" even if they did adopt a "paternal, if not patronizing manner." Extremely negative views of American culture, though "highly conspicuous," "were relatively few in number" and "[n]ot only did most critics aim to be fair, but many of them showed an eagerness to welcome American writings."[7]

Though one may accept much of Cairns's revision, he himself appears to have been biased against the contemporary effort to establish American writing as legitimately "distinctive" from that of Great Britain: "There are few American writings," he told his students, "that require careful analysis and merit intensive study as masterpieces."[8] A rather more even-handed account of the "literary war" of the early nineteenth century is provided in a multi-authored survey of American literary history, the first volume of which appeared in 1917. Though published by Cambridge University Press, the editors and authors were American scholars, such as Lane Cooper, a professor of English at Cornell who had written on De Quincey and Wordsworth. Cooper's contribution emphasized the "dismal chorus" of bitter attacks on American work by Southey and many others in the pages of the *Quarterly*, the *Edinburgh*, the *British Review*, and *Blackwood's*, and treated them, surely correctly, as a legacy that would inform many of the travel books of the 1820s and 1830s. "Prospective observers" would cross the Atlantic "with the prepossession that democratic institutions in America had corrupted good manners." They would give "the English public the reading it enjoyed" and would themselves be confirmingly reviewed in the monthlies and quarterlies and weekly magazines, as in one arm-chair commentator's casual observation: "As yet the American is horn-handed and pig-headed, hard, persevering, unscrupulous, carnivorous … with an incredible genius for lying."[9]

A sensitive American readership might indeed have over-reacted to an acerbic style found generally in the new British literary criticism. Beyond the monthly reviewers it was possible to encounter praise for the "very energetic and concise" speech and writing of Americans, as Benjamin Silliman found when he visited Britain in 1805–6 to buy books for Yale's library—though his pronunciation raised some comment. At the Royal Society the geographer James Rennel told him that he actually believed "the Americans had improved the English tongue."[10] It can hardly be denied, however, that the tone of much reviewing of American works often hinted, like many of the travel memoirs, at expectations of vulgarity and provinciality. This could color even the grudging praise of the occasional American piece that came up to their "standards," as in an 1808 review in the *British Critic* of John Marshall's monumental *Life of Washington*: American writings often deviated "from the purity of the English idiom," "Mr. Marshall deviates occasionally, but not grossly, and his composition, on the whole, although not of a high class, is creditable to him as a scholar."[11] Later, reviewers suggested that the very popular stories of Irving somehow (surprisingly) rose above one's expectations. As Cairns rightly saw, British reviewing, whether damning or praising American work, sought for and expected to find *difference* rather than comparability. Their British readership wanted to know what made American work characteristically American. It was James Fenimore Cooper's Americanness that made his adventures popular with an English readership, not the fact that his story-telling was clearly informed by the fiction of Sir Walter Scott.

Through the first half of the century, some familiarity with America through British and American fiction as well as from the published histories of pre- and post-revolutionary America that were commonly available[12] encouraged a growing interest among the British in transatlantic travel. The antebellum era saw, decade by decade, a significant increase in the number of visitors who contributed to a largely new genre of amateur reportage.[13] Reviewing these travel memoirs became a staple of the monthlies and quarterlies, which themselves helped to focus and promote the themes and tropes of such literature, establishing the questions and issues (such as the institution of slavery, the forwardness of American women, the prevalence of eye-gouging and Bowie-knifing, or the in-door habit of spitting tobacco-juice) that any tourist journal would be expected to address. They constructed, or at least encouraged, a well-populated literature that served to inform, through a highly selective vision, both the British public about the identity, peculiarities, and overall difference of Americans and the American public about what "the English" thought about them.

Though many travelers were not exactly tourists in the modern sense, and came to the New World to visit friends and relations, or as paid lecturers, speculative businessmen, journalists, theatrical players, abolitionists, evangelicals, and scientists, tourism of the more familiar kind grew throughout the period. A domestic tourism "industry" in America was encouraged by the advertising, guidebooks, and growth of railways that saw the cultural commodification of sites such as Niagara Falls.[14] But the growth of tourism among the British as a middle- and upper-class entertainment was also to a considerable degree driven by an especially imperial view of a world ripe for exploration and enabled by the leisure and means of its traveling classes.

British observations of American life and language collectively began to assume the character of a self-replicating, self-referential body of popular literature. By mid-century there was almost the expectation that a sustained trip to North America would, as a matter of course, be followed by a published memoir, and a number of London publishers such as John Murray's, Richard Bentley's (which promoted a series on "modern travel"), and Macmillan's had embraced this genre as a sub-specialty of their houses. In 1851 one traveler, considering whether he should add to the number of published memoirs (he did), feared that the British public were "nearly bored to death with Travels in the United States ... produced so plentifully, of late years." America, he thought, had become, through the tourist lens, satiatingly familiar: "Increased facilities of communication have brought New York and Philadelphia as near to us as Edinburgh and Dublin were, in the days of our grandfathers ... we know almost as much about Boston as we do about Manchester and Leeds."[15]

As the century progressed, and as the cost of and time spent in transatlantic travel diminished, the attraction of an American tour over "foreign" travel on the Continent or farther abroad was enhanced by the convenience of a holiday among people who more or less spoke English and were by and large Protestant. Like the reviewers of American literature, British travelers nevertheless came with the *expectation* of finding difference and reported (and exaggerated) that rather than a less-interesting sameness.[16] Many tourists however wished to find this entertaining difference within a degree of reassuring sameness. As James Aitken would later tell the readers of the *Greenock Herald*, "[e]verywhere our common language is spoken (a great convenience in travelling); everywhere is the intercourse civil and courteous, and everywhere we found ourselves among a God-fearing and law-abiding people."[17]

Nevertheless, within this sameness the discovery or confirmation of the nuances of language and manners continued to serve to confirm the national self—what it meant to be respectably British in a world of industrialization, commercialization, democritization, and globalization—while Americans, or some of them, were inspired to *perform* difference for the foreign audience they incessantly interrogated. The British search for what was acceptable in language led, on the one hand, to a domestic "myth of stasis" and the exaggeration of American deviance. There was an obsession with the identification of "Americanisms"—not only in the back-woods, frontier patois found in James Fenimore Cooper's Leatherstocking tales, but in the everyday usage found in American literature, letters, and journalism. On the other, there was the dawning of a popular philology that would search for the evolution of language and speculate about the perhaps *mutable* rules of grammar and pronunciation, the possible etymological, that is historical, origins of common-usage vocabulary (as national speech), and the reform of spelling.

Noah Webster and Anglo-American English

In spite of his famously reactionary political views, Samuel Johnson, in his celebrated *Dictionary* of 1755 and in the subsequent editions commonly found in American as in British libraries, had not been much interested in citing American difference (there is hardly any reference to American English as a separate or corrupted field). Nor was he much interested in pronunciation, a subject that subsequently came to play a large role in discourse about American language and American*isms*, though he was concerned, more generally, that "tongues, like governments, have a natural tendency to degeneration."[18] Nor did Captain Francis Grose give much space to specifically American argot in his 1785 *Dictionary of Buckish Slang, University Wit, and Pickpocket Eloquence*, save to note that "to gouge" ("To squeeze out a man's eye with the thumb") was "a cruel practice used by Bostonians in America" (backwoods violence, and gouging in particular, would become one of the favorite topics of travelers' accounts of the American South and the trans-Allegheny West).[19]

It was apparently the British who first labeled their colonial cousins across the Atlantic "Americans;" the colonists themselves before the War of Independence generally preferred to be regarded as a rather special category of British subjects, with all the rights and privileges to which a Briton of the Glorious Revolution might aspire. Culturally of course they were, and often saw themselves as, provincial, a further (if long) step beyond the West Country and Bristol. Naturally the course of the Revolution powerfully shifted sensibilities and encouraged—demanded—the construction of a separated identity, as did the forced or self-removal of some 50,000 loyalists and the justificatory rhetoric of victorious Patriots. As with the French Jacobins a decade later, the new Americans were faced with the need for a project of national self-creation. In the heady utopian air of the 1780s, it was not unusual for such schemes to extend well beyond the political to the cultural—to the need, not only for an evolving corpus of *American* law, but for American fashions, American manners, an American literature, and, indeed, a written and spoken language that signaled the emergence of a new nation and the dissolution of ties of social and cultural deference to the aristocratic norms of the mother country. On both sides of the Atlantic there was a sharp late-eighteenth-century interest in grammar—often, in the American case, leading some to attempt to sort through the problems that arose when local usage was in conflict with *analogy* (i.e., the standards imposed by grammars written by "a few men in London").[20] Among the founding fathers, Benjamin Franklin was most prominent in encouraging reforms to help make the English language in America more appropriately American. Like Jefferson, he foresaw, within a few generations, an American tongue that would evolve away from British English just as Portuguese separated from Spanish or Swedish from Danish.[21]

Among those who took direction from Franklin's speculative hopes was a young graduate of Yale College, Noah Webster (1758–1843). Webster, long regarded as the father of American lexicography, began as a passionate patriot and cultural separatist who in the 1780s renounced the grammars and dictionaries of most English scholars as furthering the aristocratic, elitist influence—like that of the pretentious elocution of the British actors commonly found on the American stage—of London-oriented, deference-inspiring cultural practices. Within the new United States, spelling reform and the standardization of word usage would both help to build and be emblematic of a new nation.[22]

Webster's early enthusiasms were of their post-revolutionary moment—he was well-read in both French and British radical thought—while also drawing on Enlightenment interest in the origin, character, and socializing role of language generally and the centrality it might play in the formation of national identity. Moreover, the contemporary spate of mostly British but also some American publications on language—grammars, pronouncing dictionaries, orthographies, amateur philological speculations—provided him the opening publicly to foment his own, properly American, critique and schema. At the time there seemed a pressing need to define just what kind of general, universal education a republic might require. Webster played to this opportunity of becoming an influential advisor to national figures, an ambition furthered by a tract of 1785, *Sketches of American Policy*, with its "Plan ... for Improving the Advantages and Perpetuating the Union of the American States," and by a following lecture tour down the American seaboard as far as Charleston. *A Grammatical Institute of the English Language* (parts were published 1783–5 and then together in 1790) expanded on these themes, as did continuing public lectures. These were published together in a lengthy collection, *Dissertations on the English Language* the year (1789) that the new Constitution of the United States came into force: "Let us seize the present moment," he wrote, "and establish a national language as well as a national government."[23]

Utopian schemes for reformed grammar or orthography (for some years Webster promoted his own somewhat crankish system of phonetic spelling) had, of course, to contend with the cultural conservatism of much of the educated quality folk of Boston, New York, or Philadelphia who continued to look to London for the fashions of dress, literature, and speech that served to define persons of their social status, just as many New England and New York merchants continued to look to British markets for their commercial prosperity. Webster regarded as "another evil resulting from this dependence upon [Great Britain]" the fact that "[o]ur people look to English books as the standard of truth on all subjects, and this confidence in English opinions puts *an end to enquiry*."[24] Cultural conservatism was further entrenched as the new nation was tested by the rise of a western, backwoods regionalism, characterized by a less-educated, rougher population and their democratic repudiation of the manners, style, and privileges of the Eastern seaboard elites. In 1786–7 Shay's rebellion frightened many of the respectable class, a concern that was amplified by a repugnance, shared with much of the middle and upper classes of Britain, at the later excesses of Jacobin rule in France and of egalitarian radicalism in general. In New England and New York, there was a political as well as cultural conservative turn, expressed in Hamilton's Federalist party and in the rising concerns of the New England merchant class; Jefferson's embargo of 1807 and Madison's War of 1812 threatened to destroy American maritime commerce and very nearly prompted the separation of New England from the new nation.

Shay's rebellion in western Massachusetts and the course of events in Jacobin France led Webster to promote himself as a Federalist spokesman and to turn from some of his more radical ideas (and hopes) of spelling and grammar reform to concentrate on the project of a dictionary of the *American* language that would better reflect American usage and pronunciation. If it fell well short of advancing the *new* language envisioned (or playfully imagined) by Franklin and Jefferson, it would nevertheless encourage an American linguistic and literary identity. By the turn of the century there was competition. Two Americans had already published new dictionaries. In Britain there had appeared since Johnson a number of expanded dictionaries, some exploring the pronunciation and etymology that Johnson had by and large ignored, as well as a rising interest in just how and how far American language had come to differ from accepted standards of (British) English in vocabulary and (mis)usage.

Philology was becoming a heightened area of international scholarly concern—especially in German and French philosophical circles—as well as of amateur speculation. Britain was perhaps slow to follow, but by 1792 there was a short-lived London Philological Society. The "problem of language" in an age of revolutions assumed a larger than antiquarian, philological interest.[25] Webster found the work of a formerly Wilkesite radical, Horne Tooke, especially interesting. Tooke, like Richard Price and Joseph

Priestley, strongly supported the American cause and had been imprisoned for a year for his unmeasured expression of these and other radical views. Subsequently he retired to an estate he had been given near London to pursue an interest in grammar and comparative philology. In 1786, he published a lengthy dialogue on these studies, *The Diversions of Purley*, that, though often eccentric in its speculations, helped establish in the English-speaking world the field of "rational philology" as one of serious scientific endeavor. This book was of interest to Webster (as it would later be to Ralph Waldo Emerson) as he groped toward ideas for an American grammar and an American lexicon, not only because of Horne Tooke's affinity for American democracy and his speculations about rather technical issues (such as his "theory of the particles"), but more generally because it led him to historical etymology and a conviction that "the peculiar structure of our language is Saxon."[26] Tooke's call for a plain English unencumbered by Greek and Latin accretions and pretensions[27] resonated with that of the Philadelphia doctor and patriot Benjamin Rush in his 1788 "Plan of a Federal University," which sought a break from British English "of the bar, the stage, and the pulpit," a new American philology that would encourage a "simplicity of writing in America." Both would have encouraged Webster in his conviction that "our modern grammars have done much more hurt than good" by trying to "persuade the English to speak by Latin rules ... the most difficult task now to be performed by the advocates of *pure English*, is to restrain the influence of men learned in Greek and Latin ... because they have not understood the original construction of the language."[28] By 1790 he had begun to argue, against "pedantic," "inaccurate and defective" transatlantic grammars and dictionaries, that "languages are not framed by philosophers ... they are spoken long before they are written,"[29] and that a purer, less aristocratic English, appropriate for a new democracy, could be found in the ancient language's Anglo-Saxon roots. Such reasoning led Webster toward his famous claim, in riposte to those British critics who condemned American language as lazy, corrupted, and prone to neologisms, that American English was *more* historically authentic than Latinized contemporary British English in, often, its pronunciation, and in its employment of "obsolete" terms and phrases that had traveled to the new world with the Pilgrim fathers and were commonly to be found in the works of Chaucer or the Elizabethans: "Our language was spoken in purity about eighty years ago; since which time, great numbers of faults have crept into practice ... and new words or modes of speech have succeeded the ancient correct English phrases."[30]

Webster's 40,600-word *A Compendious Dictionary of the American Language* (1806) took most of two decades of thought and research. He promoted it as an improvement on Johnson's dictionary, "the fund from which modern compilers," especially Thomas Sheridan and his pronouncing dictionary and grammar of 1780, "have selected the substance of their works," and attacked those "whose criticisms would sink the literature of this country, even lower than the distorted representations of foreign reviewers; whose veneration of trans-atlantic authors leads them to hold American writers in unmerited contempt." *A Compendious Dictionary* also defended and promoted American (i.e., New England) pronunciation as more authentic than the fashionable English of upper-class London, as "the pronunciation which prevailed in England anterior to Sheridan's time and which I am assured by English gentlemen is still the pronunciation of the body of the English nation."[31]

As a work that was intended to advance the project of both preserving and crafting a *national* language at the heart of a *national* culture, *A Compendious Dictionary*, among its various competitors (such as Caleb Alexander's *Columbian Dictionary* of 1800), disappointed Webster's hopes. It may, in fact, be considered less a beginning than, as Vincent Bynack has claimed, "a dead end."[32] Its prospectus and preface retained enough of the idealism of his early schemes—the universal education in a dialect-free tongue of an egalitarian people and condemnation of British pronunciation that was regulated by "the distinction of ranks"—to now draw the cutting sarcasm of a Federalist press, sympathetic to Britain and opposed to the cultural corruption and degradation of a coming nation of Irish and Continental immigrants. The dictionary's prospectus of 1800 was attacked by the Philadelphia editor of the once-Tory and now Federalist *Gazette of the United States*, Joseph Dennie, who published crude fictional letters in support of Webster's scheme from semi-literate Irish, Blacks, Germans, and women. Webster was attacked for promoting, not a new American language, but bad English.[33]

The work that followed another two decades of labor, and which would make Webster's national and international reputation, the *American Dictionary of the English Language* (1828), was a differently inspired work. The title change is significant, as is the fact that in 1807–1808 Webster himself underwent a personal, evangelical conversion. Though he continued to argue that American English was unriven (as he thought) by significant dialects of region or class, and thus superior to the modish linguistic fashions of London's beau monde, this virtue made it appropriate as a *universal* rather than uniquely North American language. Henceforth, his philological interests became the expression less of a radical nationalism, than of a commitment to unify rather than divide the (Christian) English-speaking world.

The so-called Second Great Awakening in America (from *c.* the 1790s to the 1840s) was an expression of the same millennialism and mass revivalism seen in England and Scotland. Though each may be situated within specific local contexts—in England the growth of new industrial communities and reactions to the anxieties of the long era of revolution and warfare, in America the mobility of a rapidly growing population beyond the Alleghenies far from the sea-board institutional centers of social and religious life—they were closely linked in theological thought and practice, by shared styles of preaching and the group experience of personal salvation. They were also tightly joined by the activities of a host of mobile, often transatlantic missionaries. Methodism, of course, had for decades been active in America, and its reliance on lay preaching and circuit riders made it especially important in the American revivalism that swept the frontier societies. Other Protestant churches—Baptists, Presbyterians, Unitarians, Congregationalists, Quakers—also had strong cross-Atlantic ties. In the early and mid-nineteenth century, revivalists crossed the ocean in both directions and formed a durable part of the nonconformist Christian network that served to unite Britain with its former colonies, and often to inspire reformist movements such as temperance and abolition of slavery in ways that ignored the boundaries of nationalism.[34]

Webster continued to frame his further lexicographical project as an assault on the famous work of Samuel Johnson (much of which he nonetheless appropriated) and the grammar of Thomas Sheridan, but with the expressed motive of creating a work that would serve the interests of both American and British users. His growing interest in etymology, in tracing the historical (Anglo-Saxon, that is, Old English) origins of the English language, now expanded into a larger attempt to establish a more romantic, if certainly dubious, biblical and Edenic etymology. Though he continued to quote American authors in his definitions—to give, that is, American English its place in establishing the language—and continued also to assert that the new, greatly expanded dictionary would serve special American needs and an American identity, there were now also plentiful biblical citations. These would make it popular with evangelical Christians on both sides of the Atlantic, and serve to make it appropriate for (reformed) British usage as well. It would be a dictionary of the *common* British and American tongue, promoting an English that would reflect "the manly character of the language and the freedom of the British and American constitutions … and perhaps act and react upon each other mutually as cause and effect."[35]

This expanded interest in etymologies prompted Webster to travel to France and England in 1824 to research early dictionaries and the origins of words at the Bibliothèque du Roi in Paris and the libraries of Oxford and Cambridge. The notable linguists he met at Cambridge, especially the Rev. Samuel Lee, a scholar of ancient languages and translations of ancient scriptures, endorsed his work. Encouraged, Webster proposed a conference of linguists from Oxford and Cambridge to promote the "unification" of the English language. Though Oxford demurred, the Cambridge philologists approved Webster's scheme, and a transatlantic linguistic community of corresponding experts was the long-lasting result.

The extended visit to Cambridge and London had not, of course, been only about research and bridge-building. As with many American authors, Webster was concerned to find a British publisher. The market for high-priced scholarly works was likely to be substantially larger in the UK than in America. And then there was the problem, one that persisted to 1891, of the lack of international copyright agreements. Generally, this worked to the advantage of American publishers, who were quick to reprint popular British authors (such as Scott, Dickens, or Anthony Trollope) with little or no compensation for the author whose works were shamelessly pirated. British publishers did the same, though in London as in Boston some of the more respectable houses might negotiate some compensation. There was advantage to be gained by British authors who were able to negotiate pre-publication agreements with an American press and thus come under American domestic copyright (established by several states and by the federal Copyright Act of 1790). The same was true of American authors in Britain who hoped to tap into the British market, such as Webster, Irving, or Cooper. They and their agents spent much time and effort, and difficult Atlantic crossings, to secure arrangements in Britain. Given the growing American market for British works, however, most of the piracy was that of the less-scrupulous of the American publishers. For much of the century a well-oiled system was in place whereby publisher's agents in London or Edinburgh were poised, competitively, to rush works fresh off the British press to New York for hurried, cheap, and often shoddy reproductions. The same was true of the scripts of successful London plays, carefully written down by agents in the stalls, and rushed to the States for unauthorized performances in New York, Boston, and Philadelphia. This literary (and theatrical) anarchy also posed a problem for guaranteeing the authenticity and integrity of works claiming to be new versions of a famous text. Once Webster's international name was made, competing works were launched in America and Britain claiming to be revisions or expansions of "Webster's Dictionary."

Webster's efforts to find a British publisher in 1825 were frustrated. Recent dictionaries, and those about to be published, had soaked up the market, or so the printers, booksellers, and publishers he sought out claimed. John Murray's, the prestigious London publisher of Byron (and later American authors such as Herman Melville), after keeping the work for some weeks, declined. Part of the problem lay in the probable small market and the great expense of publishing a work heavy with erudite etymological and pronunciation scholarship. One of Webster's reasons for searching for a British publisher was the difficulty of finding an American house that had the appropriate printer's type for such a work. Another was its size (it included 12,000 more words than the most recently expanded version of Johnson's dictionary, as well as pronunciations and more precise and lengthier definitions and etymologies). In the event, Webster managed to find a New York publisher to take on the work (and import the necessary type). He also got his cousin Daniel Webster to push through an amendment of American domestic copyright law that (in 1831) extended protection for authors in the United States to the twenty-eight years which British law provided for books published there. The work that appeared in 1828, in two quarto volumes, dedicated to God, was priced at a hugely expensive $20.

Before he returned to America, however, Webster had been able to find a solicitor, John Miller, who promised, vested with a power of attorney, to act in his interest in the pursuit of any future negotiations. In 1829 Miller managed to find an editor (who was also a linguist and Cambridge graduate) to take on the task of producing a British edition—and to promise Webster one-sixth of whatever profits it might produce. A work of this expense naturally involved solicitation of subscribers and the advertising of their support—in the event, the publisher, Edmund Henry Barker, got a number of suitably aristocratic "names," including Palmerston, Aberdeen, the Duke of Gloucester (as Chancellor of Cambridge), Lord Grenville (as Chancellor of Oxford), the Duke of Grafton, and the Earl of Carlisle. Barker had high hopes: "if the speculation answers, as I may well expect, I can make a good thing out of it, & I can make it the foundation of a *national* work such as we all want."[36] In fact, Barker promised an edition (also a two-volume quarto work) of more copies (3,000) than the first, New York, edition. After its appearance in London, "the most learned book ever published in America … the most perfect Dictionary in existence,"[37] the list of subscribers and booksellers continued to grow.

In the years following, the British edition proved a success in establishing the work's reputation as a transatlantic lexicon of the English language rather than a work promoting a special American national identity. In fact, Webster's "American Dictionary" became the standard in England, and when Webster's American publisher, Sherman Converse, went bankrupt, copies of the English edition were sold in the United States.[38] Over the following decades Webster and his heirs and designates worked to maintain control over what was now seen on both sides of the ocean as the premier dictionary of the English language. In America, there were competing dictionaries, most notably Joseph E. Worcester's *A Comprehensive Pronouncing and Explanatory Dictionary of the English Language with Pronouncing Vocabularies* (1830) and *A Universal and Critical Dictionary of the English Language* (1846). Worcester, a former associate of Webster's, remained popular in America—and in England—until his death in 1865. Others took advantage of Webster's renown, borrowing substantially from or abridging Webster's two volumes. These opportunists were to be opposed and suppressed. There were also competing new dictionaries in Britain, also along etymological lines—such as *A New Dictionary of the English Language*, published in London in 1837 by the British lexicographer and linguist, Charles Richardson (a disciple of Horne Tooke). Through the 1830s and early 1840s, Webster labored to revise his own work, producing the edition of 1840. This was promoted by another trip to Britain, where he had the American Minister, Andrew Stevenson, present a leather-bound copy to Queen Victoria. Stevenson observed that the work would "manifest to the British nation that Americans have not forgotten the language of their Fathers."[39] In his own published message to the Queen (the presentation was of course a marketing ploy), Webster emphasized the Anglo-American ambitions of the work, confirmed by its critical reception on both sides of the ocean. Victoria instructed Melbourne to "convey to Mr. Webster her warm thanks for the mark of attention, & assure him that Her Majesty will highly value the Work, as well on account of its merits, as of the author & the kindred Country from which it comes."[40]

Webster's "American" dictionary, as a universal lexicon, would, he thought, accompany and enhance the ever-expanding realm of the language itself. He told his colleagues that within two centuries English would be "the language of one third or two thirds of all the inhabitants of the globe ... the instrument of propagating sciences, arts, and the Christian religion."[41] Shortly after he returned to New York, Webster had a "pleasant conversation" with Captain Basil Hall—soon to be infamous in America for his memoir of his travels there. Touching on the subject of Americanisms and the future of English as more than a national language, Webster acknowledged that there was an "interchange" across the Atlantic in both directions of new words, a kind of "inevitable" hybridity, and that his dictionary was intended to be "as complete as possible a picture of the English language, as it stands at the moment, on both sides of the Atlantic ocean."[42]

The attractiveness to the British of a major work of scholarship from a "kindred country," to the point of making it for more than a generation the most widely regarded reference work on the English language, can be attributed not only to the softening of the American nationalism of Webster's text and perhaps the biblical nature of some of his etymologies, but also simply to its unparalleled heft, the substance of its two quarto volumes, and the fact that, unlike some of its British competitors, it contained words drawn from the modern fields of commerce, manufacturing, and science—of interest to the middle-class urban world of mid-century England. It may also be the case that challenges to the aristocratic character of the British state, advanced by the Great Reform Act and subsequent liberal reforms, made the contrast between elitist England and democratic America a less compelling divide—to both Webster and his readerships—than had earlier been the case. Webster's dictionary, especially the expanded (to 85,000 words) but cheaper "royal octavo" edition of 1847, secured a place in the British marketplace until after the 1860s, when a competing *Imperial Dictionary* by John Ogilvie (originally borrowing heavily from Webster and first published in 1850) was substantially revised and enlarged to four volumes and became the preferred British standard. Though both Worcester in America and Ogilvie in Britain played to their national bases, presenting their tomes as the American or imperial, respectively, alternative to Webster's international legacy, they themselves drew heavily on Webster's dictionary. As late as the late 1870s the *New York Tribune* could still reasonably boast that (by then) Merriam-Webster's *An American Dictionary of the English Language, Unabridged* (the right to Webster's dictionary having been sold by his heirs to the G. and C. Merriam Co. of Springfield, Massachusetts, in 1843) "is generally regarded as the dictionary of highest quality in the language, and has a sale all over the civilized world. It is regularly issued in London, and in English, as well as American Courts of Justice, is considered as the leading authority on the meaning of words."[43]

H. L. Mencken, in his 1919 book on *The American Language*, would take Webster to task for ignoring the wide field of American speech in its particular, idiosyncratic character ("staggering proof of his defective observation").[44] By the 1840s Webster had however largely removed himself from the defense of such Americanisms, committed as he was to the idea of producing, not an American, per se, but a larger, deeper, Christian understanding of English words and their origins.

2 Americanisms

It may be, as Christopher Flynn has argued, that Americans "were an epistemological problem for the English throughout the eighteenth and nineteenth centuries."[45] The political separation of the colonies from the mother country after 1783 and the War of 1812 certainly made the issue of how, exactly, to regard America—in its politics, its literature, its language, its cultural peculiarities—an acute one and encouraged the search for cultural and social, as well as political, difference. Nevertheless, many Britons continued to view Americans as provincially familiar, comparable to those parts of the UK that were farthest, culturally, from the urbane center of fashion. English and Scottish emigrants often preferred to go to the United States, as they imagined it from the letters home of those who had gone before (British but without an aristocracy, where an idealized yeomanly independence might be had), over the sometimes subsidized attractions of the distant and more exotic settler colonies of the expanding Empire. Even those who opted to take the (cheaper) passage to British North America (the Canadas) often migrated south shortly thereafter. Such transatlantic networks perpetuated back in the mother country the sense that the United States, though politically separate, was in some sense home ground. It says something that, unlike the Irish or German immigrants, British migrants generally did not form into tight neighborhoods of their own ethnicity; they did not become hyphenated Americans.

Americans were often viewed as a distant mirror of those unsatisfied classes that contested the British state from within. They were, in this view, but a liberated version of the English common folk—the emerging working and middling classes, especially in the North of England, with their growing self-consciousness and antagonism to social and economic subordination. Indeed, many radicals in the 1820s and Chartists in the 1830s and 1840s looked to America as the fraternal paradigm of a coming British democracy, and some fled there after the failure of their populist movement in 1848. It is also true that many among the liberal-minded middle- and upper-middle classes, those who from the late eighteenth century were increasingly uncomfortable with social deference, resented the Corn Laws and aristocratic privilege, and demanded a more meritocratic state, looked to and found in America (*sans* of course its "peculiar institution") a kind of cousinly beacon.

Witherspoon, Boucher, and a Philology of American Error

Perhaps to avoid such uncomfortable parallels, American cultural as well as political separateness became a reiterated theme in the monthlies, in travel literature, and in British fiction, where one might see, as Flynn suggests, the "literary construction of an Other … for a popular English audience" (audiences may be of course both anticipated and created, as well as cultivated). By the early nineteenth century many of the educated, literate class, the broadsheet-reading professionals, and gentry simply came to acknowledge American difference as a conventional way to "understand" the inevitability of separation, but also perhaps as a way of distancing—to avoid confronting the parallel "America" at home. English accounts of America, Flynn claims, went through a series of stages—from the abandonment of an optimistic hope that spatial distance could be surmounted by an emotional affinity, to the view of America as a land of utopian possibilities, as a place where the heavy history of the old world could be escaped, to a final, anthropological taxonomy of difference: "By the Victorian period, British writings almost always depicted Americans as a separate breed—ill-housed, ill-mannered, badly spoken, under the sway of dangerous religious enthusiasms, vain, shallow, whiskey-soaked, and constantly given to spitting on the carpet." However, chaw-induced expectoration aside, it will be clear that many of these negative representations were also exactly those ascribed to the new laboring poor of England and Scotland (who would also by mid-century be subjected to an anthropological taxonomy) by the increasingly numerous respectable, comfortable, rising classes—just those who read reviews, novels, and travel memoirs. Tropes of similarity and tropes of difference of course long *co-existed* in unresolved tension, a "composite view" of Americans as "a breed apart,"[46] as extended "family," and as a hybrid people, both savage and civilized—a characterization that would seem to owe something to America as locus for the half-breed, the métis, the mulatto.

Webster's dictionary of the *shared* (Anglo-American) English tongue may have carved out a dominant place in both British and American libraries. In Britain, however, where the fashion for travelers' memoirs flourished in the 1830s and beyond, publishers found or anticipated a thriving market also for guides to "Americanisms." Both the many travel memoirs and the glossaries of Americanisms reinforced what Webster had ultimately rejected, that American language was different and emblematic of larger differences. Philologists and lexicographers, and British observers generally, continued to debate for much of the nineteenth century the lively—then conventional and hackneyed—thesis that American speech (or lack of articulate speech[47]) was curiously ("peculiar" remained the inevitable adjective) unlike that of the mother country. It evinced a kind of decay or degeneration of proper English (Frederick Marryat, for example, wrote of the way American English had in a short period of time become "very debased"[48]), and the peculiar way Americans talked and wrote was, in often unflattering ways, reflective of American character.[49]

There were a half-dozen or so dictionaries or glossaries purporting to identify words peculiar to Americans that were published (in Boston, Philadelphia, and London) in the era of the New Republic down to the American Civil War, at least one of which (Bartlett's) went to several editions. They, and the reviews they elicited on both sides of the Atlantic, fueled a general discussion about the particular character of the literature and speech of Americans (their vocabulary, both newly invented and obsolete, and its usage and misusage; their phraseology, grammar, and pronunciation). While the subject had attracted some attention before the War of Independence, it is in the partisan era that followed that one finds the unfolding of a specific, heated dialogue characterized by, often, defensive American apologetics and British mockery. Whether self-consciously or not, these "handbooks" of American speech served the overall purpose in either a positive or an unfriendly way of confirming cultural separation. Beyond this, apart from the way they were used and abused by reviewers, and whatever the motives involved, the compilations can be regarded as fruit of the antiquarian and scholarly obsessions of lexicographers and philologists everywhere—to isolate, organize, and thus claim a field of knowledge.

The word "Americanism" was apparently coined—by analogy to "Scotticism"—in 1781, by a Presbyterian clergyman, John Knox Witherspoon (1723–94), who, invited by Benjamin Rush, had come to America to take up the presidency of the College of New Jersey (later, Princeton) in 1768. A low Kirk Protestant with a deep distrust of Episcopal meddling in colonial affairs and with republican convictions, he became influential in American Presbyterianism and was a prominent supporter of independence, helping to draft the Articles of Confederation and, in 1789, to advocate adoption of the Constitution. His views on American language were mixed. On the one hand, as others, including Webster, would note, the speech of the common folk in America was less divided by dialect than in Britain, and thus more comprehensible: "The vulgar in America speak much better than the vulgar in Great Britain, for a very obvious reason, namely, that being much more unsettled, and moving frequently from place to place, they are not so liable to local peculiarities either in accent or phraseology."[50] On the other hand, literary English, that is, the speech and writing of the educated classes in America, was unacceptably prone to "error" and abuse: "I have heard in this country, in the senate, at the bar, and from the pulpit, and see daily in dissertations from the press, errors in grammar, improprieties and vulgarisms which hardly any person of the same class in point of rank and literature would have fallen into in Great Britain."[51]

Witherspoon is here more concerned with colloquial usage and phrasing, and with the errors of those who should have known better, than with the vocabulary and manner of speech of the American nation. And of course he is offering his criticisms, and his praise, from within, as one who became a committed American patriot. His near-contemporary, Jonathan Boucher (1738–1804), another transplanted Briton, had more of an axe to grind. A teacher in Cumberland (Cumbria), he had emigrated to Virginia in 1759 to tutor planter families, left for England to be ordained by the Bishop of London, and returned to America to take up the rectorship of various parishes. Though a confirmed Tory he was also a popular preacher who criticized British policy in America as "oppressive" and "unjust." His opposition to violent measures, however, and his Tory Episcopalianism put him on the wrong side of history. When the crunch came in 1775, he embraced the Loyalist cause, had to read his last sermon over a loaded pistol, and, not yet forty years of age, emigrated back to the mother country with his American wife—to be rewarded with a government pension and a living as vicar of Epsom.

Having been forced to decamp from Maryland, Boucher spent the several decades remaining to him compiling a glossary of "archaic and provincial words," an antiquarian work to supplement Johnson's dictionary. This glossary did not, however, see publication until the success of Webster's 1829 English edition made, no doubt, the topic of somewhat greater interest to a London publisher. It was brought out, posthumously, in 1832–3, and included a lengthy introduction Boucher had written in 1800. Though he "set down a few Americanisms," he did not, in spite of the relevance of American speech to the general theme of the work, include very many. Acknowledging that in at least one example (that of using "been" or "being" for "because") American usage was likely brought over by Puritans from the western counties of England, he did not choose to follow this line of argument as Webster and others had done to justify peculiarities of American speech as authentic, uncorrupted old English. Nor, though he notes the lack of difference of dialect among Americans, is he willing to consider American speech as a whole simply a provincialism. Indeed, the lack of dialect among themselves was hardly the virtue some imagined, and had resulted, he rather oddly maintained, in "a want of diversity of character, a lack of comic humour, and original character; together with a corresponding scantiness of cultivation and improvement … [w]ith little or no dialect, they are particularly addicted to innovation." Boucher, in fact, went to some length to hold in contempt the effort of (unnamed) American philologists. The Americans, with their "passion for innovating" (he cites, for example, their use of "advocate" and "progress" as verbs), were "very poorly … qualified to set up as reformers of language."[52]

But by the time Boucher's glossary was published the debate over Americanisms—at least among lexicographers, if not more generally—had passed beyond the early, partisan era of warring reviews. As one of Boucher's editors observed rather unconvincingly in a note, "Had Mr. Boucher lived to revise his manuscript in 1832, he probably would not have passed so harsh a censure on the Transatlantic section of the English nation."[53] For Frances Trollope and Dickens, a drawling "I guess" (or "reckon" or "calculate")—"[t]here is no word for which New Englandmen are more teased"[54]— had become, whether or not it could be proved to originate in old English, simply a commonplace, clichéd, and satirical way of identifying Yankee characters in British literature and on the British stage, and would remain so for the rest of the century. While philologists might view American linguistic peculiarities as regionalisms or the errors of the semi-literate or historical relics of an English past, they came to be used more generally—not only by British observers but by many Americans themselves—as a kind of shorthand for national attitude, character, and style. Samuel Clemens' public persona, Mark Twain, would be compounded of them.

Dictionaries of Americanisms, from Pickering to Bartlett and beyond

The same year Boucher wrote his introduction dismissive of American linguistic "innovation," Caleb Alexander (1755–1828), a New England clergyman with an interest in the classics, grammar, and orthography, brought out a *Columbian Dictionary of the English Language*, published in Boston, the first substantial (550-page) dictionary by an American author. Though not a glossary of Americanisms per se, it did, as he advertised on the title page, include "Many *New Words* peculiar to the United States … not found in any other English dictionary." He was attacked for doing so—as well as, on the other hand, for simply appropriating, it was said, much material from dictionaries published in England by Samuel Johnson, William Perry, and Thomas Sheridan. The attacks on Alexander for seemingly justifying by inclusion uniquely American vocabulary, and the rising tempo of anti-Americanism generally in the British reviews, focused attention on the "problem" of linguistic corruption and innovation, and elicited both a defensive response among some and, more generally, a quasi-scholarly interest in discovering and organizing evidence of American linguistic difference.

John Pickering (1776?–1846), with his eye on a transatlantic readership for American literature, tried to thread his way between criticism and justification of American linguistic peculiarities. He was a son of Timothy Pickering, a high-ranking officer during the Revolutionary War who served in Washington's and Adams' cabinets as an Anglophilic Federalist.[55] His famous (or infamous) Napoleonic war era toast, delivered at a Boston dinner for a British minister recently declared *non grata* by Madison, "The World's last hope—Britain's fast anchored Isle," drew praise from some in New England, though hardly elsewhere, as did his encouragement of regional opposition to Madison's war.[56] He was in any event too peevish and fractious to succeed as a national politician. His son, John, was educated at Harvard College and spent a couple of years in London (his father then serving as Adams' Secretary of State), as a young private secretary to the American minister, Rufus King. He returned to Boston in 1801 to pursue a legal career and amateur philology with an interest in the classics and in native American languages. In 1816 he published the first dictionary of Americanisms, a work that, as one American scholar summing up the field early in the twentieth century claimed, "exerted an influence over vocabularies that followed, which … has never disappeared entirely." Like Witherspoon's essays, it was also concerned with usage, and many of the 500 or so words it included, rather than of purely American origin, were derived from *British* "[a]rchaisms, provincialisms, colloquialisms, and Scotticisms."[57]

A Vocabulary, or Collection of Words and Phrases Which Have Been Supposed to Be Peculiar to the United States, published in Boston, caused something of a stir in the transatlantic philological world, and received mixed reviews. It launched what would become a genre of glossaries of purported Americanisms, as well as a long-lasting critical discourse, scholarly and otherwise, about their nature, origin, and meaning. Pickering's work contained some 500 terms. That of John Russell Bartlett in 1848 would offer 412 *pages* of Americanisms (rising to 813 in the edition of 1877 with over 5,600 entries). By the end of our period Richard Harwood Thornton's *American Glossary* of 1912 contained in two volumes fewer terms (over 3,700) but some 14,000 etymological citations.

Pickering's dictionary originated in a paper presented to the American Academy of Arts and Sciences, founded in Boston in 1780 by the Massachusetts legislature and scholar-patriots (including an uncle and namesake of Pickering's who had served as Speaker to the Massachusetts House of Representatives). As he tells us, his own interest had been piqued by his residence in London from 1799 to 1801, when he "began the practice of casually noting *Americanisms* and expressions of doubtful authority for my own use." In compiling his *Vocabulary* he was further aided by two English friends who had lived some twenty years in America. Pickering does not attempt to justify peculiar words and usage in American literature. American authors, he claimed, are often amateurs pursuing other occupations, and consequently "[o]ur writings … too frequently want that *finishing*, as the artists term it, which is acquired only by long practice … and this is a defect." Though there were corruptions "which English critics have [justly] censured in our writings," most of the words he treated were, he observed, "provincialisms"—including obsolete terms, old words given "new significations," and some "new-coined" words ("senseless novelties")—though he claims, no doubt with an eye to an American readership notoriously sensitive to criticism, "[t]he reader will not infer from these remarks, that *our right* to make new words is here to be denied." In the end, there was a good, practical reason for American writers to preserve in their work the English of Milton, Pope, Swift, and Addison: "if they are ambitious of having their works read by Englishmen as well as by Americans," they must learn to write in a purer language rather than in "a *dialect* of English," however uniform such a dialect may be throughout the United States.[58]

For the next three decades or so the philological exploration of Americanisms proceeded as a kind of transatlantic back-and-forth of snide criticism and touchy justification, though when Webster included several in his *American Dictionary* of 1828 as a kind of inclusive gesture, he did so without making much of their peculiar quality or importance. He told a surprised Basil Hall that "there were not fifty words in all which were used in America and not in England."[59] However, in the larger literary and social world the subject swelled and popular interest in identifying American difference in speech and writing very much grew apace.

British critics tended to praise Washington Irving's work because it did *not*, in its use of language, demonstrate or draw attention to its Americanness. Irving had come to England in 1815, stayed in Europe for the next seventeen years, become well-known among the British literati and their publishers, and matured in Britain his story-telling style. The work of James Fenimore Cooper (1789–1851), especially the Leatherstocking novels, also found a wide popular audience in Britain, but for rather different reasons. While Irving's tales had been often set in the America of old, Knickerbocker New York, they had not drawn attention especially to American linguistic difference. Cooper, by contrast, introduced in the speech of his most familiar character, Natty Bumppo, a.k.a. Hawkeye or the Deerslayer, a whole mid-eighteenth-century American backwoods vocabulary of words, phrases, and drawling expression which British readers might take to be the authentic, continuing voice of rural America. In *The Last of the Mohicans* (1826), Natty Bumppo's own identity is frontier-liminal, as he shifts back and forth between the tongue of the Delaware Indians who helped raise him and English, "a language he was apt to use when a little abstracted in mind."[60] His language is the language that would come to represent the plain speech of the southern or western hinterlands—somewhat obsolete words such as "afore," "atween," "varlet," "atwixt," or "hereaway;" familiar words but pronounced with a countryman's drawl such as "sarpent," "sartain," "l'arn" (for learn), "natur," or "oncommon"—many of these no doubt had a near analogue in the rural dialects of Britain, but there were also new words created in the American way—"judgmatical" or to "musickate." These words and usages do express something of the authentic vernacular and can be found in eighteenth-century grammars; several were included in Webster's 1828 dictionary. As Harry Morgan Ayres, in the 1921 edition of *The Cambridge History of American Literature*, put it, "There is not an oddity in the coarse, uncouth dialect of the Deerslayer … that has not its root deep in the soil of the eighteenth and preceding centuries" and such words "cannot be made to serve as illustrations of any wanton perversity on the part of Americans."[61] In the decades that followed the use of backwoods and Yankee dialects proliferated in American and British fiction where American settings or American characters were involved. James Russell Lowell, one of the New England "Fireside Poets" of the 1840s, used Yankee speech in his *The Bigelow Papers* (1848), and would later (1889) help found the American Dialect Society for the study of spoken English in North America.

Unlike Irving, Cooper had little regard for the sophisticated society of metropolitan Britain. He had been to England briefly as a young sailor at a time (1806) when merchant ships were often stopped—as was his—by the British navy to search for contraband or to impress into the Royal Navy sailors whom they regarded as British subjects. Though he married into a family that had been loyalist during the Revolution, and, much influenced by the novels of Scott, his own first novel, *Precaution* (1820), was set among English society, Cooper of course found his métier—and his transatlantic readership— as chronicler of *American* adventure tales. Rather like the early Webster, he idealized

America's democratic culture and denigrated what he took to be the influence of British aristocratic prejudices, especially in the realm of transatlantic publishing and taste. This created an awkward tension between his avowed dislike of British snobbery and affectation and his need for a British reputation and a British publisher; he was criticized for this apparent hypocrisy in the British reviews: "We think Mr. Cooper's sneers at a country which he may thank for all his literary success, are equally contemptible and ungrateful."[62]

Like nearly all aspiring authors of the time, Cooper courted publication in London as a route to a larger, more profitable readership than was likely in America. He traveled to Paris and London in 1826, 1828, and 1833, meeting Scott in Paris and the aged radical philosopher William Godwin in London, and was widely received in London—in spite of his objection to the custom of presenting letters of introduction—but he was never comfortable among metropolitan Society. His memoirs of his time in Europe, compiled of letters to mostly American correspondents and published in 1837, are those of a prickly, rather irritable man ready to draw attention to what he saw as the "fundamental differences" between Britain and America. Oddly, one finds little in it of the then raging debate in Britain over parliamentary reform and the challenge English radicals and the middling sort were offering to aristocratic privilege. Instead, Cooper dwells on the widespread "deference to hereditary rank" and the "irritating social ambition" of those on the social ladder beneath the nobility. "The English," he said, "do not like the Americans" in spite of the profound "deference" many Americans show toward the English. Complaining that many Americans resident in Britain "wish to conceal the fact" of their birth across the Atlantic, he concluded that in all, England was "a country that I could fain like, but whose prejudices and national antipathies throw a chill over my affections."[63]

Cooper's antipathies were encouraged and confirmed by the monthly reviews that were widely read in America, and which he thought, with a degree of paranoia, were often used by the British government to plant articles unfavorable to the United States. Cooper's antipathies were also encouraged by the growing number of opinionated travelers' memoirs such as, especially, that of Basil Hall, whose strong views about the inferiority of American education and quality of mind were those of "[a]lmost every English traveller, who has written on the republic."[64] While in Europe, Cooper himself had written in the year Webster's *American Dictionary* first appeared a kind of fictionalized satirical corrective of this emerging genre in *Notions of the Americans: Picked Up by a Travelling Bachelor*, published in London as well as Philadelphia, in which he admonishes the reader that "There is, perhaps, no Christian country on earth in which a foreigner is so liable to fall into errors as in the United States of America … The European … has a great deal to *unlearn* before he can begin to learn correctly."[65]

Hall's appalling, to many in the States, *Travels in North America* (published in London but also in Philadelphia in 1829), was eagerly if angrily read to confirm American expectations of the elitism and anti-democratic prejudice of British visitors. Sharply contrasting, as it did, with the by-and-large sympathetic views of America found in Frances Wright's travel memoir of 1821,[66] it was the harbinger of other travel memoirs that in the following decade were to antagonize and further inflame American sensitivity to British criticism: especially Frances Trollope's well-known *Domestic Manners of the Americans* of 1832, but also Harriet Martineau's *Society in America* of 1837, Frederick Marryat's *A Diary in America* of 1839, and a spate of others—followed by nearly twice as many (including Dickens' *American Notes* of 1842) in the next decade, and about twice as many again in the 1850s. The ever-growing number of travelers' memoirs before the Civil War made it increasingly likely that those entering the more crowded field would build on previous publications. Already, in 1807, Charles William Janson admitted that he "occasionally had recourse to the writings of others" in crafting his own memoir of America. Hall and Trollope, especially, became latterly the reference works for subsequent memoirs—as John Robert Godley noted in his own of 1844: ever since Mrs. Trollope "every succeeding traveller has been ringing the [same] changes."[67]

In 1833, Marryat, in a satirical piece on "How to Write a Book of Travels," had recommended that first one had to read up on all the other memoirs covering the same ground. Hall, though he claimed to have deferred reading previous travel accounts in order to arrive at his own conclusions, nevertheless was clearly well-versed, as he said, in "the sentiments prevalent in England" which he intended to confirm or challenge. By the time Dickens came to write his own *American Notes* in 1842, he had collected in his research some twenty-four such works of what had become "an unusually standardized genre."[68] It was a genre that, along with novelists' and playwrights' growing use of American dialect, served not only to highlight the Americanisms of the philological glossaries and dictionaries of the era (perhaps drawing from them as much as from traveled experience).

While philologists debated the expanding boundaries of an ever-growing lexicon of Americanisms, paradoxically the popular understanding of what was essentially and characteristically American in speech and literature narrowed (as with "I guess") to a few signifiers of American difference (amounting by the 1840s to perhaps a half-dozen or so commonly cited examples of American peculiarity of vocabulary). These, expressed in what came to be almost universally known in Britain as the expected American "nasal drawl" or "twang," became an enduring caricature—an actual caricature in British satirical journals and in the representation of Americans on the London stage—of American speech found in travel literature. Straddling those genres (of fiction and travel memoir), Dickens makes much in both *American Notes* and in the novel that followed it (*Martin Chuzzlewit*, serialized 1842–4), of the comic nature of peculiarly American speech, as in, famously, his treatment of "to fix":

> There are few words which perform such various duties as this word "fix." It is the Caleb Quotem of the American vocabulary. You call upon a gentleman in a country town, and his help informs you that he is "fixing himself" just now, but will be down directly: by which you are to understand that he is dressing. You inquire, on board a steamboat, of a fellow-passenger, whether breakfast will be ready soon, and he tells you he should think so, for when he was last below, they

were "fixing the tables": in other words, laying the cloth. You beg a porter to collect your luggage, and he entreats you not to be uneasy, for he'll "fix it presently": and if you complain of indisposition, you are advised to have recourse to Doctor So-and-so, who will "fix you" in no time.[69]

Six years after Dickens' send-up of peculiar American words and phrases, and after a decade or two of travelers' reiteration of (often the same) examples of American speech, the most substantial, and enduring, of the antebellum American philological glossaries appeared, John Russell Bartlett's *Dictionary of Americanisms*. It established itself as the fullest and most orthodox of such guides and, greatly expanded in successive editions, would later in the century be heavily referenced in Britain by the compilers of the *New* (later Oxford) *English Dictionary*. Bartlett (1805–86) was born in Providence, Rhode Island, and spent his childhood and early adult years in Canada. Back in the United States, he turned first to banking and then to bookselling—which allowed him to develop interests as an antiquarian, lexicographer, and ethnologist. He cast his net more widely than some more pedantic philologists, including words used, not only among the less educated "rustic" classes, but also among the educated. He also included, albeit hesitatingly, some colloquial terms common in both England and America on the principle that "a word now used only in some out-of-the-way locality in England, but quite general here, may be regarded as a peculiarity of the English language as spoken in America." Bartlett noted newly coined words, words borrowed from native American languages, and "Negroisms" (often then avoided in glossaries of American speech). He excluded "purely technical" and "obscene and blasphemous" words—avoiding thereby the colorful palette of backwoods and southern cursing much commented on in tourists' memoirs. In the first edition he apologized, being a New Englander, for his deficiency in knowledge of "Southern provincialisms."[70]

Though Bartlett's rationale emphasized what one might call an inclusive, scientific philological approach relatively free of the "war of words" axe-grinding of the British reviews or the early American defensiveness and idealism, he acknowledges his debt to Witherspoon, Pickering, and Webster, and confronts some of the charges leveled by British critics against American language and writing. He claims that "the English language is in no part of the world spoken in greater purity by the whole mass of the people than in the United States," an observation, he says, that has "repeatedly been made by intelligent Englishmen who have travelled in the United States." But he also gives the English reviewers their due, quoting from a letter by a Dr. Lieber of Columbia College that, compared with the florid exaggeration common in American writing, "[t]here has been no period and no country in which perspicuity, simplicity, and manliness of style are so general as at present in English Reviews." He is also willing to admit, along with the "ripest of scholars among us," that the best writers and public speakers of Great Britain employ a style and "idiomatic vigor" which "few or none of our [American] writers can attain."[71]

Bartlett notes peculiar regional differences in pronunciation—the New England "nasal twang" and the southern and western broad vowels as in many words Cooper used ("whar" for where, "bar" for bear)—but is not much concerned with them. He does however convey the kind of schoolmarmish tut-tutting that would become common to the pedantry of late nineteenth-century transatlantic philology. Among the terms reiterated in the travel literature and satirical British commentary, he agrees that "fixings" was a "word used with absurd laxity" and that "to guess," to which he devoted more than a page, was, like "to fix," evidence that Americans "have a passion for coining new and unnecessary words and often in a manner opposed to the analogies of the language." "Gouging" he dismisses as a practice known largely through probably no-longer relevant travel literature and Grose's dictionary: it "appears to have existed at no time except among the lower class of people in the interior of some of the Southern States. An instance has not been heard of for years." He cautions that the "greatest perversions of the English language" arise from the vulgarisms of uneducated people that work their way up to "the floor of Congress" (he was particularly unhappy with the careless language of politicians and journalists), from the misuse of legitimate words, and from the invention of hybrid "and other inadmissible expressions" by educated men, such as "to eventuate," and, increasingly, from foreign immigrants.[72] Perversion of a purer Pilgrim Yankee language by newer (Irish and German) immigrants was not a new concern—Irish speech, especially, had come to be much caricatured in both America and Britain. But it was one that gained in resonance in the United States along with the rise of political nativism in the 1840s and 1850s. When, in the 1850s, Franklin Pierce's Secretary of State issued a circular requiring diplomatic agents of the United States to make all communications "in the American language," it called in question perhaps, not only the use of diplomatic French or British English, but just what the authentic American idiom was.[73]

Bartlett's substantial dictionary of Americanisms, and its ever more extensive subsequent editions, came to dominate the field on both sides of the Atlantic. It was of course vulnerable, in the small but heated world of nineteenth-century philology, to sharp criticism of this or that inclusion or exclusion. In 1854 the New York literary critic and Shakespearean scholar, Richard Grant White, challenged Bartlett's reading of "well" (as an interrogative exclamation) and "guess" as erroneously labeled Americanisms: "Milton uses both, as Shakespeare also frequently does, and exactly in the way in which they are used in America ... [they] have lived here while they have died out in the mother country."[74] Bartlett responded of course in the next edition of his dictionary, and was joined by a Scottish scholar resident in British North America, the Rev. Archibald C. Geikie, who read a paper on Americanisms before the Canadian Institute in 1857. Geikie fumed that American usage of such words threatened to creep into modern English, "if some check is not put on the present tendencies of our colloquial speech, and the style adopted in our periodical literature." He in turn was subjected to White's sarcasm, which took him also to task for making too much of the different British and American usage of "hanged" and "hung."[75]

Access to Bartlett' dictionary, as it became well-known on both sides of the Atlantic, opened the field of Americanisms to tourists struggling, perhaps, to write up their experiences. When in the late 1850s, the Scottish poet Charles Mackay penned his "transatlantic sketches" for the *Illustrated London News*, he emphasized "Americanisms" and American "slang." The memoir that followed, *Life and Liberty in America*, included a chapter on this subject and a listing of American words newly-coined or those "that have lost their original [British] meaning:" "the study even of 'slang' is profitable, whether the student be a philosopher in the largest sense of the word, or merely a philologist ... During my residence in America I noted down from day to day ... single words ... phrases ... which grated harshly or sounded strangely to my English ears."[76]

Throughout the century Americanisms (of words, phrases, or pronunciation) feature prominently in the vast literature of the tourist memoir, either directly as subjects for (usually negative or amused) commentary or indirectly in remembered or fictionalized quotation of Americans encountered or imagined, often for comic effect. Henry Bradshaw Fearon has a Black New York barber liberally use the favorite Americanism of the genre: "Why, I guess as how, Sir, what you say is mighty elegant ... I guess, that you come from [England] from your tongue; you have no hardness like, I guess, in your speaking; you talk almost as well as we do, and that is what I never see, I guess, in a gentleman so lately from England"). John Benwell recalls the "nasal" observation of an American fellow-traveler: "'If twarnt for that ere man [Kosciusko], wher'd we be, I waunt to know; not here I guess'" eliciting "half-a-dozen 'do tells' and 'I waunt to knows' from those around."[77] The writers of travel memoirs, like the philologists who both followed them and inspired them, cited American speech both for comic effect and, in a broader sense, to establish the foreign and somewhat exotic realm of the tourist gaze—or, rather, ear. This was a matter of language—of "vulgarisms" and "barbarisms," neologisms or different American usage for familiar words (such as "sick," where an Englishman would say ill, or "clever," meaning pleasant rather than talented), and especially the reiteration of certain words and phrases such as "to guess," "to calculate," or "to fix." It was also a matter of pronunciation and "tone," of emphasis or accent (as with "en-GYNE"). Most commonly, it involved the genre's nearly universal allusion to the Yankee or more generally American "nasal twang"—a sharp, loud, and vulgar "hard," "unmusical," "harsh," "peculiar," "almost ludicrous," "sing-song" sound.

Transatlantic philology, ostensibly more "scientific" than the observations of travelers, grappled, in the era of the new Republic down to the American Civil War, with a set of issues arising out of the original war of words and out of the casual representation of American speech in the travel memoir: whether the "peculiarities" of American speech and literature were evidence of provincialism and a lack of proper education, or whether they might signify an evolving, legitimate and alternative world, markers of a new American identity, as some American idealists maintained. Somewhere in the middle ground was the argument over whether many so-called Americanisms were obsolete or archaic terms (i.e., words still in use in America that had once been common in Britain but were no longer), and if so, whether they ought to be regarded *as*, exactly, Americanisms. These terms, no longer good English in Britain, were evidence on one level of growing distance and division of the Anglo-American world, but also on another of a deep linguistic unity, buried in the past, and perhaps fit to be re-incorporated in a transatlantic philology newly sensitive to a racialized appreciation of world-wide Anglo-Saxonism.

One would have thought that *this* long-debated issue (of obsolescence and authenticity) would have run into the ground by the mid-nineteenth century, but Alfred Elwyn's *Glossary of Supposed Americanisms*, published in Philadelphia in 1859, was still defensive about "English travelers and authors" who "twit us upon the peculiarity and oddity in our use of words and phrases," when "all those words and phrases that we have been ridiculed for using, are good old English; many of them are of Anglo-Saxon origin, and nearly all to be heard at this day in [provincial] England."[78]

Late Victorian Philology and the Continuing Debate

In the second half of the century, down to the First World War, the expanding and refining of lists of Americanisms mounted (there were another half dozen or so published in New York, Boston, Chicago, and London). The increasingly pedantic debate surrounding them reflects the scholarly back and forth of a transatlantic philology situated between an amateur past and a "scientific" future. The Philological Society in London, refounded in 1854 by specialists in ancient western and Asian languages but also by gentlemen scholars and clergymen interested, often, in Anglo-Saxon studies, was influenced, at least the more academic members were, by the German philologists Franz Bopp and Jacob Grimm. It was followed by an American Philological Association some years later, in 1869, established chiefly through the efforts of its first president, the Orientalist William Dwight Whitney, who had studied in Berlin under Bopp. Whitney had helped revise definitions for Webster's 1864 edition. Like the London society, the American association sought to establish philology as a social science committed to the close study of linguistics, often through a comparative and etymological, that is historical, approach.

By the end of the nineteenth century, there was some coalescence of scholarly opinion around the idea that American literature and language were evolving, if not separately from, at least more distinctly from those of the mother country (Whitney had promoted the idea that languages were best understood as being "socially situated"). This is not exactly what Webster had, eventually, come to envision. Nor were armchair "philologists" who wrote for the higher journalism of America and Britain much involved in the increasingly technical world of Continental social science. For many of them, "purity of language," common standards, and all-inclusiveness remained important considerations.

Most of those who grappled with Americanisms in the second half of the century were interested in issues of definition. What, exactly, might properly be considered a true Americanism? Should such lists include the exotic terms and phrases often derived from the languages of native Americans or the new world Spanish and French; those that were merely local or regional rather than common, nationally used, "American" terms and phrases; neologisms? Language purists were especially concerned with newly invented terms and phrases (including "initialisms" such as PDQ and OK), portmanteau words, words that turned nouns into verbs—by adding "-ate" or "-ize"—or verbs into nouns—by adding "-ization." These were often seen as a particularly offensive result of the

American habit of linguistic "innovation," possibly influenced by German immigrants and already creeping into good British English. There was also embedded in much philological debate the problem of class. Were words to be included that were found, not in commonly acceptable American literature and speech, but only among "the lower sort"? Isabella Bird was not the only sympathetic visitor to claim, in defense of American culture, that "[t]he peculiar expressions which go under the name of Americanisms are never heard in good society."[79]

As the century drew on, America came to be seen as particularly the home of street *slang*. There was an older, eighteenth- and early nineteenth-century tradition of quasi-pornographic glossaries of obscenities and vulgarisms, such as Captain Francis Grose's *Dictionary of Buckish Slang*. In 1859, the amateur ethnologist and connoisseur of erotica John Camden Hotten published in London *A Dictionary of Modern Slang, Cant, and Vulgar Words* that both looks back to these somewhat sub-rosa interests and forward to a growing philological concern. On both sides of the Atlantic "slang" became by the late nineteenth century an important part of a new sociological approach to language. Rather like the argot of the east-London Cockney, the American slang of most interest to late nineteenth-century American philologists was almost uniquely lower-class and metropolitan rather than that of the rural America of Natty Bumppo's dated frontier speech, the much commented on variety of, especially Southern, cursing, the later Western lingo popularized in travel memoirs and novels, or the drawling talk of the huntin' and shootin' upper classes. This focus resonated of course with contemporary fears of the social, political, and linguistic influence of poor immigrants (Irish, Yiddish, or Italian) and was associated especially with the rougher areas of New York City and Boston.

Both among linguists and more popularly, *British* interest in American slang and, more generally, in American manner of speaking (in pronunciation, accent, rhythm, inflection, as well as in Americanisms of vocabulary and grammar) grew throughout the century. A shift from the monthly reviewers' concern with American literature to later preoccupation with the speech of Americans "in the street" may reflect not only the growing academic and antiquarian interest in dialects and phonetics, but also a larger milieu that saw a great increase in British tourists traveling through the States and beyond the drawing rooms of Boston and New York and also the significant rise in the number and type of American tourists in Britain by the end of the century.

When Oliver Bell Bunce, New York playwright, publisher, and humorous sketch-writer, published *Don't: A Manual of Mistakes & Improprieties More or Less Prevalent in Conduct and Speech* in 1883, he claimed he had in mind a readership of "the better class" of Americans going abroad. If that is true, he meant the little book as a kind of joke at the expense of the new rich who might in fact need such advice. An amusing "guide to the usages of polite society," it would, he said, "admit a flood of daylight behind the scenes of Transatlantic social life." Along with advice about correct table and drawing room manners and dress, there was, inevitably, a section on proper "Speech." It touched on the expected topics—avoiding a "nasal tone," Americanisms of pronunciation (such as "pertater" for "potato" or "ketch" for "catch"), unBritish usage (of, say, "right away" rather than "directly" or "immediately," or the widely caricatured American use of "fix" and "guess"). Chiefly his advice was that the visiting American should *listen to* and emulate the pronunciation of "cultivated people." But it was also a mistake to adopt fancy words in an attempt to sound posh: "Good, plain, vigorous Saxon is never nauseating."[80] Richard Grant White had, less humorously, issued some of the same warnings in 1880. The speech of common Americans "in the omnibus or the railway car" was marred by "that nasality which is not a snarl, a whine, or a grunt, but which yet partakes of the qualities of all these graces," while "[d]eliberate elegance in language is now the sign either of an extreme of pedantry and affectation, or, more generally, of inferior social and intellectual culture."[81]

Differences of pronunciation had provided material for philologists searching out Americanisms of speech from the time in the late eighteenth century when dictionaries, such as those of James Buchanan (the earliest, in 1757) or Thomas Sheridan (1780), began to include guides to proper pronunciation, when, that is, the issue of just how a word should be pronounced came to play a role in class stratification and the division between the provincial and the sophisticated metropolitan. British critics of Buchanan's dictionary unkindly drew attention to his being Scottish (and later that Sheridan was an Irishman) and thus not himself a native speaker of the English of the fashionable, metropolitan world—he and his readership had to teach themselves about proper speech rather than having been reared hearing it: "Mr. Buchanan does not appear to *know* how English is pronounced by polite and just speakers."[82]

Though both Webster and Cooper had stressed, somewhat idealistically, the lack of American dialects, the many travelers' memoirs of the period and after often remark on the regional diversity of speaking throughout the United States. For his part, Frederick Marryat thought that diverse American pronunciation—their refusal to speak "according to our standard"—was the result of both their ignorance of Greek and Latin and their democratic insistence on speaking however they chose: "every one appears to be independent, and pronounces just as he pleases." George Perkins Marsh, who prepared an American edition of a *Dictionary of English Etymology* by Hensley Wedgwood, Darwin's brother-in-law, and helped co-ordinate the early stage American contributions to Murray's New English Dictionary project, suggested that differences between American and British pronunciation simply resulted from the fact that many Americans, a "nation of readers" scattered throughout a lightly populated country, learned their language by reading rather than by listening—carefully pronouncing each syllable as it was written, a "conformity to the very letter of orthography" that accounted for both American stiffness in speaking and the characteristic American drawl. Twenty years later Richard Grant White made much the same observation—that many Americans spoke dictionary or spelling-book English, carefully pronouncing as written "War-wick," "Wor-ces-ter," or "Loo-tenant."[83]

In spite of this, Marsh at least emphasized "elective affinities, the powerful harmonic attractions" of American and British English, over vast distances and growing separation in time. Not in fact "separated by a common language" as Shaw (supposedly) quipped,

Britons and Americans were "brothers of one blood, one speech, one faith" and "the Anglican tongue on both sides of the Atlantic, as it grows in flexibility ... will also more clearly manifest the organic unity of its branches, that national jealousies, material rivalries, narrow interest will not disjoin and shatter that great instrument of social advancement." But such rhapsodizing remained relatively rare among philologists until the political rapprochement of the end of the century and the idealization of transatlantic Anglo-Saxon racial bonds. For much of the rest of the era, "differences" tended to be the red meat of philological discourse—as it was in many of the British travelers' memoirs. Edward Money, who had gone out to Colorado to try his hand at ranching (he returned after only five months), found that "[s]ome Americans seem to forget that England was the birthplace of their language." When one American acquaintance claimed to find, to Money's amusement, the *British* accent "when speaking our language" to be peculiar, "I laughed, and remarked that unless I mistook, *we* had spoken it before Americans existed. He did not answer." Other British travelers took similar umbrage at being told they spoke with an accent—though Edward Freeman did not, simply observing that "Americans constantly notice what they call the 'English intonation,' the 'English accent,' and I have even seen it called the 'horrible English intonation,'" though he suggested that British visitors twitting Americans for their "twang" were perhaps "less civil." In 1891 Rudyard Kipling, having first visited the States in 1889 en route to England from Asia, however, made a (prickly) joke of it: "They delude themselves into the belief that they talk English—the English—and I have already been pitied for speaking with 'an English accent' ... the American has no language. He is dialect, slang, provincialism, accent ...."[84]

The publication of expanded dictionaries of Americanisms continued to provide gist for philological debate to the end of the century and beyond. Though some of the older attitude and argument remained, these glossaries often suggest a growing acceptance of an American language that is authentically, rather than perversely or peculiarly, different. In 1871, Maximilian Schele De Vere (1820-98), a Swedish-born professor of modern languages at the University of Virginia, offered a guide to *Americanisms, or the English of the New World* that quickly went through two editions. As he put it, though (he thought) there was as yet no uniquely American literary language, the colloquial language of ordinary conversation was, especially from the impact of slang and immigration, changing daily: "we still speak English, but we talk American."[85] The Rt. Rev. Samuel Fallows, who had emigrated from Manchester, England, age eighteen, published a guide in 1883 that drew heavily on Peter Mark Roget's *Thesaurus of English Words and Phrases* (London, 1852, and subsequent editions) and on Bartlett's 1877 edition. He claimed to offer, evenhandedly, a dictionary of colloquial and provincial words and phrases that included *both* "Briticisms" and Americanisms. Finally, a substantial text on Americanisms by a Briton published in Britain, John Stephen Farmer's *Americanisms—Old and New* (1889), came rather late in the day. He admitted to having drawn substantially on the more recent work of both De Vere and Fallows, as well as on Pickering, Bartlett, and Elwyn.

Farmer (1854-1916) was an eccentric, a believer in the occult (spiritualism was fashionable in late nineteenth-century London), who shared with his predecessor John Hotten not only an interest in slang (publishing with William Ernest Henley seven volumes on *Slang and its Analogues* [1890–1904]) but perhaps also an interest in erotica. "Americanisms," Farmer claimed, "in the main, have long been a bug-bear to purists, the despair of etymologists, and an unfailing source of wonder, amusement, and, in many respects, a puzzle to the general reader." Far from adopting the critical stance of much of the long tradition, he relishes the "life" of American writing and speech. He takes the field in its "wider meaning," beyond the niggling concerns of philology, and extends it to "the racy, pungent vernacular of Western life." The lingo of the romanticized American West was especially prominent in late nineteenth-century travel literature, transatlantic journalism, and fiction. When Iza Duffus Hardy, herself a novelist, visited Colorado in the early 1880s she noted in her inevitable published memoir the local words and phrases (such as "bronco-busting") that would have been "unintelligible as hieroglyphics … not so long ago." She had studied her "well-worn copies of Mark Twain and Bret Harte" for the "manners, customs, and phraseology of the great West."[86]

The language of the American West in particular fascinated Farmer—a reflection perhaps of the great increase in the number of British tourists west of the Mississippi after the opening of the transcontinental railway in 1869, and the corresponding scores of sometimes romanticizing travel memoirs published in London about Western adventure, hunting, fishing, camping, mining, and cattle ranching, as well as an increasing number of memoirs by British women such as Iza Duffus Hardy or Isabella Bird who now felt comfortable traveling into what had previously been perceived to be a largely rough male preserve (by the 1880s Bird would travel alone unchaperoned). Western colloquialisms, Farmer asserted, "have impressed the stamp of their life in a remarkable degree … on what Mark Twain aptly calls 'the vigorous vernacular.'" This was a language that, if "often coarse; sometimes cynically brutal too," was "yet always sententious, full of pith and point … overflowing with wit and humor—of a kind."[87]

3 Standard English? Coalescence, Coexistence, and Shifting Hegemonies

Richard Grant White (1822–85), a well-published New York literary and music critic and prominent Shakespearian scholar who had earlier been drawn to the debate over the Elizabethan origins of American usage, developed in the 1870s a more sustained line of interest in American vocabulary, and especially in Americanisms. During the American Civil War, he had contributed "Yankee Letters" to the London *Spectator*. A cultural Anglophile, he toured England in 1876–7, published a travel memoir of his experiences there in 1881 and in 1883 a humorous novel that followed two Americans— one a gentleman (like himself), the other an Irish-American poseur—in Britain.[88]

White's interest in Americanisms was that of a scholarly amateur who rejected the label "philologist." A "real philologist," he dismissively observed, "horsed upon Grimm's law, chases the evasive syllable over umlauts and ablauts into the faintly echoing recesses of the Himalayas." He was chiefly interested in "taste and reason" rather than deep historical etymologies which, he complained, were unfortunately coming to dominate ever-expanding dictionaries, or the study of prescriptive rules of grammar ("I am not like Sir Thomas Overbury's pedant, 'who dares not thinke a thought that the nominative case governs not the verbe'").[89]

White's distrust of the "science" of philology and his dismissal of historical etymologies was greatly and painfully deepened in the 1870s, thanks to an acerbic, and he thought personally insulting, confrontation with the eccentric philologist, Fitzedward Hall (1825–1901), an American Orientalist who had weathered the Indian Mutiny and returned to London in 1862 to take up a chair in Sanskrit at King's College. He lived the rest of his long life, with occasional visits to America, in England.[90] Expelled from researching at the India Office for drunkenness and from the (London) Philological Society for the ad hominem tenor of his public denunciations of those with whom he disagreed, he retired as a recluse to Surrey and from this refuge continued for years to publish (he was a confirmed letter writer to journals), attacking those, such as White, whom he dismissed as unqualified. In 1872 he devoted much of a book on "false philology" to savaging White's uninformed "tirade" on usage and Americanisms in White's *Words and Their Uses*, and for his presumption to "teach others English": "We shall search in vain,—for all the world as if he had been bred at Oxford,—to find him conceding, as within the compass of the credible, the fallibility of his private judgements, or the inexhaustiveness of his meagre inductions." White's work was speculative and, "in the highest degree, unscientific and anti-historical," and reached "monstrous conclusions." White's *Words and Their Uses* bore "the same relation [to philology] that alchemy bears to chemistry."[91]

Writing as a gentlemanly litterateur for a larger and different audience than the academic and professional philological community, White responded with a sense of personal injury, declaring in the *Atlantic Monthly* and in new editions of his books that Hall, as a scholar of Sanskrit, was himself incompetent "to pronounce upon [English] usages," that, being "insufficiently informed," he displayed "an enormous pretense" and a disposition to contradict all other writers, whom he treated "with the most offensive disrespect."[92] Hall, who seems to have relished such feuding, responded, in an attack on American "would-be philologists who collect waifs and strays of antipathies and prejudices, amplify the worthless horde by their own whimseys, and, to the augmentation of vulgar error, digest the whole into essays and volumes." For such, philology was "mere avocation and pastime," a "piddling and nibbling" kind of philology.[93]

White continued to pursue, in an extensive series of articles for the *Atlantic Monthly*, and in other articles gathered together and published in 1880 in *Every-Day English*, a sustained analysis of Americanisms of vocabulary and usage. He took the familiar position that many such words and phrases—such as "well," "fix," "guess," "fall" for autumn, or "different from" rather than "different to"—not only originated in earlier British usage but continued to be heard outside London, that dictionaries of Americanisms were too prone to include mere "slang and cant," and that generally the "distinction sometimes made between English literature and American literature is factitious." Throughout, his position is that much of the philology of Americanisms encouraged, by emphasizing "that which is peculiar" rather than that which is similar, "the erroneous assumption" that Americans spoke a "barbarous, hybrid dialect of which English is only the stock, upon which Indian, Dutch, French, German, Irish, and Negro stems and branches have been freely grafted."[94] In particular, he took on the popular prejudicial anti-American views of Henry Alford, Dean of Canterbury, who, in his *The Queen's English* of 1864 (a work that by 1888 had gone through seven editions), had conventionally asserted that there was in America a "process of deterioration" of language.[95]

Alford's book was widely available in America and widely discussed. When the Marquis of Lorne, soon to become a son-in-law of Queen Victoria, toured North America in 1866, he found that conversation about Americanisms "afforded me some amusement," and that Dean Alford's book was "handed about" and commonly discussed "in the railway cars."[96] However, by the 1880s it appears that Alford's views had ceased to be taken seriously by most philologists. Albert M. Tucker, journalist, amateur philologist, and member of the Albany Institute and later the American Dialect Society, dismissed him with the observation that the "insular prejudice or crass ignorance" of his book—if still occasionally parroted in British newspapers and popular journals—was hardly to be found among British philologists of the present day.[97] Fitzedward Hall, who seemed to relish annoying *both* British and American philologists, was, however, perfectly pleased to echo Alford: American language was "daily becoming more and more depraved."[98] This elicited a sharp, if in Hall's case unmerited, response from Tucker that Hall was "one of those extraordinary Americans of the Henry James, Jr., stripe, who seem to regard it rather as a matter of regret than otherwise that they were not born in Europe."[99]

In fact Hall also took issue not only with White's unprofessional assault on studies of grammar and historical etymology, but with White's cultural Anglophilia. White had claimed that writers and speakers of "good English" in America do and ought to "find our standard English, whether in word, in idiom, or in pronunciation" in Britain, and "in so far as it [American English] deviates from the language of the most cultivated society in England it fails to be English." Preferring good taste and common-sense, economical reasoning to philological nit-picking, White also was exasperated at the ever-increasing size of dictionaries that insisted on padding out their work with multiple definitions (as in the most recent Webster's fifty-six definitions of "run" as a transitive verb) and especially at exhaustive citations of historical usage, with "wearisome superfluity and puerile iteration." Etymology was "the least valuable element in the making of a dictionary," and Webster's, now edited by a German, "has gone over to etymological definitions" to an absurd and obsessive degree.[100] White may or may not have been aware that by the late 1870s, Hall had become an important contributor to the most significant philological project of late-Victorian and early-twentieth-century publishing, the New (later Oxford) English Dictionary, devoted to establishing exhaustively the historical etymology of English words and usage.

The New English Dictionary

The idea for a complete dictionary of the English language grounded in an etymological, that is historical, approach, was first floated in the late 1850s at the Philological Society in London, but the projected New English Dictionary did not significantly get underway until the 1870s. Released in alphabetical segments ("fascicles") over the decades, it was finally published together in ten volumes in 1928, well after its editor James Murray's death in 1915. Among the hundreds of researchers involved over a half-century, a number of Americans who had the time and expertise to invest, such as reclusive (and possibly unbalanced) Fitzedward Hall, were recruited or volunteered—including the genuinely unbalanced William Chester Minor, sent to Broadmoor for killing a man he believed was following him.[101]

In a sense, the New English Dictionary was heir not only to the empire-reach of Ogilvie's *Imperial Dictionary*, but to Webster's (perhaps somewhat reluctant) pursuit of a general, non-nation-specific guide for all the English-speaking world. James Murray, the third and longest-serving editor, scouted for (unpaid) contributors throughout Britain, its Empire, and the United States. His 1879 "Appeal to the English-Speaking and English-Reading Public," apparently widely distributed as a leaflet inserted into books ordered by Americans, elicited an enthusiastic response from American scholars, amateur philologists, and antiquarians who, organized in the United States by Professor Francis A. March of Lafayette College in Pennsylvania, sent, in the first year, some 17,000 citations: "I cannot sufficiently express my appreciation," Murray wrote, "of the kindness of our friends in the United States, where the interest taken in our scheme, springing from a genuine love of our common language, its history, and a warm desire to make the Dictionary worthy of that language, has impressed me very deeply."[102]

In following its etymological rationale, the NED project folded into its scheme the large corpus of lexicological research into "Americanisms." In the beginning, though Murray may have encouraged *American* researchers to volunteer, it had not been his intention to illustrate specifically American usage and development. Later, however, it was decided to include American variations, and Bartlett's expanded dictionary served as an important source. The thick use of historical citations confirmed and clarified some of the long-standing arguments over the archaic or obsolescent character of many American terms (in the earliest stages of planning it had been proposed that American volunteers might be relegated to identifying eighteenth-century usage[103]). Ultimately, the overall effect of the dictionary was, however, not to highlight American difference but to collapse it into a *general* presentation of the English language as written and spoken among English-speaking peoples, in the mother country, the Empire, and North America.

Special Transnational Languages of the Anglo-American World: Religion, Business, and Technology

Within the language of the Anglo-world ultimately enshrined in the OED, there were throughout the nineteenth century special sub-sets, as it were, of words and phrases familiarly shared and circulated by kindred communities on both sides of the Atlantic. Arguably the most powerful of these was the language of evangelical nonconformity, drawn from the King James Bible, sermonizing on sin, justification, grace, and redemption, the enduring rich metaphors of Bunyan's *Pilgrim's Progress*, or the phraseology of Anglican, Methodist, and Baptist hymnals. A few months before his death, Lincoln told the visiting Scottish poet and journalist Charles Mackay that, though he knew little Latin, "[w]e Americans are content to talk the language of the Bible, and of old John Bunyan."[104] Moreover, "revivalist" moral crusades carried their language and passion into the heart of much secular reformism. On both sides of the Atlantic, abolitionism and the temperance movement, as well as labor unionism and social reformism, shared missionary-like advocates and employed the language of religious enthusiasm.

The British nonconformist and American evangelical worlds shared a language of piety, obligation, and practice that worked against what many philologists considered to be the tendency of national speech to separation, and was a powerful reinforcer of the familial, social, and sectarian networks of extended Anglo-American Protestantism (within not only the transatlantic sphere but in the wider world of African, South Asian, Oceanian, and Caribbean missionary activity). The Quaker activist abolitionist Joseph Sturge could travel from Edgbaston, near Birmingham, to Philadelphia, New York, Wilmington, or Baltimore, guided by American "Friends" such as the poet John Greenleaf Whittier, and befriended by local "meetings" wherever he went—"I received much kindness, and many more invitations than it was possible for me to accept."[105] In 1844 the Rev. George Lewis, a Scottish Free Church minister and abolitionist, celebrated in his travel memoir "the reopening of an intercourse between churches that have a common parentage, a common creed, and in these latter days are, we trust, to wage a common warfare for the faith."[106] When a former East India Company chaplain, the Rev. Robert Everest, published his recollections of *A Journey Through the United States* in 1855, he noted that "the Protestant Episcopal Church and the different sectarian bodies" in America "have each peculiar sympathies with their respective brethren at home [in Britain]." Even war between the two nations "was a family affair ... As we are the Englishmen of King Charles, they are the Englishmen of John Milton."[107] Two years later a Wesleyan Methodist minister from Bradford, who toured the United States as a representative of the Wesleyan Conference at Leeds in 1856, reported that "[t]hough more than 3000 miles from home" he found himself surrounded by men and women "speaking the language with which he has been familiar from childhood ... 'We are all brethren.'"[108] A Liberal nonconformist from Liverpool, the Rev. Newman Hall, who traveled to America in 1867 to help restore good will after the American Civil War, could feel at home in Boston as no stranger: "We read together the dear familiar words [from the family Bible]."[109] And the popular revivalists Dwight L. Moody and Ira D. Sankey could in the 1870s travel in the other direction, sure of finding in England a familial reception and emotional mass meetings that featured gospel songs and "come-to-Jesus" preaching.

Of course there were many Britons for whom the language and zealous practice of dissenting nonconformity were regarded as part of the vulgar culture of shopkeepers and commercial travelers and somewhat beyond the pale of polite society—even after political disabilities were lifted in 1828 and the great and good of this varied community came to achieve great wealth and political influence. For those who maintained a traditional, often Tory prejudice against such "outsiders," the transatlantic *unity* of the American and British sects was at the same time emblematic of a religious, social, and political *division* of the nation. Frances Trollope had written with some disdain about

American religious camp meetings.[110] Her dislike was echoed by others, as in John Delaware Lewis's complaint of loudmouthed preachers, hymns sung by bumpkins, hysterical women in fits, and instantaneous conversions.[111] For many British, especially of the Anglican, educated upper classes, American religious difference would continue to resonate with their suspicions of nonconformity at home well into the twentieth century, though perhaps not with the same fervor that some travelers such as Richard Parkinson displayed at the beginning of the nineteenth century: A "dissenter" preaching at Baltimore, Parkinson reported, used language that "was extremely vulgar and profane, as I thought ... like an auctioneer selling razors and cutlery-ware in a market, or a mountebank-doctor on the stage."[112]

But for many others, the language of fundamentalist belief and evangelizing practice was a great transatlantic bond, and reached down, as Anglicanism often did not, into classes well below the polite society of the political and religious establishments. Missionaries to Britain for the proselytizing new Mormon church, though widely denigrated and caricatured by mainstream clergymen, journalists, and politicians, were able to recruit easily and deeply from middling and working-class communities in England, Scotland, and Wales.

One may regard the vocabulary, metaphors, and analogies of commerce and industry if not exactly as another unifier of a virtual transatlantic community, though they could be that, at least as a shared language that crossed oceans in an era of rising laissez faire, economistic thinking, and transnational commercial enterprise. In the early and mid-nineteenth century it was often a language that was as much a matter of idealism as of profit-making—though for a railway promoter *and* Anti-Corn Law League organizer such as Richard Cobden's friend Edward William Watkin the boundaries are easily blurred. His own American tour in 1851, the memoir of which was written he said for businessmen such as himself who had "little time to travel," offered a chance both to search for railway investment opportunities and approvingly to report on "the growth of the American economy and population": it was irrelevant that "Americans speak through their noses." He observed that steam navigation and railways had opened up the American hinterland to British immigration, tourism, and commerce, and generally advanced "the development of the Anglo-Saxon race."[113] For his part, George Combe found the American metaphorical use of the language of commerce and finance—in the new-to-him phrase "political capital"—to be "so pithy, so expressive, and every way so excellent, that it should be transferred into the English language ... we [the British] have the thing which it signifies in perfection, and want an adequate name for it."[114]

The hard-headed, utilitarian, individualistic mentality and discourse of "business" that came to be associated with American commercial, financial, and industrial acumen and sharp practice had its precursor and its parallel, if not exactly its origin, in the North of England, in the cockpit of the first industrial revolution. This religion of self-improvement was evangelistic as well as transatlantic. By mid-century its homilies were to be found in parallel texts such as Samuel Smiles' *Self-Help* or Horatio Alger's "rags-to-riches" fiction. Indeed, as Boyd Hilton has taught us (and Tawney and Weber before him),[115] there was a close connection between the language of Protestant, evangelical religion and that of commercial enterprise, in their mutual discourse of saving and redemption, in the language of atonement and personal salvation, that spread out from theology into economics and the sciences, as well as informing entrepreneurial practice. When the commercial traveler Adam Hodgson visited the United States in 1819 he approvingly found, among the few books in an obscure Vermont inn, a copy of Whitfield's sermons (along with Paley's *Moral Philosophy*, the poems of Walter Scott, and a grammar and dictionary of the English language).[116] On both sides of the Atlantic Quakers were especially connected to commercial and industrial enterprise; Joseph Sturge had himself, before he became a wandering evangel for a host of causes, been an active member of a family involved in the grain trade, manufacturing, and speculative investments in railways and docks.

Richard Cobden, the coming avatar of the evangelism of Free Trade, visited America for the first time (he would travel to the States again in 1859) as a young businessman and calico printer in 1835, the same year he published the first of his free trade tracts, *England, Ireland, and America, by a Manchester Manufacturer*. He prefaced this pamphlet with the well-known quotation from Washington's Farewell Address admonishing America to abjure foreign politics "in extending our commercial relations." Cobden's central message was that the United States had greatly and quickly prospered—without the national debt and corn laws that, in Britain, sustained "idle pomp and luxury," and without the vast armed fleet needed to promote Britain's Continental and imperial foreign policy. A friend of nonconformists in the struggle against the Corn Laws and in campaigns for peace, international arbitration, and abolition of slavery, he thought that the charge against American religion and morality found in the quarterly reviews, and in the books of some conservative travelers such as Mrs. Trollope and Basil Hall—grounded often in the absence there of an established church—was spurious and offered no sound reason not fully to develop close commercial ties. The "quicker mechanical genius" of the Americans, the "spectacle of commercial enterprise" of their vastly expanding railroads, and (with the glaring, and hopefully temporary, exception of duties to protect American manufacturers) the "peaceful principles of Free Trade" would lead the United States to a future where England and America would be "bound together in peaceful fetters by the strongest of all ligatures that can bind two nations to each other,–*viz*, commercial interests."[117]

If most American men of commerce and industry, fearing what we might call the informal imperialism of British global competition, did not exactly embrace the "Gospel of Free Trade" (though some did), other "sacred laws" of political economy seemed as central to American drive and national character as they had been to the money-making ethos of Manchester and Birmingham. Indeed, British home-grown entrepreneurial discourse met in mid-Atlantic, as it were, American "smart-dealing" and veneration of the "Almighty dollar," as well as Carnegie's exculpatory "Gospel of Wealth."

British visitors to an industrializing America, from the Radical godfather of political laissez faire, Richard Cobden, to North of England commercial tourists simply scouting out what clever tricks the Americans had for their particular commercial or industrial sector, brought and found there a language of commerce, the tongue of the transatlantic business community. They also found what many, such as the phrenologist and friend of Cobden's, George Combe, regarded as a striking religiosity—attractive to some, offensive to others: "I was struck with the far greater frequency and freedom with which religious opinions are introduced and commented upon."[118] The religiosity of some American businessmen, their mixture of commercial and scriptural language, certainly had a resonance among similar communities in Britain, and especially in the nonconformist British north—but not only there. The Christian language of personal responsibility was, like that of free trade and free speech, grounded in conceptions of an open market-place of choice, the pre-condition of the individualist liberalism enshrined in the writing of John Stuart Mill and in the ethics of profit-seeking and self-improvement.

The Rev. Newman Hall, on visiting the Stock Exchange in Wall Street, was asked "as an Englishman, a friend to America," to speak to the traders. "I addressed to them a few earnest words on the importance to commerce of peace between the two countries, assuring them, all opinions to the contrary notwithstanding, that the British nation were their true and stedfast [sic] friends. At the close of my brief address, hearty cheers were given for Great Britain, and some one starting 'God Save the Queen,' all joined in the anthem with enthusiasm."[119] Not all American businessmen of course would have endorsed such sentimental attachment to the land of their fiercest competitors, nor did those British businessmen who visited America always find the entrepreneurial, get-ahead climate and culture there attractive. Andrew Bell, though he "was brought up in republicanism" and wanted to visit the States from the early days of his youth, had "become less sanguine" about them by the time he actually traveled there the same year as Cobden. The language and mentality of the fraternity of commerce did not, in his case, compensate for much in American society that he found offensive, quite apart from the slavery issue—their "shallow and frothy newspapers," their political "jargon," and their "prevailing mania" for "speech-making." They were a "thin-skinned nation," likely to be "very cold and distrustful" to "aliens."[120] The default of some American states on British loans in the 1840s raised deep suspicions in Britain of American probity and trustworthiness and tarnished the reputations of many who traded in American bonds on the London market. London financial dealers, however, were themselves often charged with the immorality of dubious unethical practices, especially following the collapse of banking houses and railway share bubbles, and latterly the financial crisis of the late 1850s and scandals of the early 1870s. As in Anthony Trollope's novel *The Way We Live Now* (1875), the hollowness of commercial ethics in Britain came to be regarded as, or was implied to be, a consequence of the Americanization of practices in London and the larger Anglo-world. The London-New York financial connection in promoting stocks and bonds (and especially American railway and, later, mining and cattle-ranching shares) was throughout the century an increasingly close and somewhat murky business, though some, like the Anglican vicar, chaplain-in-ordinary to the Queen, transatlantic traveler, and antiquarian the Rev. Foster Barham Zincke, were prepared by the 1880s to find in the Anglo-American capitalist "belt around the world" the promise of an advance in both world-wide morality and prosperity.[121]

Language that suggested or claimed a special entrepreneurial morality and character had of course hardly convinced those on both sides of the Atlantic for whom the combination of preaching and love of money-making came to be caricatured as "cant"— by Transcendentalists, Ruskinian and Carlylean social critics, Tory moralists, humanist novelists, muckraking journalists, or Wildeian aesthetes—whether expressed in Lancashire, Birmingham, Pittsburgh, or Chicago. Some philologists such as Bartlett were content to draw attention to the role of money in American speech, while others such as Schele De Vere saw it in its transatlantic context: "America has sent a fair supply of cant terms to the home-country, and they have been welcome and readily adopted by English politicians and English merchants especially." He regarded the especial *American* love of mammon imputed in the phrase "the almighty dollar" as libelous however: "It may even be doubted whether the dollar is as powerful in America as gold is in England."[122]

British charges of Yankee mammonism persisted throughout the century, often echoing a familiar American self-critique. During the financial panic of 1857 James Stirling noted that "Wall Street 'mammonism'" was denounced in the New York press, though he argued in his travel memoir that, though excessive, it sprang from "a noble desire": American "'dollar worship' is but overstrained ambition … a perverted passion for liberty."[123] A harsher judgment is generally found in the very common, indeed hackneyed, critical complaints in most memoirs of those British visitors not themselves connected to transatlantic networks of finance and commerce. It was a complaint that was played and replayed throughout the century in the casual invocation of love of the "almighty dollar" as almost part of the genome, as we might say, of the American character. As Frank William Green reported back to the readers of the *Wakefield Herald* in the mid-1880s, "that all-absorbing topic, the 'Almighty dollar'" could be heard around the campfires even of the Far West—"as to how much Jay Gould and Vanderbilt are worth, or whether [Dublin-born John William] Mackay made fifty or only fifteen million dollars out of the Comstock mines. It is astonishing to find what pleasure an American takes in talking about or pointing out some rich man … Here almost everything depends on what a man is worth."[124]

Finally, there was a language of innovation and innovative technologies, of processing and manufacturing techniques and consumer gadgetry, and of promoting (that is advertising) these that reached back, in Britain, to the early days of industrialization, to Wedgewood and Bolton. By the mid-nineteenth century it was, however, held by many to reflect a particularly American obsession with (or genius for) inventions and mechanical devices and by philologists to be a source of much American slang and jargon. Flowing from the technological advances in steel and iron making, steam engines and railways, and later the generation of electrical power, industrial *metaphor* flourished, not only in America of course but especially there. Webster had introduced the language of commerce and industry in his dictionary. Bartlett, in his glossary of Americanisms— though he included "the Almighty Dollar"—excluded "purely technical words, and those only known in certain trades."[125] These had however assumed more importance with the growth of industrial cities such as Pittsburgh, ever more sophisticated processes and machinery (like the metaphor-rich blast furnace or electric dynamo), and the emergence of a professional and popular journalism devoted to the industrial and commercial sectors. Well before the late nineteenth-century rise of American industrial prowess as the basis for a coming American global hegemony, they acquired something of the character of an especially American mode of speaking, a voice of practical modernization which circulated back to Britain in the early twentieth century as a siren sound, resented by traditionalists, an invitation for emulation and a threat.

In 1869 A. J. Mundella, a Nottingham hosiery manufacturer and Liberal M.P., drew attention, as did many others before and after, to America's "technical inventiveness," a trait he traced in part "to her excellent patent laws."[126] Henry Adams later observed that the American mind differed from the English mind in being remorselessly practical,[127] repeating what had long been something of a cliché—a supposed national trait that worked its way into characterizations of matter-of-fact, "un-literary" American writing and what many thought was the dry, ironical economy of common American speech. In fact, in the course of the century the representation of the American businessman had taken over from Lancashire the language of practicality. Charles Whibley, a Tory literary critic and historian on a visit to New York City in 1907, was not a fan, one can imagine, of either Lancashire and Yorkshire plain-talking ("Where there's muck there's brass") or American "practicality." He dismissed, as did some philologists for whom it was a form of slang, the technology-heavy language of American innovation as so much obfuscating jargon: "America delights in the mysteries of a technical vocabulary; it is happiest when it can fence itself about by the privilege of an exclusive and obscure tongue."[128]

Fin de siècle Transatlantic Philology: Americanization and Anglomania

Perhaps the most widely published American philologist writing for the general public in the era between the Spanish-American War and the Great War was a professor of English language and literature at Yale University. Thomas R. Lounsbury (1838–1915) was a distinguished scholar of Chaucer and Shakespeare, though he had also published a popular life of James Fenimore Cooper. In his later years, Lounsbury turned to philology, writing books on the history of the English language (1879, 1894), English pronunciation (1904), usage (1908), and spelling (1909). Between 1903 and 1913 he offered the readership of *Harper's Magazine* a series of articles on British and American colloquial speech and pronunciation. These interests reflect the trend of much philological writing from the late nineteenth century away from the well-worked ground of a peculiar American vocabulary to issues of, often, class differences in how English is spoken, contrasting literary and colloquial English, the English of the educated and that of the uneducated, and the *spoken* language of Americans and that of Britons. As he wrote in 1903, "If one topic more than another can be selected as the subject of perpetually recurring discussion and controversy among the educated men of our race, it is that of the pronunciation of particular words."[129]

The rising popularity of pronouncing dictionaries was, Lounsbury observed, clearly related to the social aspirations of "the imperfectly educated middle class." In America, it was clear, he thought, that Joseph E. Worcester's popular *Dictionary* of 1847, a major competitor of Webster's, was so successful because "he loudly professed to conform the pronunciation authorized in it to the usage of London." But Worcester was also popular ("in vogue") in England—among, one may suppose, the same class of people eager to speak properly, leading to the irony that when a Londoner of the aspiring classes "wished to satisfy his mind about the exact quality of that pure and perfect pronunciation, to the possession of which he is supposed to have been born, he proceeded half the time to consult the pages of an American lexicographer."[130]

Lounsbury's discomfort with drawing a sharp distinction between the national speech of America and that of Britain was heightened by his understanding of the ways in which American English had for a hundred years been caricatured ("the language imputed to Americans in English comic papers and English novels ... speech which has never actually been spoken by any collective body of human beings anywhere"). Such differences as there were had been exaggerated by comparing the "cultivated speech" of the British upper classes with that of the common American—and were in fact often simply illustrations of "what is proper or improper in speech itself." Moreover, it was clear that "differences tend to become fewer with the increase of [transatlantic] intercommunication."[131] By the 1880s if not earlier, some version of Brunel's dream had become reality. As William Edwin Adams enthusiastically told the readers of the *Newcastle Weekly Chronicle* after his visit to the United States in the spring and summer of 1882, "[a]ccess to America is now ... easy, pleasant, and expeditious ... Vessels ... cross the Atlantic with all the regularity of railway trains."[132] Others of course were precisely concerned with the seepage of American influence across failing linguistic borders.

Much of the somewhat obsessive nineteenth-century debate over Americanisms held, as does any concern with the rules of "correct" spelling, pronunciation, and grammar, a *moral*, prescriptive element[133] which later scientific philology would try to abandon, if not entirely successfully. As late as the early twentieth century, the Fowlers declared in their widely regarded guide to "good" English, *The King's English* (1906, and subsequent editions), which lumped Americanisms together with "malaprops" and "bad formations," that, while it was true enough that American speech contained archaisms once acceptable in England, in the modern world their use (wherever English was spoken or written) was nonetheless not good English: "though ['I guess'] is good old English, it is not good new English ... we have it not from Chaucer, but from the Yankees."[134] There was of course all along a moral message embedded in fears of "corruption" or "debasement" of the language, a message that carried over from the earliest discourse about Americanisms and resurfaced in the Edwardian age among philologists on both sides of the ocean uneasy about the impact of (often American) slang in common speech and in literature. In the early nineteenth century the somewhat sneering tone of the Fowler brothers would have been, in the monthlies, a mark of an easily assumed superiority over transatlantic provincialism. By the early twentieth century, it takes on a subtly different implication in a world where aggressively marketing American businessmen had acquired control of that artifact of the British Enlightenment, the *Encyclopedia Britannica*, where America's commerce and its banking and its projection of power and influence threatened to turn the tables, as it were, and leave Britain and its language in an embattled and defensive position, with a need to tutor the coming hegemon.

Fear of "Amer-English" in an era of "transatlantic intercommunication" and linguistic consolidation was not of course universal. Travel memoirs from the 1870s on often seem somewhat less concerned than previously about the corruption of the English language by Americans, simply accepting the difference as an inevitable national characteristic. William Fraser Rae, who took the newly completed transcontinental railway out to San Francisco, told the readers of the London *Daily News* (and of the memoir that followed) that Americanisms were merely "the inevitable change which is being wrought in language," and that he was "unable to side with those who profess to be shocked at the alleged deterioration of the English language in America; nor can I see the propriety of taking the people to task on account of their accent."[135] By the turn of the century, however, those who persisted in denigrating American English often reflect a shifting locus— from the operation of language in America to the corruption of language in Britain itself. Some casual writers simply continue to replicate a long tradition in the travel genre; others were social and political conservatives deprecating the infective vulgarity of a coming competitor. Some of these, such as Charles Whibley in his *American Sketches* of 1908, reverted to the tone of much of the early nineteenth-century critique. Whibley was not unfriendly to (at least Anglophilic expat) American writers and artists such as his brother-in-law James McNeill Whistler or later T. S. Eliot. His memoir of his visit to the States, however, thickly reproduced clichéd observations about drawling speech and peculiar vocabulary, about "barbarous" and "pompous" Latinisms[136] and the slang "of the pavement" heard from "vulgar Americans." American language was "peculiarly rich" in the "small change of meaningless words" that are "gathered into dictionaries, and survive to become the sport of philologists." And yet Whibley's tone of superiority conceals an element of almost supernatural uneasiness: "To the English traveller in America the language which he hears spoken about him is at once a puzzle and a surprise. It is his own, and yet not his own. It seems to him a caricature of English, a phantom speech, ghostly but familiar, such as he might hear in a land of dreams."[137]

The Society for Pure English, founded in 1913 by the British poet laureate, Robert Bridges, and among others a senior editor of the *New English Dictionary*, Henry Bradley, as well as Edith Wharton, the only American, was not, at least not overtly, anti-American. Indeed, its expressed concern with the "pedantry" of grammarians and its belief that language should be "democratic," that its "best wordmakers are the uneducated," was perhaps intended to encourage Americans to support the preservation of "our heritage." And yet, its apprehension of the vulnerability of good English to the importation of scientific terms and foreign words and its recommendation of the Fowlers' *The King's English* (which a *New York Times* reviewer of the Society's agenda called "offensively insular" and "parochial"[138]) suggest a fear of linguistic contamination from across the Atlantic. As the Fowlers more clearly and directly put it, "[t]here is a real danger of our literature's being americanized [*sic*], and that not merely in details of vocabulary … but in its general tone."[139]

Fears that American peculiarities or corruptions of speech and writing might influentially travel, like cablegrams, newspapers, and steamship passengers, eastward across the ocean were voiced throughout this fin de siècle period. As the journalist and poet, T. W. H. Crosland put it more generally in 1907, the "gradual Americanisation of this grand old country is not only flattering to American vanity, but gratifying to American greed … an evil which every Britisher ought to be prepared to make any sacrifice to avoid."[140] One might note that such fears of cultural miscegenation do not seem to have accompanied the great increase in the late nineteenth century of loan words derived from the Raj in India. But then the vocabulary presented in Sir Henry Yule and Arthur Coke Burnell's *Hobson-Jobson: A Glossary of Colloquial Anglo-Indian Words and Phrases*[141] could be treated, not as evidence of the Oriental corruption of English, or even of the Anglo-Indian establishment going native, but rather as a reassuring sign of an Anglo-world with Britain in charge, familiar with and comfortable in its ability to pick and choose from the languages of those whom they ruled. It was otherwise with the "rising" Americans.

The introduction and assimilation of Americanisms in Britain were enabled, it was feared, by the increasing availability of American journals, newspapers, and humor magazines in London bookshops such as W. H. Smith's or in the street kiosks of common news-agents, the circulation of Americanisms by returning tourists, and the significant increase of American tourists in Britain through the end of the century. According to John Farmer in 1889, "England swarms with Americans, and Englishmen themselves, visiting America, are struck by the new and racy phrases that they hear"; "the influence of" such "transatlantic words, phrases, turns of expression, and construction" was "daily gaining ground."[142] The rise of the New Journalism in Britain, journals specializing in sensational exposés such as W. T. Stead's *Pall Mall Gazette*[143] and cheap, mass-circulation newspapers such as Alfred Harmsworth's *Daily Mail*, was widely thought to be inspired by the mass-production technology, gossipy themes, and marketing tactics of the American press. American newspapers, with, British observers claimed, their low standard of often over-inflated writing, casual coinage of new vocabulary, lurid themes, and demagogic editorial politics (often anti-English and pro-Irish) had been a consistent and prominent part of the indictment of American literature and language in travel memoirs from Frances Trollope ("there are more direct falsehoods circulated by the American newspapers than by all the others in the world") and especially Dickens ("licentious Press," "scurrilous," "this frightful engine," the "*New York Sewer* … this morning's *New York Stabber* … the *New York Family Spy*") through much of the antebellum era and beyond. In the second half of the century, the charge most frequently leveled by British visitors was that of sensationalism. James Burnley reported back to the readers of the *Bradford Observer* that American papers had to dress up the "small beer" of their content with "blazing," "eye-opening" headlines about "[d]esperate murders, frightful accidents, disastrous explosions, disgraceful scandals, stupendous robberies, and wonderful romances." There was of course a sensation-seeking, penny-dreadful literature in Britain, but as usual in this kind of critique, the comparison being offered or suggested was that between a local (and second-rate) American press and the first-class broadsheets of metropolitan

Britain—which Burnley assumes Americans would find "heavy, indigestible, formidable, and uninteresting."[144]

Toward the end of the century, alarms raised moved from the critique of journalism "over there" to apprehension about the "Americanization" of the *British* press. Matthew Arnold, that defender of English high culture, wrote in 1887 of a "contagion" entering Britain from across the ocean.[145] Though he denied calling Americans vulgar, he did claim in his travel memoir that "the great bulk of the nation" were "Philistines." He also found their newspapers to be contemptible: "The absence of truth and soberness in them, the poverty in serious interest, the personality and sensation-mongering, are beyond belief."[146] After the 1880s it became more difficult for critics to continue to contrast American journalistic vulgarity with the higher standards of British journalism. Whether due to the corruption of the British press by the American model or simply the technological and economic forces of the times, the popular press in America and Britain had become, according to a recent historian, "the joint products of a common culture and indefinably transatlantic in sensibility."[147]

By 1919 H. L. Mencken could, looking back, claim with some exaggeration that "[s]o many Americanisms have gone over into standard English of late that Englishmen tend to lose the sense of their foreignness."[148] The Fowlers could chide even the poet of Empire, Kipling, for "Americanizing" the language. In 1897 Mark Twain had twisted the knife, offering as a "Pudd'nhead Maxim" in his travelogue of a tour of the British Empire that "[t]here's no such thing as the Queen's English. The property has gone into the hands of a joint stock company and we own the bulk of the shares."[149] One standard British philological "property" did in fact move to America when a new, 11th, edition of *Roget's Thesaurus*, a popular and much reissued and expanded school and autodidact's guide to vocabulary since 1852, was brought out by a New York press and edited by an American philologist, Christopher Orlando Sylvester Mawson (1870–1938) in 1911. Mawson was a kind of international maven of English dictionaries—an associate editor of the American *Standard English Dictionary*, a "consulting specialist" to the *Oxford English Dictionary*, a revising editor for *Webster's New International Dictionary*, and member of both the London Philological Society and the American Oriental Society (née the American Philological Association). As editor of the new *Roget's*, Mawson "introduced for the first time in any edition of the *Thesaurus*" Americanisms, "these virile specimens of our language." Looking back at the century of debate ("What is an *Americanism*? The answer is essentially complex"), he went to some length to set out the categories acceptable for inclusion: obsolescent words, provincialisms, and words assimilated from other languages, including "Negroisms," and "words of strictly American coinage."[150]

One should, perhaps, be careful of taking much of the apprehension of American take-over at face value. It might be argued that the most significant change in the *popular* representation (as opposed to that of the philologists) of the relationship between American and British English in the late nineteenth and early twentieth century seems to be some lifting of the earlier high Victorian seriousness about the whole subject in favor of a satirical, humorous approach. Twain, whose *Life on the Mississippi*[151] was published in Britain the same time it appeared in the United States and whose *Adventures of Huckleberry Finn* came out in Britain before it appeared in America, had been doing this from the early 1880s. He both affirmed the robust separateness of American English ("When I speak my native tongue in its utmost purity in England, an Englishman can't understand me at all") and—writing in the wake of Oscar Wilde's much-publicized tour of the United States—warned that "Aesthetes in many of our schools are now beginning to teach the pupils to broaden the *a*, and to say 'don't you' in the elegant foreign way."[152] Though the *Westminster Review* agreed that Samuel Clemens' own English was "an other thing from native English" and where such American English was most different it was "for the most part vulgarisms,"[153] Twain's jokey defusing of the subject is entirely resonant with the contemporary witticisms of Oscar Wilde or Bernard Shaw.

> There was an Englishman in our compartment, and he complimented me on—on what? But you would never guess. He complimented me on my English. He said Americans in general did not speak the English language as correctly as I did. I said I was obliged to him for his compliment … but … I did n't speak English at all,—I only spoke American.[154]

In the longer view, of course, the fear that American English would become powerfully global and either corrupt or replace proper English (i.e., British English) would remain a common theme in British representations of the "special relationship" throughout the twentieth century, heightened significantly by the ever-growing presence in Britain of Americans abroad—tourists, businessmen, and, dramatically in the Second World War, soldiers—and would become a commonplace of both popular and academic media critiques with the coming fashion for American music and film, radio and television. Within America however there was a powerful counterweight to "linguistic democratization."

Wealthy Americans, as Webster knew and deplored, found in British pronunciation, grammar, and vocabulary, in British enunciation and elocution, a model with which to assert their own social distinction—sustaining what linguists call a "diglossic" language culture of the high versus the low. They sent their sons to prep schools that taught the value of the heritage of not only British literature but British style and speech; a few of the traditional elite, and those new rich who had the money to do so, even sent their sons to Eton or Harrow, Oxford or Cambridge. Socially conservative, Anglophilic litterateurs such as Richard Grant White embraced their inner Britishness, especially in the face of a democracy of non-English immigrants. In 1891 Charles Hamilton Aide, a London novelist and well-connected man about town who had recently visited the United States, observed that "New York has grown more and more European. They are called 'Anglomaniacs' who imitate our manners and customs, and, as far as possible, our mode of speech."[155] Eight years later as the century came to a close, William Archer, a London theatre critic visiting New York, cited "the influence of club life in keeping America in touch with England. At all the leading clubs one or two English daily papers and all the more important weekly papers are taken as a matter of course."[156]

The "Anglomaniac" as a risible type served, from the American perspective, to fix the metropolitan monocle-wearing dandy as an *inauthentic* American. The culturally Anglophilic American gentleman had long been a familiar type—a type that Richard White, certainly, did not see as comic, but as simply a matter of "class." Early in the century manuals of correct behaviour, like pronouncing dictionaries, had proved popular, and these etiquette books were often written by English men and women or were based on British originals.[157] That the comic image of the pretentiously British-accented East Coast Anglophile became a trope of satire in the 1890s—not least in the newspapers of Chicago, Denver, or San Francisco—suggests an America, and its language and literature, that had taken on a more trans-continental character. As the loci of population and wealth multiplied westward to the Pacific coast, East Coast metropolitan Society came to be regarded with some of the same suspicion as had the London elite earlier in the century. By the turn of the century if not earlier, "American" had come to evoke, less its historic origins in New England, the Eastern seaboard, or the old South, than the mythic heart of a continental nation somewhere near Peoria, Illinois. When just after the First World War, Harold Spender, journalist and father of the poet Stephen Spender, visited the United States, he found that mid-westerners, no longer "merely a type of provincial Englishman," "were tired of being told that they talked bad English. They were glad to meet a visitor who recognised that they just 'talked American.'"[158]

The derisive *British* representation of the Anglomaniac plays differently. Here it was used in fact to reinforce a familiar charge of American provinciality—as one who tries but fails to meet the British standard of style or language, who does not quite understand the codes of behavior and speech and thus is prone to faux pas and becoming an object of ridicule. In 1891 Rudyard Kipling condescendingly observed from Buffalo, New York, that one man, pointed out to him as a "glass of fashion," "was aggressively English in his get-up. From eye-glass to trouser-hem the illusion was perfect, but—he wore with evening dress buttoned boots with brown cloth tops!" Others played polo and rode "in the English manner, in neatly cut riding trousers and light saddles." But it was all unconvincing. "They can't do it, any more than an Englishman, by taking a cold, can add that indescribable nasal twang to his orchestra."[159]

British style and speech among Americans were, as Sir Lepel Henry Griffin observed, most evident in the eastern cities "where the imitation of British manners and amusements has become for the time [the 1880s] the fashion." Farther West, he claimed to have found "little love for England or English ways, and criticism is almost uniformly unfriendly." Yet Colorado, "which is being largely developed by English settlers and capital," was, he thought, an exception.[160] In fact, even in the rough American far West, suspicion was mixed with a degree of awe. William Howard Russell, the famous correspondent for the London *Times*, while on a tour with a party that included the Duke of Sutherland and his son the Marquis of Stafford in 1881, was surprised to discover that the local papers were well-informed by *Burke's Peerage* and *Debrett's*, and "gave full accounts of the ducal house of Sutherland—of its history and possessions … with most un-Republican enthusiasm."[161]

Late nineteenth-century literary and artistic Americans abroad, such as the much-commented-upon expatriates Henry James, James McNeil Whistler, or Bret Harte, were widely ridiculed, even by some among the privileged classes. Henry Cabot Lodge disapprovingly declared in an 1883 article, "Colonialism in the United States," that "[t]he first step of an American entering on a literary career was to pretend to be an Englishman, in order that he might win the approval, not of Englishmen, but of his own countrymen."[162] A generation later, a young Van Wyck Brooks, recent Harvard graduate and literary critic and historian on the make, complained that "[l]iterary English with us is a tradition [that persists], not as the normal expressions of a race, ... but through prestige and precedent and the will and habit of a dominating class largely out of touch with a national fabric unconsciously taking form out of school."[163] Lounsbury had resentfully noted that deference in language "on the part of the best-informed American to the least-informed Englishman" was still to be found, and had been common even in the era of the vigorous young nation.[164] In matters of language, as in style (Theodore Roosevelt disapproved of his brother Elliott's social world of foxhunting and polo), the "Anglomaniac" remained a persistent object of comment. It was a name Mencken scornfully applied to those American "collaborators" who signed on to the agenda of the Society for Pure English.[165]

And so back to Shaw's (probable) aphorism of two nations and the English language. The Anglophilia of the aspiring or newly arrived American upper class was a target *en passant* of his 1913 play *Pygmalion*. As Professor Higgins explains to Col. Pickering, teaching better English to those wishing to be passed off as someone of a superior class "is the sort of thing I do for commercial millionaires. ... I've taught scores of American millionairesses to speak English."[166]

CHAPTER 2
THEATRE/THEATER

Pygmalion opened at the Park Street Theater in New York City on October 12, 1914, a few months after its acclaimed run in London of over a hundred performances and a few weeks after Britain declared war on Germany. Much of the original cast sailed on the Lusitania with the production. In New York as in London the role of Liza Doolittle was played by Stella (Mrs. Patrick) Campbell, a rather mature actress for the part, though one who was a very popular transatlantic "star." The New York transfer was "a great success," and "Mrs. Pat" also gave benefit performances at Wallack's Theater of Pinero's *The Second Mrs. Tanqueray* for her new sister-in-law the Duchess of Westminster's hospital for British and allied soldiers. Simultaneously, the British actor-manager Johnston Forbes-Robertson's "farewell tour" of the United States—a matter of eight freight cars hauling sets and costumes and two passenger carriages for the actors—reached Chicago and opened there with a successful production of Shaw's *Caesar and Cleopatra*.[1] In December, the *Pygmalion* company followed with its own tour to San Francisco via Pittsburgh, Detroit, and Chicago.[2] Such busy transatlantic and transcontinental traffic by British actors, managers, and plays popular on the London stage was by the beginning of the twentieth century not at all remarkable.

British players on the American stage had been commonplace from the earliest years of the new Republic. Professional drama—the plays, the productions, the managers, the actors, except in the far reaches of provincial America, and often even there—was largely imported from the mother country. Colonial American cities had not developed much of a domestic theatrical tradition or many permanent venues for public theater. It might be expected that after the Revolution, as urban life multiplied and new places for performance began to proliferate, the more sophisticated classes in the metropolitan centers—New York or Philadelphia or Baltimore—would continue to look to Britain for traveling troupes and actor-managers while rougher, provincial, trans-Allegheny America shunned them. But such was not the case. Theater, and the British professionals who enabled it, marched westward with the expanding American nation, and often playhouses were among the first public buildings to grace the rough new towns of the west.

"American" theater was, not only in its transatlantic origins but throughout its long nineteenth-century course of development, enmeshed with and dependent upon British material and British means (actors, managers, performance style, and theatrical architecture). This continuing cultural hegemony of the mother country requires some re-examination of the essentializing concept of "American" itself when applied to nineteenth-century drama. By the dawning of the twentieth century, the idea of "British" theatre itself in turn begs to some extent not only the importation of Continental modernism but a growing transatlantic hybridity impelled by American impresarios, American productions, American money, and, especially, American-style entertainments—well before cinema, radio, and television made cultural dependency a matter of general apprehension and discussion. Such an angle of vision might encourage an approach to the history of theater (broadly considered) that is more concerned than it has been, at least in the United States, with a wider perspective of cultural interactions across domestic *and* international social boundaries.

Theater and opera were not quite the elitist institutions in the early Republic that they would later come to be. In the cities, of course, audiences drew heavily from the professional and leisured classes. This elite may indeed have sought, as Noah Webster feared, to emulate the rituals and fashions of London Society. The elite in question of course changed over time—from the relatively narrow patriarchal gentility of colonial times to the broader, richer, professional, and leisured classes who came to patronize theater in the growing Republic. But, as in Regency Britain, antebellum audiences also had their demotic, artisanal side, and not only at the lower-class entertainments of some venues such as New York's Chatham Garden or Thomas Hamblin's Bowery Theater. In even the fashionable metropolitan theaters "the crowd," indoors and outdoors, was often a participating, contesting presence—loud in the gallery or pit, and thronging out of doors to cheer favorite performers and, sometimes, to jeer despised foreign actors unwise enough to have expressed, as Edmund Kean was thought to have done, reservations about American national character. It was this popular side of theater-going, and the riotous side of theatrical protest, that made the theater a special danger in the eyes of some social and political conservatives.

With their shirtsleeves and their spitting, American audiences—even those found in "the boxes"—were much maligned by Mrs. Trollope. Their taste, however, extended beyond comic entertainment and sentimental melodrama to, also, a reverential appetite for Shakespeare. Americans were wont to claim Shakespeare—and Milton and Chaucer—as their particular cultural heritage, one that, according to some philologists, spoke to them more historically and directly than it did to contemporary Britons. The contrarian and sometime radical British journalist and patriot, William Cobbett, who sought refuge in America in the era of the French wars and who detested the "obscenity" of Shakespeare, wrote of Americans who "claim [Shakespeare] as *their countryman*."[3] Alexis de Tocqueville reported that when he toured America in 1831 there was "hardly a pioneer's hut that does not contain a few odd volumes of Shakespeare."[4] Though visiting Britons might carp at the way "American players murdered Shakespeare's language,"[5] they were also impressed and amused by the rapt seriousness with which the citizenry of the western towns endured long hours of *Hamlet* or *Lear*—with, one imagines, some of the same concentration and endurance required of long Sunday sermons. At least in the era of the early Republic, Shakespeare can be said to have been part of "a shared public culture," however much it might be argued that a contested shift was under way in which "high culture" generally, and Shakespeare in particular, was being appropriated by the polite upper middle class and the wealthy.[6]

The popularity of theater and the rapid growth of domestic theatrical establishments in New York and Philadelphia at the beginning of the nineteenth century cannot, however, belie the fact that there was in America as in Britain also a long-standing resistance to "the stage" as a moral danger like dancing and other popular amusements. Webster himself, though he had as a young man performed in amateur theatrical productions at Yale and (guiltily?) enjoyed the theater in New York, had reservations: Vanbrugh's *The Provoked Husband* contained, he confided to his diary, "low scenes and indelicate ideas." In 1787, in support of his diatribe against the corrupting influence of London pronunciation ("in language, what the stage-strut is to walking"), he deployed the familiar Puritan charge that theatrical entertainments encouraged "the vices of all classes of people" and that all who "attend constantly on the exhibitions of vice, become equally depraved." His later conversion to evangelical Christianity simply amplified this especially New England bias, as well as anticipated the coming middle-class priggishness of the Victorian era: in 1823 he wrote that "[v]ery few plays are … free from sentiments which are offensive to moral purity."[7]

In New England, Puritan divines had long railed against the stage, and an anti-theatrical ordinance had been adopted by the Boston town council in 1750. Public performances had been banned from time to time in several of the other colonies but without much effect. While the first Continental Congress passed a resolution against "shews, plays, and other expensive diversions and entertainments" in 1774, this was ignored in the southern colonies and did not apparently interfere with George Washington's own enjoyment of theater. Moreover, private and collegiate amateur entertainments continued before and during the Revolution. In New England both patriot and loyalist "pamphlet plays," a form of partisan propaganda, were "privately" read and (perhaps) performed, and the British sanctioned public theater in Boston during the occupation.[8]

It was not until 1793, however, that Massachusetts formally ended its prohibition, the last of the new United States to do so. Though its first, wooden theater was opposed by "puritanical sects" and pulled down, thereafter Boston began to emulate Philadelphia and New York with an elegant, Bulfinch-designed, purpose-built theater in Federal Street where legitimate repertoire was performed by a company from London managed by an actor celebrated at the Theatre Royal.[9] Touring companies from Britain and Ireland, such as that of Lewis Hallam (the brother of a bankrupted manager of a London theater), had played before avid theater-goers in Philadelphia, New York City, and some southern cities well before the Revolution.[10] After Hallam died, David Douglass, a Scot who married his widow, continued to have some success (not however in Boston) up to the Revolution. Manager of a traveling troupe and theaters in six colonies and Jamaica, Douglass intended, a recent study claims, to appeal to a colonial elite eager for London fashion and London manners, though the rise of the Patriots—his theater in New York was burned down in an anti-British riot—and the death of his wife ended in his removal to Jamaica in 1773.[11]

The lifting of the not-very-effective formal bans on public theatrical performance in the 1780s and 1790s was in part spurred on by civil libertarian debate, partly by the rise, as in Boston, of a highly partisan mobilization of theater by Federalists and Democratic-Republicans, and partly by a rising middle-class demand for the regular performance of a repertory that had been relegated to amateur, private, and collegiate stages. After the revolutionary hiatus, the John Street Theatre was established in New York by members of the Hallam family, and a professional repertory company was based there in 1785. Even in New York there was indignant opposition from some quarters and a petition of 700 names was presented the next year to the legislature demanding the theater's closure. The successful counter petition of 1,400 signatures, however, indicates the growth, at least in New York City, of a popular audience for theatrical productions and a thriving market for the importation of British managers, actors, and plays.[12]

Apprehension about the morality of the theater however continued throughout our period to have some traction, in Britain as in America, among those who saw in it a danger, like that of novels, to the seriousness that fundamentalist, Sabbatarian religion demanded. In Britain, there was some interest between the first two Reform Acts (of 1832 and 1867) in expanding the provision of "improving" drama—especially Shakespeare—as part of educating an expanded electorate. But many in the nonconformist churches remained highly skeptical of drama in any form. In 1844 the Rev. George Lewis, a member of the (narrowly sectarian) Scottish Free Church visiting the American South, pronounced that he was "sorry to learn that the theatre is much frequented, both here [in Mobile] and in New Orleans, even on the Sabbath." Revealing, no doubt, the excessively limited range of his own acquaintance, he claimed that "[n]obody now goes to the theatre in Scotland … It is not the present fashion."[13] Ironically, of course, the sermons of popular divines and the excited emotionalism of revivalist meetings were themselves a species of theater, in competition perhaps with the entertainments of the stage. Mrs. Trollope had said as much, commenting that in Cincinnati "the places of worship were the theatres and cafes of the place." When Richard Cobden—who enjoyed the theater wherever he traveled in America—heard Henry Ward Beecher preach, he noted in his diary that "he ought to have been an actor on the boards."[14]

In early nineteenth-century America, venues for "low" theater—pantomimes, comedy, and "species of musical entertainment"—thrived, as at Philadelphia's South Street Theater, at the same time that a lively competition also emerged among new houses in both Philadelphia and New York that were established to be permanent bases for a more serious repertoire—most importantly, Philadelphia's Chestnut Street (opened in 1794) and, in New York, Park Street (opened in 1798). The design for the Chestnut Street Theater originated with John Inigo Richards, chief scenic artist at London's Covent Garden who sent drawings, a three-dimensional model, a drop curtain, and sets of scenery.[15]

These companies were not simply dependent on the chance of snaring the services of visiting Irish and British thespians; they relied for decades on actors recruited and contracted in London by their agents. They were often, at least initially, run by immigrant British managers and, in the next generation, their sons, who had close ties and frequent communication with the mother country. Transatlantic theater was a significant factor in *both* maintaining an Anglo-American closeness *and* furthering the culture wars and identity politics of the era—an influence that extended into the far corners of the political, social, and cultural history of the times.

Of course, if one considers "theater" in the broadest, metaphoric sense—as "liminal spaces" in which a reciprocal relationship is played out between performer and audience, between the observed and the observer[16]—then much of the story of British and American nineteenth-century culture can come within the "theatrical." Musical performances, circuses, literary readings, and public galleries of painting and statuary offered a chance for those rising in the world to see others and to be seen. Here however we are chiefly concerned with what the formal theater—the stage, its venues, its actors, managers, and promoters, and its audience—as a particular form of the Anglo-American special relationship in the long nineteenth century can reveal about the times and the transatlantic bridge between Britain and America. Some political historians have treated aspects of the subject, but have tended somewhat narrowly to focus on the dueling reputations of American and British actors and moments of protest as micro-studies of national jealousies. More may be done, for instance, with the role of the theater in the construction, amplification, and proliferation of national stereotypes—of the British aristo or the sharp-eyed Yankee—and how these memes were deployed in wider contexts.

Individual American actors and other popular entertainers who had come to prominence in the States had occasionally made their way to the London stage earlier in the century. After the Civil War the traffic became brisker and perhaps more successful, as in the tours of Joseph Jefferson, Edwin Booth, Lawrence Barrett, and, by the 1890s, many others. From the host of minstrel shows and P. T. Barnum's traveling curiosities (he took "General Tom Thumb" to London in 1844) before the Civil War to the Fisk Jubilee Singers or "Buffalo Bill" Cody's Wild West show thereafter, organized tours to London by companies of entertainers became commonplace. For their part, British companies heading the other way came to see by the end of the century American touring as ever more necessary for their financial survival. Even the most renowned of late nineteenth-century actor-managers, Henry Irving, relied on the receipts of his company's repeated American tours to stave off bankruptcy in London, just as Irving's heirs in the next century came to survive on the number of seats filled by American tourists.

The Anglo-American theatrical world was, as were other elements of the nineteenth-century special relationship, a matter of shifting, reversing hegemonies. London represented "the biggest [rising from two to six million], most exciting audience in the world" and after mid-century the most flourishing concentration of playhouses in its West End.[17] By the end of the century, however, New York, with its rapid growth in population [to three and a half million], and its own electric-lit Broadway theater district, the "Great White Way," offered an American challenge to London's predominant position in a transatlantic industry that would be increasingly organized by American impresarios such as Henry Abbey, George Tyler, David Belasco, or Charles and Daniel Frohman.

1 Transatlantic Relations: American Theater and the British

By the early nineteenth century theatergoing was more important to urban social life in America than it had been in colonial times or would be in the next century when the entertainment and public intercourse it offered would be substantially displaced by cinema and the more private realms of radio and television. In Britain, though there were repertory theatres beyond the capital, London had long been more central to British theatrical culture than any American city—even than rapidly swelling New York—could ever hope to be, and, as the hub of the expanding rail network, was becoming more so even as the industrial revolution was making metropolises out of northern provincial towns. English actors and repertory companies had long fanned out from the capital in the off-season to provincial cities—to Exeter, Bristol, Bath, York, and Edinburgh, and, as they grew in population and wealth, Birmingham, Manchester, or Leeds. With steady improvements in ocean transport, *transatlantic* nomadism came as a natural extension, and one that was often much more remunerative. As these crossings became commonplace, some American nationalists complained that reliance on British actors and managers inhibited the growth of domestic theater. But, at least in the antebellum era, such dependency was both inescapable and necessary for the sustained development of this important, well-patronized part of American cultural, that is, collective social and public life.

Given the relative paucity of American dramatic material—there was some truth to Sydney Smith's further jibe, "Or who goes to an American play?"—or an adequate supply of trained and experienced domestic actors, it may even be that London was, at least in the Anglo-world of theater, as important to American as to British provincial cultural life. Its plays—from Shakespeare to the modish dramas of contemporary times—provided the core of American repertory from Philadelphia to Louisville. In the early Republic and for some time afterward there was a dearth of American drama, at least at the level of formal stage performance. The few American playwrights often parroted the playwrights of fashionable London simply to get an audience. There long remained in fact, among the American critics[18] and American theater-going public, tangible prejudice against an American-made play, however much some might claim there was a pressing need for an authentic, democratic American drama. In 1812, for instance, the American playwright James Nelson Barker's play *Marmion* was actually presented as *being* an English play; William Dunlop, the "father of American drama," also attempted to hide the "native origin" of one of his plays.[19] Throughout the antebellum era and beyond, British actors were everywhere on the stages of American cities and towns performing British plays, and British-born managers ran the best theaters in the most populous American centers. This fact, as much symptom as cause, played a part in establishing the much-commented-upon century-long lament that the American stage struggled and largely failed to realize its own identity. As the playwright, actor, and manager, Dion Boucicault said from his perspective both outside and inside the phenomenon, "There is not, and there never has been, a literary institution, which could be called the American Drama. We have produced no dramatists essentially American to rival such workers as Fenimore Cooper."[20]

It is also apparent that the major shift that historians of American theater have emphasized—from local community-based stock companies to the so-called *star system*—was to a significant degree a product of the rise of the new metropolitan theaters whose managers imported British celebrities. By the 1830s, a phenomenon that had originated in London—a commercial system that encouraged hero-worship organized by manager-impresario "star-makers"—had come to characterize domestic American theater as well.[21]

In order to see rising or confirmed stars, but also simply to observe America at its leisure—and in part, no doubt, because their American hosts and friends insisted on taking them to theater—British visitors to the States throughout the antebellum period attended theatrical performances wherever they traveled. The recorded itineraries of theatrical attendance run through their published memoirs of travel and confirm that they sought out, in both the metropolitan east and the raw west, stage drama as entertainment, social ritual, and a chance critically to compare American and British acting, stage-craft, venues, and audiences. Ironically, Such comparisons of a shared theatrical tradition often served to reinforce their views of American difference. When the British dramatist and novelist George Rose came to write up his own travel memoir in 1868, he found little to praise: "I saw no [American] actor in that country worthy of being called a first-rate artist ... The popular taste is decidedly low; there is a love of over-acting, over-dress, and what is technically termed stageyness, which must be fatal to the growth of good acting."[22] Like Frances Trollope before him, Rose was especially prone to faultfinding, but they both sought out performances.

It is true that Lady Emmeline Stuart Wortley, a daughter of the fifth duke of Rutland who traveled widely after her husband's death, appears to have dismissed American theater unseen ("There are numerous theatres in New York. We visited none of them") and was sardonic about provincial American culture. Buffalo, she noted, had twenty churches and one theater.[23] Many British tourists, however, found theater in antebellum America interesting enough to attend everywhere they visited. John Robert Godley went to that theater in Buffalo ("the 'legitimate drama' at Buffalo!—what think you of that?") and saw "a curious medley" there of *King Lear*, comedy, farce, and melodrama, with songs between the acts. It was, he thought, "a good house," even if the audience was "disreputable-looking."[24] Charles Murray found the theater in Natchez, Mississippi, though "not remarkable for elegance or decoration," to be as good as that found in country towns in England, with a good orchestra and the audience "neatly dressed, without any pretension or display of finery." The three theaters he visited in New Orleans were all "respectably decorated," if small.[25] Inevitably, there were disappointments where local theaters, with local management and players, were hardly comparable even to those of provincial England. Fanny Kemble recalled a performance in Washington at a shabby theater where "[t]he proprietors are poor, the actors poorer; and the grotesque mixture of misery, vulgarity, stage-finery, and real raggedness, is beyond every thing strange, and sad, and revolting."[26]

As they swung through their itinerary, from New York, Philadelphia, and Boston, to Baltimore, Washington, New Orleans, or Buffalo, Cincinnati, and Louisville, British visitors not only looked to compare British and American theatrical experience, but often simply sought out the familiar. Many of the actors, and the plays they performed in, were already known to British visitors from their London theatergoing. This is especially true of the well-known principals of Shakespearean drama. Charles Lyell, for example, made sure to see Charles Kean perform in Boston, and again in New Orleans. Frederick De Roos, who had not been impressed with the class of audience when he attended the theater in Portsmouth, New Hampshire, had been nevertheless concerned to seek out a performance by Kean's father, the famous Edmund Kean, when he visited New York in 1826.[27] Tourists often comment on the British and Irish "stars" they manage to catch in America.

Managers with Connections

British actors had been drawn (or driven) to perform on the American stage from the earliest years of the Republic—by hopes of better remuneration, sometimes to escape from wives or threatening creditors, or to revive a failing London reputation. By the turn of the century, not only Price at the Park but the managers of most major American houses like the Chestnut Street Theater in Philadelphia took an active role in searching out and recruiting talent in London. In 1797 English-born Thomas Wignell secured for the Chestnut the prominent actor-manager John Bernard with a thousand pounds and a twelve-month contract with an option to extend for five more years.[28] He relied on well-oiled machinery: agents in Britain on the look-out for movable assets were armed with contracts and ready cash, and their successes served to cement the dependence of the American stage on transatlantic talent. British-born managers—often themselves, like Wignell, transplanted London actors—had an obvious advantage in this business, as they could draw on their own contacts, but an astute American-born manager like businessman Stephen Price might also play the game.

Price, who would become the first foreign lessee of the Drury Lane Theatre in London,[29] had an English actor, Edward Simpson, as his assistant (and later partner) in running the Park Street Theatre. He not only booked well-known British actors such as George Frederick Cooke, Edmund Kean, William Charles Macready, and Charles Mathews. He also, according to Francis Wemyss (an immigrant British actor-manager himself and historian of the early American stage), developed the "bold idea of *farming*" them out on contract to other theaters in Philadelphia, Boston, and Baltimore—"acquiring for himself in England the title of 'Star Giver General to the United States.'"[30] One of Price's prominent stage acquisitions, Macready, was lured in 1826 to New York for two years by a contract, signed by Price in person in Liverpool, guaranteeing £50 a night. Macready complained in his diary that dealing with a "boastful and overbearing" American speculator, who he waspishly claimed clearly "knew nothing" about "dramatic art" other than what the public seemed to want, was demeaning ("he was not a gentleman"). But Macready took the money. His characterization of an American manager-impresario as rich vulgarian resonates enduringly with what other British writers and actors—who attempted both to profit and to preserve their dignity—would claim through the nineteenth century down to the buying of British talent for Hollywood in the 1920s and 1930s.[31]

Wheeling and dealing in thespian "properties" was not a strictly native-born, sharp American practice. The British actor-manager at the Chestnut Street Theater (and later at both the Arch Street and Walnut Street Theaters) in Philadelphia, Francis Wemyss, London-born son of a Royal Navy officer and an undoubted "gentleman" with respectable connections, played as well a very competitive game. Searching in London for talent that could be persuaded to cross the Atlantic for the 1827–8 season at Chestnut Street, he came armed with a shopping list and instructions.

> I think you can get a lady to play high tragedy, of middle age, not old, of good appearance … Let me recommend to you to call upon the stars in London, all you think may come here, and tell them not to sell themselves to Price & Co. Put an article in the Theatrical Messenger … This will break up the New York plans.[32]

Nor were managers on the lookout only for stars, or, as Wemyss said, the "big fish." The demand in the States was such that the "*minor* order of stars … found their way by the dozens into the United States, possessing no talent above mediocrity,"[33] as well as a host of simply run-of-the-mill out-of-work actors recruited in their hundreds by managers with connections or personal experience in the British and Irish theatrical marketplace. Others simply made it to America and hoped, as did a Mr. Prigmore, "a very poor man and a very poor actor," who abandoned England at the turn of the century owing his manager £10, having been "seduced" by the prospect "of every dramatic adventurer" of "making his fame and fortune" there.[34] What was important to the managers of American theaters, as at Chestnut Street, was to find actors who could suit the American audience's demand for "polished manners, good exterior, and a guarded sense of decorum"—that is, one might conclude, those who sounded and acted politely British. Wemyss returned to Philadelphia in 1827 with sixteen new recruits, and more to follow.[35]

In the era immediately following the Revolution and for some decades thereafter American theater was perforce dependent on the continued supply of acting and managing talent that could only come from Britain. It might be thought, however, that, as the decades rolled by, these seasoned professionals would progressively and quickly be replaced by rising American talent. This was not, however, the case—at least among the major playhouses. Partly this was because theaters proliferated and grew in their ambition, along with the growth in the populations they served, faster than the domestic supply of competent talent—at least that which could meet the demand for "polished manners" and "decorum." There did of course emerge in due course a generation of domestic actors, often groomed in provincial American towns and local thespian clubs, who managed to transition from the nomadic troupes serving the western and southern circuits—such as most famously the first American-born star, Edwin Forrest (though he was half Scottish). But at the top of the profession they remained exceptional for much of the antebellum era. In fact, even good American talent had at every level to contend in the 1820s, 1830s, and 1840s, with a surfeit of British competition, and not only in the eastern cities and not only from the "big fish" brought to the United States on contract. Before the Civil War temporarily turned off the tap, the volume of British and Irish acting migrants in America continued to grow due to the progressive improvement in the speed, ease, and safety of travel. Indeed, a kind of commuting back and forth developed whereby contracts of a year or two might be engaged alternatively in London and in the major American metropolitan centers.

Not all theatrical managers in the American metropolitan centers were keen to import British and Irish stars. They either lacked the ability to compete, because of the cost, effort, and connections required to nurture the transatlantic egos of those already acclaimed as stars, or, from a sense of national obligation or calculation, they felt the need to provide home-grown, domestic talent to that part of their public likely to value domestic talent, even if rough-edged, over the smooth elocution of British style. Ironically, the manager who best followed this patriotic course, Thomas Sowerby Hamblin (1800–53), was British—an actor who had been born in London and, following some early success there, left for New York at age twenty-five to perform Shakespearean roles at the Park and the Albion Theaters. Five years later he took over the management of the Bowery, a theater that, as fashionable society moved northward in Manhattan, had become increasingly isolated in a rougher, older district and came—though its audience remained in fact largely middle-class—to be thought to cater increasingly to lower class "Bowery B'hoys." Hamblin provided blackface minstrels, circus acts, spectacles, and farce, as well as higher drama. As a marketing ploy no doubt, Hamblin advertised the fact that he intended to cultivate *American* talent, and in 1831 renamed the Bowery the American Bowery apparently to draw audience away from the Park where there had been an anti-British riot.[36] He died, in 1853, a wealthy man, though one whose career—both as actor and as gentleman-manager—was often denigrated. Chronicler of the New York stage Joseph Ireland referred to him condescendingly a few years after his death as "vastly over-rated as an actor" who catered to "the million" rather than attempting to "elevate" drama and its audience.[37]

In advancing the Americanness of American theater, Hamblin's story is however unusual for the times, at least among those actor-managers who were themselves migrants from Britain, and when American-born managers did become more common, these were often a second generation of the original emigrant actor-managers from Britain. The profession, of both acting and managing, often took on a distinctly dynastic character—as was true in Britain of the Keans (father and son), the Mathews (father and son), or the Kembles (father and daughter), and in America of the Booths (father and sons), the Jeffersons (grandfather, father, and son), or, at the end of the century, the Barrymores (father, sons, and daughter). Among the actor-managers, the Wallacks were especially prominent as a theatrical clan that maintained an active and entrenched presence on both sides of the ocean for much of the century. Such familial continuities across the century suggest that the "international era" of American theater, what one scholar has called the "cross-oceanic reality of theatrical culture,"[38] long recognized as characteristic of the *early* Republic to about 1830, extends more deeply and longer than this.

James William Wallack (1791–1864) and his brother Henry John Wallack (1790–1870), reared in an itinerant acting family in Britain known for "genteel comedy," came to America in 1818—James (already a star in Britain) to play Macbeth in New York,

Henry to take a number of roles in Philadelphia and Baltimore. Neither became exactly settled immigrants—spending the best part of two decades playing both in London and in America. James crossed the ocean a dozen times before 1837, when he became manager of the new National Theater in New York. Continuing transatlantic travel allowed him personally to recruit in Britain for his New York productions. In 1852 he committed himself to a more settled American life, became an American citizen, and took on the running of the New York Lyceum, then the Broadway (the first of several "Wallack's" Theaters). Henry, who also roamed back and forth across the Atlantic (his second wife was a British provincial actress), played a number of venues in New York, including the Bowery, in the 1820s and 1830s. In 1837 he took on the management of the National. After three years it was back to London where he became manager of the Princess's and (unfortunately) lessee at Covent Garden, which bankrupted him. He continued thereafter a transatlantic acting career, playing alternatively on the London stage and in New York. Three of his children carried on the family acting tradition in both Britain and America.[39] James's eldest son, John (Lester) Wallack (1820–88), born in New York, continued the managerial dynasty. Though an American citizen, his early life was transatlantic; he was educated in London before beginning a career on the stage in Dublin. Lester, as he was known, performed at a variety of New York theaters before becoming manager of the new Wallack's Theater (the second) built by his father. Though he continued to act, he became a prominent manager-impresario in his own right, opened another Wallack's (the third) in 1882, kept the family tradition of life shared on each side of the ocean, and married a sister of the British artist John Everett Millais.[40]

The itinerant, transatlantic character of the acting and managing careers of a family such as the Wallacks—a prominent example, but one that was not unique—may suggest that the world of Anglo-American theater was often a matter of nomadism in search of opportunity wherever it led on either side of an oceanic divide that, for them at any rate, did not seem to constitute a significant national boundary. That is, the *family* world, even into the third generation, was neither, exactly, American nor British—or rather American and British as suited the purpose of the moment. With family and friends and enduring associations on either side of the Atlantic, identity must have involved a kind of chameleon-character—American when playing New York (or Cincinnati, or New Orleans, or San Francisco), British when in London (or Leeds, or Edinburgh, or Dublin). There were no doubt costs in such periodic displacements, and repeated moments of family crisis. One can imagine family debate, as when Fanny Kemble decided to remain in America to marry, rather than to accompany her actor-father back to London (or when she separated a dozen years later from her slave-owning husband and returned to London and the stage, with two daughters in tow). But there were advantages as well, not least being able, in a failure-prone, bankruptcy-filled environment of sometimes fickle audiences and sharp competition, to fall back on engagements thousands of miles away. Even the minor advantage cannot be discounted of being able to have serial "farewell benefit" performances (a significant device in the nineteenth century for raising cash in hand) to celebrate a transatlantic move that would, in the event, be but temporary.

Boucicault

The Wallacks were a family firm with British origins that drew throughout the antebellum era and beyond on transatlantic resources of experience, opportunity (including marital opportunity), and useful connection. Others were often freebooting individualists, unattached and self-created without the resources and obligations of the Wallacks' extended genealogy. For these, the English-speaking Anglosphere, extending by the later nineteenth century across the American continent and as far afield as Australia or Southern Africa, was a vast potential gold mine, a California of opportunity. The theatrical career of Dion Boucicault—neither American nor British, but quondam Irish—can serve as an example of an outsider making it in such a shrinking, boundary-less world. If anything, Boucicault was even less bothered by national, that is, political, identity—a crafted and exaggerated cultural identity as a stage-Irish actor and author was perhaps a different matter—than were most of the Wallacks.

Dion Boucicault's career as actor, playwright, and theater manager lies across much of mid- and late nineteenth-century theater in America and Britain, and across these national boundaries. Born in Dublin in 1820 into a declining middle-class Protestant family, he attended several schools in England, including University College School in London. By age eighteen he had taken up acting in the English provinces, making use of his pronounced (and perhaps cultivated) Irish brogue. He also became at an early age a prolific author of plays and by twenty-one had his first success with *London Assurance*. Within five years he had offered some thirty plays, mostly hasty adaptations, to London West End theaters. Boucicault's colorful self-making and lively opportunism—unlike prouder young authors, he had no qualms about casually making whatever changes to his plays actors or producers might wish—came to define his rise to prominence. In the 1840s he took advice, it appears, from P. T. Barnum about the importance of publicity—how to manipulate the press and to satisfy the popular audience's appetite for sensation and sentiment. Such insouciance, his cheerful willingness to try anything, indeed suggests something of the character of the stage-Irishman he both performed and scripted—boastfully loquacious, friendly though unreliable, and a bit of an opportunistic outsider.[41]

Many of Boucicault's successful London plays had been quickly performed without his consent in New York (and thus without profiting him). He was therefore already pretty well-known there before he decided on an American tour. He would later claim that in London he had spent hours socializing ("talking American") with American actors and with British actors who had been to America, convincing himself that direction offered new horizons for his talent.[42] An American trip would also give him the chance to claim something from pirated performances of his own work there and on arrival he would set about promoting, ultimately successfully, the extension of American copyright law to plays. More immediately, America offered a quick exit from London where he had been writing scripts for Charles Kean, but with whom he had a falling out over his relationship with Kean's ward, the actress Agnes Robertson.

By the time Boucicault made his speculative transatlantic venture with Agnes in 1853 (they were married shortly thereafter in New York), Irish actors on the American stage had become a very familiar presence and plays with stage-Irish roles were proliferating. By 1849 the *Irish American* newspaper could rejoice that "the largest number of Irish actors ever assembled together, are at present among us."[43] For many their accent was their chief, perhaps only, asset. In New York, the plays, generally comic and sentimental pieces with perhaps some singing and dancing, were earlier written for the largely Anglo audiences that expected and enjoyed stereotype and caricature (just as they expected to see grinning Black servants named Pompey). Increasingly, however, audiences might also include some of the growing population of Irish immigrants—or at least those who could afford a cheap seat at the Bowery.

The stage Irishman had been, from at least the mid-eighteenth century, a familiar type in British drama, and actors who specialized in such roles naturally looked to try their luck in the States as the demand for comic Irish sketches grew there. The best in these roles of vulgar mimicry became stars of a kind, able to draw large audiences and command substantial salaries not only in arenas of popular, that is, low entertainment, but in major play-houses on both sides of the Atlantic. Some Irish actors who found success in Britain were able, with some difficulty, to rise above stereotyped, low-comic roles. Making his early reputation with his ability to deploy different styles of brogue, the Irish actor Tyrone Power (1797–1841) achieved an avid following in more legitimate comedy roles in both Britain and America before his untimely death at sea. He was quickly replaced on the New York stage by Dublin-born John Collins, who had debuted in London at the Haymarket before specializing in "the Hibernian dramatic" and crossing to America. Aiming to occupy the ground between low farce and legitimate theater, he added Irish ballads and humorous songs to his performances and specialized in characterizations of the "impudence and reckless assurance" of "a gentleman of his nation."[44]

Though the critics might prefer Collins, with his background in major repertory houses in Britain, over the "buffoonery" of the more vulgar of the comic Irish performers on the American stage, the lasting, widespread vogue for Irish plays, from Boston to New Orleans, encouraged playwright hacks to churn out entertainments that assured stage-Irish performers a flood of roles from the 1840s to the 1860s. Buffoonery and an exaggerated brogue characterized the majority of these routines. The most successful of self-caricaturing Irish players was "Barney Williams" (Bernard O'Flaherty, 1824–76), born in Cork, who came to the States in 1840 to play at the Franklin Theater in New York and later the National. Trying at first comic blackface minstrel roles, by 1845 he had adopted his future stage persona, one that achieved great popularity, by portraying "the peculiarities of Irish and American low life." By the 1850s he was an acclaimed star of Irish comedy and toured throughout the States before recrossing the ocean to perform at the Adelphi in London from 1855 to 1859. Here as well he was a great success—playing for Victoria and the Royal family and touring the English provinces and Ireland. Williams was the most popular of the stage-Irishmen of his generation, performing "the ranting, roving, blarneying blade, or … the more dull and stupid of bogtrotters" and giving rise to "a host of imitators and competitors." In 1863, he played for Lincoln and entertained Union troops.[45]

Boucicault, when he came to America with Agnes (they sailed separately) in 1853, cannot simply be typed as a "stage-Irish" actor or author—though as he settled into a professional career in New York he may have profited from the popularity there of the genre. It was his soon-to-be wife who had the greater appeal to audiences: though Scottish-born, she played an Irish boy in Boston for nine weeks, netting the manager of the theater there some $20,000, before setting off on tours that took her through the midwest to Chicago and south to New Orleans. Boucicault debuted to rather less acclaim in Boston in *The Irish Artist* and then in New York in a play of his own. Staying in the States for some years, Boucicault tried his hand at lecturing (for a fee) at "soirees" on subjects that appear randomly chosen—European literary life, the rights of women, the stage. These were only modestly profitable.[46] He carried on writing, producing, and acting in his own plays. These were often adapted from French farces or were potboilers inspired by events much in the news, such as the Sepoy mutiny and the relief of Lucknow, or sensational subjects, such as Mormonism (*Brigham Young; Or, the Revolt of the Harem*). In 1857 he had great success with a work suggested by a French play but given a contemporary theme and local setting, *The Poor of New York*—enlivened by sensational special effects. He tried his hand at dramatizing Dickens and, in 1859, sought to cash in on the huge popularity of stage versions of *Uncle Tom's Cabin* with *The Octoroon*, a tragedy of interracial love that, unlike Stowe's work, seemed noncommittal on the great slavery debate. It proved a box-office success.

Boucicault later claimed to have been won over by the city, with its myriad nationalities and its lively street life of bands, "poles of liberty," and flags, bunting, and banners: New York, he later wrote, "was not a city. It was a theatre. It was a huge fair." He would also claim that "American theatres [were] superior in every respect to the theatres in England" and that the New York audiences were "keener and more sincere; their taste was of a finer kind; their appreciation was quicker."[47] One may take this with a grain of salt. It was written years later when, late in the day, he was attempting to sustain his career by affirming an American identity he had hardly ever possessed.

In the spring of 1860, Boucicault had a major success with his first Irish play, *The Colleen Bawn* ("the fair-haired girl," played by Agnes). With the two successful Irish plays that followed, it can be regarded as both "a commercial commodification of Ireland" and "an internationalisation of Irish drama."[48] It also established him as *the* dramatist and actor of the Irish diaspora. Controversy would later rage into the twentieth century, through Yeats to Synge, over Boucicault's character, commercial intention, and influence—whether he simply perpetuated stage-Irish stereotypes or advanced a kind of Irish humanity and the politics of liberation. In *The Colleen Bawn* at least, it may be argued that Boucicault, as in *The Octoroon*, does not overtly advance a political analysis or radical solution to a notorious social and political question of the day but pursues a somewhat middle-of-the-road, noncommittal, even culturally hybrid course—the Irish tongue is the voice of passion, English, a language of order and reason. And there are no ranting anti-British nationalists in the play. Instead, Boucicault took a minor character out of the story he had adapted and made this lazy, loquacious, shabbily dressed rogue, Miles-na-Coppaleen, the central figure—a comic role with a heavy brogue which he took himself and with which he became identified for the rest of his career. In the event it was a very profitable success in New York, prompting Boucicault to try mounting it in London, and in Dublin. He and Agnes quickly returned to London's Adelphi, where Boucicault produced and again took the male lead in *The Colleen Bawn*, and where the production became a huge, long-running hit.

This was an entrepreneurial venture that Boucicault closely directed: he presciently chose to take, as author, half the nightly receipts as royalty payments rather than, as was customary, an actor's or director's contracted fee. This proved ultimately influential in the British theatre world, where the "Boucicault revolution" would "help to wrest the contractual initiative out of the hands of the manager and put it into the author's."[49] He also carefully organized the companies that he sent out to tour the British provinces. The play throve and ran for 230 performances in London. It was also a great success in provincial towns and in Dublin, where he and Agnes were followed through the streets as celebrities. Victoria and Albert saw the play four times, and it made Boucicault rich— earning £23,000 in royalty payments the first year alone.

In the years that followed, Boucicault moved from London to New York and back again, and the British and Irish successes reopen the question of just where the center of gravity of his transatlantic life lay, or whether, in this world of theatrical scene-shifting there *was* a center. However much he may later have insisted on his American rootedness, much of the proceeds of *The Colleen Bawn* went immediately to paying his British creditors, purchasing a London mansion in the Brompton Road, and (unwisely as it proved) building his own theater on the South Bank. Three years later when he returned to London, an adapted version of *The Poor of New York*, changed to *The Poor of Liverpool*, proved so profitable that he followed it with *The Poor of Leeds*, *The Poor of Manchester*, *The Streets of Islington*, and *The Streets of London*. Back in the money (provincial productions of *The Colleen Bawn* were also still minting substantial profits) as probably England's best-paid playwright, Boucicault moved into a fashionable new home in Regent Street.[50]

Boucicault came to cultivate in Ireland and America the image of a playwright and actor of "a subjugated nation" (his own words), however much his roguish lay-about and tipsy Miles might seem to lack the heroic nature of the Irish patriot. It was a reputation that was sustained by two, more overtly political, Irish plays: *Arrah-Na-Pogue* ("Arrah of the kiss"), set in the Irish rebellion of 1798, and *The Shaughraun* ("the wanderer"), set in a western Ireland of contemporary Fenian plotters and arguably written chiefly for an Irish-American audience. Whatever their political motivation, together these two plays were clearly intended to build upon the huge success of *The Colleen Bawn*, and it can certainly be argued that their political turn was dictated as much by Boucicault's search for themes sensationalized in the contemporary press, as by political conviction, nor were they received by the more radical Irish-Americans as furthering the "cause." Whether motivated or not by a rising sense of his own Irishness, Boucicault characteristically, and adroitly, employed material, such as his own version of the rebel anthem "The Wearing of the Green" included for the London opening of *Arrah-na-Pogue*, that was especially likely to fill seats. *The Shaughraun* proved very profitable. Boucicault toured the play to Boston and San Francisco, earning perhaps half a million dollars in America before taking it across the ocean to London.[51]

"The Wearing of the Green" was widely published in America and embraced by Irish-American nationalists, as was the Boucicault-encouraged myth that it had been banned throughout the British Empire after the Clerkenwell Prison bombing of 1867. It remains something of an open question however just how much Boucicault intended to advance Irish-American radicalism or the politics of Irish liberation. The claim that he played the nationalist card out of personal conviction always seems a little unconvincing. He was quick to denounce the Fenian atrocities of the late 1860s, and in the decade after *Arrah-na-Pogue*, though he wrote some thirty-two plays only two of them, both failures, were Irish dramas. His fall-off in reputation as a playwright forms the immediate context of the third of his profitable Irish plays and his return to popular success. When in January of 1876 *The Shaughraun* opened in London, Boucicault wrote an open letter to Disraeli demanding the release of Irish political prisoners, but one remembers the advice he was given years earlier by P. T. Barnum about the need for press manipulation and publicity. Though he publicized a touring *Shaughraun* "benefit night" for Irish political prisoners, the proceeds to go to a "Boucicault Fund," there is little suggestion that very much of the very substantial profits of his successful Irish plays were donated publicly or surreptitiously to Irish nationalist causes.

The question of Boucicault's Americanness must be equally an open one.[52] Though he turned to American life for the subject of his 1857 play *The Poor of New York* and to the American Civil War for his 1874 play *Belle Lamar*, he and Agnes spent the Civil War years safely in London. And when they returned to America in 1871, they left their children behind in England. They (finally) took American citizenship in 1873, but Agnes almost immediately returned to Britain. Boucicault followed the next year, and again in 1875–6 and 1880–1, and spent the long summers of 1881, 1882, 1884, and 1886 there.[53] He continued to the end, as his powers and successes began to fail, to open plays in London as well as New York and San Francisco, and in the mid-1880s there was a tour to Australia and New Zealand. Connections among the London theatrical world remained close—as with Henry Irving, for whom in 1876 he revised his early play *Louis XI*. It became a long-retained and successful vehicle for Irving as he established his own remarkable career. In the end, the *New York Times* obituary for Boucicault in 1890 called him "the most conspicuous *English* dramatist of the nineteenth century."[54]

It may be that it is misleading to pose the question of just who, that is, what Boucicault was—whether Irish, British, or American. Was he a proto-nationalist or an opportunist; was he more British, in spite of the cultivated brogue, than Irish in his eager self-advancement on the English stage and as script-writer for English productions or did he, as a naturalized American exploiting the Irish-American market, seek to craft a new self in the new world? Like the Wallacks, though even less anchored, he was neither one thing nor the other, or rather he was all of these. It is a characteristic of the nineteenth-century transatlantic world that identities, like careers, could be malleable, transitory, and mobile rather than fixed and confirmed.

2 Daggers Drawn

We have, thus far, emphasized the thickly networked connections of the nineteenth-century transatlantic theatrical world as a reality that counterpoised mutuality, interdependence, and fluidity to fixed national narratives and confirmed identities. Those national narratives—and especially the American self-narrative—nevertheless constitute a reality that it would be misleading to suppress. But there may be a need more closely to examine the sometimes acrimonious competition between some British and American actors and between British actors and those who sometimes took to the streets to air grievances about them. Rather than simply invoking textbook nationalism and nativist populism in understanding these moments, it bears considering their dynamic—how jealousies and suspicions can escalate (and why at one moment and not at others) from a commonplace language of ill will to exceptionally violent action, how public assumptions and misunderstandings may be manipulated for the calculation of private advantage. Who led and who followed, and why did some actors become lightning rods for the angry expression of American tribal identity while many others did not?

Unsurprisingly, the sharpest confrontations between visiting British actors and some among their American audiences in the antebellum era arose not so much from the carping of philologists such as Webster about the threat to American democracy of British elitist stage elocution, as from the crowd's extreme sensitivity to expressed, implied, or imagined criticism by "foreigners." Well-informed actors hoping for success on the American stage learned when to keep their mouths shut. Those with a large London reputation and egos to match often did not. Famed Shakespearean tragedian Edmund Kean (1787–1833) was the first British star to find a widely anticipated and profitable American tour to be seriously endangered by his loose talk and the overheated, populist imagination of his audience.

When he sailed to New York in 1820 to commence a year-long tour with a performance of *Richard III*, Kean was self-consciously following in the footsteps of his mentor, the great romantic tragedian George Frederick Cooke (1756–1812). Cooke, at the apex of his career, had surprised the London theatrical world in 1810 by taking up Stephen Price's offer to play *Richard III* at the Park in New York City. He stayed for a very well-attended tour that included Boston, Providence, Philadelphia, and Baltimore. Separated for some years from his English wife, he (perhaps bigamously) married an American woman, but died, of cirrhosis, in New York in 1812, shortly after the outbreak of war. Cooke, who set the pattern for subsequent successful star "turns" in the United States, was off the stage a kind of John Bullish figure who made no secret of his patriotic Britishness and of his dislike for James Madison—"The contemptible king of the Yankee Doodles … I'll be damned if I play before him." This apparently did him little harm (especially, one imagines, in Federalist Boston) with audiences who, it seems, enjoyed rather than resented his reputation for outspoken, sometimes drunken gruffness (in London he had a reputation for "insolence and contempt"). The reputation that preceded him made him larger than life and his acting style proved hugely influential in America—according to Rick Bowers, it "interpenetrated American consciousness."[55]

Popular knowledge of Cooke's American success almost immediately seems to have inspired less renowned actors to follow in hopes of transatlantic fortune and fame. "Induced by the great success of Cooke," Joseph George Holman took his actress daughter to the States after the war ended in 1815. They both had some success on the American stage—and she married the manager of the Bowery.[56] The Holmans of the theatrical world crossed the ocean often on speculation, seeking out agents in London for what they could get; those with really large reputations—unless they were desperate to escape London for financial or other reasons—required close nurturing by the agents of American managers. In 1820, in their biggest coup since Cooke, Price managed to sign Cooke's successor as best-known Shakespearean of the day—Edmund Kean.

Kean and Mathews

While Kean's 1820–1 tour proved financially successful, some audiences it appears were less willing to grant him the license the loudly opinionated Cooke had enjoyed. Trouble began in Boston where Kean, miffed at a thin house, expressed his contempt and refused to appear as advertised. Outrage traveled ahead and on his return to New York there was such "severe and universal" public condemnation that he cut short his tour and returned to England.[57] When Kean returned for a second tour in 1825, though he was able to attract large audiences and considerable enthusiasm wherever he played, there was also a highly visible and this time often violent opposition—amplified in the press perhaps by the public notoriety his private life had received in England as correspondent in a divorce case. In Boston, the Debating Society posed the question "Would the public be justified in expelling *Kean* the tragedian from the Stage on account of his private character?" And then in New York, "indiscreet remarks" attributed to him caused "one of the worst riots ever known in the city" and his performance at the Park was "interrupted by the most vile and disgusting proceedings." A letter of apology smoothed things over, but an attempt to perform in Boston caused such violence inside the theater that "flight alone preserv[ed] his safety." In Philadelphia "[r]otten eggs, children's bullet buttons, and other small missiles, were thrown upon the stage in countless numbers." Active opposition pursued Kean on his subsequent tour of western and southern cities—though so did the enthusiasm for the "genius" of his performances. In Baltimore Wemyss claims to have had to "extricate him from a most unpleasant and dangerous situation"—a riot that he says, without elaboration, was provoked by Kean's own supporters.[58]

Kean's reception in America indicates, it has been argued, "a new spirit of contrariness" on the part of American audiences when confronted with British actors they suspected of anti-American hauteur.[59] And yet, it is difficult to reach firm conclusions. The American nation did not en masse reject Kean. He filled houses with enthusiastic supporters wherever he went. When Frederick De Roos saw Kean (twice) at the Park in 1826, he found a "particularly respectable" audience that rewarded the actor with "great applause."[60] Where there was trouble, there was likely to be, as with Boston's Puritan anti-theater tradition, local contexts that contributed to the furor. Moreover, demonstrations were often fomented "in the street" and spearheaded indoors by eager troublemakers who were not regular theatergoers. It is likely that the opposition to what Kean may or may not have said in public or private about America and American audiences was amplified—perhaps maliciously elaborated—by a newly aggressive anti-British press and by partisan political elements. Rather than simply reflecting a new and general anti-British spirit, theater riots, or at least some of them, were also signs of a growing politicization and polarization of audience participation, a kind of inter-class war pitting demos against the respectables. In Philadelphia, Wemyss reported a "nearly equal" antiphony of "hisses and applause."[61]

Kean's American embarrassments proved not to be unique in the decade or so that followed. Other British stars such as, notably, the comic actor Charles Mathews (1776-1835) and, subsequently, the Shakespearean William Charles Macready encountered similar difficulties. Though these moments stand out—especially the Macready vs Forrest feud, which was indeed raised into a major matter of injured national pride—they occurred within an enduring general context in which literally hundreds of British actors continued to cross the Atlantic and perform profitably throughout the Republic. In part, it may simply be that the star system and the publicity it generated in the press encouraged the targeting of highly visible visitors, or that the greater the reputation, the greater the likelihood of a certain professional arrogance. There was a learning curve—British actors aspiring to sell their services at a good price in the States came to know how to stroke their audiences and what pitfalls to avoid.

Mathews, a well-known comic caricaturist, was inspired by the financial success of a colleague's 1817 tour and by Kean's first tour in 1820. While his own first American trip encountered none of the difficulties Kean had experienced, nor was it as profitable. He hoped however to turn the experience to advantage by producing in London a humorous one-man show, *A Trip to America*. This pastiche of American types, while not seriously anti-American, did include comic sketches that introduced the stage Yankee in the form of "Jonathan Doubikin" who, with his runaway slave Agamemnon, became a great favorite of London audiences, and was often replayed in Mathews' perennially popular "At Home" monologues. This, and the fact that Mathews performed in another play, Richard Brinsley Peake's derivative satire, *Jonathan in England*, convinced many in the States of his malicious intention to defame America. When he returned to Philadelphia and then New York for a second tour in 1834, though he played to good houses in both cities, he also met with ugly opposition. As a notice stuck up at one theater read, "The Scoundrel ought to be pelted from an American stage … This insult apont [sic] Americans ought to be met with the contempt it deserves."[62] Mathews, who was already an ill man, cut his tour short, returned to London, and died soon thereafter.

Macready's difficulties in America were altogether of another order of magnitude, and suggest more than traditional suspicion and sensitivity. The rising phenomenon, in both Britain and in America, of battling admirers or fans shares much of the blame. Kean's adherents, his "Wolf Club," in London theaters had "conspired to hoot down every other actor who essayed Kean's favourite characters."[63] Such warring factions helped turn Macready's testy relationship with his American stage rival, Edwin Forrest, into an exaggerated drama of national confrontation. Macready, who had made his own successful first tour of America in 1826–7, was well established on the London stage in mostly Shakespearean roles by the time the younger Edwin Forrest made his debut at Drury Lane in 1836.

Forrest (1806–72), son of an immigrant Scottish father, had been the rising star among American Shakespearean actors since Kean discovered him on the provincial circuit in Albany, New York, and took him on as Iago to Kean's Othello.[64] The next year, 1826, Forrest broke into national prominence with his own Othello at the Bowery in New York. In the following decades, much was made of the fact that he was *America's* tragedian, able to hold his own, his admirers claimed, against the best Britain could send—a role Forrest himself was happy to embrace. Britons who saw him act were often more guarded in their praise—typically, Frances Trollope, who first saw him as Hamlet in Cincinnati and later at the Park in New York, had little good to say.[65] Captain Thomas Hamilton, a devotee of theater who made a point of attending several plays in New York when he visited America in 1832, found Forrest to be "a coarse and vulgar actor, without grace … utterly commonplace." The "energy" for which he was known (and which he had learned from Kean) degenerated, Hamilton claimed, into mere "rant." "The audience, however, were enraptured."[66] Though advised against by some of his friends, Forrest's decision to tour Britain was no doubt driven by an ambition to court the favor of British critics on their home ground. Disappointment led to anger, confrontation, and gratuitous insults.

The Forrest-Macready Feud

At first, Macready was generously inclined and welcomed the younger American to his home, but within a week or so rival factions had asserted themselves; there was a "set" which Macready was told was "making against me to elevate Mr. Forrest … it is very indelicate, to say the very least, that an American should thus make himself a party in such a business."[67] For his part, Forrest took umbrage at what he deemed to be partisan critical reviews that drew attention to his "Jericho-trumpet voice" and "provincial flavour." His Richard III at Drury Lane had to compete with another production of the play mounted by Macready. And so by 1837 a contest of sorts began—with substantial paranoia all round. There was in fact some praise for Forrest's provincial and London performances, which were well attended, but the failure to get wholehearted endorsement soured him and encouraged a sense among his followers that there was an anti-American British conspiracy at work. Forrest returned to America, his patriotic suspicions of the British confirmed—but with a new English wife.

Macready's second trip to America in 1843 was predictably marred by agitation on behalf of the injured Forrest, who followed Macready from city to city, deliberately performing identical roles in competing houses. Sensationalist newspapers such as (Scottish-born) Gordon Bennett's *New York Herald* tried to stir up a storm of newsworthy protest: "forty or fifty unfriendly persons could, if they pleased, drive even Mr. Macready from the stage."[68] Nevertheless, the tour of American cities—New York and Boston, but also out to St. Louis and down to New Orleans and Mobile—was a financial success. His Hamlet "has brought me more money than any [other] play in America."[69]

Forrest's return to the London stage in 1845-6 kept the rivalry going. His Lear went down well enough, but not his Othello (he was criticized for his Yankee accent) and Macbeth. He also chose to play (there were four performances) a noble savage in *Metamora: or, The Last of the Wampanoags*, a favorite of his. This piece by an American author was, like another American play, *The Gladiator*, with which he had opened his first London tour, a romantic (and coded) affirmation of patriotic heroism and resistance to tyranny. *The Gladiator* was thought by some to be anti-British and he received a rebuke from the *Times*' critic for a curtain speech in which he charged the audience to prove with their applause for his Spartacus their present good will toward America and Americans.[70] The nadir was reached when Forrest wrote to the *Times* confirming reports that he had himself loudly hissed a performance of Macready's in Edinburgh in retaliation for Forrest being hissed in London. In consequence, when Macready next sailed to America in 1848, he rightly feared that his performances there would be met by hissing and perhaps worse "outrageous conduct" as well as by vicious reviews planted by friends of Forrest.

In the provinces, Macready was in fact plagued by "indecent outrage and malevolent barbarism," and at a performance of *Hamlet* in Cincinnati half a dead sheep was thrown on the stage.[71] Finally, in New York, Forrest's "partisans," inflamed perhaps by the actor himself and by placards and handbills calling for the ousting of "aristocratic" foreigners, infiltrated and disrupted the Astor Place Opera House where Macready was to play Macbeth. Seats were thrown onto the stage and an ensuing melee spilled outside the theater where hundreds, perhaps thousands, of demonstrators, recruited from among the disreputable of the Five-Points and Bowery district had gathered. Police and eventually militia went on the offensive, and when the smoke had cleared there were more than twenty dead and hundreds wounded. Macready had to flee the city in disguise.[72] The Astor Place Riot was the worst civil disorder in New York before the Civil War draft riots. "[A] struggle for power and cultural authority within theatrical space,"[73] it also resonates more widely. It came only months after the revolutions of 1848 in Europe and the last great Chartist demonstration in London, a fact cited by those respectables who defended sending in the militia and its firing on the stone-throwing crowd.

There had been a long history of theatrical disruptions and urban unrest—in Georgian Britain as in America. Violent disruptions might be sparked by xenophobia— as at Drury Lane in 1755 over the employment of French dancers—or, increasingly, by management's attempts to increase the price of admission and restrict the attendance of the boisterous, lower classes—as in the abolition of half-price tickets which provoked riots in 1763 at both Drury Lane and Covent Garden and in 1809 at Covent Garden. The 1809 OP (Old Price) riots sparked by attempts to raise the price of seating rocked London with massive protests lasting for three months.[74] In colonial America, the Stamp Act had provoked a major riot in New York (the Chapel Street riot) when a mob pulled down and burned the Hallam-Douglass theatre there as a symbol both of

English tyranny and the immoral luxury of the patriarchal elite. In the early Republic, clashing political factions at theaters were commonplace, leading often to disruptive behavior led by plebeians in the pit or gallery: as one scholar observes, "the republican street theatre of the revolutionary era had been brought inside."[75] There were serious turn-of-the-century hissing, disturbances, and destruction at the Federal Street Theater in Boston and at the Chestnut Street Theatre in Philadelphia. Working-class rioters often targeted English stars and actor-managers in the 1820s and 1830s—as in New York City where there were riotous disturbances at the major venues for legitimate drama every few years.[76]

Common, frequent, and casual disruption—well-short of exceptional rioting—was a part of an eighteenth-century Anglo-American theatrical culture that regarded theaters as open public spaces belonging to the people, "a forum for public dialogue." A large degree of "dialogic participation," that is back and forth between audience and stage, was tolerated and expected.[77] This customary popular tradition was under increasing assault by theatrical managers and owners by the early nineteenth century, as part of the advancement of bourgeois-culture-as-national-culture that was marked in both countries . There was a shift toward class-segregated institutions—music hall and rough entertainments for the less well-off, opera and legitimate theater for polite society. Though there had been a concern with preserving social distinction and respectability from the first development of legitimate theater in post-Revolution America, in the early nineteenth century raising seat prices, designing theaters without pit and with reduced gallery space, and imposing a dress code further advanced this project and caused resentment. One of the grievances shouted out at the Astor Place riot was that "You can't go in without kid gloves on … and a white vest, damn 'em!"[78]

Social grievance was easily deflected onto British interlopers and their cultural allies among New York's Anglophile elite. The disruptions of the 1830s and 1840s, however, appear to mark the end rather than a reinvigoration of the old tradition of protest. As previously in Britain, in America the new commercial theater managed to squeeze out plebeian attendance and workers turned to their own entertainments. Rioting, branded now as mere criminal behavior, largely disappeared from "bourgeois" playhouses after 1850.[79]

During the era of the Forrest-Macready confrontations, American provincial theaters, long dependent on traveling British performers, experienced some of the same populist protest that bedeviled theatrical life in the eastern cities—though agitators there lacked the crowds of the impoverished that helped inflame the New York riots. British talent, however, continued to be imported and welcomed by many right up to the Civil War. James Robertson Anderson, a Glasgow-born, modestly successful actor, for instance, made repeated "financially productive visits" to America—six tours in all—throughout the 1840s and 1850s. During the first of these, in 1844–5, aggressive admirers of Forrest demonstrated against him as yet another British interloper. There were fracases involving police and arrests, and yet he took home a very tidy £5,000.[80] Violent demonstrations against British theatrical touring ran out of steam, while populist nativism turned its guns 180 degrees to bear on the "invasion" of poor Catholic Irish immigrants.

3 Performing Americanness (and Britishness)

Our American Cousin

On October 15, 1858, the British playwright Tom Taylor finally had his comedy *Our American Cousin* premiere—at a New York theater. Written in 1851, the year of the Crystal Palace when London had received thousands of American tourist-visitors, the script had languished unperformed in England before being picked up and produced in New York by the English-born actor-manager Laura Keen seven years later. It proved a surprisingly long-lived success, both in New York where it ran for 140 consecutive performances and in London when it was produced there two years later. An enduring piece of light entertainment, it made stars of its principals on both sides of the ocean, lifted its main characters—the Yankee rustic Asa Trenchard and, especially, the dimwitted British aristocrat Lord Dundreary—into popular culture figures, and was frequently revived in the decades that followed.

Taylor (1817–80), a civil servant, humorist, and playwright, was known as a prolific adaptor of French farces who also rushed to produce a London stage version of *Uncle Tom's Cabin* in 1852—in competition with the very successful adaptation by the American George Aiken the same year. Taylor was, it has been suggested, motivated to write a play featuring an American visitor to home-county England by the "Yankee mania" in London caused by the American exhibits at the Great Exposition and the unprecedented "throngs" of American visitors to the British capital.[81] His delineation of country-house guest Asa Trenchard, who, with his feet propped up on a table, whittles while smoking cigars, nevertheless followed what was by then a decades-long theatrical convention of the stage New Englander "with a strong nasal twang, and a decided taste for tobacco and [whiskey] cobblers." It incorporated a caricatured regional dialect drawn from clichéd Americanisms. Asa's speech is littered with "I guess" and "fixins."[82] The twist that Taylor provides in the part is to take the humor and combine it with a positive representation of a somewhat crude, but plain-speaking outsider juxtaposed against the artifice of the polite British upper class. As Florence, daughter of Sir Edward Trenchard, Bt., says of Asa, "And they call that man a savage; well, I only wish we had a few more such savages in England."[83]

The role of Asa—and the play itself—had been, in fact, originally written for and offered to a then-popular American stage-Yankee comedian, Joshua Silsbee, who, however, declined to produce it. It was ultimately performed, in New York, by Joseph Jefferson (1829–1905), whose English immigrant grandfather and father had been actors, and whose own career was confirmed by Taylor's play. Before *Our American Cousin*, he had played the stage-Yankee role of Sam Scudder in Boucicault's *The Octoroon*, and would follow his Asa Trenchard with another "American role" as a young (and old) Rip van Winkle in a dramatization of Irving's 1819 story, rewritten by Boucicault. He would be identified with "Rip" in Australia, London and New York for the rest of his long career.[84]

The most enduring of *Our American Cousin*'s characters, one that moved beyond the stage into transatlantic popular culture, was that of the feckless, dandified, drawling, silly aristocrat Lord Dundreary, a role that owed more to the embellishments of the Liverpool-born actor who came to be identified with the part, Edward Askew Sothern (1826–81), than to Taylor's forty-seven lines of script. Originally a minor role, Sothern's Dundreary (formed, he said, on "studies … made from real types" and suggested "by people whom he had known since early boyhood"[85]) ultimately came to upstage the rest of the cast in one of the most immediately recognizable comic parts in nineteenth-century Anglo-American theater. The long frock coat (borrowed from Boucicault for the New York premiere), eyeglass, and exuberant side whiskers came to typify on both sides of the Atlantic the aristocrat-as-fop.

The play lifted Jefferson to "star" caliber and a successful tour of Australia; for Sothern, it provided a meal ticket for the rest of his life. For us, the play has some interest for its double role in national and class stereotyping—of American and Briton, common man and aristocrat. It can be "read" from either side of the Atlantic. From New York or Britain, Asa Trenchard can be seen as a plain American come into an English inheritance who brings to that mannered and perhaps effete country a dose of American candor and common sense. This submerges Taylor's use of the derisive clichés of Yankee speech and behavior into a larger rendering of the unmannered but admirable American abroad. Vain and ignorant Dundreary presents the opportunity for a more complicated reading. In America he would have been seen as a long-familiar caricature of the elitist Briton of the mother country—invoking the self-regard and assumed (but false) superiority Americans had found in the turn-of-the-century review writers and the most egregious of the travel writers. In London, however, the theater critic of the *Athenaeum* complained that the part was "a vile caricature" of a nobleman, though allowing that it might be accepted by the audience as a "type of any class whatever."[86] The manager producing the play had worried that a "gross and insulting caricature" of a British aristocrat, while it might be popular in New York, would be found in London "wanting in humor, taste, and judgment," and that class prejudice of this kind would fall flat, especially among the beau monde—the swells and dandies—of the theater-going public. In the event, the play ran before enthusiastic audiences at the Haymarket for some 400 consecutive nights and Buckstone cleared £30,000.[87] It may be that enthusiastic British reception had something to do with the renewed demands for political and social reform in the late 1850s and 1860s, when anti-aristocratic humor, as in some of Gilbert's later work for Sullivan, came to have a sharp, contemporary edge.

The Stage Yankee[88]

The Yankee caricature was made generally known to London audiences by Charles Mathews' routines in the 1820s, and by the popularity in the 1830s of the Nova Scotian author Thomas Chandler Haliburton's series of sketches featuring the wisecracking character Sam Slick. In the States, the stage-Yankee role was taken up by numerous comedians who developed their turns on the eastern and western American stage and then took these to London, where they came to constitute a familiar genre. Often derided by critics, these performances could prove popular with audiences with a less discriminating appetite for low comedy. They were broad—if increasingly hackneyed—humorous representations of the American Other, whether performed by British actors such as Mathews or by touring Americans such as James Hackett.

Seeing the stage as a site for performing national identities, one's own and those of imaginary others, and for the enacting of "narratives of the nation," owes much to the general interest in identity and performance in cultural studies. This would seem to offer an especially appropriate approach for considering the history of a new nation deeply invested in self-creation, where "the very ontology of America seems ambiguous."[89] It may be argued that an America constantly constructing and reconstructing itself through immigration is naturally a "performed trope."[90] But if *American* nationality is "susceptible to performance," the same might be said of other constructed nations—revolutionary France or Bismarck's Germany—and indeed of older countries as well as they transitioned from royal patrimonies to nation-states. Negative stereotypes that serve to set off the positive sense of the English nation have of course a long history in British literature and theater—the arrogant Spaniard, devious Italian, or lascivious Frenchman, or their counterparts in the canny Scot, thieving, sing-song Welshman, feckless and drunken Irishman, and the rude rustic of the uncivilized agricultural hinterland.

The early nineteenth-century British representation of the American, of Brother Jonathan, inherited much from that of the English provincial—especially the rural Yorkshireman. By the time however that Charles Mathews came to portray on stage in London his own humorous sketches of the American in the 1820s, the image had evolved to give Jonathan a generic Yankee character in speech and manner at a time when, in America, parodies of differentiated *regional* speech and manner were advancing the politics of geographic sectionalism—metropolitan east and backwoods west, Yankee New England and planter and slave south. In the British popular mind elements from each of these regional types might be rolled into one general idea of the American as slavery-condoning, hard-drinking, spitting, log-cabin rural. The literary and performing caricature that came in Britain to signify antebellum Americanness most specifically was that of the dry, sharp-witted, calculating, and, above all, nasal "Yankee." While the Yankee on the American stage was a clearly sectional figure,[91] on the British stage he was a character that in a sense floated free of his New England origin, and became a conveniently recognizable trope for Americanness. As the American John Neal, writing anonymously in *Blackwood's* in 1824, protested, "those who have been employed in getting up Brother Jonathans for the English market ... have jumbled everything together, true and false—all the peculiarities of all the different people—and called the composition a Yankee."[92]

Mathews' enduring stage-Yankee creation, Jonathan Doubikin, was, like Richard Brinsley Peake's satire, *Jonathan in England*, informed by the rustic "Jonathans" of the American stage. This was a tradition that reached back to the American Royall Tyler's satire of 1787, *The Contrast*, a piece that had been played before President Washington. Ironically that role was taken by an English actor, Thomas Wignell, and played, apparently, with a kind of Yorkshire accent. The Philadelphian James Nelson Barker's addition to the genre, his play of 1807, *Tears and Smiles*, also used an immigrant English actor, the subsequent founder of an American acting dynasty, Joseph Jefferson. This was hardly surprising, given the prevalence of British actors on the American stage in these early years. In 1809, another Yankee play, performed at the Park Street Theater, *Love and Friendship, Or Yankee Notions*, by a young Abraham Lindsley, used a more genuine New England dialect and pronunciation. By the time New Englander David Humphreys produced his *The Yankee in England* a few years later, the drawling stage-Yankee speech he employed had apparently become expected in Jonathan roles. It appears that others, such as Mathews, used the text of this play, published *c.* 1815, as a kind of reference book for their own Yankee characters (Mathews loaned his copy to Peake). And so the tradition developed out of these origins. It included representations that were sometimes contradictory—as in the quick and too-clever versus the laconic and slow Yankee—and was subsequently deployed not only on the American stage in Philadelphia or New York but in London.[93]

When, in 1827, James Henry Hackett (1800–71), a New Yorker who had some success in Shakespearean roles,[94] brought his own Jonathan to Covent Garden, he was seen as an inferior imitator of Mathews. In response he developed a second version which juxtaposed satirical representations of both British and Yankee stereotypes. *John Bull at Home, Or Jonathan in England* adapted material from an English play featuring a comic Yorkshireman, Solomon Gundy, transformed into the Yankee Solomon Swap. This went down well enough in New York, and Hackett was encouraged to try Britain again, in part by a belief that the success of Frances Trollope's book would have encouraged greater curiosity among the English about Americans. But when he took Solomon Swap to London's Drury Lane in 1832 critics were again unkind ("a damnable substitute," "sheer vulgarity"[95]), though audiences were more generous, and Hackett received praise for other roles—one of them a comic backwoods Kentucky "Colonel"—while in London. He would return in 1836 and 1839 in other roles but reserved further stage-Yankee routines for American audiences in Boston and New York where he was able to develop a witty Jonathan who turned Mathews' satire back on the English themselves as dullard cousins. Other American dialect comedians followed Hackett to Britain. The most successful was George Handel Hill (1809–49), who had performed *Jonathan Doubikin* in Philadelphia and *Jonathan in England* in New York. He had a better reception with the critics in London, and, as "Yankee Hill," came to be regarded as an "authentic" satirist of Yankee character in the late 1830s and 1840s.[96]

The stage Yankee flourished in Britain in the pre-Civil War era as somehow representative of the national American character, rather the way the stage-Cockney's dropping and adding of "aitches" was often taken, in America, to be characteristically British. At the hands of some actors, the role came to enfold quite disparate kinds of mythic American. Danforth Marble (1810–49) presented a Yankee, Sam Patch, who was "part Jonathan, part Davy Crocket, part Mike Fink." Successful when he took Sam to the western American towns of Cincinnati, St. Louis, and Louisville, he had less success with the theater critics in London in 1844. He persevered, however, touring the English provinces until 1848. Marble's stage Yankee still retained, behind the comic elements, something of the buried negative qualities—the conceit and cunning—of earlier representations.⁹⁷ A decade later, it is this side of Yankee character that has largely disappeared from Jefferson's Asa Trenchard.⁹⁸

There were other stage-Yankee actors who followed Marble to Britain but after the American Civil War, the role rapidly waned, surviving as a mere regional, New England, stereotype that itself was ultimately replaced with the quite different, by and large uncomic representation of the wealthy guidebook-scanning, Gilded Age American abroad, in an era that saw an Anglo-American literature, as in the early novels of Henry James, abandon mere dialect satire in search of an understanding of national character that was far more complex. The representation of the American on stage shifted from that of a comic rustic figure to a more or less cultivated member of upper-middle class, urban and suburban polite society on the one hand, and on the other the get-ahead, efficiency-driven competitor set to displace the Lord Dundrearys in the coming globalized commercial world. When he visited America with Henry Irving in 1876 and 1880, the editor and novelist Joseph Hatton was surprised to find nowhere the Yankee familiar in the earlier travelers' memoirs or on the London stage, "a very pronounced and *outré* sort of person, with a grating nasal twang in his speech, and in his manners a vulgar disregard for the decent customs of social life."⁹⁹

Elements of the early stage stereotype survived in the pages of humor magazines and in the editorial cartoons of late nineteenth-century journalism. If in these an imperial, trident-armed Britannia came to compete with if not displace the traditionally corpulent roast-beef-eating farmer John Bull, cartoon representation of the nation in America also shifted from the young, cloddish Brother Jonathan to the tall, thin, bearded, and elderly Uncle Sam. Sam remained rural (as was most of the United States well into the twentieth century) and something of a hayseed—a term that was invented in its modern sense in the 1870s—rather than metropolitan, though characterized by red, white, and blue patriotism rather than the crafty, self-serving calculation of the New Englander of the early Republic. By the First World War he had become not so much a figure of humor as a stern, if laconic, reminder of the larger duties and destiny of America-in-the-world.

A Sort of Binary

The stage Yankee as emblem of Americanness, of *the* American, had, in its heyday before the Civil War, depended on a sort of *binary*—of Americanness versus Britishness, of rude democrat versus urbane or foppish aristocrat. In antebellum America the two caricatured identities marched, as it were, hand in hand; subsequently, as the representation of the American shifted to embrace the rising wealth and prospects of the nation, the image of the British aristo endured. In the American playwright Bronson Howard's successful play of 1887, *The Henrietta*, the American is a Wall Street financier made very rich by investment in a western mine. The British suitor to his daughter's hand, Lord Arthur Trelawny, however, is still the Dundreary of thirty years earlier: a fop with a monocle who delivers quaint Briticisms.¹⁰⁰ The image of the Briton as supercilious and effete grew naturally out of the experience and patriotic ideology of the Revolution. The flight of often wealthy Loyalists thereafter sharpened that understanding—however much many Loyalists may have been, not Tory snobs, but in fact persons of very modest means. America, the patriots suggested, had expelled its own would-be aristocracy. Those Americans who traveled to Britain or who had close connections with kindred communities there—evangelical Protestants, abolitionists, commercial entrepreneurs, or the literary elite of Boston—of course knew that Britain was itself socially diverse and that the aristocratic element was on the defensive, caricatured increasingly as useless, or worse, in its own homeland. Ralph Waldo Emerson's friendship with caustic Thomas Carlyle would not have encouraged him to believe that Britain was wholly defined by an exaggerated traditional sense of social deference. But most Americans, especially the growing, rural part across the Alleghenies, had little personal experience or knowledge of life over the ocean beyond the patriotic texts of school books or the exaggerated expostulation of popular journalism and the stump speeches of politicians. This misinformation or, at least, vacuum of knowledge encouraged fanciful imagination and parody. British travelers were sometimes shocked and amused by the eager and willful ignorance, as they saw it, of Americans about the mother country—those they met who assured them that the Queen lived in the Tower of London and that the House of Lords daily tyrannized the country.

The antebellum stage Yankee then, in America, might be taken as a savvy character able, finger alongside his nose, to put the affected Briton in his or her place; in Britain, the American as Yankee-doodle braggart provided both amusement and confirmation of an untutored America and, as well, of a Britishness that was defined, not exactly by condescension, but by an ability judgmentally to stand above and observe the provinciality of their country "cousins." This binary of Americanness and Britishness continued, if in a sometimes lighter vein, in the era that followed the Civil War, to be cultivated long after the stage Yankee ceased to be its prominent vehicle. In the American North and West, thanks in part to the awareness of pro-Southern attitudes among, especially, the British upper classes during the war, and in part to the growing prominence in American politics of the aggrieved Irish-American, politicians like James G. Blaine promoted a convenient Anglophobia well beyond the era of the settlement of the Alabama claims. The image of the supercilious Englishman lay beneath much of the remarkable outpouring of populist Anglophobia during the Venezuela Crisis, and even Grover Cleveland, who was inclined to improve relations with Britain, had to be seen to respond aggressively toward British imperial encroachment, as it was widely portrayed, in Latin America. At the same time, the image of American difference proved useful in domestic British politics on both sides of the long-lasting debate over political and social reform. The Second Reform Act risked, as Carlyle put it, "shooting Niagara," and radical-liberal Joseph Chamberlain's attempts thereafter to organize national politics on a foundation of local associations were, his conservative critics claimed, but the importation of the corrupt American ward-politics of Tammany Hall.

And yet, American audiences flocked to see and hear British theatrical troupes in the late nineteenth century. These were ever more organized and frequent and were carried by the convenience of rail across the entire continent. The attraction of a Henry Irving, an Ellen Terry, or a Lillie Langtry perhaps depended as much on the allure, among some

Americans, of their well-advertised Britishness as on their art. Among that part of the nation that retained a robust suspicion of Britons, the bitterness and anger of previous representations were softened by a new, amused appetite for British self-parody. Gilbert and Sullivan's operettas were hugely popular throughout America and inspired literally dozens of local production companies ready to perform, without, of course, royalty payments, each of these entertainments soon after they were introduced in London. The humor allowed them to share, with Gilbert and Sullivan's enthusiastic middle-class English audiences, a contempt for the vanity and incompetence of the privileged, and to stroke and confirm their own democratic American view of a Britain of incompetent

Figure 1 "Side-by-Side—Britannia" (1918), by James Montgomery Flagg [Library of Congress].

First Lords of the Admiralty, garrulous modern Major Generals, elderly, lascivious Lord Chancellors, or a fairy House of Peris. For his part, Wilde, dressed as a "real Bunthorne" advocating an aesthetic of art and artifice, also advanced—at least in some circles—the familiar trope of a dandified effeminacy that was already part of the common American caricature of the affected Briton. At the same time, imported Wild West entertainments or novels of the romanticized American West advanced a special American masculinity.

One might, in conclusion, note that the stage Yankee, closely resembling the canny Scot or commonsensical Yorkshireman, was paralleled, in American *and* British theaters, by another pronounced, if contrasting, stereotype—that of the stage-Irishman. Both were formed around a comic manner and by pronunciation and phraseology that typed them as distinctive and predictable characters—as feckless and drunken "Milesians" or dry, sharp-practicing New Englanders (drinkers but not drunkards). Both types shifted over time. Boucicault developed a more sympathetic Irish stereotype with a hint of pathos behind the crude humor. The Yankee shifted as well, or rather elements of the Yankee may be found within the transatlantic representation of the American most favored in Britain by the end of the century—the laconic, drawling, plug-chewing westerner, the cowboy of Buffalo Bill imagination. Without much adjustment, Asa Trenchard—who came to Britain to claim his inheritance, and who is romantically, if wrongly, imagined by Augusta Mountchessington to be "an Apollo of the prairie"[101]—can be seen, beneath his comic boorishness, to anticipate the square-jawed, racialized Anglo-Saxon of the turn of the century. This was a type that Bram Stoker, in his most famous novel, would employ in the plain-speaking, kukri-knife/bowie-knife wielding Quincey Morris, or that poster art in the First World War would portray as an Uncle Sam armed and arm in arm with helmeted Britannia.

4 "The Great Wet Way":[102] Theater and the Growth of a Transnational Industry

American Actors in London after Forrest

In the early Republic and antebellum eras American actors appearing in serious theatrical roles—chiefly Shakespearean tragedy and comedy—were not unknown on the London stage, but they were uncommon there and regarded by many as a curiosity. When the young John Howard Payne, a friend of Washington Irving who was regarded (in Boston and New York) as an "American Roscius,"[103] came to London in 1813 to play at Drury Lane in a romantic tragedy, he met only modest success. One critic declared "it remarkable that a youth from a remote country—a country nearly 200 years behind us in the improvement of every art—should have the courage to come before a London audience under every possible disadvantage."[104] His chief disadvantage was, apparently, his provincial-sounding American accent; he would prove more successful in Britain as a playwright and a manager at Sadler's Wells. Critics were not often generous in their estimation of American artists, finding or claiming to find American acting style coarse and informal (i.e., untutored by the conventions of early nineteenth-century British stagecraft), and of course American accents were never quite right. This, in spite of the fact that many American actors, like Forrest, modeled themselves on Edmund Kean's own impulsive style, what Coleridge called his "flashes of lightening," and his rejection of declamatory formality.

Some American actors came to find a niche as performers of Americanness, as stage-Yankee humorists, and the popularity of this genre probably served, until the performing cliché faded in the second half of the century, to restrict somewhat the prospects of those who were ambitious for larger roles. When just before the Civil War Boucicault brought four American actors to London for *The Colleen Bawn*, preferring not to rely on local stock companies, they were not successful with audiences that, presumably, were used to low-comedy stage-Yankees and preferred their own stage-Irish.[105]

Generally, however, when prominent American actors of the second half of the century, such as Lawrence Barrett (1838–91), Joseph Jefferson, and, especially, Edwin Booth (1833–93), toured Britain, they could count on a reasonably unprejudiced reception. It had become nearly as common for Americans of the classical, Shakespearean tradition to try a British tour as to tour across the United States. Booth appeared in London for the first time in 1861, Barrett, in 1867 after the hiatus of his war service. Subsequently their reputations flourished, and both returned to London numerous times in the 1880s. If, despite the occasional disappointment, they were generously treated by London critics, this should be seen in the general context of the greater familiarity of things American in the second half of the century, the softening of the critical tone in mid-century travelers' memoirs, and the growth, generally, of an eastward as well as westward transatlantic theatrical exchange. This is not to suggest that British criticism ever abandoned unfavorable national comparisons. Lesser-known actors in the classical tradition, those without a star reputation, often fared indifferently unless they enjoyed the advance publicity and active promotion that the fin de siècle Broadway impresarios would provide for their "properties." In 1884, Sir Lepel Henry Griffin, a diplomat, dandy, and later proposer of an Anglo-American union, observed that "Booth, and to a less degree, Jefferson, may be held to possess something of this power [of dramatic art as the mirror of nature], but it is altogether absent from the work of most American actors, as might be seen this season in London."[106]

In the early 1880s even Edwin Booth could have hard going in competition with the rising national reputation of Henry Irving. Though both Booth and Irving were known for the naturalism of their delivery, Booth's was of an older, powerful though quietly thoughtful kind compared with Irving's livelier subtlety and versatility. In London each attracted a following and their dueling Hamlets were sometimes characterized there and in New York as reflecting competing national styles.

The personal relationship of Booth—only five years older but whose career had matured earlier—and Irving remained apparently cordial and fraternal, with none of the ill-will of the Forrest-Macready feud. In 1882 Irving arranged for Booth and himself to play *Othello* at the Lyceum, exchanging the parts of Iago and Othello on alternate evenings. As Irving generously replied when asked if he had seen Booth's Hamlet, "No;

but I have the highest respect for Mr. Booth. I played with him when he was in England the first time [in 1861] ... I am glad of Booth's success here. It is a good thing, apart from the advantage to art, in the way it strengthens the real friendliness that now exists between England and America."[107] One may suspect that some of this public bonhomie suggests Irving himself was careful of his reputation in America where he intended to continue to make highly profitable tours. But late in the century there does seem to have often been a kind of cozy male camaraderie in London among the actors. "Booth, Barrett, Boucicault, McCullough ... and others of their craft" would of an evening sit around the table at the Beefsteak Club at the Lyceum, smoking Havanas.[108]

Until late in the century most of the notable American actors to cross the ocean were men. There were exceptions, as with Charlotte Cushman (1817–76), an actress-manager at Walnut Street who performed with Macready on his 1843 tour of the States, and who became well known for, especially, trouser roles such as Romeo and Hamlet when she came to Britain the next year.[109] But in an era when British actresses such as Fanny Kemble and Agnes Robertson commanded significant attention in America, American thespian traffic eastward was mostly male. By mid-century, however, there were a number of acclaimed American actresses briefly notable on the London stage, such as the sisters Isabel and Kate Bateman, and this relatively thin record began to thicken by the 1880s. Mary Anderson (1859-1940), an American actress who achieved an early fame in the American West and South and who debuted to acclaim in New York in 1877, had a famous success in London in 1883–4, where, according to Emily Faithful, in a phrase echoed by Ellen Terry, she "has simply taken the whole of Britain by storm!"[110] Lepel Griffin, characteristically, was less impressed. Anderson, he thought, was merely "a pretty and picturesque woman." Faithful, however, an advocate of female employment and emigration who had toured the States, pressed her feminist case that Anderson represented much more: "Mrs. Anderson emphatically represents what the stage still wants in both countries, well-bred, educated, accomplished ladies, whose principles have been tested and whose culture is the result of thought and experience."[111]

However much the self-narrative of the transatlantic late nineteenth-century theatrical world may have emphasized its achievement of bourgeois status and professionalism—with a knighthood for Irving and, ultimately, the entombment of his ashes in Westminster Abbey—it never managed entirely to shed its subversive reputation, especially with regard, on stage and off, to actresses "loose" in their morals if not actually prostitutes.[112] Cushman's sexuality was more or less an open secret, and the image of the courtesan-magdalen, and of sexual dalliance, secret liaisons, divorces, and illegitimate births, clung, enticingly perhaps, to many of the British stars "with a past" who toured the United States later in the century—from Ellen Terry and Lillie Langtry to Mrs. Pat (who, in her renowned role as Pinero's Mrs. Tanqueray played a woman "with a past"). The effort that went into representing American exports to Britain such as Anderson and others as great beauties may have served to enforce this unspoken tradition. The public, *pace* Emily Faithful, was not it seems especially interested in "well-bred, educated" ladies, but in actresses with a rumored past (or present). By the end of the century long-standing expectations of the immorality or amorality of actresses were more than suggested by the fashion for vampire roles (metaphoric or otherwise) and by the "new woman" of modern, Continental drama represented in the plays, most vividly, of Henrik Ibsen. An American actress in London became especially associated in the 1890s with these roles.

Kentucky-born into a middle-class professional family, Elizabeth Robins (1862–1952) was raised by a grandmother who gave her the complete works of Shakespeare. At age twenty she became a member of Edwin Booth's touring company, married another actor and, after his suicide in 1885, toured the United States with Barrett and Booth before traveling to London en route to Norway in 1888. She embraced the work of Ibsen especially, and roles playing women of strength and independence. In London, she established a close relationship with the actress and "non-commercial" stage manager Marion Lea to create "a theatre of independent management and artistic standards." The two introduced *Hedda Gabler* to the British public in the spring of 1891, a role with which Robins would be identified both in Britain and on occasional tours back in the States. In the Edwardian era she became an articulate and active feminist and suffragette whose writings circulated back to America where, she claimed in a speech delivered at the Albert hall in 1912, "the Americans have taken fire from the English torch … from the Atlantic to the Pacific."[113]

British Theatrical Touring in Late Nineteenth-Century America

From George Frederick Cooke on, some nineteenth-century transatlantic actor-managers made (and lost) very substantial fortunes. Boucicault, like the Wallacks, was highly attuned to ways in which the business he attempted to organize from the ground up might be made a money-spinning one, in London as in New York. In Gilded-Age America the scale of great enterprises such as the oil, steel, railway, and financial interests grew exponentially and were ever more concentrated in fewer hands. This world of Rockefeller, Carnegie, and Morgan, of trusts, monopolies, and horizontal and vertical amalgamation had a parallel of sorts in the more modest realm of a commercial theater that a generation of new entrepreneurs were integrating into "an expansive, unified system of production, distribution, exhibition, and reception."[114] This phenomenon was most pronounced on the American side of the ocean, in a new breed of deep-pocketed Broadway broker-dealers, often not themselves primarily actor-managers any longer but negotiators, arrangers, and speculative investors in a wide spectrum of shows and touring companies.

The growth in the scale and organization of theatrical commerce which one may observe from the early 1880s was however not an American monopoly. Regular, programed transatlantic touring was, with the improvement in transport, a logical evolution of the Atlantic-hopping of individual stars to that of whole theatrical troupes. In the most famous example before the end of the century, that of Henry Irving's traveling Lyceum productions, American tours, expensive affairs, were a calculated, entrepreneurial response to the growing debt incurred by Irving's ever-more ambitious London stage operations. Irving's tours were preceded, and perhaps encouraged, by the London producer and impresario Richard D'Oyly Carte's ambitious and successful plan to "bring the aesthetic movement to America," by importing to New York his popular London production of Gilbert and Sullivan's *Patience*, with much of the London troupe of singers, actors, and orchestra, sets and costumes, in September 1881.

D'Oyly Carte's interest in American touring had not, however, been motivated solely by the anticipated profits of a successful tour, but by the need to deal with extensive American pirating. *H.M.S. Pinafore* had within weeks of its opening in London been performed in New York without authorization, and within a year there were perhaps 150 other unauthorized productions throughout the country. To secure American copyright, D'Oyly Carte traveled to New York with Gilbert and Sullivan to open *The Pirates of Penzance* there in December 1879—*before* the London opening a few months later. Unauthorized productions in the United States continued however to be a problem, and the bringing of the London production of *Patience* was in part an attempt to undermine the market for pirated versions by offering the authentic, original production in New York and by directly organizing authorized traveling companies. This was a course D'Oyly Carte would follow again for *The Mikado* in 1885, though the conflicted legal issues surrounding copyright remained largely unresolved.[115]

The opening of *Patience* in New York in December 1881 was followed in January by Oscar Wilde's lecture tour—coordinated by D'Oyly Carte to proceed across America during the on-going engagement in New York of the operetta and as the provincial productions also organized by D'Oyly Carte spread out across the major cities. Wilde's success was immediately followed by the decision of Lillie Langtry—urged on by Wilde— to venture her own, elaborately publicized, extensive, and quite profitable tour through the United States, involving nine cities and a private train lent to her by Diamond Jim Brady. D'Oyly Carte's ambition and success, and both the Wilde and Langtry "crazes," would have suggested new and promising possibilities for a financially hard-pressed actor-manager such as Irving.

Irving, in fact, turned what had been an occasional recourse into a *system* of well-placed agents, public relations, highly publicized promotions, and steamship and Pullman car transportation. This was the organization, that is, not merely of a few stars, but of a whole multifarious and numerous transplanted company with the sets, costumes, lighting, and stage managers, not for one or two London "hits," but for a repertoire of plays, some familiar vehicles for Irving and others associated with the Lyceum's recent seasons. Irving boasted, "[i]n the history of the stage the Lyceum Company is the first complete organization which has crossed the Atlantic with the entire equipment of a theatre."[116]

Irving's preparations were focused and thorough. The journalist, Joseph Hatton, a convenient friend of Irving's and a foreign correspondent for the New York *Tribune*, arranged for "favourable intelligence" to reach New York well before the entourage arrived there. Austin Brereton, who would become Irving's biographer, was the representative of a syndicate of English newspapers sent out ahead of the first tour. Irving departed in a blaze of publicity, a send-off at the Garrick Club and dinner with Prime Minister Gladstone. In New York the company was met by the American actor Lawrence Barrett (due himself to perform at the Lyceum in the next season). Barrett "had a great share in organizing this meeting of welcome," which included some thirty newspaper reporters.[117]

Irving said to a friend after the first tour, "[t]he seed we have sown, I mean to reap."[118] Between 1883 and 1904, his company visited the United States eight times, staying for months. They traveled as far as Chicago for the first tours and as far as San Francisco for the fourth in 1893.[119] These tours were exhausting for all involved—that of 1895-6 included fifteen different plays performed in some twenty-nine cities (sometimes six different venues in a single week), but the total receipts, Brereton tells us, came to nearly three and a half million dollars. Expensive as the tours were to arrange and carry out, total profit nevertheless amounted to well over half a million dollars.[120] Though some suspected that the 209 weeks Irving spent in America between 1883 and 1904 weakened the Lyceum by his absence (there were losses in London in the 1890s and a devastating fire), there is little doubt that the financial difficulties which finally overtook him after 1902 would have dragged him down earlier had it not been for the American cash.

John Henry Broadribb (Irving) claimed a special relationship with America—his stage name, he said, was taken "through his admiration for the author of 'The Sketch Book," just as he would claim that Booth, with his fine voice and natural interpretation, was, from the first time he saw him in 1861, "the actor of his dreams."[121] It would be misleading, however, to assume that these strenuous and well-orchestrated tours were chiefly motivated by a personal special relationship. They were business ventures organized with the intention of both immediate profit and the establishment and massaging of a long-term reputation that would continue to provide bankable value.

By the turn of the century Irving's famous successes in the repeated touring of his company to America no doubt encouraged others. Looking westward as a last recourse in a financial crisis was, of course, no new thing for individuals. It was the scale, ambition, financial planning and organization, and casualness of such a remedy that came to mark the era. When, late in 1901, the resourceful Mrs. Campbell was informed that bankruptcy was imminent, she and her London advisors immediately agreed on an American tour and contacted George Crouse Tyler. Tyler (1867–1946) had co-founded a firm in New York in 1896 to acquire the rights to British and European plays and to import the actors to perform them (by 1908, under Tyler's management, it was bringing from fifteen to twenty new plays a season across the ocean to New York theaters). A Liebler and Company agent was quickly sent across to arrange a contract, though it took a month of negotiation for a deal to be closed. Not only was Campbell booked for a twenty-two-week tour of the major American cities, but fifteen members of her company, her dresser, her maid, her "businessman" (a Mr. Bertram) and her lap dog Pinkie Pankie Poo, were to accompany her on a "fast ship" to New York. Up to half of the earnings she might realize would go to pay off her creditors.[122]

Fin de siècle Impresarios and the Americanization of a Transatlantic "Business"

From early in the nineteenth century the transatlantic business of finding and engaging actors, whether known stars or simply available repertory performers with some experience on the London or Dublin stage, was in America mostly in the hands of

British-born or British-descended actor-managers such as the Wallacks, who ran the major theaters and employed their own agents abroad. There were of course always local managers and brokers who scouted for talent and helped negotiate contracts, but until late in the century these were relatively modest enablers rather than the driving force behind the growth of this particular industry. By the 1870s this situation was beginning to change. The rise of a new generation of native-born, not-British managers and stage directors such as John Augustin Daly (1838–99) presaged an inevitable shift away from hegemonic British transatlanticity in the theatrical world. North Carolina-born Daly, son of Catholic Irish immigrants, began as a drama critic and playwright before turning to the management of a New York theater in 1869. He eventually opened his own on Broadway and, after growing success there opened another in London in 1893. As an "arriviste" transatlantic owner-manager, Daly sent his company on tour to England and the Continent in the 1890s, promoting rising American stars such as Ada Rehan and Maurice Barrymore and reaching for a more popular audience with abridged Shakespeare texts (a vulgarity attacked by Shaw) and unconventional productions.[123]

At the same time, though some of the emerging big impresarios of the late Gilded Age may have started as actor-managers attached to a particular New York, Philadelphia, or Boston theater, their entrepreneurial operations were evolving into detached, general agencies with an elaborated business model as middlemen to a host of clients in an industry that ran from classical theater, opera, and light comedy to popular entertainments of all kinds.[124] One can find in Britain similar firms (such as the concert management specialists, Ibbs and Tillet, founded in 1906) and impresarios of the new type, following perhaps the lead of Broadway.

Pointing to this future, the first of Irving's tours (subsequent tours would be taken more completely into Irving's own hands) was coordinated by the American theatrical impresario Henry Eugene Abbey (1846–96), who had arranged Sarah Bernhardt's first American tour, a coup that made him famous. He subsequently oversaw the first of Lillie Langtry's two American tours of 1883–5 (she reportedly held out for more than Bernhardt had negotiated).[125] From the early 1870s Abbey had managed a number of New York theaters. Recruitment of British and European stars for these led to a larger interest in facilitating the needs of actors and theaters beyond those of his own management. In 1882 he formed a partnership with John Baptist Schoeffel, a Boston theatrical manager, and Maurice Grau, an Austrian-born New York opera promoter (who, as manager of the Metropolitan Opera and, briefly, of Covent Garden, intended to "put opera on a business-like sound financial basis"[126]). The partnership promoted opera and theater productions and the singers and actors imported from Europe to play in them, as well as negotiated the London reception of American stars—in 1883 Abbey booked Irving's Lyceum for an eight-month run for Mary Anderson.[127]

Inevitably, the new style impresario and agency, with wide interests, transatlantic deals, and deep resources, came to exercise rather more control than had been generally true at mid-century—especially if the actor, manager, or production in question was facing financial difficulty or lacked a significant reputation. When George Tyler of

Liebler & Co. agreed to underwrite and organize Stella Campbell's first American tour, there were drawn-out negotiations in London. He claimed an option on any further tours, and, with his London agent, intended to "conduct" the whole operation. They began by insisting that "some well-known leading man" accompany her to New York as a further insurance of success. Lesser members of the cast who were dragged along to America might also feel aggrieved at over-management, though touring might open unexpected opportunities. A supporting actor in the troupe, George Arliss, included at the last moment, felt that he "was obviously regarded by the Liebler Company as of no real importance."[128] Once he arrived in America, however, he received competing offers from other impresarios such as Belasco and Frohman, left Mrs. Pat's troupe, and stayed on for twenty years.

That there were inevitable tensions between exceptionally empowered impresario-moguls and supplicant actors was inevitable. Mrs. Pat claimed to regret the publicity "stunts" that turned her 1901–2 stay into "a circus," and threatened to go to another American impresario, Charles Frohman, for her next tour. When she returned for a tour in 1907–8, again arranged by Tyler's Liebler & Co., she would bitterly complain of his "particularly odious" staff and would, in fact, for her next tour, choose another American producer, David Belasco—a popular playwright who had been secretary to Boucicault in the 1870s and who by the end of the century was on his way to becoming one of the most powerful of the early-twentieth-century Broadway and film moguls. The twentieth-century transatlantic stage and film industry was in its way symptomatic of a more general, if gradual, shift of political, cultural, and economic hegemony from Britain to America. When in 1913 the doyen of New York theater criticism, William Winter (1836–1917), published his memoir of more than a half-century, he came to muse that the theater in the United States had grown in his lifetime into a powerful force in the life of the nation. "[B]uilt by British actors" and "a continuous influx of the dramatic spirit of the mother land," it "has only of comparatively late years become an independent power." American drama, like American music and Broadway reviews, had also become a profitable cultural export.[129]

Arguably, before the First World War the most influential of those American facilitators of transatlantic entertainments was Charles Frohman (1856–1915). Of an Ohio family that moved to New York City when he was eight, Frohman was Jewish-American, as were many other fin se siècle impresarios and producers such as Belasco, Abe Erlanger, and the Shubert brothers[130]—a common background in the late nineteenth and early-twentieth-century stage (and later film) industry, and one which would sometimes trigger a degree of anti-Semitism from their journalist critics and from British actors and managers who both profited from and resented dependency and subordination. In the early 1890s, Frohman, who had with his brother Daniel prospered as agents for minstrel shows and managers of comedy and other light entertainments, founded the Empire Stock Company and acquired a theater of his own on Broadway. Productions of plays, often with well-known British and American actors, led to a significant reputation and useful connections as part-owner of a growing number of theaters in Boston as well as New York. In 1895 he produced the New York premiere of *The Importance of Being Earnest*, and by the end of the century had acquired a larger character and influence than that of a mere theatrical manager.

Frohman was well positioned to profit from what has been called "the infrastructural politics of global performance" that emerged from changes in copyright law, technology (electric stage lighting, theatrical signage, and wireless telegraphy). In an era of business "wars" between 1893 and 1914, rival managers and impresarios of serious drama, musical comedy, and opera reached across the Atlantic for "new connections, partnerships, and joint ventures." Frohman was especially quick to use Marconi's shipboard wireless "to micro-manage transatlanticly." He also was a practiced believer in personal brokerage and hence transatlantic journeying in the furthering of his many projects. Marlis Schweitzer's study of Broadway and ocean liner travel calls this an emerging "networking the waves."[131]

By the end of the nineteenth century, fast steamship traffic had, as we have seen, facilitated a new era of systematic transatlantic theatrical touring between Britain and the United States (and indeed farther afield in the Anglosphere to Australia and New Zealand) that would be negotiated, planned, and conducted by Broadway impresarios such as Tyler, Abbey, Belasco, and Frohman.[132] Frohman had moved quickly into this world of transatlantic, transnational opportunity. In 1892 he acquired his first Broadway theater, established a London office a year later, and co-founded a Theatrical Syndicate or trust in 1896 that attempted, unsuccessfully, to corner the American theater industry through a national booking system. In 1897, he took a nineteen-year lease in London of the Duke of York's Theatre, where he "did away with the statues of … Shakespeare and Garrick … and replaced them with large photographs of his live American stars."[133] Barrie's *Peter Pan* would debut there in December 1904, and in the United States the next year. Frohman boasted that he would send a hundred American actors to London, transporting "not only his stars, but stage managers, musical directors and chief electricians."[134] He devoted his personal, close attention to these enterprises and treated the transatlantic liner as a mobile office which, by the first decade of the new century, could provide telegraphic communication back to New York and forward to London the entire week or so he was at sea. He especially enjoyed the luxury of commuting on the new Cunard liners *Mauritania* and *Lusitania*.

Between 1897 and 1915 Frohman produced 125 plays and musicals in London; on occasion as many as five of his productions would run at the same time in the British capital. These were scattered across the wide theatrical spectrum, from serious drama to musical reviews and variety shows, light comedy, and dramatizations of novels of intrigue and mystery. An American Jew who embodied turn-of-the-century Broadway and the rapidly expanding world of global entertainment, Frohman was driven for twenty years by his determined transatlanticity. Even the outbreak of war was not allowed to interrupt the routines of this life—his melding of Anglo-American theatrical business through all those crossings in First Class cabins. His last crossing (one not quite completed) would be aboard the Liverpool-bound RMS *Lusitania* in early May 1915.

CHAPTER 3
TABLEAUX OF RACE

In May of 1825 a black American actor, Ira Frederick Aldridge, just seventeen years of age and recently arrived from New York City accompanied, it appears, by James Wallack, debuted his Othello before a small audience at the Royalty Theatre, a non-patent playhouse in Whitechapel, east London. A few months later he moved to the more prominent Royal Coburg Theatre in a role long familiar to London audiences, that of Oroonoko in Thomas Southerne's 1695 tragedy, *The Revolt of Surinam, or A Slave's Revenge*. The special attraction—to both a skeptical press and an intrigued public—of these performances, as with the several tragic and comic roles that followed in London and, especially, the provinces, was that of an actual black man, not a white actor in blackface, performing theatrical blackness. As a "tragedian of colour" *and* an American on the British stage, Aldridge was a double curiosity.

Born in New York City and educated at the African Free School there, Aldridge had received from the age of thirteen a vicarious tutelage of sorts as a spectator in the gallery at the Park Theater and at William Henry Brown's African Grove pleasure garden and theater, where an all-Black company entertained mixed though mostly black audiences in the early 1820s. At some point he attached himself to the Wallack brothers' entourage, and Henry Wallack would provide him a letter of introduction to the London theater world.

The African Theater, established by 1821 in Mercer Street, lower Manhattan, not only provided an open venue for black spectators, but also, it would seem, encouraged the kind of lively audience-player interaction that was increasingly being discouraged in "legitimate" theater. It and its principal star James Hewlett were well enough known for Charles Mathews, searching for material for his humorous sketches of American characters, to have formed upon them his parody of a black actor playing Hamlet: "I have studied their broken English carefully."[1] At the words "whether him nobler in de mind to suffer or lift up him arms against one sea of hubble bubble and by oppose 'em end 'em," Mathews' Black Hamlet is interrupted with shouts of "opossum, opossum," and he steps out of the play to sing and dance a well-known Negro song, "Opossum up a Gum Tree."[2]

Though exaggeration and invention are central to Mathews' comedic reproduction of African-American speech, it is likely that his parody of the liveliness of the black audience at the African Theater, their eager reciprocating, back-and-forth participation, and a non-reverential treatment of Shakespeare's text suggests something of the actual character of the venue as reported in the New York press (Blacks in the pit and boxes "cracking jokes with the actors"[3]). Somewhere between what would become the audience-presenter antiphony of both minstrelsy and music hall and the solemn "high culture" of legitimate theater, audience participation persisted in some theaters cultivating a lower- or lower-middle-class clientele. Walt Whitman could remember that in the 1830s the audience at the Bowery was "as much a part of the show as any."[4] It was, however, the liveliness of an undisciplined *black* audience inside and outside a black theater—a space that served openly to legitimize black cultural presence in the city— that provided an excuse for police raids and harassing white mobs. This harassment was, it appears, urged on by the Park Theater's long-time manager Stephen Price. By the mid-1820s the African Theater had been forced out of business, and Aldridge, who had debuted there as Rolla in Sheridan's *Pizarro*, was persuaded and assisted by the Wallack brothers to try his luck in the London theatrical world from which they themselves had recently come.

Aldridge spent a half-year in London performing a half-dozen or so roles, attempting to achieve quick recognition as a young but coming artist. Even if reviews dripped, often, with racial insults, Britain would have had for him, as for many African Americans, an aura of liberation. It is unclear whether, even had he encountered clear failure on the stage, he would have returned to the States. As it was, he spent the following eight years traveling from one playhouse to another in British provincial towns and cities. And at the end of this period of seasoning he returned to London in 1833, married to a white woman, and prepared to present a more mature self to audience and press.

In the years Aldridge crisscrossed Britain he presented "white" roles such as Shylock or Richard III, and "Gothic" roles as in *The Castle Specter* or *The Divan of Blood*. It was however his overt performances of blackness, both tragic and comic, his Othello and Oroonoko or the slave Mungo in *The Padlock*, that drew audiences to see him. Later, when he made a reputation in Europe in the 1850s, he may have been able to transcend, to a degree, this fascination. But in a Britain attuned to the ongoing debates over the abolition of slavery in the British Empire, and, after 1833, the prominence of the American slavery question, it was inevitable that audiences would expect Aldridge's routines to reveal something of himself. Indeed, he played to these expectations, as the *Black* Roscius, a "tragedian of color." But the identity he promoted was more fluid than this suggests, and his blackness, as both an asset and a liability, was adjusted from time to time. Later he would invent a spurious heritage, as the son of a mythic prince of the Fulani of Senegal, that would serve to displace his actual birth as an African *American*.

What can Aldridge's Othello and its reception in Britain tell us about transatlantic racial representation?[5] How might it resonate with other kinds of black Atlantic traffic, and what does it reveal about the expectations of white British audiences? Aldridge, as an exotic, may have encountered, in the provinces at least, more curiosity than animosity. Preconceptions however were influenced everywhere by cultural lore about blackness, the abolitionists' image of the poor Black as object of charity, and coarse and demeaning caricatures borrowed from planter propaganda from the Americas.

Aldridge's mix of tragic and comic roles, of serious theater, melodrama, and song-and-dance, sometime in the same evening program, might resonate with audiences' different expectations of blackness—farcical, pathetic, and Gothic. But they also reflect the contemporary custom of the early nineteenth-century stage (especially in the non-patent theaters) where serious drama was often mixed with "burletta."[6] He commonly played both Othello and Mungo on the first evening of a provincial engagement—tragedy *followed* by buffoonery, as a way perhaps of engaging audiences' expectations of finding Black buffoonery *in* his Othello.[7] In this, they were encouraged no doubt by the contemporaneous popularity of Mathews' satire of an American black actor playing Hamlet. Indeed, Aldridge would satisfy these expectations, not by rendering his tragic roles ridiculous, but by providing on request an entr'acte rendition of "Opossum Up a Gum Tree." As Bernth Lindfors has speculated, "[p]eople came expecting to see a comic spectacle and left with a chastened appreciation of black virtuosity."[8]

The other area in which Aldridge as African-American thespian engaged British expectations of race and performance lay in the way in which his Othello related to that of his most immediate, renowned predecessor, Edmund Kean. Kean's realism had broken with the tradition of a heavily blacked-up Othello, presenting a lightly-darkened "tawney Moor," and thus, it can be claimed, offered "a visual erasure of blackness as a locus of meaning in the play."[9] Though Aldridge, a black American playing a stage Black, was twitted in some derisive reviews for not being black enough to play "a genuine nigger,"[10] his performances in fact challenged, Joyce MacDonald has claimed, the whole travesty of white actors acting Black, not by lightening up as did Kean, but by embracing the "signs and meanings" of Othello's racial difference.[11] Aldridge's insistence on Othello's Africanness, as in the Africanness of many of his other roles, suggests his own fictive imagining of an African self-identity. Both can plausibly be traced back to Aldridge's need to confront an American theatrical history where performances of *Othello* were deemed unsuitable for black spectators, where a white Desdemona could not be seen to be "pawed" by a real Black. When the water colorist John Lambert wrote up his memoir of travels in America in 1810, he noted that on the stage in Charleston, South Carolina, Blacks were never used for "appropriate roles in Shakespeare," and that in fact "white actors playing these roles do not blacken their faces so as not to be seen to imitate Negroes."[12] When thirty-some years later the British actor James Robertson Anderson went "down South" to play Othello in 1844–5, he was told that the play had never been popular there [New Orleans], and that "to see a nigger make love to a white woman causes a Southerner's gorge to rise, I tell you sir."[13]

When Aldridge returned to London to reprise his Othello—at Covent Garden—in 1833, it was as a modestly successful and much more experienced actor. Though, arguably, repugnance at racial intermarriage in Britain was nothing like as intense, especially below the polite classes, as it was in the American South, it has been argued that Aldridge's marriage was at least in part to blame for the barrage of negative reviews he received in the press. In 1825 Aldridge's debut had drawn a kind of flippant, sneering humor—comments about the novelty of a "monkey-man" with thick lips attempting to pronounce the King's English. By 1833, in the midst of a national debate over abolition of slavery, this jocular dismissal had hardened—one journal bragged of having "hunted the Nigger from the boards of Covent Garden"; the *Times* and the *Atheneum* complained that his accent was "vulgarly foreign" and doubted whether he actually understood the meaning of the matter he delivered, and were outraged that an American Black could take it upon himself to present "the master-work of the [national] master-mind [Shakespeare] … a sort of theatrical treason." The *Times* reviewer went to the heart of the matter: that propriety and decency protested against the indignity of a white actress, Ellen Tree [Desdemona], being "pawed about by Mr. Henry Wallack's black servant."[14]

The language of racism, as well as that of paternalistic abolitionism, was a transatlantic phenomenon, even if the popular culture of the British middling and lower classes had yet to absorb the intensity of the race-hatred found in America. Though Aldridge's interracial marriage may have been distasteful to the West Indian interest, the broadsheet reviewers who socialized with them, and London Society in general, it did not seem to bother Aldridge's provincial audience. When, nearly thirty years later, Boucicault's *The Octoroon* toured provincial Britain, with its theme of interracial romance, it proved, as we have seen, modestly successful. A more pronounced racial loathing would come in time. Racial assumptions among the British in the long nineteenth century were not static, but, as Hazel Waters has reminded us, "evolved … to a greater rigidity, elaboration and entrenchment."[15]

Aldridge played his Othello at Covent Garden for only two nights before retreating to the provinces where he resumed his quite profitable nomadic routine of performances, expanding his repertoire to the roles of Shylock, Macbeth, and Lear before appreciative crowds well away from the *bon ton* of a less encouraging London. In 1852 he left Britain on a first Continental tour, and would achieve a substantial renown in European capitals, especially in eastern Europe. He returned briefly to Britain from time to time, and in the late 1850s would perform his Othello at the Lyceum—this time to some acclaim from the critics. A few years later he applied for and was granted British citizenship.

Aldridge died, during his sixth Continental tour, in Poland in 1867. In the end, as argued by Nicholas Evans,[16] he may have not quite resolved a "struggle of consciousness," that is, his own duality (triality?) of social identities—African American, African British, or simply African. In Europe, he had become, by effort, persistence, and talent, a prominent interpreter of the British national poet, but he remained an American Negro by birth and in some of his comic routines. It is possible that he intended to return to the United States after the Civil War to tour his emancipated homeland. Had he done so, he would have discovered that his international fame had preceded him. In 1863, a group of African-American minstrels performing in Philadelphia before a mixed audience called themselves the Ira Aldridge Troupe. After the Civil War a number of African-American theatrical companies emerged, many performing Shakespeare—and at least four of them named themselves after Ira Aldridge.[17]

1 The Performance of Race

It is far from clear that Aldridge recited his lines with a pronounced American or African-American accent, and one may imagine that whatever characteristic style, tone, and pronunciation he may have brought with him as a teenager from New York was over the years in Britain disciplined to a degree by English norms. His manner of speaking, however, was a common subject in the London press reviews—in 1825, 1833, and beyond. These claimed he had a "foreign" oddness of elocution, emphasizing, not the "twang" of which white American actors in London were likely to be accused, but "vulgarisms" of an especial "Negro" character and an assumed lack of understanding of meaning: "owing to the shape of his lips, it is utterly impossible for him to pronounce English in such a manner as to satisfy even the unfastidious ears of the gallery" (the *Times*, 1825); "[i]t is impossible that Mr. Aldridge should fully comprehend the meaning and force of even the words he utters" (the *Times*, 1833). It is hard to judge how much of this criticism was grounded in some oddness of Aldridge's delivery and how much was merely what they expected to hear. As late as 1858, the *Atheneum* reviewer, though admitting Aldridge spoke with correct "elocutional emphasis and propriety," still could not help referring to "this Othello's 'labial peculiarity.'"[18] It is likely that such charges say more about decades of mocking white mimicry of the exaggerated malapropisms and ungrammatical speech of poor Caribbean and American Blacks than of Aldridge's actual speech. In the 1820s, 1830s, and 1840s, the derisive clichés of African-American speech would be fixed in the humorous anecdotes of British travel literature, the comic routines on the London stage, and, especially, the formulaic staples of transatlantic minstrelsy. In his Shakespearean roles, Aldridge might speak perfectly acceptable English, but was *heard* as a black man who had been "in service" to the Wallacks, a distinctively British demeaning combination of race and social class.

We began this study using the nineteenth-century philology of Americanisms and, then, the cross-traffic of legitimate theater as routes into shifting Anglo-American transatlantic cultural relations. This section will broaden those applications by extending "Americanisms" to include (caricatured and real) *African*-American speech that was generally excluded from philological discussion. It will also draw a broader picture of "theater" to include popular entertainments and different kinds of performance, within and outside the playhouse and music hall. This involves moving beyond a discourse of "national" (that is, American *vs*. British) separation and entanglement to other—narrower and broader—ways of approaching affinity, difference, and exchange within the Anglo-American sphere. The field here is the important one of "race" in a long nineteenth century that began with transatlantic discord over American slavery. It is well to remember, however, that American defense of bondage drew not only on Southern domestic experience and anxieties, but on the convenient propaganda of British West Indian planters and their London lobbyists, just as antebellum America's own (Northern) abolitionism owed much in its evangelical zeal and program to its successful counterpart across the Atlantic.

Criticism of American slavery, even if pro forma, was a prominent element in many, perhaps most, British travelers' memoirs before the American Civil War. These commonly condemn, as did Adam Hodgson in 1824, the "barbarity" shown to Negro servants, and the "profane, licentious" language employers use toward them—"beyond even what I had anticipated." A year earlier, William Faux had deplored the "contempt" shown to poor Blacks, "or niggers, as they are there called"—"the national sin of America." And not only in the South: a decade or so later Mrs. John Felton tells us that in New York City

Negroes were a "despised class," and white children were "taught to be contemptuous of them."[19] Since the Revolution there had of course been an element of British superiority in such observations. The ironic juxtaposition of the much-touted American ideal of liberty and the inalienable rights of man with the reality of American slavery is reiterated throughout British travel memoirs of the antebellum era.

After the war, the end of slavery, and the failure of radical Reconstruction, as British tourism surged in the 1870s and 1880s, the travel genre came to display more consonance than dissonance with white American racial stereotyping, with the threat of "amalgamation" both corporeal and cultural that resulted from Black emancipation, non-Anglo-Saxon immigration, and territorial expansion. In the British Empire and the American nation, white elites, and the populisms they manipulated, co-elaborated strategies for racial definition, separation, and subordination. This study, informed by a generation of post-colonial, post-modern scholarship on identity and performance, will highlight some cultural resonances and reciprocities that reflected, shaped, confirmed, and sometimes contested the understanding of "race" in an era of ever-increasing transatlantic (and global) communication.

Black Language

Throughout the nineteenth century linguistic peculiarities (peculiar, that is, from the perspective of the elite or dominant culture) were made to signify a range of often demeaning and comical differences. British critics often mobilized the grating twang of Yankeedom or the drawl of bowie-knife-toting Westerners to paint a new Republic that was as a whole crude and unlettered. Some (not all) American philologists tended to be more generous and heard not *mis*pronunciation and *mis*usage but the legitimately various character of American speech, with all its archaisms and regionalisms—as a legitimate part of the transatlantic patchwork of Anglo-American culture.

Interestingly, learned treatises on how Americans spoke rarely, and then only briefly and casually, dwelt much on the ways in which the language of other tongues had been woven into early American speech, though borrowings from native Americans or from French and Spanish colonials were occasionally invoked. And they remained almost entirely silent—other than by the merest, usually comical, allusion—on what would have been the most obvious and at least in the South, influential source of dialect within the new American nation—the African- and Creole-influenced speech and manner of expression of millions of African Americans. One reason for this lies in the fact that many early American philologists like Webster were deeply committed to affirming the authentic Old English heritage of the seeming peculiarities of American language. Moreover, those who compiled such dictionaries—often New Englanders of the educated classes—simply lacked much personal contact with distant Southern or African-American sources. The most ambitious of the antebellum philologists of Americanisms, John Russell Bartlett, tells us that "[i]n Southern provincialisms I find myself most deficient" and apologizes for the fact that he was unable "to avail myself of the assistance of persons residing in various parts of our country … words here brought together have been, with very few exceptions, collected by myself."[20]

Those who did pay attention to (upper-class, plantation) Southern dialect, at least before the Civil War, tended to assume that, with its genteel drawl and colorful cursing, it reflected a historical debt to the "Cavalier" speech of seventeenth-century England—an assumption that of course flattered the self-regard of "gentlemanly" Southerners. Some, it is true, regretted what they regarded as the ongoing amalgamation of white and African or African-Caribbean argot. The Yorkshireman, geologist, and railway promoter George William Featherstonhaugh, long resident in the United States before returning to Britain in 1839, used his memoir of a tour of the Southern states to attack the "vulgar corruption" of the English tongue by "a sort of Creole dialect"—a view that seems to have been shared by Dickens and Fanny Kemble.[21] Slave or free, black Americans were racial Others who could not legitimately be considered part of the linguistic, social, or political nation. The patois of black America had to be caricatured and relegated to the realm of "the nigger joke" and the minstrel show, and in these genres treated as a class of deformed and degraded speech that confirmed the difference, separation, and, in the dictionaries at least, near-invisibility of the American Negro. Serious linguistic scholarship on varieties of African-American dialect, like the pioneering work of Howard- and Harvard-educated Lorenzo Dow Turner (1890–1972) on the coastal Gullah speakers, would not appear until well into the twentieth century.

Bartlett did indeed concede that American language had been influenced by "Negroisms," but only as a few "borrowed words"—as if from outside authentic American discourse—like those from other foreign languages. His large 1848 work, *Dictionary of Americanisms*, an opus that grew from edition to edition, included very few of these borrowings. More common among the philologists was the citation of white language (nearly always degrading) that referred to Blacks, though Russell includes only a few of these—"Darkey," and also "Snowball."[22] Like Bartlett, William Fowler, in his 1850 work on *The English Language in Its Elements and Forms*, classified "negro words" as "foreign" and "borrowed"—like Dutch words in New York or native American words that had passed into common usage, such as "tomahawk." In America as in Britain, English itself was properly "the soul of the Anglo-Saxon race."[23]

After the Civil War and emancipation the problem of black speech as a corruption of good English drew more attention. It became necessary, many thought during Reconstruction, to tutor the children of freed slaves in reading and in the proper (and respectful) way of speaking. Such freedmen schools were, of course, promoted by white paternalism, but one may also imagine that there was a wider motive—to engage the threatened penetration of national English by emancipated African-American language. The post-war "professor of modern languages" at the University of Virginia and philologist of Americanisms, Schele De Vere, argued that it was time to consider more directly the African American's English, which previously had been unlikely "to influence the speech of his masters." As a transplanted Swede who had owned slaves and supported the Confederacy, De Vere had a complex position in 1871. On the one hand, he blames the African American's "ignorance, his carelessness, his inability, with peculiar organs of speech … to repeat certain sounds at all" for "the havoc he played with the king's English." Those teaching the children of freedmen faced "almost insuperable difficulties," even when these children had "mental capacities" that were "fully equal to those of the white race, and the zeal to learn almost irrepressible." On the other, he admits that our (white) understanding of the Negro and his language is unjustly misinformed by the clichés of minstrelsy, just as "no American ever spoke like the Yankee on the boards of minor theaters in London." There was lyricism and poetry in black speech which, he suggests, might fill a need in a national language deficient in these attributes.[24]

There would come a time when, after the failure of radical Reconstruction and after southern whites had resecured their racial ascendancy, when African-American speech would be romanticized as part of the nostalgic retrieval of the Old South, beginning, most famously, with Joel Chandler Harris's Uncle Remus tales of 1880, or in the sustained, amplified popularity of Stephen Foster's antebellum songs. Northern abolitionists had prepared the way by attempting to publicize authentic black dialect in works such as William Francis Allen's collection of spirituals, *Slave Songs of the United States* (1867). But in the world of American lexicography, De Vere's inclusive sense of the "poetry" of black language as a potentially valuable constituent of the national tongue did not find much footing. As one might expect, the Anglophile Shakespearean scholar Richard White had little use for a philology that regarded American English as "only the stock, upon which Indian, Dutch, French, German, Irish, and Negro stems and branches have been freely grafted." Mere birth in America—as with the "lately arrived son of Ah Sin"— did not, he dismissively claimed, make one (or one's language) "American"—"what is the worth, the distinguishing value, of a name which lumps Anglo-Saxon, Celt, Teuton, Negro, and Mongol together?" A dictionary such as Bartlett's, by lumping "foreign" words together with "English pure and simple," had an effect that was "one of gross and injurious misrepresentation."[25]

Nevertheless, in the late nineteenth century, American and British philologists did develop some interest in black English, just as they worried and sparred over "slang" that often derived from European immigration. The London philologist John Stephen Farmer published a quite substantial dictionary of Americanisms in 1889, often accompanying definitions with examples of usage drawn from American literature and from works such as Allen's *Slave Songs*. He tells us that he intended his dictionary by and large to be concerned with "a word or phrase, old or new, employed by general and respectable usage," but "[l]anguage," he acknowledges, "like everything else is progressive." "All these [non-Anglo-Saxon] people, whether German, French, Spanish, or Dutch descent … and with these … the negro and the Chinaman" were contributing to the American "stock."[26]

Farmer's dictionary is the first, in fact, to pay substantial attention to the contributions of African-American speech—to "Negro Ballads and Negro Melodies." But most of the citations of "Negro" words in Farmer's dictionary that are not sourced from ballads and melodies are described simply as "corruptions" (either "pleonastic" [garrulous], as in "all two" for "both," or abbreviated, as in "darsnt" for "dares not") of proper speech, and are often drawn in fact from white literature that employed familiar (to their readers) stereotypes of black dialect—as in Stephen Foster songs, Harris's Remus tales, or Mark Twain's stories and novels.[27]

Bringing the African American directly into the dictionary also encouraged philologists to include, as Bartlett clearly had hesitated to do, the host of crude, white vulgarisms that degraded and humorized Blacks. Farmer includes a dozen or more of the familiar (in the British Empire, as in America) terms for black and other non-white persons: "Quashie," "Cuffey," "Sambo," "darky," "nigger," "buck- or bull-nigger," etc., as well as phrases such as "There's a nigger in the fence" which he explains is "an allusion to the thieving propensities of the negro."

It is worth noting here that such inclusion of racial vulgarisms shows less concern than earlier work did with violating the sensibilities of a polite readership. Earlier, the use of "nigger" for instance, though no doubt widespread in Britain in popular parlance, would have been avoided by many in polite intercourse. Following the Sepoy rebellion in India in 1857 and the "massacre" of whites in Jamaica in 1865, the declaration of martial law there, and the hanging of black insurgents by Governor Eyre, an intense debate ensued in which crude, demeaning Anglo-American planter language about Blacks was unapologetically injected into mainstream public discourse by Thomas Carlyle, Charles Dickens, J. A. Froude, Charles Kingsley and other pro-Eyre arbiters of Victorian literature—with lasting effect, as one can see in the casual employment of such terms in British traveler accounts in the late-Victorian era.

Certainly the British Empire came to embrace a language it shared with the Americans—in the Caribbean and in the Raj where dark-colored Indians were casually referred to as "niggers," as were aborigines in Australasia and Oceania as well as Africa. Both humorous and Gothic, the language of race and racism in the late nineteenth-century Anglo-world was transatlantic, indeed global, and easily transposed from the American South to Sydney, Cape Town, or the plains of Maharashtra. As Farmer says, "[t]he works … of the popular exponents of 'American humor' … have made the English people familiar with transatlantic words, phrases, turns of expression, and construction … Their influence is daily gaining ground."[28]

When the American dictionary compiler, C. O. Sylvester Mawson, set out to explain how the new 1911 edition of *Roget's Thesaurus*, recently removed from London to New York, was to include Americanisms for the first time, he drew attention to the several categories of Americanisms that would be included. The seventh, and last, was "negroisms." Mawson, like Farmer, was in fact little interested in black language per se, but generous with the British-American lexicon of racial terms whites applied to Blacks: "negro," "blackamoor," "nigger," "darkie," "Ethiop," "buck," "buck-nigger [U. S.]," "coon [U. S.]," "sambo."[29]

British Travelers and Black Americans

As we have seen, Henry Fearon, in his 1818 *Sketches of America*, recalled for his British readers an encounter with a black barber in New York. But the anecdote does not reproduce the kind of black speech that would become commonplace in later travelers' memoirs. The barber is made to exaggerate *Yankee* speech—full of "I guess"—rather than the comic clichés of what would become the standard blackface language of minstrel performance of both antebellum America and Victorian Britain. By the 1830s and 1840s, British memoirists are likely to offer a formulaic reproduction of comical black speech—the ungrammatical, "gibbering," slurring voice of the "blubber-lipped Negro," full of contractions and difficulty with "th" ("dat" for that, "de" for the) or "v" ("ribber" for river), learned perhaps as much from Mathews' routines or Thomas Rice's Jim Crow as from much close attention to the speech of the few African Americans they met in their travels—waiters, cab-drivers, or barbers. This is of course not to deny the reality of a variety of black speech that can be found fixed, however prejudicially, in the comic anecdotes of British letter and memoir writers, or indeed in minstrel routines. A few tourists, often those with a special sympathy with abolitionism, made some effort to distinguish the speech of northern from that of southern blacks, or refused to subscribe to the categorical dismissal of "nigger gibberish," North or South. Mrs. John Felton, who spent two years in America with her husband and children in the late 1830s, "frequently conversed" with black women in New York City and found that "they generally express themselves in good language, and with an enunciation as bold and clear as any Englishman."[30] James Stirling, a wealthy Scot who retired from the family Glaswegian dyeing firm to sail his yacht and travel abroad, observed in 1857,

> even here, in Kentucky and Tennessee, I have heard little or none of it [nigger gibberish]. On the contrary, the coloured men in America seem to me to speak better, or at least more agreeably to an English ear, than the whites. They have no twang, and no sing-song …[31]

Such "listening" was, however, somewhat exceptional among those Britons who offered their readers tales of American Blacks they had encountered. Most, even those sympathetic to the slave's plight "heard" untutored ignorance, a lazy way with grammar, and "slave slobber." Very few were likely to admit hearing what Stirling heard: something "soft in their voices, and this, with a certain native courtesy and gentleness, gives quite a charm to their manner."[32]

Other than those who sought out black church services and camp revivals and black abolitionist lecturers in the northern cities, the first contact most British travelers of the middle and upper classes had with an African American was a hotel waiter in New York City. As with the white servants, these encounters were framed and shaped by British "sensitivities about class"[33]—as well as by ethnic and racial prejudices and preconceptions. On the whole, the travel memoirs are more generously inclined to black American servants than to that bugbear of the Victorian middle and upper classes, the Irish domestic, made, many thought, offensively impertinent (and expensive to hire) in egalitarian America: "whatever their faults, [colored attendants] are better adapted for domestic service than the uncouth, slovenly Irish waiters so very general in the New York hotels."[34] The practiced deference the smiling black waiter showed, in spite of the difference of color, was a reassuring confirmation of the upper-class English man and woman's view of hierarchical social relations. In 1849, Lady Emmeline Stuart Wortley found an old black waiter at Yale to have "the manners of a quiet, highly respectable English butler."[35] Charles Mathews wrote to his wife that "[i]n short, all the Whites of the order [American servants] are born blackguards, and the Blacks—above them in being *genteel*."[36]

The black waiter, a commonplace like the black railway porter in Gilded-Age America and well beyond, could be an elegant exotic that, for some, might exercise a kind of sexualized allure. Lady Mary Rhodes Carbutt was sure that "[s]ome of the large establishments must choose them for their looks, as I never saw a good-looking negro anywhere else." Winifred, Lady Howard of Glossop, went further: one "picturesque" Negro "who particularly waited upon us, was a perfect Adonis, 'black but beautiful,' and always stood, between whiles of serving, in the most elegant and aesthetic of attitudes, smiling sweetly upon us."[37] Nor was it only women who experienced a certain ambivalence in the attentions of young Blacks. Walter Gore Marshall found a "nigger" waiter in New York to be "very diligent in his attentions, and every now and then during the repast would come up and bend down over me, and, putting his face close to mine, say, 'Are you all right?'"[38] Especially in the late-Victorian era, British travelers were prepared to find aesthetic qualities in the smooth skin and manners of a well-groomed waiter. Anticipating Oscar Wilde's observation that the African American was almost an aesthetic *objet*, "their half-naked bodies gleaming like bronze," in 1876 Montague Davenport described one "very civil" waiter in Philadelphia as a work of art: "Black as ebony, he stands out in strong relief against the snow-white walls and marble columns, the contrast having an effect almost theatrical."[39] James Burnley mused that Negro hotel servants "watch you with the eye of a lynx, and seem to search deep down into the desires of your heart." And the poet Robert Anderton Naylor found colored waiters to be "especially susceptible to the charms of kindness [and] innocent flattery … I like these coloured 'gentlemen' and admire their eye-speaking intelligence."[40]

Those who held the African-American waiter to be interesting and attractive—either because he suited their conception of how a servant ought to behave, or because of his exotic charm—though numerous, were admittedly something of a minority among the many visitors who commented on American black servants and found in them simply a source of amusing anecdote. This was the prevailing mode in the antebellum era, but can be found throughout the long nineteenth century. It is a mode of observation clearly related to, perhaps determined by, the black minstrelsy tradition, as well as the comedic revues of Rice and Mathews (in one of his sketches, he acted the part of Maximilian, a jolly, voluble black waiter at a New York boarding house). Samuel Reynolds Hole at the end of the century could still comment that, though he found the black waiters clean and honest, "one almost expects … to hear a conundrum from 'Bones,' or an exhortation from the head waiter to his troupe, 'Sing, darkies, sing.'" A year later, Hare Booth found that his party "were pleased with our 'darkie,' and were amused when he asked if he might 'replenish' our glass with iced water."[41]

After the Civil War, when all black waiters, North and South, were free men, the text seems often more determinedly racist, having perhaps lost some of the antebellum sense of African-American comedy and abolitionist sympathy, and with prejudices further entrenched by Darwinian schemas: John Francis Campbell, though he found the Irish waiters at Boston's Parker House to be exasperating, thought that the black servers in Springfield were "born waiters without much brains ... the darky's head is like that of the Neander-thal man who was like a monkey."[42] A dyspeptic observer like Frederick Trench Townshend echoes many when he dismissed both Irish (who seemed to think they were doing one a favor "to obey an order") *and* African-American servants ("even worse than the whites"), who "are sulky, lazy, and dirty."[43] As free black servants came to prevail on the railways, in hotels, and in domestic service, the commentary of many British tourists simply echoed the phenotypical and ethnological racial observation and assumptions of the Anglo-American world. In 1885 Mrs. Emily Jane Pfeiffer wrote of "the array of negro waiters, all lounging lazily on a bench" at her hotel in Saratoga Springs. "All had the same reluctant, shambling gait, with the same splashy sounding fall of the flat, splay feet, the same air of groaning under the slightest burthen ... with a grotesque sort of swagger."[44] Rose Pender found the black waiters at Wormsley's Hotel in Washington to be "very civil and obliging, but terribly slow. The black man's intellect is far slower than his white brother's."[45] And one may turn to Rudyard Kipling's characteristically pungent notes of his journey across America in 1889 for a full-throated denunciation: "Now let me draw breath and curse the negro waiter, and through him the negro in service generally ... as complete a heavy-footed, uncomprehending, bungle-fisted fool as any mem-sahib in the East ever took into her establishment."[46]

Many British tourists who were favorably impressed, and sometimes surprised to be impressed, by the black waiter's capable, well-spoken, and attentive service in the face of the dominant prejudice, North and South, against the African race admitted that those they encountered in service—like the "house-nigger" of the plantation—were an altogether separate, specially chosen caste, not to be compared to the wretchedly poor shanty-town black, the ragged unemployed pauper, and the lowest-class field hand or share-cropper. If many upper-class British visitors approvingly found their black servants to "have all the humility of an inferior," "attentive without being ... self-important," and "anticipating every wish,"[47] in a country where white waiters were likely to regard themselves as equals, they could hardly be representative of the race as a whole. As James Wentworth Leigh remarked of his visit in 1873, "in order to understand the negroes" one should go live with them in the South. "An American might as well get his idea of an English agricultural labourer from a waiter at the Langham Hotel."[48]

Most British observers, one assumes, did not go out of their way to engage black Americans in the street. Those who did were likely to be already sympathetic and seeking some confirmation of the errors of prejudice. The young Isabella Bird, who, like millions of Britons, had read *Uncle Tom's Cabin*, and, convinced of the cruelties of slave owners, found a couple of self-manumitted black women she met to be "agreeable and *naïve*." They "chattered" with her until two in the morning and said that they wanted to emigrate to England, "which they have been taught to look as to a land of liberty and happiness." If the Negro did not have "intellectual powers of the highest order," providence "had given him an amount of *heart* and enthusiasm to which we are strangers."[49] A year later, the financially independent feminist Barbara Leigh Smith Bodichon, on her honeymoon in America, had a more ambiguous recollection of her encounter with "a dozen black women" on a Mississippi steamboat. One of these, "working for her freedom," was "very hideous, very black, and looks very low on the human scale, yet she has the strongest desire for liberty." In March the next year, however, she met on the Savannah River "some negro women" who "talked very pleasantly," said they loved the Queen, and, like the black women Bird met, wished to emigrate to Britain.[50]

Bodichon, like Frances Trollope before her and many others, also sought out an African church—almost a form of entertainment expected of antebellum visitors. As late as 1880 James Burnley could claim that African-American camp meetings were "looked upon as Sunday amusements … there is much more fun to be got out of this burlesque of a Christian service than in many a week-day entertainment which is given in the usual places of amusement."[51] Here in New Orleans Bodichon's reactions to the excited responses of the black congregation to a white preacher's evangelical fire and brimstone were conventional—"The negros shrieked and howled and repeated words … jumping up and howling them out until they fell down exhausted at the bottom of the pews."[52] Her description is so commonplace among such travel memoirs, that it is well to remember George Coombe's sympathetic comment on having a few years earlier heard a sermon delivered by a black preacher in an African church in Philadelphia: "Many persons … would expect to hear the minister and congregation mistaking and mispronouncing the English language … but … [t]he service was read and the sermon delivered in pure good English … and the whole demeanor of the congregation was becoming and devout."[53]

Transatlantic Blackface: Comedy, Song, and Dance

Mathews' popular comic sketches of American Blacks, repeated in his "At homes" for a decade until his death in 1835, prepared the ground for humorous representation of African Americans on the London stage and in popular culture more generally[54]—for Ira Aldridge's burletta routines, for the American Thomas Dartmouth Rice's[55] Jim Crow act, and for the blackface minstrel shows that became fixtures of British popular entertainment for the rest of the century and beyond. Much has been written about transatlantic minstrelsy, whether performed by blacked-up whites or African Americans, in both America and Britain. Beginning with, most famously, the various incarnations of the Christy Minstrels—in Britain provincial troupes adopting this name proliferated from the late 1850s—blackface minstrelsy presented the stereotypes which "came to dominate, even in vehicles—like the *Uncle Tom* plays—that might, at first sight, seem antithetical to them."[56] Just how blackface minstrelsy can be placed into wider contexts presents a complex set of issues. Minstrelsy's reception in Britain as in America can be situated within the great growth generally of popular entertainments with "a much enlarged audience and a widening social base" from the 1840s on.[57] There are, therefore, questions in both Britain and the United States of its relationship to legitimate theater. In America it can, at least in its Jacksonian beginnings, be said to signal "parody of the legitimate 'official' stage"; in Britain, it appears to have had from the beginning "a wider, upper-crust" appeal, but Rice's Jim Crow tours clearly worked to lower generally the social status of his audience whether he appeared in legitimate theaters or otherwise.[58]

Rice's blackface performance of a ragged, deformed, clownish black man who weirdly leaps about, dances, and sings ("Jump Jim Crow") in black vernacular was, perhaps, based on slave lore from the deep South, though it also may have owed something to Irish or Scots folk music. Debuted in 1828 in Louisville, it came to enjoy an immense popularity in the 1830s, from Kentucky to New York, where Rice brought his comic song-and-dance routine to Hamblin's Bowery and then the Park Theater—often as a closing piece following serious drama—before taking it to Britain. By the autumn of 1836, Rice's performances in various theaters in London and the provinces—he also performed other blackface comic roles, including a burlesque of Othello—had established his reputation and created popular enthusiasm for vehicles for Rice and his imitators, what the *Times* called "novel species of entertainment," black "extravaganzas," and "black operas."[59] According to the Scottish poet Charles Mackay (1814–89), looking back from 1887, "nigger mania broke out with a virulence that has never since wholly subsided … small beggar-boys of the streets" performed "'jumping Jim Crow' in the public thoroughfares by day and by night."[60] Commercialization followed, with Jim Crow hats, pipes, and knick-knacks on sale (just as later blackface minstrelsy would turn London into a center of minstrel sheet-music production).[61] He repeated his very profitable year-long 1836-7 tour of Britain with another in 1839 and again in 1842-3, when he performed in a Jim Crow spin-off play written for him by Edward Stirling. Rice's routines were widely imitated for the rest of the antebellum era on both sides of the ocean.

Back in America, Fanny Kemble (Butler) gushed to a friend in 1839 that she had been to a "Negro Ball" in Georgia and "Oh, my dear E, I have seen Jim Crow—the veritable James … that ineffable black conception."[62] It may be debated how much of the song and dance of Rice's routine and of the minstrel tradition drew from the actual culture of African Americans in the South, as Kemble here suggests ("the things these people did with their bodies, and, above all, with their faces, the whites of their eyes, and the whites of their teeth"), but it is of interest that she and others were now prepared to "see" *actual* ("veritable") black performance through the lens of the (white) blackface performances of Rice and others. Though the origins of blackface minstrelsy had an earlier provenance in America, "Daddy" Rice's parodies and those of his imitators did much to establish the minstrel show and whet the popular appetite for it.[63] In Britain, the years following the "nigger mania" inspired by Rice saw a flood of imported entertainers such as the Virginia Minstrels, the Ethiopian Serenaders, and the Christy Minstrels, and their domestic imitators, as well as a host of blacked-up street singers and dancers. By the time Henry Mayhew surveyed the London poor at mid-century, there were scores of these strolling blackface "nigger-singers" or "Ethiopian serenaders," offering entertainment as individuals and as groups—"gangs" or "mobs" that could be found any day from St. James and Regent's Street to the East End, and in the seaside resorts. They were mostly white English, but also Irish and Scots. Mayhew's informer could only name one out of forty or fifty who was "a real black—an African."[64]

Mayhew considered these to be among the "better class of ballad-singers," though one informant complained that latterly too many without much skill or presence were crowding the streets: "It wasn't everybody as could be a nigger then [i.e., three or four years earlier] … It's got common now." Expanding opportunities for performance reflect the spreading fashion for blackface not only in the theatres and on the London streets. Blacked-up street performers might earn a little extra if they could get to the seaside resorts for special events, or find a "gent" who wanted someone special to be serenaded, or they might get a job singing at a wedding. Another way of earning something, interestingly, was by doing "nigger-statues" in concert-rooms, where "tableaux vivants" of Negro life were to be presented: "We illustrate the adventures of Pompey, or the life of a negro slave." As in scenes from the later *Uncle Tom* novel and plays, this meant posing as a slave cutting cane, a slave being flogged, a vengeful slave killing his overseer and fleeing—with one of them "doing the orator and explaining the story."[65]

Representations of the black body, black speech, and black character spread throughout mid-century urban culture in a kind of ripple effect from the theatrical minstrel show into the street and beyond, where they became something more, or other, than crude comedy. Putting on blackness ("posing") in public spaces, like putting on whiteness by a black performer, might raise complicated issues for performer and audience alike of the mutability of identity and of "the [permeable] borders of the material and epistemological in transatlantic performance culture."[66] The history of white blackface minstrelsy, in Britain as in the United States, has often simply stressed its "symbolic inversions of white, civilised values … a *Mundus Inversus* of the white world,"[67] and yet, the inherent problematic of the theatrical profession's grappling with multiple identities has opened other issues of the ambiguous meaning of blackface for *both* player and spectator and the ambivalence of crossing racial (and perhaps gender and class) boundaries.[68] However much blackface minstrelsy may have settled into crude racist stereotype as the century wore on, in the beginning *some* minstrel troupes in Britain offered a sentimental, anti-slavery message that resonated with widespread abolitionist philanthropy—as in the very popular "slave lament," "Lucy Neal," introduced by the Ethiopian Serenaders. Thomas Rice followed his comedic blackface Jim Crow of 1836 with the lead role in a stage version of *Uncle Tom's Cabin* in 1852. As Eric Lott has provocatively said, blackface was "a far more unsettled phenomenon than has been supposed … Without the minstrel show there would have been no *Uncle Tom's Cabin* (1852), no *Adventures of Huckleberry Finn* (1884)."[69]

If we are to "decode" minstrelsy, there is, first, the problem of the comparability of the phenomenon in Britain and America—that is, whether British minstrelsy was simply a replication of the American original that carried much the same signification for its audience in London as it did in New York, or whether, as Michael Pickering has suggested, it resonated within the specific contexts of the British class system and the British colonial empire.[70] Second, some more recent scholarship has explored, within this particular "commodification of black culture," issues of racial transgression, ambiguity, and subjectivity. Rather than simply operating to confirm the racial identity of both the white audience and the white actors whose (removable) shoe-polish or burnt-cork only advertised the exaggerated racial otherness of those they were aping, performing blackness might, however temporarily, invoke a degree of subjective confusion and inject through performance a largely unintended sense of racial mutability.

If black performers of blackness were presented with an opportunity both to exploit and, by mocking it, transform a white representational tradition,[71] white parodies of the black body predominated. These allowed the apprehension of Negro threat to be rewritten as humorous rather than dangerous. In the empire a similar displacement might be said also to have operated: just as in the United States comedic blackface minstrelsy followed Nat Turner's rebellion of 1831, in Britain the South Sea and African cannibal joke can be said to have dismissed (black) Gothic horror by humorizing it.[72] In the last analysis, the transatlantic parodies of black language, black music and dance, and black bodies—through blackface minstrelsy, burlesque theatrical performances, or the common prejudicial humor found in jokes and cartoons—whether imported wholesale from America or shaped and redirected by the British class system, political culture, and colonial experience, are complicated with multiple meanings. As Jacky Bratton has observed, there was not a single phenomenon, but rather a multiplicity of performances "adapted for every kind of audience in Britain."[73] The Ethiopian Serenaders from Boston, for instance, aimed at a genteel audience. *The Freeman's Journal* found them to be "free from the coarseness and vulgarity which has banished nigger dancing and singing from the stage to the taverns."[74] They had played for President Tyler before traveling to London twice (1846–7 and 1848–9) to play at the St. James Theatre and for Queen Victoria. The rowdier Christy Minstrels, originating in Buffalo, New York, aimed at a more popular audience. In 1857 they too crossed the ocean and played in London and provincial venues before settling in at the new St. James concert hall (seating 2,000) after 1858. Anticipating the appeal of the late-Victorian music hall, they were especially popular among the British working classes and in Ireland.

At the most obvious level, blackface minstrelsy served to create a "spectacle"[75] of blackness in transatlantic culture, what Daphne Brooks has called "a dynamic transatlantic cultural matrix,"[76] within which black witnesses of slavery such as Henry "Box" Brown[77] might develop "counter-constructions" of blackness. Those who brought their slave narratives, that is, their own performances of race, from America to Britain where they lectured in British public halls, churches, and philanthropic institutes in the 1850s were offering themselves on that particular kind of stage as a species of theater.

Blackface minstrelsy itself, however read, was in some sense subverted by the appearance, from the 1850s in America and the 1860s in Britain, of troupes formed by African Americans, often former slaves, performing blackness without blackface (as a kind of parody of a parody).[78] Sam Hague's Slave Troupe of Georgia Minstrels came to Liverpool in 1866 and then entertained (albeit with only modest success) the same white audiences in London that had applauded white blackface; Callender's (later Haverly's) Coloured Minstrels, managed by the Frohman brothers, were more successful and played before Queen Victoria in the early 1880s. And at the end of the century there was a surge of individual African performers, singers, dancers, and comedians, who took variety acts throughout Britain. These were no longer simply imitations (or parodies) of white blackface.[79]

One might question, of course, the degree to which the authentic blackness of these performers "subverted" the routine racism of the genre—they often simply replicated (though perhaps with a subjective "difference") the "banjoes and bones" acts and Stephen Foster melodies expected of blackfaced white performers. On the other hand, the growing appetite in Britain for (albeit somewhat "whitened" versions of) black spirituals clearly did open a chance to undo the tightening knot of racist derision and stereotyping at a time when from the 1860s on, according to Robert Nowatzki, blackface minstrelsy in Britain was becoming *more* denigrating of African Americans as the abolitionist era waned.[80] The famous Jubilee Singers from Fisk University in Tennessee brought an emancipated, younger, and mixed-gender black seriousness and humanity to Britain in 1873 and thereafter.[81] They were especially popular, as one might imagine, with the genteel, erstwhile patrons of abolitionism like the Earl of Shaftesbury; they played at Moody and Sankey's revival meetings, and they ended their first tour in 1873 with a concert at that iconic evangelical site, Exeter Hall. Offering a sharp contrast to blackface "Bones" in rags, they were respectable, well-dressed, "inveterate abstainers" from both tobacco and alcohol, and "irreproachable" in their religious morality.[82] The antithesis of the minstrel players' "symbolic inversion" of the white world, they were well-received in polite society—though they too occasionally sang, as no doubt their audiences expected, Stephen Foster songs.

Slave Narratives as Theater

There is clearly a theatrical element in the well-orchestrated touring throughout Britain and Ireland of ex-slaves with their well-crafted narratives of hardship. Their dramatic story-telling, from the 1820s to the Civil War, commenced in roughly the same era as the blackface stage-caricatures of Mathews and Rice, and proliferated in the 1850s following the Fugitive Slave Act in the United States. This decade witnessed together the greatest amplification of the African-American narrative "voice" in Britain, the publication and theatrical dramatization of Harriet Beecher Stowe's *Uncle Tom's Cabin*, *and* the flourishing of American-exported blackface minstrelsy. On stage and in lecture hall, often contrasting performances of blackness became highly visible to (albeit somewhat different) British audiences.

It has been argued that the slave narrative—telling of the progress of the poor fugitive from despair to hope, from darkness to liberation—would have resonated in Protestant Britain with that staple of popular reading, *The Pilgrim's Progress*, and its invocation of questing resolve, will, and persistence in the face of obstacles imposed by satanic forces.[83] But slave narratives of flogging, mutilation, and rape also conveyed the dramatic horror of the Gothic tradition, as well as a certain eroticism.[84] Though the staid venues of ex-slave narration were usually quite different from those of the melodramatic play, the caricature skit, and the minstrel show, presentation was inescapably histrionic. The well-organized touring of a star performer like Frederick Douglass followed the route of theatrical troupes in the provinces and gave Douglass three hundred opportunities to speak in nineteen months.[85] Both the minstrel show *and* the ex-slave narrative invited audiences to anticipate a distinctive voice, and educated, articulate Blacks in Britain sometimes found that they were, like those performing blackface comedy, expected to speak with the familiar stage dialect of a blackface minstrel.[86]

The narratives themselves were only part of a panoply of abolitionist propaganda and of sympathetic representation that could, in fact, be found on stage as well as in the lecture hall: during the 1850s the Royal Princess's Theatre in Oxford Street, London, put on a "panoramic entertainment" of "Negro Life!" that included tableaux of the Mississippi, the plantation house and its slave quarters, and "Negro Dancing."[87] In coordination with the staging of slave narratives in the lecture hall, abolitionists could dramatize their case, as in panoramas and tableaux vivants of Negro life and victimization, in the most public sphere. Following the revelation that the Free Church of Scotland had raised money from white churches in the American South, British abolitionists mounted a campaign in 1846 based on the slogan "Send Back the Money!" In Edinburgh, Frederick Douglass helped cut these words into the turf of the highly visible mountainside below the peak known as Arthur's Seat.[88]

The theatricality of the ex-slave narrator was cited negatively in the contemporary, anti-abolitionist criticism that "witnessing" ex-slaves sometimes drew. Such critiques stressed the practiced artificiality of their voices. An unsympathetic John Delaware Lewis complained in 1851, after visiting the States and observing the real, "inferior" Negro there, that "Exeter Hall philanthropists" in Britain only knew "some half-dozen specimens" of black men who were "victims of tyranny by profession"—the "lions of clerical dinner parties," "sipping their wine with ease and grace" in "faultless black clothes and snowy neckcloths."[89] When in May 1864, an anti-slavery southerner in London addressed a meeting of the Negro's Friend Society, a Baptist minister from Birmingham, England, the Rev. Charles Vince, rose to warn against a romantic view of black people, a view that was especially promulgated in Britain by the practice of sending freed slaves "up and down the country." They were "rank imposters" who were "spoilt by over-patronage."[90] At the end of the Civil War abolitionism, amid its difficult campaign to find assistance for the freedman, began rapidly to lose popular appeal while Britain was greatly agitated by the black Rebellion in Jamaica. An anonymous writer in the *Saturday Review*, a London weekly, claimed that the public had been misled all along by the anti-slavery Sunday-school image of the Negro promoted by philanthropy, "a black but good-looking man," with "a soft and gentle countenance ... men of no inconsiderable intelligence, and of very remarkable comity of manner." The public had been, that is, urged to overlook the matter of "race," and to disregard the sage and skeptical views of those who had actual knowledge, not of the dressed-up, performing Negro among them, but of the real Negro abroad, with all his "faults and impertinences."[91]

The ex-slave who found his or her way to Britain or was sent or brought there by American and British white abolitionist patrons, sustained by the hospitality and donations of anti-slavery campaigners, often clergymen, and by the small fees to be had from speaking, was of course not exactly representative of those on whose behalf he or she spoke. Manumitted or fugitive, these narrators had, even when slaves, generally not lived among the most wretched of the deep southern sugar cane, rice, and cotton workers, and were literate and articulate. This does not, of course, mean that they were, as their accusers charged, inauthentic actors out to make a comfortable living among their British and Irish sympathizers. Most—and there were many, both men and women—came to Britain to "witness," as the Quakers called it, against a great evil. The most effective and best-known among them, such as Douglass and William and Ellen Craft, were promoted by the familiar Exeter Hall philanthropists who had been the chief paternalist patrons of supplicating blacks since the late eighteenth century. But by the 1840s new activists had developed a voice of their own that was less supplicating and more demanding.

There were, by the mid-1850s, dozens of these black Americans on one circuit or another throughout England, Scotland, and Ireland. Though they retailed familiar stories of victimization—of tortured, broken bodies, of families torn asunder, women raped and tender children abused by slave-masters—the role they themselves played in Britain was at least ambiguous. For their sympathetic supporters, they comfortably fit one side of a familiar black binary, that of the black object of pity. Their doubtful critics, however, associated them with another side, that of the black trickster. Henry "Box" Brown, who had achieved freedom by mailing himself in a box to Philadelphia, played both roles, as a narrator of slave life who also took up a later career as a performing magician called "the African Prince."[92]

The passage of the Fugitive Slave Act in America in 1850 not only pushed many of these witnesses out of the United States to wander about Europe for years (more black Americans visited Britain between 1848 and 1854 than at any time since the freed slaves who found their way there after the American Revolution[93]). It also lent immediacy to their message, amplified their cause, and furthered their attempts to raise money in Britain and Ireland for black schools and chapels, and to buy relatives out of slavery in America. Some of the ex-slave narrators of course—Douglass is the prototype—projected anger and impatience, and, while appealing for the support of white people of influence, were determined to tell their own histories in their own voice. In their testimony from inside the peculiar institution they were much harder to attack than the distant idealist Dickens had egregiously assaulted in his caricature of the negrophilic philanthropist, Mrs. Jellyby. Their lectures and their memoirs floated on the same sea of interest that made *Uncle Tom's Cabin* nearly ubiquitous in high-street book shops and news agents, railway book-stalls, and lending libraries in county towns.

African Americans in Britain did not of course speak with one voice. They were divided, as were the anti-slavery societies that supported them, on important issues such as the African colonization movement, militant or non-violent tactics in the United States, gradualism *vs.* William Lloyd Garrison's (no compensation) radicalism. For some, activism could mean simply offering themselves in British residence as "a living lie to the doctrine of the inferiority of the African race," as important perhaps as lecturing. Life in Britain could offer, without words being spoken, a public affirmation of equality, as when

William Wells Brown and the Crafts strolled through the Crystal Palace Exhibition in 1851, "a salutary rebuke to the numerous Americans present."[94]

In the second edition of his "landmark" *An Appeal to the Coloured Citizens of the World* (1830), David Walker, a free black journalist living in Boston, repeatedly asserted that "the English are our friends … our best friends."[95] His "fervent Anglophilia" reflected the "arc of refuge" that British North America and Britain itself provided to those escaping slavery, and was, especially after the British parliament abolished slavery in much of the British Empire in 1833, widely mirrored among the free African-American community. British travelers in America often commented that blacks there had a high regard for Britain and her Queen and celebrated British slave emancipation day, August 1st. When, in October, 1860, the Prince of Wales visited Boston, its "colored citizens" presented an address expressing their "gratitude and grateful attachment and respect for the Throne"—in sharp contrast to the indifference, or worse, of the city's Irish diaspora.[96]

Unsurprisingly, many of the black visitors to Britain, in crossing the Atlantic, acted upon such sentiments and praised what they claimed to be the (comparative) lack of race prejudice there—attending British universities,[97] walking "arm in arm with whites," and (some) taking English partners. As Harriet Jacobs recalled of her feelings on disembarking in Liverpool, "[f]or the first time in my life I was in a place where I was treated according to my deportment, without reference to my complexion. I felt as if a great millstone had been lifted from my breast. … My visit to England is a memorable event in my life."[98] William Wells Brown, though well aware that Thomas Carlyle had defamed blacks in his recent writings, on the whole found life in Britain as sympathetic as might a white New York Anglophile, a sympathy that extended beyond the issue of race-prejudice: the British shared with Americans "a common origin and identity of language … and have the same literature." But Americans, he observed, had "mobbed" the English actor Macready in New York. If "the American is better treated in England than the Englishman in America," it was attributable to "John Bull's superior knowledge of good manners, and his being a more law-abiding man than his brother Jonathan."[99]

The Slave Auction as Spectacle

Ex-slave narratives commonly invoked the slave auction in their tales of horror. Indeed, the southern slave auction—especially that in New Orleans—had become a species of theater,[100] not only in the ex-slave narratives, in white abolitionist propaganda, and literally so in the *Uncle Tom's Cabin* plays or *The Octoroon*, but also in many of the travel memoirs of those British tourist-voyeurs who sought it out for a later retelling. The nonconformist minister Ebenezer Davies, en route from South America to Boston, professed his burning "indignation" at the New Orleans slave auction, not only with the cigar-chewing white "soul-drivers" who asked him if he was "[l]ooking out for a few niggers this morning?" but also with the fact that the sale, being scheduled for Sunday morning, profaned the Sabbath.[101] Burning indignation was not, however, universal. Henry Ashworth, touring the American South in 1860, and looking to present, in that agitated time, a more "balanced" view on the "Slavery Question," claimed to be "surprised to observe," at the central New Orleans auction held in the rotunda of a large hotel, slaves for sale who "did not appear dismayed, but on the contrary, tried to show off to the best advantage," though he admitted that for him and his party "the spectacle was a very humiliating one."[102] The actor James Robertson Anderson, in New Orleans to play Othello, echoed the common accounts (he was "shocked and disgusted"), though his actual description has a certain lightness of treatment: "the biggest knock-down was that of a handsome buck-nigger, who realized 600 dollars."[103] For Barbara Bodichon, a casual inquisitiveness seems to be the motivation for seeking out the auction in New Orleans: "As all my paintings are finished and my easel packed up I seem to have unlimited hours in the day, so I went to a Slave Auction ... [and told the auctioneer] that I was English and only came from curiosity."[104] Her reticence may, of course, have simply been precautionary. Southerners were more than likely to do violence to those they suspected of gathering abolitionist "evidence." When the young painter Eyre Crowe, serving as secretary to the touring novelist William Makepeace Thackeray, set up his easel in a Richmond slave market to sketch the scene, "the people rushed on him savagely and obliged him to quit."[105]

In fact, the slave auction was often designed as a kind of theatrical event. Especially in New Orleans, it was carefully arranged. It took place in a theater-like rotunda, accompanied by orchestral music, with the slaves themselves elegantly costumed before their at least partial public disrobing. Those attending included, as well as the interested buyers, many who, like our British observers, were a non-purchasing audience.[106]

There were of course many lesser auctions, or "slave bazaars" as they were sometimes called, throughout the slave states—some were large affairs, many others small and less theatrical. In 1852, Marianne Finch saw slaves being sold in Richmond and in her memoir registered, somewhat pro forma perhaps, her "increased disgust of slavery," though she admitted that (in Virginia at least) slave habitations were better than she expected—better than Irish hovels, she thought—and, in a veiled riposte perhaps to the excitement recently caused by *Uncle Tom's Cabin* and to abolitionist propaganda generally, she "saw no delicate, half-starved mothers; no sore-eyed, sore-eared, miserable-looking children."[107] The same year, the confirmed abolitionist John Benwell witnessed a "slave-vendue" at a large store in St. Louis, Missouri. His description touched keys familiar in the literature—the "grief-worn countenance" of a middle-aged negress being displayed, parentless children, the coarse auctioneer, overseers and "negro-dealers."[108] Such repugnance was no doubt genuine, and shared by many such as the Chartist William Aitken ("horror and revulsion")[109] or Charles Mackay ("a feeling of nausea"),[110] and there may have been, as J. W. Reed has claimed, "the quality of epiphany" in these experiences.[111] Surely though most would have anticipated what they were to see in such a place. For others, responses were somewhat ritualized, learned from the familiar abolitionist denunciation of human trafficking, just as indignation, shock, and disgust were no doubt expected by their British readers.

In the end, for many, whatever the depth of feeling elicited and retold, British memoir writers were in the antebellum era compelled to include the spectacle of the slave auction by the travel memoir genre itself and the expectations of its audience. In fact, relatively few of the travel writers ventured down South, and were left (like their readers back in

Britain) to imagine the horror. For those who did travel into Dixie, recounting the slave auction could serve two purposes, to confirm the appropriate Christian sensitivity of their own natures, and, secondly, to add weight to that very common trope of many antebellum travel memoirs—the hypocrisy of an America dedicated to the "self-evident truth that all men are created equal."

2 Slavery on the Anglo-American Stage from *Uncle Tom's Cabin* to *The Octoroon*

It is likely that the slave auction scene in *Uncle Tom's Cabin* provided a central tableau in most of its many stage adaptations. Harriet Beecher Stowe's iconic novel of 1852 (serialized in 1851), as is well known, was a transatlantic publishing wonder, with an unprecedentedly wide readership. It was also, like many of Dickens's works, almost immediately adapted for the stage on both sides of the ocean. Both the novel and the plays can be said to have built upon slave narratives of the 1840s, just as they themselves no doubt served in turn to shape the performance of ex-slave narrators who traveled to Britain in the decade thereafter.

While the sympathetic portrayal of African Americans in the novel draws from the familiar abolitionist stereotypes of victimization and passive resignation, childlike innocence, supplication, and gratitude, Simon Legree's black enforcers, Sambo and Quimbo, seem in their sadistic cruelty to be drawn from another (threatening) side of contemporary Negro representation. Both the novel and the plays, in their *visual* language, also advance contrasting representations—some editions of the novel in Britain were illustrated by satirists such as George Cruikshank with big-eyed, wide-grinning Blacks.[112] Moreover, in the plays Blacks portrayed by white actors in blackface could hardly help suggesting, however much such portrayals were sentimentalized, the familiar visual representation of Blacks by white minstrels. *The Nonconformist* thought that Topsy's antics "surpassed the humour" of blackface minstrels, an association that would have been encouraged by the southern black speech used in both minstrelsy and in the novel and plays. Douglas Lorimer has observed that the black dialect used by Stowe (novels were often read aloud in the mid-Victorian era) "provided an opportunity for English readers to try an imitation of the speech and mannerisms of a black slave."[113] Stowe's use of dialect also promotes a kind of social/biological hierarchy that would have been resonant with British class-consciousness: Tom, his wife Chloe, Topsy, and the comic characters Sam and Andy all speak, as Hazel Waters has observed, with a pronounced slave dialect, while the speech of the lighter-skinned George and Eliza is closer to that of the white characters.[114]

The Many Uncle Toms as Popular Entertainment

Stage productions began in New York while the novel was still being serialized, while in London Tom Taylor rushed to produce his own adaptation. In America, the dramatizations of George Aiken (with George C. Howard) and Henry J. Conway proved to be the most successful of the many staged versions before the Civil War, and were followed after the war by hundreds of circus-like "Tom Shows" that proliferated throughout the States to 1900 and beyond.

The Uncle Tom productions of the 1850s often made, it would seem, some effort to anticipate regional expectations (as in Baltimore where some were concerned that "good," that is paternalistic, plantation owners be represented fairly), and to offer entertainments that met the various purposes of abolitionist idealism *and* melodrama. Aiken's production moved from upstate Troy to New York City in 1853 and proved a great success there. It offered an audience not known to be fond of abolitionism a kind of "entertainment mingled with edification," making, as Laurence Senelick has put it, a more "generalized appeal to the emotions." Moreover, blackface and "a 'darky' accent" drew out associations with minstrelsy, and could inspire laughter from gallery audiences "preconditioned to accept stage negroes as comic figures."[115] These plays generally emphasized humanity (and inhumanity), a sentimental family ideal, and the corrupted economics of the slave system without confronting the issue of "race" and racial difference. In some, as in Aiken's *Uncle Tom*, the focus shifts to the humanized and refined mulatto, George Harris and his family, and to the benevolence of white patrons. In others, interest was simply directed away from the politics of abolitionism by melodrama and special effects.[116]

Conway's play, produced by P. T. Barnum, was an extravaganza that ran for three years with twelve to eighteen performances each week. It has been called the "Missouri Compromise Uncle Tom," a "happy, jokey" version where Tom survives to enjoy freedom and family.[117] Aiken's play, however, proved with its sentimentality and sensational effects[118] to be the most popular of the early *Toms*, and was, according to T. Allston Brown, well-attended by clergymen. It ran for more than 200 performances in New York City, day and night, and was "the great dramatic event of the season" attracting "all classes of the community."[119] Though Aiken stayed closer to Stowe's story than some, he added a comic Yankee role, played by Joseph Jefferson and C. K. Knox. In January 1854, T. D. Rice of Jim Crow fame, playing the role of Uncle Tom, opened a new version that suggests an overlap with the clichés of minstrelsy—something some of the advertising poster illustrations of banjo-playing, singing slaves would also indicate. Rice had a modestly successful run of several weeks at the Bowery Theater in spite of what must have been a glut of *Toms* by then on the American stage.[120] There was a spate of other "slavery plays" that followed, including one by the ex-slave William Wells Brown in 1858 (*The Escape; or, A Leap for Freedom*), and the next year Boucicault's *The Octoroon*.

These plays aimed to entertain—often with accompanying minstrel music as back-up[121]—a variety of different audiences (a less-abolitionist *Uncle Tom*, called *Uncle Tom's Cabin As It Is*, was produced in Baltimore), though such calculations did not, one imagines, often include strategies to attract black spectators. T. Allston Brown recounts numerous versions in the early and mid-1850s alone—from New York and Boston to Chicago and Detroit, as well as two competing versions in Paris. In London, Uncle Tom adaptations drew criticism from the mandarin press (the *Times*, the *Spectator*) more for their popularity among the "weak intellects" of the uncultured "mob" than for their quality as plays.¹²² Tom Taylor's play *Slave Life* opened at the Adelphi in November 1852. A year or so later Aiken's production came to London on a transatlantic tour of England, Scotland, and Ireland. Half a dozen or more others found homes in a variety of London theaters. Some of these productions included rhyming doggerel and songs pulled from blackface routines, along the lines of the advice (perhaps tongue-in-cheek) one reviewer offered that the reiterated "barrenness" of abolitionist sermonizing "might have been supplanted to advantage by the bones and banjo."¹²³ In all of these dramatizations, excepting presumably that of William Wells Brown, the black characters on stage were as a matter of course performed by blackfaced white actors, as would have been true of the four different Uncle Tom pantomimes that appeared in London during the Christmas season of 1852.¹²⁴

We are left with the near-impossibility of unraveling art and reality in, especially, an important source such as the travel memoir. The British observer recreates the American black for us, but his vision may owe much to expectations and imagination prepared by the stage and the music hall. As James Burnley nicely observed when attending a "nigger camp meeting,"

> we could see the negroes … looking like the Uncle Toms, the Chloes, the Zoes, the Gingers, the Sambos, and the Petes with which our fiction, our stage, and our pictorial literature have long familiarized us. One almost expected to hear the deep chuckle and the obtuse conundrum of the minstrel of our popular entertainments proceed from the persons on the platform.¹²⁵

But of course not everyone saw and heard the fictional or performing blackface Negro in the same way. Did the British and American Tom plays appeal to different national audiences, were they heard and seen with different expectations and understandings, and differing theatrical traditions? Obviously the abolitionist message spoke to a particular audience within both national cultures, while some productions, in a crowded field, shifted toward audience-catching entertainment, and elements of minstrelsy. As Tracy C. Davis has written, in Britain *Uncle Tom's Cabin* "refracts a plethora of ideological positions, historical circumstances, and emplotments beyond those known in the United States of the 1850s."¹²⁶

In 1855, the British political economist, Nassau W. Senior, in the midst of the Uncle Tom sensation, sounded a cautionary note about the abolitionist hopes that, while embraced by many in Britain, faced entrenched bigotry in America. Though "[t]he sale of 'Uncle Tom's Cabin' is the most marvellous literary phenomenon that the world has ever witnessed,"

> [t]he contempt, the loathing, with which the coloured race is avoided in those [free *northern* American] States, deprives of all public sympathy every one that is suspected of being stained by the least drop of black blood. No one, who has not

been raised by a better education far above ordinary prejudices, looks on a negro, or on the descendant of a negro, as a fellow creature.

This raised at least one further important transatlantic issue. Senior went on to argue that at least part of the popularity of Stowe's story *in Britain* arose, he thought, not solely from sympathy for enslaved black people, but from its encouragement of "national jealousy and national vanity." "We have long been tired of hearing America boast that she is the freest and the most enlightened country that the world has ever seen. Mrs. Stowe taught us how to prove that democrats may be tyrants."[127]

Boucicault's The Octoroon: Or, Life in Louisiana

Whatever his private convictions about American slavery, Boucicault had a sharp sense of the opportune moment. He however held back from entering the lists with his own contribution in a very competitive marketplace. When finally, in 1859, he did mount a slavery play, only days after John Brown was hanged, it was a reworked story of the Irish-born novelist, Capt. Mayne Reid. In the febrile environment of the approaching election of 1860, he avoided outright abolitionist piety and substituted universal tragic romance (and exploding steamboats) for anti-slavery hectoring. The central theme—interracial intimacy—was perhaps unlikely to find much popularity among southern whites, though the sympathetic female Quadroon or Octoroon was a familiar enough figure in popular literature North and South. The play was, in the American version, after all a tragedy in which the (near-white) mulatta heroine dies before love could be consummated and biological boundaries crossed. With his sensational effects and melodramatic plot, Boucicault could reasonably have expected an audience beyond the northern metropolises. The success of the play in the United States and its profitable run in Britain does, however, beg the question of different popular contexts.

One might begin with the observation that the London stage had a longer and more frequently acted tradition of black characters and themes on the serious tragic/comic stage than was true of New York, Philadelphia, or Boston—one reason, after all, that Aldridge left for London. Moreover, there was far less likelihood that a play about slavery and interracial relations would stir up aggressively critical complaint in Britain than in America. In New York, the *Herald* had unfairly charged Boucicault's play as a piece "calculated to fan the flames of sedition," "imported into this country from the British hot-bed of abolition." Boucicault was like "the other English abolitionists who participated in the recent conspiracy" at Harper's Ferry and his play was the end result of "twenty-five years of niggerism."[128]

Boucicault's play was, it appears, received in an America on the verge of the great national schism as much more of an anti-slavery piece than any read-through could possibly support. It was a sell-out in abolitionist Boston, and in Portland, Maine, an excited member of the audience leaped on stage to save Zoe from the poison she was poised to take with his own histrionic words "fly with me, and I will place you in safety in Queen Victoria's dominion."[129]

The play as performed in New York was a tragedy about the doomed love of a young white plantation owner for a light-skinned mulatta slave, Zoe (played by Boucicault's wife Agnes). In London, Boucicault, as he himself suggested, may have been resentful or at least "ambivalent" about changing the play's tragic ending, out of a sense that this would weaken the play's (not very pronounced) antislavery message.[130] It is doubtful, however, that his quick substitution of a happy ending in the face of the London audience's negative reaction to Zoe's death caused him much concern. Boucicault was a most flexible author and adaptor who often seems to have, with a nose for profit and popularity, accommodated local taste, expectations, and social mores—notably in his Irish dramas. His own credentials as an antislavery advocate were not very impressive, and the original ending (for an American audience) could just as well have suggested, not the tragedy of race prejudice, but an affirmation of the common view that in the end racial barriers could not/should not be crossed.

So what can be inferred about the transatlantic reception of the *Uncle Tom* plays and *The Octoroon*? First, the Anglosphere received these performances with something like comparable degrees of enthusiasm. There were, of course, regional differences of reception in antebellum America and perhaps class differences in London and the provinces, especially in the popularity of the variety of *Toms* on stage in both countries as well as in audiences' reactions to the interracial theme of *The Octoroon*. Both countries had been prepared by a generation of stage performances of comic Otherness, one legacy of which was the wide expectation and reception of these plays as entertainment rather than as mere explorations of familiar antislavery themes. Does Boucicault's shift in his ending of *The Octoroon* necessarily tell us much about the different character and expectations of his British and American audiences? Though the "improved," non-tragic *Octoroon* certainly had considerable success in London, Boucicault received some contemporary criticism there as in America for either ending. It is likely that, however much productions were crafted for a particular audience, the slave play phenomenon represents a kind of unity rather than a sharp division in the transatlantic Anglo-world, just as Boucicault's productions generally "did much to stylize a transatlantic form of spectacular theatre."[131]

In the years before the outbreak of the American Civil War, a person in search of black representation in London, the provincial cities, and seacoast spas, would have had a generous menu to choose from: there were minstrel players on stage and in the streets, a number of Othellos, competing *Uncle Tom* adaptations, and in 1861 Boucicault's *The Octoroon*. There were educative panoramas and artistic tableaux vivants of African-American slavery, competing perhaps with displays of exotic species of aboriginal life from the colonies, with missionary exploits in the South Sea islands and Africa, and with narratives of the terrible events in India. For much of the long nineteenth century, what has been called an "ethnological show business" brought instructive and exotic entertainments to London featuring Africans—Bushmen, Hottentots, Zulus, Pigmies, Ubangis—in native dress and partial nudity, in "theatres, fairs, amusement parks, and circuses."[132] In some sense, American ex-slaves telling their tales in a variety of evangelical and abolitionist venues were themselves a species of such display, as were learned (and perhaps lantern-slide illustrated) lecture-hall expositions by phrenologists, ethnologists, and amateur anthropologists on racial difference.

Though nearly everyone assumed the reality of racial difference—of body, language, and character—this did not yet, in Britain, translate into the "scientific" racism of the late-Victorian era. At mid-century, black difference could yet be perceived by many as being as much about heritage, class, and education as about biology. That this was swiftly to change in the 1860s, 1870s, and 1880s is owing not only to the kind of pseudo-scientific, "race is everything" theories of biological and social hierarchy that arose from the British intelligentsia's loose interpretations of Darwinian evolution. Nor, alone, to prejudices that were driven into popular culture by illustrated and highly sensationalized media coverage of the violence in India, the Jamaican rebellion, reports of cannibalism in the South Seas, aborigine wars on the Australian frontier, and the series of "little wars"—with the Zhosa, Ashanti, Zulu, Matabele, and other peoples—in Africa. It can also be related to close transatlantic connections—to the debates in Britain spawned by the American Civil War and the significantly American obsession with "miscegenation," to the wide discussion of the parallel "problem" of the freed slave in post-bellum America and the subjugated non-white in the British Empire. Latterly, the American Indian wars and resettlement also found a significant place in British popular culture via short stories, novels, and mass entertainments. The starker language and representation of racial difference that were pushed along by such gathering phenomena may be traced in the continuing genre of the travel memoir.

3 Anglo-American Racial Representation in the Mid- and Late-Victorian Era

In the post-Indian Mutiny, post-American Civil War, and post-Jamaican Rebellion era, there was a growing Anglo-American convergence of concern with the problematic of race relations that resulted from black emancipation, non-Anglo-Saxon immigration, the spread of white settlement areas, and the governance of non-white populations: as the British travel writer, John James Aubertin, succinctly put it in 1888, following a tour that ranged from Hawaii to the Bahamas, "what is to become of the negro question? This is a profound problem."[133] Fear of the "mixture" of races encouraged a sense that "assimilation" threatened not merely social obloquy but a (white) existential crisis of racial decline, a powerful apprehension that was met, in a sense, by the prevalent late nineteenth-century theory (a classic example of wish-fulfilment) of the inevitable extinction of primitive races. Imperial and American responses came to be marked by a similarity, one might almost say a coordination, of rhetoric, motive, and policy. The reimposition of white control in the Old South and the genocidal Western Indian Wars were both pre-figured and accompanied by the extirpation of aborigine cultures in New Zealand, Australia, and southern Africa, and by administrative schemes for disciplining and containing native peoples within increasingly restricted areas. Such coercive imperial designs, programs, and institutions were contemporaneous with the development of the removal, control, and territorial "reservation" policies of mid- and late nineteenth-century American commissioners of Indian Affairs. Both can be seen in the general context of the entrenchment throughout the Anglosphere of the domestic, quotidian bigotry in the spreading realm of settler communities. Where there had once been a certain British smugness, however unjustified, about Britain's anti-slavery credentials in the face of the American "peculiar institution," in the late nineteenth-century British Empire and in expanding America there came to be a shared and mutually-massaged, defensive "race-awareness" that led to a politics of segregation, legal and supra-legal subordination, surveillance, and, often, (white) community-condoned violence.

The British, African Americans, and the Coming of the Civil War

Having in 1853–4 done the now-familiar circular tour out to Cincinnati and down the Ohio and Mississippi to New Orleans, then by rail across to Mobile, Columbia, and Richmond, the Rev. Robert Everest, a retired East India Company chaplain, published his memoir of travels. A moderate emancipationist who advocated gradual manumission, with compensation for the dispossessed owners, he used his travelogue, as many had before, as a kind of running commentary on the institution as he found it. He was informed by second-hand stories of lynchings, beatings, hangings, and burnings of Negroes, but also by his own observations and casual conversations on the road. He saw an unprovoked five-year-old white boy hit in the face and kick a black slave child; he spoke with two young white men at Vicksburg who raised hounds for the sole purpose of "hunting niggers." He concluded that race hatred and arrogance were bred into southern whites from the earliest age and were almost universal.[134]

Everest was well-traveled, with experience in the British East, and often put his views of life in the American South in a comparative perspective. Slavery, he thought, was "worse in this part of the world" than among Muslims who, provided the slave accepted the Koran, often treated a slave as one of the family who might rise to "freedom, affluence, and power." Unlike American whites, Muslim slave-owners were themselves "dark" and less likely to harbor racial animosity, while their slaves were likely to regard their condition as but the will of God—unlike the American Black who "feels that he is wronged and ill-used," suffers from a sense of injustice, "and becomes, in consequence, what masters everywhere call 'troublesome.'" Nevertheless, the Southern white and the Asiatic slave owner shared something in their character: each is "brought up from his cradle to know no control of his will, and he consequently becomes a tyrant."[135]

For a liberal like Everest, comparisons were also available with the British domestic social structure, with the landed gentry with whom southern planters liked to compare themselves. In Baltimore he encountered landowners who were said to live lives devoted to "field sports, racing, fox-hunting, and deer-shooting, a pretty exact counterpart of the type from which they descended." Drawing parallels between the southern gentleman and the British landed gentry was something of a commonplace in the British travel memoir. Charles Lyell, commenting on his travels in South Carolina in the early 1840s had observed that, like English country gentlemen, the prosperous plantation owners, whose "mansions were surrounded by deer-parks," had "well-appointed carriages and horses, and well-trained black servants." Their conversation "turned chiefly on agricultural subjects, shooting, and horse-racing."[136] Everest gave the parallel a more critical twist. The "lords of the South" were, like "all other privileged orders devoted to pleasure and luxury," "a bold and unscrupulous oligarchy." Even so, this was a different, a perverted landed society that (perhaps as European lords had done in the ancient past) despised the servile class they depended upon and regarded labor itself as "degrading." Consequently, beyond the elegant plantation, "the towns and villages were filthy," "everything wore a dirty, slovenly appearance," and, as with the British in the East, "every fellow, who can possess a slave to fag for him, fancies himself a 'gentleman' and passes his time in lounging about and gossipping [sic]."[137]

In the circumstances of the mid-1850s, with the implementation of the fugitive slave law and the aggressive determination of "bowie knife and revolver" southerners to expand the slave system into new territories, Everest found himself no longer sure that slavery would "die out" in America: "Unless the people, that is, the working classes, can be fairly roused to this question" and "made aware that the very object and end of slavery is to cheapen and degrade labour, ... the cause of liberty is gone." And yet, as other travelers had remarked, the problem lay not only in the South. In the Northern states "the coloured race," though free, remained "degraded." Everest's solution anticipates, perhaps, the radicalism of the post-Civil War Freedmen Aid cause and raises the central issue of how the emancipated Negro is to be enabled—by being taken "in hand," educated "in the same schools" with white children, given equal political rights, "in short" made "one with themselves [the white majority]." The alternative was an emancipation that would but lead to "a new [Anglo-Saxon] aristocracy of race."[138]

As the likelihood grew that the American system would fall apart due to divisions over slavery (Everest himself thought that the slave-holding class, "like all other privileged orders devoted to pleasure and luxury, wants also the excitement of war"[139]), British visitors were prone to find confirmed their long-held anticipation that the American experiment, based as it was on hypocrisy and bumptious arrogance, would fail. The breakup of the Union, many thought, was inevitable, and either regrettable or desirable, depending on where one's (domestic social) sympathies lay. Some were prepared to imagine that the Southern plantation owner was, like genteel landed society in Britain, a force for good, bringing culture and refinement to a rough society otherwise dominated by the bowie-knife wielding, tobacco-chewing, poor whites as in the wilder parts of Tennessee or Kentucky. Plantation society might be imagined rather as the benevolent landowning class in Britain was imagined, that is, idealized. Certainly those travelers who, unlike Everest, were invited into the genteel world of wealth and polite pursuits amid elegant parks and tree-lined avenues were likely, even if opposed to slavery in principle, to find the clean, well-dressed black domestic who held their reins or served their table or helped them to dress to be altogether better off than, say, the wretched Irish in the Northern cities.

William Makepeace Thackeray, who had little regard for blacks or for abolitionism and claimed to prefer "the 'imitation nigger' of the minstrel stage to the 'genuine article' as represented in antislavery discourse,"[140] made two extended trips to the United States in 1852-3 and 1855-6, lecturing profitably in Boston and New York. Like another British author, John Delaware Lewis, he also traveled south to Virginia where, also like Lewis (slaves Lewis passed en route were "merry, exchanging jokes"[141]), he was not shocked with slavery as he found it among the "good families" whose Blacks were, he thought, "the comfortablest race of menials."[142] Britons who were, like Lewis and Thackeray, welcomed into southern society often parroted the biases they found there: Lewis asserted "the plain and simple fact, that the negro is an inferior race."[143] Some others, who did not visit the South and did not wish to be seen to be upholding slavery, nevertheless sympathized with what they imagined to be the American equivalent of a generous and paternal landed gentry and aristocracy. Amelia Matilda Murray wrote from Boston that she had met a southern planter, a "kind person" who assured her that the childlike American Blacks, like those in Britain's colonies, had to "become men in experience and intelligence before they can take care of themselves." She "was inclined to hope that the 'Legrees' are as much exceptional beings, as idle and profligate landowners [are] among ourselves."[144]

In Richmond Thackeray observed that "[t]he negroes don't shock me or excite my compassionate feelings at all … little black imps are trotting and grinning about the streets, women, workmen, waiters all well fed and happy. The place, the merriest little place, and the most picturesque I have seen in America."[145] His young secretary, Eyre Crowe, seems to have had a more thoughtful and questioning view, if one can judge from the painting he made from a sketch he drew at a Richmond slave auction—for which Thackeray chastised him lest it be thought to insult their hosts.

Figure 2 "Slaves Waiting for Sale" (1861), by Eyre Crowe [Alamy].

The secession of the southern states after the election of Abraham Lincoln, the bombardment of Fort Sumter, and, in July 1861, the Union defeat at the first battle of Bull Run and the rapid evolution of skirmishing and stand-off into a full-scale Civil War caught by surprise most British travelers who were already in the States. Others, like the Conservative MP for Ayrshire Sir James Fergusson or Anthony Trollope, novelist son of Frances Trollope, were preparing to depart for America; Fergusson set sail at the end of the summer and Anthony Trollope in the autumn of 1861. They would tour (Fergusson enjoyed shooting quail, prairie chicken, plovers, and snipe in Illinois) and lecture (as did Trollope in both the North and the South) without much hindrance. In December, Fergusson, back home, told the readers of *Blackwood's* that "[t]he war, perhaps, is not one to awaken our warm sympathies for either party," though it is clear where his own sympathies lay—the North was a "Democratic Absolutism" employing secret police and nighttime arrests, while in the South, though slavery deprived it of the "moral encouragement" the Briton often gave to peoples struggling for self-government, the negroes seemed content: "Numberless are the tales of the happiness of the slaves, in which, as a rule, I really believe."[146] Most visitors carried on, at least until movement across lines became difficult or impossible, and assumed that the creation of two Americas, one slave and one free, was more or less inevitable. Few anticipated that the war would become one of slave emancipation.

The British and the American Civil War has been a topic of interest for some time. In Britain, there has been significant historiographic debate over the so-called Lancashire Cotton Famine and working-class attitudes toward the American conflict, and over the extent of sympathy for the Southern cause among the British landed, upper classes.[147] The tracing out of Anglo-American representations of race through the long nineteenth century suggests continuities and gradual shifts in attitude that were already underway before the conflict began and accelerated in the decades after it ended. Something may be learned, of course, through British journalism and from the letters and memoirs of visitors to America during the war—travelers who often, as in the case of Edward Dicey, took on the role of "special correspondent" to a newspaper or a weekly or monthly journal.[148] The flow of transatlantic travel, however, was significantly attenuated—before surging beyond the annual pre-war numbers in the 1870s. Such accounts of the war years as we have are often those of war correspondents specifically sent out from London— such as William Howard Russell of the *Times* who became persona non grata in the North after his reportage of the disastrous first battle of Bull Run[149]—or those private individuals who traveled out with an already formed personal commitment to one side or the other.[150] There was a significant number of volunteers, often young men with some military experience and a taste for adventure as well as a commitment to either abolition or a romantic idea of the Southern cause. There were others, though many fewer than before, who like Trollope even in wartime (at least in the early years of the struggle) continued to follow the familiar routines dictated by the hope of profitable lecturing or simple curiosity.

University men, often liberals such as Goldwin Smith, Edward Dicey, Leslie Stephen, or Henry Yates Thompson, who went out were drawn to their counterparts in Boston and tended to have Union sympathies, as did many less privileged young men who, like Robert Livingstone, eldest son of the missionary explorer David Livingstone, volunteered to serve in the Union army. Livingstone would die in a Southern prisoner-of-war camp. Some, such as Thomas Conolly, an Anglo-Irish MP, were drawn to the South to see for themselves the "nation" being built there. Others, sympathetic to the Southern cause and often with a military background, went to serve as volunteers. Henry Wemyss Fielden of the Black Watch, son of a prominent Lancashire mill owner, would serve in Tennessee to the end of the war and marry a South Carolina judge's daughter before returning home to Britain. The Confederate leaders were eager to cultivate British supporters among the influential class, and some visiting observers, such as Major Garnet Wolseley, on leave from his duties in Canada, or the Marquis of Hartington, later the 8th Duke of Devonshire, were flattered to meet Jefferson Davis and other southern leaders and military men. Subsequently, Wolseley wrote an admiring piece about General Lee, and Hartington, a young Whig-Liberal, claimed that he had "liked them all very well, & they all talked in a very moderate & sensible way … I have certainly become much more Southern since I came here."[151] In these memoirs, as in Britain itself, the character and condition of the enslaved or free black in America attracted less attention than the drama of the fighting, at least until the 1863 Emancipation Proclamation, the use of Black troops by the North, the anti-Negro Irish mobs in New York, and the passage in 1865 of the thirteenth amendment finally signaled a future that would center the "problem" of the African-American citizen, North and South.

The British Observer in the Post-Bellum American South

With the end of the war, there was a sharp uptick in tourism, often now focused around a wish to see and report on the condition of the devastated Southern states. There was a corresponding rush into print by transatlantic tourists such as Henry Latham, a tutor (later master) of Trinity College, Cambridge (*Black and White: A Journal of a Three Months' Tour in the United States* [1867]), John Henry Kennaway, a young Oxford graduate soon to become a Conservative MP (*On Sherman's Track; Or, the South After the War* [1867]), or the Rev. Foster Barham Zincke, a Suffolk vicar (*Last Winter in the United States* [1868]). On the other hand, many were eager, like Zincke, also to explore the American far West, opened for an easier tourism by the progressive extension of the transcontinental railway.[152] These Western memoirs, as we shall see, were much less likely to dwell on the long tradition in the genre of black and white race relations in the North and South, though "race" remained an important, wider category as traveling Britons were drawn to comment on the "red Indians," Mexicans, and immigrant Chinese.

During the war, those Britons who managed to visit the South hardly challenged the views of the southern slave that their hosts embraced. These were relayed back to a British public torn between the images found in the slave narratives, abolitionist pleading, and Stowe's novel, and those spread through the representations offered by the stage, the minstrel show, and the Confederate propaganda project active in Britain. Lt.-Col. Henry Charles, for instance, having managed to get a pass from General Sherman through to the Confederate lines in Tennessee, found that he had to explain to his southern hosts that all Englishmen did not "form their ideas of slavery from such books as *Uncle Tom's Cabin*." The slaves he encountered, he told the readers of the *Cornhill Magazine* in 1863, lived up to their familiar comic representation. They were "a most ridiculous set of beings, and always appear to be caricaturing themselves. No representation of their manners can be too ridiculous or extravagant for the reality."[153]

A breezy or angry dismissal and disparagement of Stowe's widely read antebellum novel characterizes much of the British reportage from the post-bellum South, standing in, as it did, for the whole, seemingly dated, abolitionist discourse in the fraught days of Reconstruction and recovery. Already, in early 1866, the actress Ellen (Tree) Kean, touring the South with her husband Charles, was writing back to friends that emancipation had freed the Black to revert to his natural "indolence" (there is here more than a touch of Thomas Carlyle's "pumpkin-eating" freed slave of the Caribbean islands): "They will not work ... and so some of them rob and murder and some lie down and die." Harriet Beecher Stowe "has done a cruel injustice to the southern people and absurdly ennobled the negro into an angel without wings."[154] A year or so later another actor, the humorist known as "Arthur Sketchly" [George Rose], visiting a Richmond still in ruins, wrote that the Negro, "an idle, thoughtless creature ... like a child," was also "terribly vindictive," unlike Stowe's "black angel," Uncle Tom.[155] When William Hepworth Dixon, editor of the *Athenaeum* and frequent tourist, published his very popular post-war overview of America and American life in 1867 (dedicated to Charles Dilke, his "fellow traveller"), he dismissed Stowe's "fancy pictures [of the sensitive, affectionate Negro]—drawn in a New England study a thousand miles from a rice field and a cotton plantation."[156] By the 1880s and 1890s such views, taken from one side of the highly polemical debate over Stowe's work in the 1850s but presented now as balanced judgments, had become more or less a standard transatlantic understanding, a condescension located in the fin de siècle effort to reestablish the integrity of a white, Jim Crow South. A reactionary British historian such as the Lancashire-born Percy Gregg, in his pro-Southern *History of the United States from the Foundation of Virginia to the Reconstruction of the Union*, could simply dismiss Stowe in a sentence or two as a New Englander with "little knowledge and less experience of the society she undertook to describe," whose novel was populated with "clumsy, polemical caricatures":

> Uncle Tom was a *possible* negro; the result of a peculiar religious teaching, of a literal faith in the maxims of the Gospel as interpreted by orthodox Unitarianism, acting on a simple, impulsive, affectionate and submissive nature, idealized to the utmost.[157]

Like many of the British visitors who were prepared to sympathize with the Confederate cause, Henry Charles unselfconsciously uses the word "nigger," as did, on the other side of the lines in the border states of Tennessee and Kentucky, John Francis Campbell. Campbell, a Scottish author and Celtic studies scholar traveling down from Canada through Chicago to Louisville, found that "niggers were not popular" there and observed that, though they were "impressed" into the Union army and "waiting for slaughter," no white soldier would, he claimed, fraternize with them. At least in the West (Chicago and the border states), "strong antipathy [to the Negro] breaks out everywhere … So, the picture of a great nation shattering the fetters of slavery, which looked so grand and bright at a distance, seems all shadow on close inspection." Campbell is as casual in his slurs about Negro character as any southerner Lt.-Col. Charles would have encountered: a "nigger" wearing Parisian fashions he observed in Louisville "was a regular darkey, with blubber lips … the type of her race."[158] While hardly new, such language became increasingly the common coinage of much late nineteenth-century British and American public (and published) discourse.

Though most of the information passed back to Britain during and immediately following the war came from roving journalists and from the snap-shot observations of tourists like Henry Charles and John Campbell, some of the transatlantic news of the South in the 1860s and 1870s was produced by more "interested" parties who, like Fanny Kemble's daughter Frances Butler (1838–1910), had personal hopes for recovering a degree of antebellum prosperity. Though she accompanied her mother to London after her parents divorced, she came to take her father's side, returned to Georgia and inherited his estates there. Determined to restore family fortunes, she found a post-war world of "conquered, ruined, and disheartened whites" and manumitted labor with, as she thought, unreasonable expectations ("all their foolish and extravagant ideas of freedom"). One of her first acts was to hang a picture of General Lee on the stripped, bare wall above the mantelpiece of the plantation house. In her attempt to relaunch a profitable, working concern (her father having died in 1867), she personally ran the estate until 1877 but ultimately threw her hand in, moved with her British husband[159] back to London, and in 1883 published her own memoir of *Ten Years on a Georgia Plantation Since the War*. In some respects, it served as a kind of counterargument to her mother's representations of both the South and the black slave.[160] Though she (or her London editors) avoided, as had her mother, the cruder nomenclature for black people, her account presents a different, much less optimistic picture of their possibilities and character. She clearly blamed feckless, freed African Americans, undisciplined either by the direct constraints of paternalism or, as yet, by the new wage-economy marketplace, for the failure of her dreams of restoration. In this, she presents her generation's (Anglospheric) views of the operation of a racialized political economy, rather than the more liberal abolitionist idealisms of her mother. They resonate in these late-Victorian times with the extension and consolidation of empire and the entrenchment of an operational racism in the assertion/reassertion of white control—from southern Africa to the Georgia rice fields. Though she was brought up in Philadelphia and London, Frances Butler Leigh (as she became in 1871) came to identify with an idealized South, and her journal shows a fierce defensiveness both of her father's world of (as she saw it) genteel paternalism and charity and of a new South struggling to emerge from the ashes. In all this her representation of African Americans is central. She projected upon them (her father had owned over four hundred slaves) a gratitude and yearning for the past, simple folk who on the one hand were "perfectly happy" to return to the estate ("missus, we belong to you; we be yours as long as we lib"), and on the other were confused about what was due to them (when she deducted advances in kind and loans from their meager wages). They seemed to be a "hopelessly lazy" people (she later recanted this when rice production rose significantly in the later 1870s) for whom "liberty meant idleness," and, like her father, she at least contemplated importing Chinese labor and investing in labor-saving machinery. Where Fanny Kemble had been equivocal, though with a certain optimism, about the possibility of black "improvement," her daughter had fixed beliefs based, she said, on experience: the Negro was "incapable of any high degree of intellectual training, or of being raised to a position of equality with the white race."[161]

Frances Butler Leigh was especially transatlantic in her parental background, her upbringing, her marriage (to the son of a landed and titled aristocrat), and her final removal from Georgia to London and a country house near Stratford-upon-Avon. While in residence at the refurbished estate in Georgia, she entertained visitors from Britain of political note and upper-class credentials such as Sir Michael Hicks Beach and the young Lord Rosebery—friends, one assumes, of her husband's family. Nevertheless, she identified as American and did not, it would appear, much care for the English. Her views about African Americans were no doubt those of her American slave-owning father, but there is something of the Englishwoman nonetheless in her dream—was it also her husband's?—of presiding over an inherited estate which in its heyday had been, if not as impressive as her father-in-law's grand house at Stoneleigh, as impressive as many a lesser English country estate.

There were, in fact, many in Britain who aspired, after the end of the American Civil War and the collapse of the old plantation class through dispossession, debt, and wartime mortality, to step into the boots of the ruined landed elite of the old South. These were a sub-set, as it were, of the more general movement in Britain to find land and status abroad for "second sons."[162] When the Scots author David Macrae traveled to Richmond in 1867, he encountered "several" who had come to Virginia to buy land— not large estates but sizeable farms, with the encouragement of the reconstruction era governor, Francis Harrison Pierpont: "If any of your Scotch farmers are coming out, now is the time for them." Macrae agreed, and told his British readership that "Scotch perseverance, Scotch 'canniness,' and Scotch farming are precisely what Virginia wants."[163] Small holdings were another matter. As William Stainer, in his 1874 book of advice to the "Gentleman Emigrant" pointed out, the small farmer would likely be competing with the "negroes and mulattos" who were able to overcome "[c]ongenital laziness," and "[s]ooner than live on terms of equality with such beings, we would sell our property for whatever it might fetch and clear out."[164]

For Englishmen with larger ambitions, the search for land in the American South may also have been inspired to some extent by the expectation of finding there a "docile" labor force that remained dependent on the land for their subsistence, at a time when agricultural unionism appeared in Britain to be organizing a significant challenge to the low-wage economy that had long underpinned the prosperity of farmer and landlord there. When the British newspaper publisher William Saunders traveled to America in 1877 he reported that "first-class negroes," who, under slavery had cost $800 to $1,000 dollars purchase price or $150 for annual hire, could now be had, as free labor, for as little as $100 a year, and "[u]nder the old system you had to keep your negro in sickness and in health, whether he suited or not. Now … he can be changed for another." There was enough interest in "the United States as a field for agricultural enterprise," he claimed, to justify a second edition of his travel memoir in 1879.[165]

Though ultimately Britons with hopes of living the life of the landed gentry in the States looked to new opportunities in the far West, in the late 1860s and 1870s land in the South seemed relatively cheap (compared to the price of arable in England) and had a social cachet which the wide expanses beyond Kansas lacked; and much of it was on the market. John Clay, who traveled to Virginia in 1874, told the readers of the *North British Agriculturist* that he found every other man wanted to sell his plantation, believed that "under an Englishman's guidance" the ex-slave could be made a good laborer, and advised that Virginia was "a land of promise" for the "middle-class emigrant."[166] Opportunities for those with capital to invest and an ambition to play the role of a modest lord of an American manor in fact proved, briefly, attractive to many young men such as Arthur Granville Bradley.

Bradley (1850–1943), educated at Marlborough College and Trinity College, Cambridge, was a son of a master of Marlborough and dean of Westminster, who in later life became a prolific author of light histories. Many of his late nineteenth-century magazine articles and fin de siècle books, such as *Sketches of Old Virginia* (1897) and *Other Days: Recollections of Rural England and Old Virginia, 1860–1880* (1913), were based on his own early years attempting to make a go of farming in post-war Virginia— an experience that seems to have been equal part agricultural entrepreneurship and enjoyment of such social entertainments of his class that he could find there. As he says, Virginia in the late 1860s "was very much talked of in England as offering, in a measure, the prospects of a new country without the accompanying conditions of hardship and isolation." Moreover, it possessed "a flavour of romance, due partly, I am quite sure, to the Christy Minstrel ballads, and to British upper-class sympathy for the South during the war." And to the great "Cavalier myth" purveyed by British writers like Thackeray in his *The Virginians*. Unfortunately, as Bradley himself came to find, the would-be American squires who invested and emigrated "knew absolutely nothing of plantation life or Society in the South." The properties required substantial capital for restoration, the soil was often exhausted from decades of single-cropping, and (as Frances Butler had discovered in Georgia) labor proved difficult to integrate into either a wage-only or sharecropping economy. The result was that "nearly all" educated middle- and gentry-class Englishmen who invested "lost heavily."[167]

In 1878, shortly after Bradley gave up hopes of a life as a latter-day gentleman farmer in the Virginia lowlands, he set down his impressions of "the Southern Negro" in an article for *Macmillan's Magazine*. Noting that "the storm of American politics" had raged since the war around the "problem of his ultimate future," he argued that the African American's fate remained undetermined. The picture he paints for his British readership avoids the cruder characterizations one can find in much of the traveler writing of the Reconstruction and post-Reconstruction era, yet he finds the freed slaves to be superstitious, their ignorance "of the lowest type," and their lives—lacking any political influence—to be tied into the wretched poverty of either the wage economy or that of a spreading sharecropping system. And yet—it is consonant with the long-familiar trope of the "happy slave"—the post-emancipation Negro enjoyed, amid his hardscrabble poverty, a "rapid succession" of "[p]reachings, weddings, baptisms, cake-walks, candy-stews, and corn-shuckings … throughout the calendar."[168]

It is a hallmark of Victorian discourse about "race" that variation within the reified category of "black" or "Negro" is suppressed. Certainly, the casual observations of British travelers generally ignore the variety of cultures represented by black people in the several regions of the slave South, or the particular African heritage that may have left a mark on their culture and appearance. To "know" such things or to have an interest in knowing them would have required more attention than the average white person, even the concerned abolitionist and freedman philanthropist, was willing to invest.

There is some indication that the cruder, demeaning language of phenotypical racial characteristics emphasized in popular Anglo-American discourse about "niggers" throughout the century became, in the late-Victorian era of scientific racism and imperial expansion, more pronounced among the polite classes, and especially among privileged women in the 1880s and 1890s. In post-Reconstruction America, as in the British Raj, there was a concern to suppress any appearance of a socially demeaning interracial intimacy and to advertise distance and distaste in the new era of emancipation. En route to the emerging Jim Crow system in the American South, some British visitors came to use a more pejorative language of physical difference, parroting their hosts, as a defensive means of pointing up the absurdity of claims for political and social equality. The charge of Negro "blubber lips" became commonplace in the memoirs of travel. Julius George Medley, for instance, wrote of the "thick blubber lips" of the offensive Negro in his travel memoir of 1873. More egregiously, the controversial social climber Theresa Yelverton, seeking perhaps to shore up her own contested status as the genuine Viscountess Avonmore, complained in her American journal of having to listen to "these blubber lips" of enfranchised "Negrodom."[169]

Yelverton finds the Black, in her southern journey to Charleston, Jacksonville, and New Orleans, physically repulsive, especially the "yellow" mulatto, an "animal man" living in "idleness and filth." She judges the black children whom Fanny Kemble had admired ("quite as pretty as white children"), to be "round black things," like "little pups, or little pigs," who were "lacking entirely that exquisite loveliness and angelic sweetness, which surrounds the rosy form of the white infant." Negro speech was "almost unintelligible," a probable result, she muses, of a "physical defect in the organs of speech," of "a tongue being too large." Confusing (as is often done) the monster with his creator, Yelverton judges the Negro man to be "that dark Frankenstein of the South" and the Negro woman commonly to "have recourse to the most horrid form of infanticide." In the world-turned-upside-down of Reconstruction, the Negro, a "coarse, revolting animal," "devoid of any sense of morality, religion, virtue, or truth," had been raised above his or her betters. It was "astonishing that any white lady can bear to have [a Negro] familiarly about her."[170]

Yelverton's extended diatribe against the African American in her travel memoir is starkly racist. Some female tourists had, it is true, much softer, more generous views— like the relatively progressive Welsh poet Emily Jane Davis who found the American black to be gracious, to speak good English, and "to compare favourably with those of the whites among whom he has been bred."[171] But the majority who traveled after white reassertion of social and political control made touring in the deep South by middle- and upper-class British women more acceptable were unlikely to risk the social *déclassement* of judging American blacks too favorably. Mary Anne McDowell (Lady Duffus Hardy), a wealthy traveling widow en route to Savannah, though she was "struck by those peculiarly sweet negro voices," nonetheless dreaded the thought, she wrote, of having to ride in a railway car with an "odorous" black family (strict segregation on southern trains meant she need not have worried). Her daughter who accompanied her, the novelist Iza Duffus Hardy, observed more directly in her own travel book that, though black people had many good qualities, the white Southerners knew well "the blot on the negro character," "believe devoutly in the inferiority of the negro," and have their reasons for resorting to lynch law. She retells, without condemnation, a story of "the Ku-Klux-Klan breaking into a gaol and killing a black prisoner."[172]

British philanthropic commitment to helping the emancipated American Negro was prominent during, and for a few years after, the Civil war. Aid organizations, like similar missionary-style efforts in the United States, were based on the model of the British and Foreign Anti-Slavery Society of the pre-war years and drew on the older, established networks of anti-slavery campaigns and aborigine protection. Funds were raised and emissaries sent over to help found negro schools.[173] The outbreak of black rebellion in Jamaica, however, significantly undermined popular support in Britain for "nigger philanthropy," while the coming era of American and British imperialism saw a popular shift away from traditions of Anglo-American abolitionism to the newly articulated ideal of a global white "Anglo-Saxon" supremacy.

A number of academics and upper-middle-class public servants made their tour of post-bellum America, including the historian Goldwin Smith, the Indian administrator and Liberal politician Sir George Campbell, and Edward Freeman, Regius Professor of History at Oxford and an advocate of, if not federation, then a mutual regard among "the English-Speaking People." Each of these came to lecture about or to observe the emerging rebuilt nation and, en passant, to comment on the prominent issue of race relations there. Smith found American Negroes to be physically repulsive, Campbell, "hideous" (though he deplored their "unjustifiable" treatment, he "hardly knew before what an ugly race some of the blacks are"). Freeman was the most outspoken in his distaste for the American Black: "The eternal laws of nature, the eternal distinction of colour, forbid the assimilation of the negro … To the old question, Am I not a man and a brother? I venture to answer: No."[174] For these, and others like them, the American South remained for decades a locus of interest as tales emerged of the progress of an often brutal white campaign to resecure power through violence, intimidation, and extra-legal suppression of the newly enfranchised.

"Lynchings" and "lynch-law" had been a familiar subject of antebellum travel literature, especially during the fugitive slave debates of the 1850s when visitors such as Benwell drew attention to the terrorizing of slaves by the threat of hunting, hanging, and burning.[175] When lynching re-emerged after the Civil War in the new South, however, it, like the Ku Klux Klan, was both deplored and reluctantly seen as a part of the messy business of recreating order. An uneasy George Campbell, in 1879, can neither approve nor entirely repudiate the practice.[176]

Other visitors had a less qualified view. William Ballantine, a well-known, retired "serjeant-at-law" touring the United States in 1883, commented on the press accounts of very frequent atrocious "outrages" committed by Negroes, and "in some of the far-away localities ... the 'nigger' met with a somewhat short 'shrift.'"[177] Samuel Reynolds Hole, dean of Rochester, touring the United States to raise money for the cathedral, found that lynch law "however shocking it may appear to Europeans and New Englanders, is far removed from arbitrary violence ... it is not often abused, and its proceedings are generally conducted with some regularity of form as well as fairness of spirit," though he admitted that there were "inexcusable cases."[178] And even in far-away New Mexico territory, the British immigrant settler Edith Nicholl, in her 1898 memoir of twenty years as a rancher, could casually observe that lynchings, while they turned white men into brute beasts, were often the result of "hideous provocation" and that "crusades" against lynching overlooked, in "their hysterical clamour against what they falsely term persecution of the poor negro" the bestiality of the offender and plunge "into that fatal error of sentimentalism."[179] The Welsh poet William Henry Davies, tramping through the South after the turn of the century, attempted a similar justification and told tales of "insulting and arrogant" Negroes with concealed razors in St. Louis, brutal outrages committed by gangs of Negroes in New Orleans, and, near Memphis, a wholly justified small-town lynching of a terrified black man taken from a jail.[180] Lynchings became part of the lore of the American South and South-West (the "unwritten law of the land") and late nineteenth-century travel literature often includes an anecdote or two about them as simply part of the expected narrative.

On the other hand, reports of Southern lynching, as a notorious practice, were also used by some British critics to score points against American society and politics generally, as did Sir Lepel Henry Griffin when he suggested that the *necessity* of lynch law (the "miserable negro," he claimed, was "as fit for the franchise as the monkey he loosely resembles"), due to the corruption of the American courts, "those parodies of justice," was "as much the disgrace of America as the outward sign of its moral decrepitude."[181] In a *Blackwood's* piece by D. J. Bannatyne in 1892, a case where "a negro was roasted to death by lynchers" was held up, like nocturnal visits from vigilantes, duels, and revenge shootings, as simply evidence of a blood-soaked anarchic society of violent, armed "self-assertion."[182] Four years later, Roger Pocock presented the hanging, burning, and flaying of black men as but a part of the "strife between black and white" in contemporary America.[183]

Through the later decades of the nineteenth century and in the early twentieth century, the American South, race relations there, and Jim Crow restrictions on black civil liberties continued to generate some interest in, especially, academic work on the American political system. For many traveling Britons, though, that which had earlier been part of the dynamic of an unfolding American saga became a less interesting, less visit-worthy static set piece—populated with by and large docile and segregated Blacks. As the *Daily Mail* journalist George Warrington Steevens observed at the century's end:

> So there the Southern nigger lives—alongside of the white man yet as far away from him as if he had never left the home of his grandfathers. ... He may not stay in the same hotel, nor travel in the same railway-carriage, nor even worship beside the white ... [yet] he is quite happy and lazy, jolly and improvident ... he is satisfied with his proper position of inferiority. The problem adjusts itself.[184]

There emerged by the 1880s and 1890s a market for entertainments, theatrical and literary, that dwelt nostalgically, if not on lynchings, then on the American Civil War, the Old South, and the doomed nobility of its "cause." This romance of the lost cause came to play well on the fin de siècle London stage and in a new late nineteenth-century genre of adventure novels for boys. In 1890, G. A. Henty, following a novel of 1883 set in the American Civil War (*Friends Though Divided*), published *With Lee in Virginia*, a tale informed by the belief that *Uncle Tom's Cabin* had been "a gross libel" against decent southerners. As he explained, with perhaps also an American readership in mind (the novel was published in New York as well as London):

> The great war between the Northern and Southern States of America possesses a peculiar interest to us, not only because it was a struggle between two sections of a people akin to us in race and language, but because of the heroic courage with which the weaker party ... sustained the contest ... Authorities still differ as to the rights of the case.[185]

Henty's story was an Anglo-American one that involved a young American, educated in Britain, whose father, a British officer "making a tour in the States," had fallen in love with and married a Virginia heiress. The family survives the war, its Virginia estates are restored, and its slaves, treated with kindness and encouragement, are carefully "prepared" to receive their emancipation. The hero and his wife cross the Atlantic for months every year to visit "home." He will, Henty tells us, "not improbably ere long sell his estates in Virginia and settle in England altogether."[186]

Henty's work, like that of Kipling and Rider Haggard, was, of course, the embodiment of the popular culture of Empire, and many of his hundred-plus adventure novels were set on its contested frontiers and in the significant contexts of late-Victorian imperial expansion and the need to incorporate neither enslaved nor fully emancipated non-white populations—from the freedmen of Jamaica to the "niggers" of India, Burma, southern Africa, or Australasia. That America was often considered an informal part of this world-wide realm of Anglo-Saxondom is suggested by the popularity of travel in the late-Victorian era that included the United States in a world or Empire-wide itinerary. Already in 1869 Leslie Stephen, writing anonymously in the *Cornhill Magazine*, observed that "[t]he grand tour of the present day is a trip through America to St. [sic] Francisco, and thence by Australia, Japan, and China, to India, and back by the Holy Land."[187] Dilke's 1866–7 tour around "Greater Britain," including America, set the pattern for many, from Anthony Trollope's Australia, New Zealand, and American tour of 1871, Isabella Bird's 1872–3 journey from Australia to the Rockies, Robert Louis Stevenson's first trek through America to the Pacific coast in 1879, or Kipling's tour from the Raj to Vermont. In 1870, Charles Mackay, writing anonymously in *Blackwood's*, laid out the historical, racial context that enabled and inspired many such excursions: "when the man of white skin goes forth to remote regions … in America, Australia, South Africa, and New Zealand, he goes as a superior being, assumes possession by the right, if not by the divinity, of his colour."[188]

The global realm of the Anglo-world also opened a host of new possibilities to Americans chafing at the bonds of Yankee isolation, just as, from the 1870s on, American authors and artists like Henry James, Whistler, and Sargent chose to make London their home; Bret Harte, Ambrose Bierce and Mark Twain sought at least a temporary refuge there, and Twain would later "follow the equator" in his own swing around the British Empire (Fiji, New Zealand, Australia, Ceylon, India, and South Africa). American actors and playwrights, as we have seen, took their plays, not only to England, but abroad through the English-speaking world. Joseph Jefferson perfected his role as Rip Van Winkle in Australia, the "white dominion" to be, before taking it to London; Boucicault very profitably toured several of his last productions in Australia in 1885. By the turn of the century, it had become relatively common for an actor to take a role that had some success in America, not only to Britain but to South Africa or Australia, or for a touring theatrical company, such as those organized by Charles Frohman, to explore the possibilities at least of empire-wide bookings.

Henry Morton Stanley, a Welsh workhouse orphan who had emigrated to the United States at age eighteen, toured Britain and America after the self-celebration of his *How I Found Livingstone* (1872) and further newspaper-funded expeditions to Africa, offering himself as a form of popular entertainment. Following a very profitable 1886 American lecture tour (he signed a contract with a British impresario for £40,000), he commenced an equally profitable one in Australia.[189] The American West, like the African veldt or the Australian outback, also offered, as in school-boy fiction, tales of Anglosphere empire. In fin de siècle London crowds flocked to see both the display of Zulu warriors at Earl's Court and William F. Cody's Wild West extravaganza.

CHAPTER 4
THE FAR WEST: IMAGINING, SEEING, PERFORMING

In the second half of the nineteenth century the American (and Canadian) far West was a vast canvas of high country, mountain passes, endless-seeming grasslands, and parched desert. Viewed from New York or London, it offered a readily mythologized vista of romance and destiny, of buffalo, rifle-and-revolver-brandishing plainsmen, of gold and silver, survival sagas, cowboys and Indians, of saloons and Mormons. The 1849 gold rush, the swift incorporation of California as the thirty-first state in 1850, and the progressive extension of the first transcontinental railway, complete by 1869, meant that San Francisco became the westward terminus (or the eastward gateway) for those tourists, commercial agents, hunters, prospectors, miners, and settler-immigrants who were drawn to explore the possibilities between the Missouri River and the Pacific. Amid those who found their way out to Texas, Colorado, California, or the Pacific Northwest, there were tens of thousands of Britons (English, Scots, Welsh) and Irish.[1]

Generally speaking, Britons who were attracted to the American West were at first mostly single young and middle-aged men—those looking for work, flâneurs just out of university, entrepreneurial investors and promoters, big game hunters, alpinists, amateur ethnologists, journalists—who were, however, increasingly joined by middle- and upper-class women as the conditions of travel became less onerous. After the Civil War an elaborating rail network weaving across the continent supported an ever more extensive, comfortable (thanks to the Pullman car), cheaper, and faster traffic in men and materiel just as the transcontinental telegraph provided a sense of unbroken connection that stretched eastward across the continent, the Atlantic, and, via the hub of Empire, the whole of the Anglosphere. Encyclopedic guides and companies offering organized "excursions" (such as those promoted by Thomas Cook and Son in London or the Raymond and Whitcomb Company in Boston) proliferated.[2]

As David Wrobel and others have argued, the American West of the late nineteenth century, its representation and what may be called its "cult," was a manifestation of a more general phenomenon. It was "one developing frontier, one colonial enterprise, among many around the globe." There was, that is, a "global West."[3]

1 Westward Ho!

In the Anglo-world generally, the American West rapidly bred, not just the lore of discovery and adventure, but an argot of "ranches" and "broncos," "renegades" and "firewater," "greenhorns" and "six-shooters," "grubstakes" and "buckaroos"—a language drawn from Spanish, native American, cowboy, and prospector usage, and familiar by the 1880s to every schoolboy in Britain. The big game hunter William Baillie-Grohman observed in 1882 that "[t]he lingo of the West" was "rich in happily-coined words," and, citing Schele De Vere, affirmed that "the language of the West *is* an intensified and strangely impulsive speech."[4]

There were of course certain continuities in the British understanding of the frontier—in, for instance, the way "race" continued to be woven into discourse and mythologies, with California as the new embodiment of the American mixing of Anglo-Saxon, Native American, Latin, Black, Irish, and now Asian peoples. As in the earlier, antebellum era, Britons who traveled to the West often offered in their journals an off-hand species of social and political criticism. Most, however, who swept across the plains, over the Rockies, and into California in cushioned comfort were unlikely to reach any deeper understanding of their hosts than does a modern tourist, and their observations are often clichéd and dependent on the prevailing narratives found in other memoirs, the press, guidebooks, and fiction of the day. Others were longer-stayers who sought a deeper relationship with place and peoples, a more profound knowledge of themselves, or simply entrepreneurial advantage. They often exported back to Britain something of the language and style of an especially Western individualism that both resonated with meritocratic Gladstonian Liberalism and clashed with its expectation of a society ruled by law and social order; others found a new social democracy relevant, perhaps, to their own world.

Tourist Itineraries: The American West of Burton, Stevenson, and Wilde

The characteristic late nineteenth-century travel memoir no longer was bound by New York and New England, Chicago and New Orleans, but spilled westward of the Mississippi and Missouri rivers, across the plains to Mormon Salt Lake City, over the Sierra Nevada range, and into San Francisco. It was a world of pullman cars, large hotels, and organized recreation that paralleled the commercial development—often prominently financed by British investors—of a West of mining and railway companies, large-scale ranching, and, at the nodes of travel, urban growth and infrastructure.

The typical travel memoir of these Western excursions might spend a chapter or two on the long, uneventful, and, once the impact of the scale of it all wore off, not very interesting journey through the plains; those who deviated off the main line to the Comstock Lode's Virginia City in the Utah Territory or to Denver and the mining towns of California Gulch and nearby Leadville might dwell on mountain scenery and the eccentricity of hard-drinking mountain men and miners; nearly everyone set aside a chapter or two on Mormon life and utopian Salt Lake City—given color, often, by personal interviews with Brigham Young and, almost invariably, loaded with observations on the moral outrage of polygamy.[5] These texts either begin or end with detailed descriptions of San Francisco, where selective sights became as obligatory as the sausage factories and stockyards of Chicago. San Francisco, though gateway to the wide world of the Pacific and home to a polyglot and often temporary population was, unlike Chicago, less a model of get-ahead America than a unique ("insane" according to Kipling), wide-open circus of alien life where nearly everyone was an immigrant—rough Australian chancers, feminine-seeming Chinese servants, Anglo-, Negro-, and Sino-phobic Irish laborers, the down-and-out of the Barbary Coast, the nouveau riche and the bohemian artists and writers they patronized—in a city that, unlike that other city of immigrants, New York, had no historic traditions or old, moneyed elite.

From the 1840s on, the British press, following the appetite of its readership, was eager to print stories of the American West. Especially after the progressive opening of new rail connections, publishing houses in London, as in New York, also turned out guidebooks and maps, and encouraged a journalism and a fictional literature that worked California, Mormons, and Colorado into tales of Western life among hunters, prospectors, and ranchers. Travel memoirs, even the most derivative and prosaic of them, invoked, in what became a ritualized retelling, something of the romance of a land of gold and silver strikes, quick fortunes, violence, Indian wars, Mexican desperados, and, especially, laconic "cowboys"—a word that had in England meant simply local cowherds before, after mid-century, the colorful American usage, like "buckaroo" from the Spanish "vaquero," came to prevail.

Richard Francis Burton Evidence of the attractions (and marketability) of the West for literary narrative can be found in the established authors who turned to it—the way Frances Trollope or Dickens sought to capitalize on curiosity about antebellum trans-Appalachian America and, in so doing, themselves encouraged the growing travel genre. While first-hand accounts of the gold rush of '49 had created in the eastern United States and in Britain a readership for Western adventure in the early 1850s, the most important of the early transatlantic narratives of the far West as travel literature was Richard Burton's very popular *The City of the Saints, and Across the Rocky Mountains to California*, a narrative of the nine-month tour he made in 1860 before the railroad made the trek West commonplace. There had been a number of accounts by American authors, most notably Horace Greeley's of his transcontinental journey to San Francisco in 1859, published first as letters en route which he sent back to the New York *Tribune* and then collected as a book published in New York just as Burton departed on his own cross-America trip.[6] It was Burton's book, however, that did most to encourage a transatlantic appetite for western narration and, specifically, a long-lasting fascination with the Mormon city in the desert.

Richard Burton (1821–90) was already a well-known author of works that promoted his own foreign adventures. His growing reputation rested on the famous account of his pilgrimage in disguise to Mecca (*Personal Narrative* [1853]) and subsequent, often violent, explorations in Africa (*First Footsteps in East Africa* [1856] and *The Lake Regions of Central Africa* [1860]). He intended, he tells us, for his American westward journey to Salt Lake City to add a new name to the list of "holy cities" he had visited. The tone of much of the book may suggest the casual detachment of the tourist (in San Francisco he said he was "grateful to *flaner* about the stirring streets, to admire the charming faces, to enjoy the delicious climate"[7]). In fact, Burton had characteristically prepared carefully for his trip by reading all the American authors he could find on the West—including Randolph Barnes Marcy's guide, *The Prairie Traveler, A Hand-Book for Overland Expeditions* (1859), and doubtless Edwin Bryant's travel journal of 1848, *What I Saw in California*, available in two British editions, along with other works by geographer-explorers and soldiers such as John C. Frémont, Howard Stansbury, and John Williams Gunnuson. He also collected all the "polemical" works he could find on Mormonism,[8] and brought along a copy of Bartlett's *Dictionary of Americanisms*, becoming something of an aficionado of American drinking slang and cursing.[9] Burton did not intend to present his travels as a mere "photographic" description for "our realistic age," but to engage the American West, and the Mormon project in particular, rather as he had sought to understand Islam—the book is full of comparisons with India, Arabia, and Africa—by getting beneath conventional representations. In this, he was, famously, an outsider in a world of middle-class Victorian religious and sexual piety.

Burton approached the West obliquely, spending weeks, first in New York with the publisher handling the American edition of his book on Central Africa, then wandering down to Washington, DC and on to New Orleans before heading out to St. Louis. From St. Louis, armed with two Colt revolvers and a Bowie knife, he launched a three-week stage-coach journey to Salt Lake City, where he stayed some three weeks before heading for San Francisco via the new mining center of Carson City. His approach to the *Book of Mormon*, the practice of Mormonism, and especially the much-sensationalized institution of polygamy (he compared Mormon "harems" with those of Africa and the Near East), was neither patronizing nor satirical. He, as had Greeley, interviewed Brigham Young (an "affable and impressive, simple and courteous man"), attended Mormon services and social events, and spoke with many of the thousands of European emigrants, British, Irish, and Scandinavian, who had trekked out to find a home in the desert and to make it bloom. To Burton's well-traveled eye, the Mormons were a tolerant and progressive people, if conservative in their religion ("the faith of the poor") and supportive of slavery.[10]

Burton's tale of his journey westward from St. Louis via army outposts and dusty, isolated staging settlements, his attempt to satisfy curiosity about the often demonized Mormons, and his exploration of the delights of San Francisco proved to be a publishing success in both the United States and London. It was influential, in spite of his heterodox opinions about religion and marriage, not in winning wide acceptance for Brigham Young's experiment but in encouraging others to follow—especially after rail service made the trip doable in a fraction of the time and with less revolver-armed precaution and more comfort. The flood of tourism, and of writers like Dilke and Dixon intending to bring the plains, the mountains, and the Pacific coast to a wide readership, would have happened anyway, but it is safe to say that Burton's account became standard reading for those planning to follow him. Indeed, he himself contributed footnotes to the 1863 edition of Marcy's handbook for tourists, *The Prairie Traveler*.[11]

Not only tourist memoirs but fictional accounts of the Wild West proliferated transatlantically in these years, in boys' weeklies and on publishers' lists, often mixing adventure, social criticism of modern life, and sometimes satire. This was a genre that had grown from before mid-century, from novels invoking the solemn majesty of nature, as in Percy St. John's *The Trapper's Bride: A Tale of the Rocky Mountains* (1845), or the frontier novels of Mayne Reid, such as his *Rifle Rangers* (1850) and *The Scalp Hunters; or Romantic Adventures in Northern Mexico* (1851)—a tale of an Englishman who lived in the borderlands among Santa Fe traders. Reid was very prolific, and the market for what he offered only grew over time. It was met in the next generation by, for instance, the Canadian and American frontier novels of the Scottish writer of juvenile fiction, Robert M. Ballantyne (1825–94)—*Fort Desolation; Or, Solitude in the Wilderness* (1874), for instance, is about a public school boy who runs away to sea and discovers "the romance of life" in western Canada. Ballantyne's stories also attempted to sustain a Cooperesque mythology of the native American in stories like *The Red Man's Revenge* (1880). *The Prairie Chief* (1886) is a tale of "a Red Indian of the North American Plains," Whitewing—a man of "courage, strength, agility, and … a deep thinker."[12]

The British appetite for tales of western adventure, of cowboys and Indians, was fed by the rising tide of travel memoirs like Burton's, by the exhibition in Britain of western landscapes and native American artifacts and portraiture, by accounts of the Indian wars in America in the 1870s and the memorializing/mythologizing of the death of General Custer. Henty, in addition to his two novels about Civil War Virginia, contributed to the late Victorian stream of Western adventure a number of stories, including *Captain Bayley's Heir: A Tale of the Gold Fields of California* (1889), *Red Skin and Cowboy: A Tale of the Western Plains* and *The Ranche in the Valley* (both 1892), *In the Heart of the Rockies: A Story of Adventure in Colorado* (1895), and *The Golden Canyon* (1899).[13] Apart from the gush of adventure fiction, there also emerged a generation of American authors published in Britain that included notably among others Mark Twain, Bret Harte, and Ambrose Bierce, each of whom came to California after the gold rush era in search of a career in journalism and would later spend at least some time in London. When Iza Dufus Hardy traveled out to Salt Lake City and San Francisco in the 1880s, she carried "well-worn copies of Mark Twain and Bret Harte which attest to our diligent study of the manners, customs, and phraseology of the great West."[14]

RLS By the end of the 1870s the American far West can be said to have become routinely accessible for British travelers—more directly accessible certainly than southern Africa, Australia, or the Raj—not only for leisured middle- and upper-middle-class tourists seeking recreation and sport, but for those, often young men of scanty resources, who were willing to endure the crowded discomfort of second-class travel. It also drew a crowd of businessmen of all kinds, speculative investors in mines, railways, cattle, and agricultural properties, as well as those promoting their own services. One finds many actors, singers, and artists who, either with traveling troupes or individually, sought to perform their trade in western cities where venues for opera, theater, and art were often among the first order of civic development[15] and in booming mining camps before enthusiastic if undiscriminating audiences. Others came searching for health in the dry air of the West or perhaps hoped to find an American wife. The young, tubercular Scottish writer Robert Louis Stevenson (1850–94) was looking for both.

Stevenson struggled in the autumn of 1879, with narrow resources and bad health, across the country to California where he was reunited with an older married (soon to be divorced) American woman he had met in France. Fanny Van de Grift Osbourne, an independent-minded short-story writer and amateur painter who had left her husband, traveled to Europe, and then moved with her children to Monterey and San Francisco, nursed him back to a semblance of health, and would become his wife in May the next year.

Stevenson had traveled out with the intention, he says, of also finding copy. His popular novels of adventure came in the next decade or so, but unlike those of his fellow Scot, Ballantyne, they would hardly ever involve American stories. He would, however, compose from his travels a number of extended travel essays derived from his personal experiences crossing the American continent. *The Amateur Emigrant*, written in 1879–80, would be published posthumously in 1895; *Across the Plains* (the continuation of the journey, also written in 1879–80), in 1892. But, like many traveling writers seeking some immediate compensation, he also offered to do pieces for periodicals. *Longman's Magazine* published an abbreviated version of "Across the Plains" in 1883. Other articles appeared in American and British journals like *Scribner's* and *Fraser's*. He wrote, but did not publish, an account of his stay in Monterey, California, in the last months of 1879, and his honeymoon trip to Napa Valley resulted in *The Silverado Squatters* (1883).[16] Some years later, in 1887, Stevenson and Fanny, accompanied by his recently widowed mother, crossed again to America. He intended to travel to Colorado for his health, but ended up spending the winter in the Adirondacks instead, where he began *The Master of Ballantrae, A Winter's Tale*, a novel that concluded with scenes set in eighteenth-century New York and the American wilderness.

Like Burton, Stevenson was something of an outsider—an agnostic bohemian with the looks of a long-haired, semi-invalid aesthete, perhaps of an ambiguous sexuality, and, in the western parlance, a "loner"—as suggested in the well-known, if peculiar, portrait by Sargent, who, like the other ex-pat American Henry James, Stevenson came to know in London and Bournemouth. His writings about his American journey have a quality of a novelist's crafted arrangement that makes them superior, as literature, to much of the contemporary one-thing-after-another travel memoir. Echoing Burton's claim that he did not mean to offer photographs of reality, Stevenson would tell Henry James that, contrary to what he took to be James's own practice, he believed the object of writing, that is the art of narrative, was not to reproduce infinite material "confusions" of detail but to offer abstracted and harmonious patterns.[17]

Traveling across the ocean in second class, and across the American continent in crowded "emigrant trains," 29-year-old Stevenson attempted to present the country from the perspective, not of a world-traveling imperial flâneur, but of a hopeful migrant of modest means for whom America seemed an open land of possibilities. If there is no evidence he packed Bartlett's *Dictionary of Americanisms* as Burton had, he did travel with the six volumes of George Bancroft's *History of the United States*, and he had read the American adventure novels of the French writer Gustave Aimard, the "Dumas of the Indians."

The Far West: Imagining, Seeing, Performing

Stevenson claimed that from childhood America had been a "favourite home of my imagination."[18] He admired Whitman's *Leaves of Grass*, and in his record of his journey invokes "the sentiment with which spirited English youths turn to the thought of the American Republic":

> It seems to them as if, out west, the war of life was still conducted in the open air, and on free and barbaric terms; as if it had not yet been narrowed into parlours, nor begun to be conducted, like some unjust and dreary arbitration, by compromise, costume, forms of procedure, and sad, senseless self-denial.[19]

But his West, a "promised land," is also already a land of lost innocence—a California where an "ugly" Anglo-Saxon Protestantism has supplanted the pastoral work of the Jesuits and has ushered in a new era of "greedy land-thieves and sacrilegious pistol shots." As in the once-quiet town of Monterey, huge resorts "for wealth and fashion" have sprung up and "the poor, quaint, penniless native gentlemen of Monterey must perish, like a lower race, before the millionaire vulgarians of the Big Bonanza."[20]

San Francisco was the end objective of most of the railway tourism into the far West. Stevenson found the city fascinating, and his accounts depart somewhat from the critical tone of his commentary about the vulgarity of Californians on the make. Though Victorian San Francisco might offer a wide range of exotic subjects for discussion and contemplation, by the time Stevenson, Wilde, and later Kipling came to write about it, British tourist memoirists, one after another, often reduced their experiences there to a Baedeker-like round of sights—first on the list, an obligatory tour of Chinatown, followed invariably by a trip to Cliff House to see the sea-lions and scenic views of the Golden Gate, the narrow entrance to San Francisco Bay. For most Britons "doing" the town, San Francisco might be said to be the first specifically "tourist-city" in America, a metropolis of new palace-like hotels and an urban experience that offered a tableau of color and a safely-distanced frisson of the strange and exotic. Sketch-artists made a profession, before Kodak, of selling views and post-cards; guides proliferated for city tours and coach excursions to see Yosemite or the redwoods.

In San Francisco Stevenson drops his identification with the modest immigrant and embraces the role of the leisured observer. Like Oscar Wilde a year or two later, he became an aesthete framing a "scene." His account opens, not, as others did, with the mundane business of collecting luggage at the rail terminus in Oakland, but with an impressionist painting-like description of the fresh, salt-aired, gleaming white hills, crowned with "palaces," as viewed from the entrance of the Bay, a "sparkling picture." Much of the fascination, for Stevenson, lies not in the comfort of finding, as in Boston, a city that reminds one of the civilized familiarity of home, but in the strangeness, the daily apprehension of earthquake and fire, and the fact that San Francisco seems not an *American* city at all, nor even an Anglo-Saxon one, but a locus for the "mingling" of races, "a strange country" with "the airs of Marseilles or of Peking." For Stevenson, San Francisco is a "magic lantern city," where one can sit and observe the Mexican, the "blue-clad Chinaman," the "soft-spoken brown Kanaka, or perhaps a waif from far-away

Malaya." Chinatown offers a "cabinet of curiosities." "Of all romantic places for a boy to loiter in, that Chinese quarter is the most romantic," where interest is heightened "with a chill of horror"—"cellars," one hears, "are alive with mystery; opium dens … unknown vices and cruelties … the secret lazarettos of disease."[21] The San Francisco of Stevenson's imagination is not a matter of "sights" to be ticked off, but both a place "to explore"— there was a hidden, secret life of the city—and a stage where crimes of violence, six-shooter revenge, and vigilantism are likely to be played out before one's eyes.[22]

Oscar Wilde Both Stevenson and his somewhat younger contemporary Oscar Wilde (1854–1900) were of a post-mid-century generation. Neither was much concerned, as hard-faced Burton, the seasoned and scarred explorer had been, to "go native" and dig down with an unjudgmental determination to discover an America from within and on its own terms. By the time they made their way westward, there remained in fact little more to be said about the familiar itinerary sights, catalogued in great detail in guidebooks such as that by the American journalist and travel writer Charles Nordhoff (*California: For Health, Pleasure, and Residence* [1873]), the same year Thomas Cook published an American edition of *Cook's Excursionist*, and, especially, the many cheap editions of George Crofutt's *Overland Tourist and Pacific Coast Guide*. The new 1879 edition[23] included "One Thousand Two Hundred Cities, Towns, Villages, Stations, Government Fort and Camps, Mountains, Lakes, Rivers, Sulphur, Soda and Hot Springs, Scenery, Watering Places, and Summer Resorts." Nor were Stevenson and Wilde ready, as had been Frances Trollope and Dickens, to hold an inquest on the country's manifest sins. Their West was one of eccentric and sometimes romanticized characters and panoramic views—human as well as geographic. Their art of telling was counterpoised against the superficiality of the conventional travel writer.

Unlike Stevenson's journey, motivated by private needs and withheld for years from full publication, Wilde's Western venture was intended to play out in a burst of immediate publicity. His 1882 travels were ongoing, unfolding public relations exercises, as well as likely "earners" (he told Boucicault, "Let me gather the golden fruits of America that I may spend a winter in Italy and a summer in Greece amidst beautiful things"[24]). It was as much a performance and promotion of himself as a discovery of the real America. Sent across the Atlantic by D'Oyly Carte to advertise Bunthorne's aestheticism, Wilde would over-perform the role in knee-breeches and silk stockings. Traveling on to the far West, where, now sporting furs, boots, and a wide-brimmed hat, he could claim, in a characteristically witty inversion of the expected, that he found there something not available in the over-valued, "civilized" East—Philadelphia was "dreadfully provincial" and Boston, a "paradise of prigs."[25] The West offered not merely a sweeping magnitude and a "paradise of beauty," but local life that, uninformed by any formal appreciation of Art, was nonetheless itself artistic.

Matinee audiences of ladies in San Francisco or rough miners in Leadville, he claimed, hung on his words as he lectured them about "The House Beautiful" or the nature of the Gothic. Wilde's posing was, of course, aimed at securing a reputation. An annoyed Edward

Freeman, on a lecturing tour in the United States, claimed that he "knew nothing about Mr. Oscar Wilde" before coming to America where his name "was then [1882] to be seen in large letters on the walls, as his photographs, in various attitudes, were to be seen in the windows."[26] Wilde, on his return, immediately commenced a lecture tour of England, speaking on "Impressions of America." His carefully crafted aperçus often inverted and contradicted the common observations of the conventional travel memoir—"from the ordinary standpoint I know little about the country," "I was disappointed with Niagara."[27]

Wilde turned upside-down British "knowledge" of the American West while at the same time acknowledging its clichés. Whether or not he in fact intended to convince his readers of anything other than his own cleverness, his collected observations, picked up and broadcast by the journalists who followed him, became probably the most visible of the late-nineteenth-century commentaries—playing their own part in the creation of a mythology of the West (as in his oft-quoted recollection of a placard at a Leadville saloon, "Please do not shoot the piano player, he is doing his best"). It is doubtful, of course, that those Leadville miners who, he claimed, "dressed for comfort and obtained the beautiful"[28] actually did hang on his every word about the Renaissance sculptor and artist Benvenuto Cellini or their countryman, the ex-pat James Whistler. In Wilde's own way, his West was as much an invention of a mobile, playful imagination as were the contemporary romances of cowboy-and-Indian fiction. And the effeminacy of Wilde's performance of aestheticism only set off, like his admiration for the bronzed body of the African-American servant or his affirmation of the unintentional beauty of the miners' flowing drapery, the masculinity of that West presented to the British public in London by the long-haired Californian poet, the "American Byron" Joaquin Miller, who dressed as a Spanish vaquero, or the ruggedly handsome, long-haired, buckskin-wearing Buffalo Bill.[29]

Hunting, Ranching, and an "Empire of the Mind"[30]

In California, the young Charles Dilke, having traveled westward "through the dry air of a continent four thousand miles across," observed "you are at last in a new world."[31] Dilke and others who traveled through the West by rail and coach in the 1860s and early 1870s had been preceded since at least the gold rush days by the more focused (and more rigorous) tourism of an often-affluent class of British sportsmen looking for American game—elk (wapiti) and mountain sheep in the Rockies and bison and antelope in the plains. Such well-published Western adventures might be regarded as yet another aspect of what Dilke would call the spreading realm of "Greater Britain." The fashion for big game hunting, like other rituals of recreational consumption, characterized a mid- and late-Victorian imperialism that was not confined to the formal Empire. In the words of Lord Dunraven,

> I hope no one labours under the delusion that hunting is a mere barbarous, bloodthirsty sport … The reward of the hunter is the same as that of the student of languages, of the archaeologist, of the geologist … His triumph is the triumph of unravelling a mystery … [32]

Francis Francis, Jr., novelist and raconteur, would comment, after a tour of the West in 1882, on "the sense of freedom and independence—of empire, in fact, that the vast stretches of open country which occupy most of the West beget in the native of a land [England] where walls and hedges, gates, fences, and trespass notices bristle at every turn."[33] Like life on the imperial frontiers generally, it also offered a largely masculine world of close male bonding—something that an outdoorsman like Dunraven, with his fondness for the companionship of his Scots gillie and his favorite guide, Texas Jack (manly but "gentle as a woman"[34]), may especially have valued.

Hunting expeditions, in America as in Asia and Africa, became ever more routinized, commercially organized, and populated by an aristocratic and an upper and upper middle class of hunter-tourists. Co-opting local guides and their lore, they came to project a kind of personal colonization that paralleled the significant British financial investment (and threat of foreign control) that drew the ire and apprehension of some Western American Anglophobic nationalists. In the 1850s, a number of extravagant hunting expeditions by the scions of British aristocracy and landed gentry were well (and often critically) reported in the American press—that of the Hon. Henry Coke, a younger son of the Earl of Leicester, and his Etonian friend Lord Durham, or the Hon. Charles Wentworth-Fitzwilliam, younger son of Earl Fitzwilliam, or, especially, the absentee Irish landlord Sir St. George Gore, Bt., who traveled out to Colorado in 1854 with a substantial entourage to kill 2,000 buffalo, 1,600 deer and elk, 105 bears, and thousands of mountain sheep, coyotes, and timber wolves.[35]

The itineraries of British hunting expeditions often began in British North America, and followed the game down through the Rockies to Colorado, accompanied by large retinues of guides, camp followers, and, sometimes, domestic servants, horses, and weaponry brought from Britain (Thornhill's of New Bond Street offered a variety of large-game hunting paraphernalia). By the 1870s the knowledgeable were more likely to fit out their expeditions among the eastern American mercantile establishments that specialized in servicing them—thus avoiding the 35 percent duty the United States levied on imported saddles, guns, and other equipment. Such hunting expeditions, challenging at mid-century due to the unfamiliarity of the terrain and the supposed dangers of hostile natives, became routine, the routes serviced by professional guides and marked by the spread of seasonal campsites and new towns. The spread of farming in the plains and the disappearance of the over-hunted buffalo meant that the more inaccessible areas of, especially, Colorado became the favored locale, but even this "wilderness" was ever more accessible by rail. Denver, which had first boomed due to the rush to explore for gold and silver, subsequently grew also due to its role as jumping-off point for hunters and tourists. Though an English emigrant settler attempting to encourage others to come out may have been exaggerating when, in 1878, he claimed that Denver was already "perhaps the most English city in America," by the 1880s, thanks to the efforts of the London homeopathic doctor and railway survey consultant William A. Bell and others, the planned community and resort of Colorado Springs had indeed become practically a British colonial town (and was nicknamed "Li'l Lunnon").[36] When young Allayne Beaumont Legard (late of the 60th Foot serving in Canada), who deeply disliked most "surly" "Yanks" ("I return with an inward loathing at the very thought of some of them"), wrote up his three-month trip to the American West in 1872, he seems to have encountered fellow Englishmen wherever he went in Colorado—farmers, ranchers, and other emigrants and visitors (including the son of the English historian, novelist, and Christian Socialist the Rev. Charles Kingsley). There was an English gentleman setting up a cheese factory (his manager was also an Englishman), another "on his voyage around the world," and, finally, a cook and ranch hand near Colorado Springs who had attended southeast London's Blackheath proprietary school "against whom I had played many a football match."[37]

Those Britons who went out for the sport of hunting, guidebook in hand (Crofutt's claimed to tell one where "to look for and hunt the Buffalo, Antelope, Deer and other

Figure 3 A Briton in buckskins: Charles William Wilson, photo *c.* 1860 [Alamy].

game; Trout Fishing, etc., etc."[38]), like those who later took up speculative ranching in the West, commonly if self-consciously adopted the dress of—that is performed—the American tracker/hunter and cowboy. Clad in furs, buckskin, or chaps, they posed before the camera, just as they scattered Westernisms in their speech, letters home, and published travel accounts. In the American West, though many tourists necessarily maintained a distance that was dictated by railway timetables and hurried itineraries, those who came to spend time there, who pursued a longer-lasting interest in hunting or ranching away from the main rail routes, often enjoyed, if only temporarily, playing the part.

Windham Thomas Wyndham-Quinn, 4th Earl of Dunraven and Mount-Earl (1841–1926), a wealthy British peer, sometime minor Unionist politician, Anglo-Irish landlord (of some 40,000 acres), and proprietor of twenty-two collieries in Wales, was the best-known of the aristocratic sportsmen in the late nineteenth century who promoted "cleansing, healing" recreation in the vast forested solitude of the Canadian and American West, and especially the sharp air of the Rockies, as a kind of antidote to the ills of modern life.[39] As the young Lord Adare, Dunraven had read all, or so he claimed, of Mayne Reid's American adventure novels (Reid "haunted my boyish dreams"[40]). Looking back to 1869 from 1922, Dunraven recalled of his first trip to America that

> I was young—not twenty-eight years of age; and my boyish brain-cells were stored to bursting with tales of Red Indians and grizzly bears, caballeros and haciendas, prairies and buffaloes, Texans and Mexicans, cowboys and voyageurs ....[41]

An avid hunter and sportsman in the West from the early 1870s, he also, famously or infamously, began to acquire—in the face of considerable local opposition—tens of thousands of acres of Colorado wilderness and promoted there the largest sequestered private park in America.

Dunraven was in the beginning dependent, as were most British sportsmen in the West, on the skills of local guides and hunters, a class of facilitators that flourished in the 1860s and 1870s, becoming themselves often a mythologized race of larger-than-life plains- and mountain-men with a cultivated reputation, such as the well-known and long-lived scout and trapper Jim Bridger (1804–81), hired by St. George Gore for his buffalo shoot in 1854, Isabella Bird's guide in Colorado, one-eyed, grizzly-bear killing "Rocky Mountain Jim" Nugent (shot dead in 1874), "Buffalo Bill" (William Frederick) Cody (1846–1917), or "Texas Jack" (John Baker) Omohundro (1846–80). Texas Jack had served both as a Confederate "boy scout" during the Civil War and as a civilian scout for the US Army during the Indian Wars. Dunraven found him, with his "laughing honest blue eyes," to be "a model for a typical modern Anglo-Saxon," and used his services from Canada to Nebraska, Wyoming, Montana, and Colorado.[42] Texas Jack died young (age thirty-three) in Leadville, already a legendary figure of pulp novels. He had also turned to acting and joined Cody in 1872 in the first Wild West show, "Scouts of the Prairie;" in 1877 he formed his own acting troupe in St. Louis to perform self-mythologizing plays such as "Texas Jack in the Black Hills" to some acclaim.[43]

Those Britons who came for hunting as sport, and who posed in the part of the American frontiersman, would return home with trophies and club-talk of the American wildernesses. Isabella Bird, a deeper explorer of the American West, knew and disliked the type. In her recollection of life in the Rockies at Dunraven's Estes Park, she told the London readers of the illustrated magazine *Leisure Hour* of a young officer in the Guards from a good family who traveled to Colorado as a companion of the "celebrated hunter" Bob Craik. "[I]n spite of his rough hunter's or miner's dress, I at once recognized [him] as an English gentleman … with a Lord Dundreary drawl and a general execration of everything." Such "high-toners" as they were called in Colorado "make themselves," she thought, "ludicrously absurd."[44]

Dunraven himself was far from a foppish tourist, though he treated Colorado as a kind of personal holiday resort to which he made annual summer excursions from Britain. However, he increasingly became the butt of criticism in the Western press as an encroaching aristocrat and absentee Irish landlord with a retired British army officer as his land agent. Though he himself had once written, in reference to the proposed preservation of Yellowstone as a national park, that "[n]othing is so abominable as the system of buying up scenery on speculation,"[45] he used the Homestead Act of 1862—intended to encourage the settlement of the West and Mid-West by family farmers—to amass thousands of acres (his agent hired land claimers and then bought up their parcels). This inevitably drew sharp criticism and legal challenges. He succeeded in keeping the titles, but the area was too vast to stop encroachment and he turned to developing his estate into a tourist attraction, hired an artist (Albert Bierstadt) to paint romantic mountain scenery, built a large hotel, set up a company in London to administer the estate, and turned tourist-promoter, telling the British readers of the *Nineteenth Century*,

> [Colorado's] scenery is varied, beautiful, grand, and even magnificent. Crystal streams of pure, wholesome water rush down the hill-sides; play at hide-and-seek in the woods, and wander deviously through the parks. The climate is health-giving—unsurpassed, as I believe, anywhere …[46]

But by the mid-1880s, disliking the loss of privacy, he ceased his own visits and eventually (in 1908) sold his holdings as unprofitable and too onerous to administer.[47]

Dunraven's was an especially notorious case of encroachment by the British, due to the size of his ambitions and his personal background as a very wealthy aristocrat. There was in fact a seeming window of opportunity in the late 1870s and early 1880s—it closed thereafter—for British and Irish landlords, motivated perhaps by the precipitous fall in income from their landed estates and a worsening political situation at home, to invest in the American West. Though in the face of the vastness of western territory the actual extent of acreage purchased by the landed British aristocracy in America was far less than many Americans came to assume, the press in the 1880s seized upon the charge of rich and titled foreign "land grabbers." The much-publicized tour through the West of the Duke of Sutherland and his heir in 1881 looking, it was said, for investment opportunities in land and railroads,[48] or the notoriety of the American land holdings of an aggressively evicting Irish landlord such as John George ("Black Jack") Adair, coincided with the rising agitation—in America as in Ireland—of Irish radicals against Anglo-Irish landlordism. In 1881 Colorado passed a resolution of sympathy for Michael Davitt and his Irish Land League. The Anglophobic *Chicago Daily Tribune* warned that the Republic was in danger "if the seeds of absentee landlordism" were allowed to grow and produce its "fruits of poverty and degradation … The ancestors of the men who are now stealing the fairest portions of the public domain stole the lands of Ireland 200 years ago."[49]

Many of the British who traveled to the States to oversee their investments in American land, while preserving a (sometimes inflated) sense of their social caste, were on the margin only of the landed aristocracy, if that—third or fourth sons of lesser landed families with little chance of an inheritance, or simply "gentlemen's" sons. Some, like Moreton Frewen (1853–1924),[50] a friend or at least an acquaintance of Lord Dunraven, were social climbers hoping to leverage some success in America into an enhanced position back in England. The Eton and Cambridge educated fifth son of an untitled landed Leicestershire Member of Parliament, Frewen went out to America, age twenty-five, with introductions to the well-connected, to try his hand at whatever entrepreneurial opportunities might arise. This proved the first trip in a transatlantic career—he claimed he made over 100 crossings—but his ventures often proved notoriously unlucky (Moreton Frewen would come to be known in clubland as "Mortal Ruin") in spite of his fortuitous marriage in 1881 to an heiress in New York City, Clara Jerome, older sister of the Jenny Jerome who had in 1874 become the wife of Lord Randolph Churchill.

From the late 1870s there was a rush to register American cattle companies in Great Britain.[51] Frewen's own ranch enterprise in Wyoming was registered in London as a joint stock company with the Duke of Manchester as chairman of the board, before collapsing—like many of Frewen's ventures (he had also invested in Texas bat guano)—in 1889. Less socially ambitious than Frewen, John Baumann had as a youth in the early 1870s gone out to the Rockies and the Sierra Nevada for a few months of sport and adventure and had, he later recalled, seen "only the picturesque side of frontier life." He returned in the 1880s, driven by "exigencies" in Britain, to "make my fortune" in Texas or New Mexico—through an "apprenticeship as a cow-boy"—by getting a position as manager of one of the many large ranches founded by English and Scot companies. Three years later, in 1886, he told the readers of the *Cornhill* magazine that, though the cowboys he came to know could be "shockingly cruel, hasty in temper, and unbridled in tongue," their life "joins courage, stoic indifference to suffering, and dogged industry" while offering an escape from "[t]he cringing servility born of centuries of strongly marked class-distinction."[52] Only a year later, however, annoyed at the distance between the romanticized image and a gritty, comfortless reality, he complained in the *Fortnightly Review* that "[t]he Cowboy has at present day become a personage; nay, more, he is rapidly becoming a mythical one."[53]

Despite the warnings of some like Baumann and the vicissitudes of the cattle industry, especially for absentee British investors who were dependent often on self-interested agents, the image of the American cowboy and the romance of the western ranch continued in the 1880s and 1890s to flourish in popular culture. In 1878, for instance, William Black, a Scottish journalist and novelist, published a story that features a suntanned and blue-eyed cowboy, "Buckskin Charlie," who works for a Colorado ranch- and mine-owning English "Colonel," actually a former ne'er-do-well known as "Five-Ace Jack" who has, nevertheless, reformed and, dying, leaves his ranch to his niece (an earl's daughter) and her bankrupted husband. They, in a happy denouement, travel out to enjoy their Western salvation.[54]

It remains unclear how much American ranch and agricultural land came under the control of wealthy foreign investors as states attempted to impose limitations on foreign ownership. There were a number of ways around these laws—through dummy corporations and silent partners or by conveniently taking American citizenship. By the time an Alien Landlord Bill made its way through Congress (in 1887), limiting, in theory, an individual or company to no more than 5,000 acres in the territories (existing titles were not affected), the peak period of aristocratic investment in American land appears to have passed. At the height of the "cattle bonanza," there were some thirty-three cattle companies capitalized at more than $37 million registered in Britain, with ten major Anglo-American companies incorporated in 1882 alone. The rush to invest in cattle land (in Canada as in the United States) saw, in Edinburgh as in London, the mushrooming of companies that were eager to send out agents to both sides of the North American border to scout the possibilities. And in 1888, amid great chagrin and alarm, the storied Chicago Union Stockyards themselves were sold to a London syndicate. By the mid-eighties, in the context of a general economic depression, however, a swift and very considerable slippage in British enthusiasm for investment in American ranching became evident. Whether this is due to apprehension of further legislation, the animosity of local governments, popular complaint and ostracism, or the severe weather of the early eighties is unclear.

Nevertheless, some British investors like William "Lord" Scully continued from the 1870s to the end of the century to accumulate, through a web of agents, substantial holdings—if not in western ranching, then in mid-west farming. Scully was misnamed in the American press as a "lord of London, England."[55] He was in fact, if not an aristocrat, a notorious and severe Irish landowner who would by the 1890s acquire through one subterfuge or another—he finally crossed the ocean to take American citizenship, and then returned to London—some 40,000 or 50,000 acres in Missouri and some 220,000 acres more in Nebraska, Kansas, and Illinois. Those opposed to British land-grabbing claimed that he "rack-rented" his hundreds of American tenants.[56] Real "lords," meanwhile, appear to have turned from direct investment in American territory to a search for the American heiresses whose dowries would enable them to continue to possess unprofitable landed estates in Britain.

Though Dunraven's Western land-hunger was, we may suppose, motivated more by a kind of personal thrill at holding empire over expanses of scenery and the wildlife that dwelt there than turning a sharp profit, the era was marked by a considerable number of would-be wealthy Britons seeking to find tangible American assets with a good rate of return. Much of the Western economy, its railways, mines, and large agricultural enterprises, was available to investors on the London stock exchange, and British entrepreneurs ran agents throughout the West seeking possibilities, just as Americans looking for capital sent agents not only to New York but to London.

The story of the British in the West was also one of the more modest enterprise of those, often of the middle or upper-middle classes with a little capital, attracted by the romance of the West and encouraged by the printed memoirs of hunters and by the promotional literature of financial investors and their agents who hoped to sell on the tracts of empty territory they had acquired. This wave of migrants came to settle, to farm or run herds of cattle that would provide a reasonable living in a West that had become (in Britain) a storied land of opportunity. Inevitably many, like those who had rushed to buy land at knock-down prices in post-bellum Virginia, were disappointed and moved on or returned to Britain. Their memoirs offer a sometimes embittered, sometimes ironic alternative to the travel literature of short-staying tourists.

In Britain, the early published accounts of hunters such as Dunraven or William Baillie-Grohman[57] evolved often into a more calculated boosterism. As we have seen with Dunraven, the line between a boyish enthusiasm grounded in one's own experiences and a subsequent need to "sell" the West was a thin one. Baillie-Grohman, after repeated tours in the 1870s for mountain-climbing and big game hunting, returned to British Columbia to combine hunting with settlement and ranching. He invested in a London-registered land company (that secured nearly 80,000 acres in BC), and worked through the 1880s to promote these interests in periodicals such as the *Fortnightly Review* or *The Field, the Country Gentleman's Newspaper*,[58] before finally returning to London where, in his later years, he followed a sedentary career as a historian of European hunting and a collector of trophies and the arcana of stalking, trapping, and shooting.

Baillie-Grohman might glowingly claim that "[i]f you would see the English character to its full advantage, hie from Pall Mall and St. James's Street to some Colorado ranche [sic] or Kansas farm" where "you will find the survival of what has gained England her grand repute—sterling manliness and uncompromising honesty,"[59] but, with an eye to the settling of the *Canadian* West, his advice to Britons intending to emigrate and "to settle as cowboys" in America also included a cautious reminder that, though land was cheap or free in the United States, it was a world where the "right of perfect equality" meant a rough society where "possession is nine-points of the law, and the tenth is that ever-present law-maker and law-breaker, the Colt revolver."[60]

The lure of the American West for Britons intending to try their hands at ranching and farming is evident in the trail of reports, memoirs, and sometimes regrets that they published—as a kind of sub-genre of the era's travel literature. Their ventures were accompanied, especially in the late 1870s and early 1880s, by accounts of the West that were meant at least to inform intending emigrants and often to encourage them. In 1876, a journalist, Samuel Nugent Townshend, was sent as a member of a British delegation to report on agriculture in the American West. As "St. Kames," he wrote prolifically for the *Field* and other British journals, encouraging emigration to ranch and farm, especially in Colorado (as "there are almost no Irishmen in it" [!]) and observing that already "almost every third ranche [sic] there" was "English property."[61] In 1877 James Macdonald was commissioned by the *Scotsman*, an Edinburgh daily, to go to the American West and report back both on the development of the beef industry (in the expectation that growing American production and refrigeration would undermine the profitability of Scottish beef production) and on the prospects for the emigration of Scots, Irish, and English farmers: "a trip to America is now thought no more of than a journey from Aberdeen to Edinburgh fifty years ago."[62] Other reports on prospects in America followed, such as James and William Close's pamphlet *Stock Raising and Sheep Farming in Northwestern Iowa* (1879), or James Selwin Tait's *The Cattle-Fields of the Far West: Their Present and Future* (1884), often with vested interests to promote: the Close brothers, after leaving Cambridge University, had helped organize the British "colony" of Le Mars in Iowa and then founded a firm there to help direct would-be emigrants to such settlements, and to advise on land purchases, the building of houses, the fitting them out with "machinery, implements, stoves, furniture … at wholesale prices," the establishing of co-operatives, etc.[63] Tait was a member of a firm of "Cattle Ranch and Land Brokers" that dealt out of Edinburgh and New York.

Promoters may have had some success in encouraging emigration, farming, and ranching in the American West, but for many young men, such as William French, a "younger son," there was also an element of serendipity in their decision to settle. Getting a letter from a friend who had gone out to northern California, he took off with little planning and happened to fall in with a trio of recent Cambridge graduates en route to a ranch in New Mexico. He "threw in my lot with my new chums,"[64] and ended up managing a large ranch for a settler who then returned to Ireland to marry and enjoy the life of an absentee landlord.

While there was some concern in the 1870s and 1880s that emigrants to the United States from Britain would thus be "lost" to a British Empire that needed them, for the most part the American West was seen by its British promoters as a logical and admirable extension of frontier Anglo-Saxondom. The actual experiences of settlers who went out, at least those who published their experiences, are inevitably more mixed, though it may be, of course, that those who "failed" at Western ranching, or at least, like French, encountered hardship (severe weather, cattle rustling, the death of partners and friends) and returned home ("I was resolved," after sixteen years, "to get away from the place as soon as I conveniently could"[65]) were more likely to write up their memoirs.

To the end of the century, the large majority of British memoirs about the American West are by men, though one finds after the Civil War that an increasing number (perhaps as much as 15 percent) of tourist accounts are written by British women—like the unchaperoned Isabella Bird in 1870s Colorado or, later, Susan McKinnon St. Maur who toured the Canadian and American West for "health, sport, and pleasure" in 1889 or Georgina Synge who rode through Yellowstone Park a year or two later.[66] Women who wrote of their experiences as *settlers*, who had gone out with husbands or friends to take up ranch life in the West, are rarer. Among these one finds Mrs. Edith Marion Nicholl[67] who, at the end of the century, published in London her recollections of twenty years as a "ranchwoman." In tone, this memoir pitches somewhere between journal and novel, with colorful descriptions of native Americans, Mexicans, and anecdotes of, say, the death of Billy the Kid. The next year, in fact, she turned to novel-writing and published several western-themed "tales" over the next twenty-three years.[68]

As a young woman in her early twenties, Edith Nicholl had, like many, gone West for her health. In New Mexico she found inspiring landscape, less gratuitous violence than she had been led to expect, but also overwork with no reliable servants (a common complaint). What one does not encounter here is much acknowledgment of the enhancement of women's position that many feminists in both Britain and America professed to find in a more gender-egalitarian West where women might drive their own carriages or ride astride. Oscar Wilde had opined—it was a common observation of the time—that American women commanded a "frank, fearless candour" and rejected "the subtle evasion and graceful mendacities of high life in Europe."[69] Edith Nicholl, however, had a different perspective. She complained, as many others of her class had long done, about the independence of white American female servants. Furthermore, as women in the West might perforce more equally share the burden of ranch-work, Nicholl emphasized the hardness, rather than the independence, of their lives—at least for those outside the cities on isolated ranches and farms. Moreover, she argued, British women found it difficult, often, to assimilate into the thin local social environment. Immigrant women like herself tended to "hug our ignorance, or our self-conceit."[70] A full American assimilation was doubtless complicated by the fact that, in some areas, there were so many other English about.

The male immigrant ranchers and ranch hands who wrote memoirs do not seem to have worried much along these lines. On the whole, intent on playing the role of cowboy and dedicated to the familiar, romantic myth of masculine independence on the frontier, they had little overt concern about preserving either their Britishness *or* social assimilation. But they were a mixed lot. Some who went out as young men began as hired hands, some bought ranches and farms, others were hired as managers, often by landholding companies based in Britain or on the east coast. Their memoirs can be divided into those, on the one hand, that were written by men who had gone out with hyped expectations and quickly returned, disappointed, and, on the other, those written by immigrants who stayed for some considerable time, dabbled in a number of ventures—from running cattle to property speculation in burgeoning western towns—and perhaps married. At the end of the day, however, they, too, often returned and published their memoirs in London—"My Life on the Range," etc.—as a species of Western lore.

One might take Reginald Aldridge as an example. A young railway engineer in Britain who had difficulty getting work on the Great Western, he happened to read Samuel Townshend's ("St. Kames") boosterish articles in the *Field* and determined to sail from Bristol to New York in late summer, 1877—without "any very clear idea of what I should turn my hand to after my arrival," but with some capital. En route he met (they had been on holiday in Britain) the son of an English clergyman and his wife who had carved out a living as farmers in Kansas, taking advantage of the Homestead Act and cheap railway land. Visiting them in Kansas he met other Britons—a Scotsman, for instance, who was in a partnership to raise sheep—and found a willing partner of his own "for the purpose of buying, selling, and handling [live]stock." Becoming experienced in this business, Aldridge bought out his partner's share and hired a hand to manage some 200 head on unfenced winter range, ultimately selling this herd to make a fresh start. Hiring two young brothers "who had come out West," he ran, with others, combined herds in Indian territory and the Texas panhandle. Living an isolated life, Aldridge nevertheless often encountered other Britons new to the area—"a couple of young Englishmen, one of them from Cambridge, and the other an indigo-planter from Ceylon," while a third "young fellow" stopped with him at his ranch for a while. They entertained themselves, he recalled years later, with singing western versions of Gilbert and Sullivan—"Then a cow-boy's lot is not a happy one, Happy one."[71]

Others, inevitably, were less savvy or less inclined to adapt. Edward Money, a novelist and author of various travel books who had served in the Bengal Army, was enticed to California, he said, by an encouraging report he read in London (written as he later discovered by an American promoter), and determined to settle his two sons—whom he sent out some months ahead—on a ranch. Finding southern California too dry to farm, he bought a cattle ranch near Colorado Springs (where he and his sons met an English lady they had known in London, along with others of "culture and refinement" from England and Scotland). But the ranch failed to be immediately profitable, and, leaving his sons in charge, he returned to Britain after "not quite five months." Back in England, Money wrote a somewhat sour book, entitled *The Truth About America*, in order "to put a certain class of emigrants on their guard against the machinations of a few [American] agents in London, who victimize them." Though the English abroad had their faults, Americans, he charged with some indignation, lacked deference and courtesy.[72]

For those British settlers and novice ranch hands who hoped to meld into the American West, adopting Western dress and attitude was less of an affectation or pose (as Frewen's embroidered buckskins surely were) than simply a necessary means of adapting to their new world. Some, it is true, clung to the dress, attitude, and language of their heritage and (however shakily maintained) class and tried to remain culturally British in a world of American egalitarianism. A number of settlement "colonies," founded on land purchased in the Midwest by a self-regarding elite of school and university men, hoped to recruit from the superfluous "second sons" of landed aristocrats, establishment clergymen, and retired military officers.[73] At Le Mars in Iowa, William Close, of Trinity College, Cambridge, and his brother Frederick set up a community of the like-minded with an Episcopalian church, a gentleman's club (by annual subscription), and a cricket team. Baillie-Grohman claimed, somewhat fancifully perhaps, that at Le Mars one might see streets "filled with English ladies and English gentlemen, and English children, and English babies" and "the heir-apparent to an old English earldom mowing, assisted by the two sons of a viscount; you can watch the brother of an earl feeding the thrashing-machine."[74] Another English colony, begun in 1873, was established by George Grant, a wealthy London silk merchant and Scottish landowner, for over a hundred British settlers in Kansas. It was named after the reigning monarch, Queen Victoria, and also had an Episcopalian church and other buildings designed by a London architect. A similar community in Kansas, Runnymede, was founded for "gentlemen farmers."

Inevitably, the hope that these communities could sustain themselves through a steady flow of elite emigrants (and their resources) from the privileged school-and-university-educated classes proved illusory. It assumed that there was a tangible upper-class population in Britain that wished to remain "British" yet could be persuaded to prefer America as a destination rather than, say, Canada, Australia, New Zealand, or South Africa. To survive, promoters inevitably came to draw from a broader social spectrum. Runnymede, for instance, began advertising, via its London office, in the London *Standard*, for "retired officers and gentlemen's sons thinking of emigrating to the Western States," then, when no doubt this proved wishful thinking, some months later simply for "small capitalists," and finally, anyone "wishing to emigrate."[75]

These communities generally failed within a few years. There was difficulty finding the farm labor that would allow "settlers" to follow an idealized life as gentlemen farmers; they were inevitably isolated with neighbors not always well-inclined to communities of overt Britishness; and those who imagined they might preserve something of England in Iowa or Kansas often moved on farther West, as individuals rather than a community. Young men who were brought out, of whatever class, were likely to find it difficult to suppress a yearning to explore other possibilities. A young Scot, Thomas Carson, had at age twenty-two already traveled out to the tea district of Cachar, India, felt hemmed in there, and was "determined to lead a country life of some kind." After his father's death he found his way to Le Mars in Iowa to join the "well-known colony of Britishers … almost entirely of the gentleman class," but quickly found that they "foolishly" clung to "the idea of social superiority over the natives," and thus had little ability to pick up the vital knowledge of practical affairs. He went on the road—to a ranch in New Mexico ("the romance attaching to it had much to do with my determination"), but soon moved on again to a frontier town where he "caught the infection" of speculation in real estate and made some "tremendous [though temporary] profits." Then, in 1883, Arizona territory called, where, still in his twenties, he found a ranching partner and settled down for some years to raise cattle, subsequently taking charge of a number of cattle ranches in New Mexico for the Scottish Land and Mortgage Company. After that, he tried, in the 1890s, his hand at running his own small ranch in New Mexico which in 1902, at the end of some twenty-five years in America, he sold and left to become a wandering tourist—in Latin America, Europe, Morocco, Hawaii, Fiji, Australasia, Japan, China, Burma, and India—returning to Britain to publish his memoirs.[76]

One imagines that a young, and not-so-young, unsettled "settler" like Carson, driven, as he said, by the "romance" of the West and a youthful wanderlust that persisted into late middle age, may have been of this special Anglo-American time and place, and have regarded the Anglo-world as his oyster. There were, of course, others, not on the make, not driven by wanderlust or the romance of performing the cowboy, but who came to America simply to find their leisure, who dressed for the English hunt and rode English saddle on imported thoroughbreds, and who armed themselves with expensive weapons from London gunsmiths. As Baillie-Grohman reported from Colorado,

The Western hunter will tell you he never knew one of 'them thar English lord chaps' "outfits," them top-shelfers who come over a' hunting, to be without "bear-coated wipes" (rough towels), rubber baths, string-shoes (laced boots), and a corkscrew in their pocket-knives.'[77]

Such "top-shelfers" were able to find like-minded Anglophiles in the East and accommodating social rituals there, but in the West they would become emblematic of the British "dude," like the "remittance man," a figure of derision. John Fox visited Cheyenne in 1885, in a brown Derby and English riding breeches, and said that he had "never attracted so much attention in his life."[78]

The fashion for mythologizing the lively individualism of the American West carried back to Britain some sense of a "new world" of social, possibly even gender, if not racial, democratization (as did the quite similar representations of Australia). It also served to rekindle Americans' sense that they would become, after all the vicissitudes of civil war and the problematic of race relations, not just a beacon but a world power, a successor state to an effete Mother Country. It was just this reborn expectation of a coming reversal of the Anglo-American power relationship that was made to serve as the humorous substance of Harry Leon Wilson's best-known novel, *Ruggles of Red Gap* (set in 1907 and published in 1915). Wilson, born in 1867 in Illinois, worked his way from Nebraska to Colorado and on to California. A contributor to the American humor magazine *Puck*, he traveled with the Indiana novelist Booth Tarkington to Europe in 1905. His Ruggles was an English manservant (memorably portrayed by Charles Laughton in Leo McCarey's 1935 film) who is lost by his aristocratic British master, an "honourable" represented with all the silliness of a Dundreary, in a poker game to an American, accompanies his new plain-speaking, nouveau-riche employer to the Pacific North-West, and at last discovers "that contact with their curious American life had taught me that their equality should be more than a name … if we were going to be Americans it was silly rot trying to be English at the same time."[79]

2 The American West in Late-Victorian Britain

The quasi-mythological, often romantic American West that was seen, read, and heard in late-Victorian Britain, was compounded of adventure novels, travel literature, illustrated periodicals, landscapes and portraiture, touring lectures and exhibitions, theatrical productions, and elaborate entertainments involving "real" cowboys and Indians. In America, hundreds of plays on the New York stage brought to life the drama of the American frontier. Roger Hall estimates that some 1,200 frontier dramas were written and staged from 1849 to 1917. Some were comedies, but most were romantic melodramas that brought cowboys, Indians, and sensational frontier violence to audiences eager to find entertainment in the clichés of the American West.[80] If rarely treated as serious theater, these pieces had a large appeal, and many transferred to London or were copied there. They promulgated themes of normative violence, masculinity, primitive instincts, and ethnic stereotypes that mirrored those of the adventure novels—drunken Irish, villainous mixed-race Mexicans, independent women (who nonetheless needed saving by heroic white manhood), comic or sinister Chinamen, conspiratorial Mormons, and Indians who were either buffoons, angry rebels, victims, or simply "noble unfortunates."[81]

The runaway success on the New York stage of a number of western plays in 1871 and after both established frontier theater as an enduring entertainment there and were often directly transferred to Britain, a "fertile ground" for such drama. James J. McCloskey's *Across the Continent* (a tale of the transcontinental railway and Indian marauders) opened at the Royal Alfred Theatre in London in 1871, and was revived in 1875, 1876, and 1882. In 1879, after some 1,000 performances in America, Frank Mayo's impersonation of Davy Crockett crossed over to England, as did, the next year, a drama about a mining camp in California, *The Danites*—following the success in London of the Californian poet Joaquin Miller. This piece (the entire New York company was imported for the production) became the toast of the 1880 season. By the end of the century, with the Western drama established as popular entertainment (an anticipation of the popularity of American cowboy films in the decades to follow), writers and producers like Belasco and Frohman were attuned to the transatlantic profits of bringing westerns to the British public: in 1893 their production of *The Girl I Left Behind Me* ran for 100 performances at the Adelphi in London.[82]

In this, the exotic and colorful "American experience" that domestic Britain found available for amusement and instruction closely resembled in form and content the contemporary popular imperial entertainments of adventure in Africa, India, and Canada. Both involved what might be called the spectatorship of empire. Though the United States was outside the formal empire and its politics often unfriendly to British imperial self-regard, it was clear to most observers that its western expansion was analogous, not only, if most obviously, to that of the western development of British North America, but to the imperial frontier more generally. Moreover, working against the familiar, entrenched narrative of American "difference" was, especially, the spreading fin de siècle rhetoric of "Anglo-Saxonism." The powerful, if not universal, belief that Britain and the United States were coming partners in a global civilizing mission was grounded in a parallel, shared intensification of the principle of race.

"Race" in British Views of the American West

As reported by visitors and reproduced in late-Victorian entertainments, race in the West was of a different character than that uniquely American discourse that arose from the South, with its focus on slavery, minstrelsy, Reconstruction, and the Jim Crow era. The African American himself largely drops out of the western tableau. He was, of course, widely present in the West but hardly visible in its lore, replaced there by the either dangerous or degenerate Red Indian and the displaced and degraded Mexican "greaser." The Indian-and-Mexican mixture (a "dusky compound of Castilian and Indian blood," as Maurice Morris observed in his *Rambles in the Rocky Mountains* in 1864) seemed to have produced, as Mrs. Nicholl complained at the end of the century, a willfully idle

The Far West: Imagining, Seeing, Performing

population with a "muddled" physiology and the vices of a "mongrel race."[83] Echoing the earlier uneasy discourse about the Caribbean or Southern mulatto, British visitors throughout the era often drew attention to the prevalence of racial mixtures in a West where the social conventions of respectable white society did not apply, finding, or imagining, that a "yellowed" black and brown (or white and brown or white and red) mixture, like that of the Negro/Indian, was likely to be unfortunate in its biology and its character. In 1879 Samuel Townshend had thought it worth noting that the expedition's Negro cook's son was half Comanche Indian, seemingly not "a bad mixture of races" as he was "a bright, hard-working, honest little fellow." One would naturally expect, he opined, that "the bad qualities of each would be combined."[84] Though rarely seen as a danger like that of the full-blooded, warlike plains Indian, and perhaps not as offensive to nature as the full miscegenation of black and white, such mixtures offered the racialist observer an easy and distinct means of contrast, one that centered the unmuddled, dominant, blue-eyed, often heroic western Anglo-Saxon.

It is, of course, the native American, the Red Indian, who populates the West as the racial Other of most prominence in the lore imported back across the Atlantic. In Britain, as in America, he had long had a double literary representation as noble if fated stoic *and* demonic savage—to which was added in the era that followed the final white conquest of the western frontier that of a pathetic—perhaps degenerate remnant mostly sequestered in "reservations" and dependent on government hand-outs or the charity of trinket-buying tourists. In Canada, native Americans (First Nations peoples) may have been able to preserve a larger independence and a firmer collective status,[85] but in the western United States native American cultures were broken and became the butt of racist derision, relegated, as fixed clichés, to the cowboys-and-Indians pulp novel, the satirical cartoon, or the Wild West show.

The Red Indian, in America and in Britain From time to time since the sixteenth century, native Americans had been brought or found their way to Britain. In the era of the colonial wars and the subsequent foundation of the Canadian provinces, some traveled to London, such as the Mohawk chief John Brant famously painted by Romney, to represent and defend their interests. Others, like the exotic animals they might accompany, were inevitably seen and represented, in their native dress, as a rare curiosity. By the early and mid-nineteenth century, the novels of Fenimore Cooper and stage representations helped to carry on the familiar theme in Anglo-American popular culture of the Indian as noble savage. Such representations created a Red man who could be both a trope for the stoical, masculine virtues vital for the Republic, *and* a signifier of a semi-mythical, rapidly receding past. Unresolved contradictions abound. On the one hand, the realm of the native American was that of "an anachronistic, atavistic world that needed to be rapidly abolished." On the other, he offered "a new spirit of idealization" in opposition to an artificial, mechanical modernity.[86]

In 1839, George Catlin, a Pennsylvania portraitist and ethnologist who had traveled West to get to know the Plains Indians on their own terms, brought his carefully painted images of types of native American, stressing their "nobility and manliness," to London's

Egyptian Hall for two years. He subsequently toured the provinces (Liverpool, York, Edinburgh, Glasgow, Belfast, and Dublin) in a popular show that demonstrated the appetite in Britain for a colorful, living ethnology. His collection, exhibited also in Paris and Brussels, included 600 of his own sketches and paintings of the Plains Indian, along with their weapons, clothing, and wigwams, in order, as he said, "to awaken a proper sympathy for them."[87]

Catlin returned in 1843, had a private showing at Windsor, unsuccessfully proposed a Museum of Mankind to house his collection in London, and raised advance subscriptions from the great and good—including the Queen and Albert—for the lavishly illustrated book he planned on *The Manners, Customs and Condition of the North American Indians*. His second tour at the Egyptian Hall included nine Ojibwe dressed in their plains garb and with their weapons. They performed twice daily, and their success as crowd pleasers led to the importation of other representative native Americans.

Catlin's proposal of a Museum of Mankind echoes a widespread mid-nineteenth-century interest in an ethnology that could present the imperial British with a taxonomy of aboriginal people who inhabited the widening realm of a British Empire that, as Catlin pointedly observed, "has more than thirty colonies … in which the numbers of civilized men are increasing, and the native tribes are wasting away."[88] Founded in 1843 by members of the Aborigines' Protection Society, the Ethnological Society of London, like the Royal Geographical Society of 1830, advanced an Enlightenment science that was attractive to many of the upper-middle-class tourists who would travel to the American far West to explore and report upon its scenery and its scattered native peoples. Both societies were closely imbricated, as useful sciences, with the global extension of nineteenth-century British imperialism and the governance of non-European peoples. Ethnology would also be enlisted by some in the fin de siècle struggle to establish global Anglo-Saxondom as more than an attachment of sentiment.

Many of the British travel writers, such as John Mortimer Murphy, would claim a kind of ethno-geological status for their observations. Murphy advanced his book as "a description of the physical geography, climate, soil, productions, industrial and commercial resources, scenery, population, educational institutions, arboreal botany, and game animals" from Washington territory and Oregon to Wyoming, Montana, and Utah. The ethnology of the region, in his telling, encompassed a kind of cosmopolitan mixture of every nationality of Europe, as well as "yellow, almond-eyed Chinese, the black, curly-headed Negro, and the brown, straight-haired Indian," and their half-breed mixtures, making "an ethnological *olla podrida* [miscellaneous assortment or stew], that changes in hue like the parts of a kaleidoscope."[89] In 1857, Thomas Gladstone, an antislavery advocate who had traveled out to report on "bleeding Kansas," offered his British readership a chapter on the "Red Races" there, detailing the variety of tribes and their circumstances. He claimed to have seen among these "examples of almost every stage, from the lowest [condition of barbarism] to the highest [near-civilized]," from the "most savage" Sioux to the prosperous and thriving, missionary-converted Wyandots.[90] Dr. William Bell's travel journal of 1869, reporting on a surveying expedition for a southern railway route to the Pacific, is organized into a first part on "physical geography" and a second on "ethnology"—"a terse account," he says, "of aboriginal tribes, well worthy of study."[91]

Anyone, of course, could be an amateur ethnologist or anthropologist, though the science of phenotypical and social/cultural classification was impossibly confused by the prevalence in the West, as many British observers were keen to point out, of the heterogeneous racial mixtures that made calculations of character more fluid and difficult than the reified concept of "race" would seem to permit. As regards the Plains Indian, though, the British travel memoir points a common theme. However proud, stoic, savage, or warlike the character of the Red Indian that the continuing romantic adventure literature or stage entertainment might project, the reality encountered and reported by the British hunter, tourist, or immigrant settler became often a contrasting one of a deflated, derogated, and diminished type, adrift and in perhaps terminal decline. Even the relatively sympathetic Robert Louis Stevenson, in a section of his *The Amateur Emigrant* on "despised races," sighed over "the noble red man of old story": "I saw no wild or independent Indian," but only those who came to the way-stations to stare at the passing train—"disgracefully dressed out with the sweepings of civilisation," pathetic in their degradation.[92]

In the contact zone—on the ground, as opposed to in the continuing romantic literary tradition— there was a general vilification of the plains Indian in the era of the Indian wars. Dilke's view in 1869 was shaped in part by these anxious times. He and Dixon had left London, he said, with an image of the dignified Red Indian "elevated on a pedestal of nobility in our hearts," but "our three days' risk of scalping in the Plains" changed all that: "disarm at any price, and exterminate if necessary."[93] The same year, Capt. Frederick Townshend, referencing the wider Empire familiar to his London readers, reported that in Utah "[t]he deserts of Africa or Asia present no more forbidding aspect, nor amongst Bedouin Arabs or African Negroes" as that of "such hideous and degraded-looking savages as were some of the Utahs, Pahutas, Shoshones, and Diggers … who inhabit this country."[94] Two years earlier, the British tourist Henry Latham, reporting on the progress of the transcontinental railroad in the West, cited approvingly General Sherman's dictum that Indian "marauders" were "so many wolves to be exterminated." War would, Latham thought, settle the matter "right off" and perhaps avoid the expensive "distant expeditions and frontier skirmishes as unsatisfactory and costly to them [the American tax-payer] as a war in New Zealand is to us." As would Dilke, he had come to the conclusion that "[t]he Fenimore Cooper age of belief in the noble qualities of the Redskin has passed away."[95] Dismissal of Cooper's romanticism had rapidly become commonplace in the far West travel literature. Greeley, who considered Indians to be "squalid … worthless, lazy, and lousy" children, claimed in 1860 that "the Indian of Cooper and Longfellow" was "only visible to the poet's eye."[96]

These sentiments were echoed through much of the rest of the century by British travelers to the West, such as Charles Mackay in an 1866 article in *Blackwood's*:

> As the Red man could not be made to work, the Anglo-Saxons resolved to exterminate him, and they have all but accomplished their purpose. Similar results

have grown out of similar causes in South Africa, Australia, and New Zealand. Philosophy, humanity, Christianity, all are alike impotent to stay the inevitable catastrophe.[97]

By the 1880s, such observations, repeating a theme that had become routinely expected perhaps, are common among the memoirs of British women traveling West as well. Mrs. F. D. Bridges, who had "expected something picturesque," found the first Indian she met in the Washington territory to be an "ugly commonplace individual, chewing tobacco."[98] Similarly, Lady Rose Pender was "greatly disappointed in the red men ... an insignificant and ugly race ... a squalid, cruel and degraded people" with "the lowest Irish type of features ... inferior in strength to the Zulu and in grace to the coolie or Tamil."[99] Lady Duffus, in her rail journey out to San Francisco via Montreal, summed up such, by then commonplace, sentiments in 1881 when she noted, of a "posse of Indian squaws and 'bucks'" with "their dark faces and black beady eyes looming out from a mass of thick unkempt hair," that

> they were the most revolting specimens of the human race. It is simply impossible to regard them as 'men and brothers' ... Civilization, with its humanizing principles ... will never overcome the inborn blindness of the savage race. They have not the power to comprehend our codes, nor to feel as we feel."[100]

One can see together in these testimonies a progression—first, the stripping out, as a justification for genocidal warfare, of the positive character of stoicism and dignity from the traditional duality of nobility-and-savagery, to be followed after western conquest by a prevailing image of the defeated and degraded Indian as a kind of fated residuum, comparable in domestic British discourse to the unreachable, unimprovable social residuum of Charles Booth's black-colored streets of urban poverty. The squalor and idleness of the pacified native American was, of course, a result, in large part, of the objective conditions in which British travelers fleetingly and superficially encountered them. It was, however, also encouraged and entrenched by other long-standing prejudices. The formerly fierce Plains Indian warrior became not only degraded but, ultimately, feminized in his dependence and passivity. Traditional representations in Britain of the noble savage had been strongly idealized and gendered as masculine in character (the native American transgendered "berdache," though known, was generally ignored in the traveler accounts[101]).

Of course, the long and continuing literary and theatrical tradition of the beautiful Indian maiden, from Pocahontas to Minnehaha, lived on into the twentieth century in romantic melodrama. Longfellow's *The Song of Hiawatha* (1855) was, like Cooper's novels, especially well-received in Britain, running through at least fourteen editions by the end of the century. There was a dramatization using Ojibwe actors transferred from New York to London's Earls Court in 1905, a year after Barrie's *Peter Pan* brought New York and London audiences the Indian maiden Tiger Lily. The same year, a British actor at Wallack's in New York, William Faversham, had great success in Edwin Milton Royle's

The Squaw Man, a western play (which transferred to the Lyric Theatre in London) about an earl's second son who goes West, is saved by an Indian maiden, and settles down incognito with her and their son on a Montana ranch. When he sends his son off to England to be educated as the presumptive heir to the earldom, the squaw-wife obligingly removes her socially embarrassing self by suicide.[102]

One can find elements of the romantic view preserved in some of the travel literature, as in the British hunter J. S. Campion's observation that among the Utes the young women were quite comparable to flirtatious "civilised" European girls—"the way they used their eyes was quite wonderful" and "their hands were very pretty and well shaped."[103] Thomas Gladstone, in his earlier, less romanticized but sympathetic reportage from Kansas, found on board a steam-boat two Wyandot women and their several children, forced to have their meals after all the whites had eaten, to be more civilized in their deportment than the white self-styled "ladies" on board.[104] In most late-Victorian memoirs, however, the Indian "squaw" is more often made the negative signifier of the loss of Red Indian character. Already in 1848, Ballantyne had noted of the Cree in his first book, *Hudson Bay*, that Indian women "were not so good-looking as the men," with "an awkward slouching gait, and a downcast look … complete drudges."[105] In the main, Indian women of whatever age become the objects of a new, unflattering "realism." H. Hussey Vivian, leaving Ogden by rail in 1877, recorded two "hideously ugly Indian squaws" looking in the window "as I write," "dirty and coarse-looking to the last degree."[106] The same year, Wallis Nash, as he traveled along the Humboldt River, saw "at every station some of the miserable Indian squaws and children [who] came to the train to beg" while their husbands "in the cast-off clothes of the white men … squatted under the shadow of the station fence."[107] And in 1886, a tourist from Yorkshire told the readers of the *Wakefield Herald* that the Indian squaws he had seen at railway stations were "horrid looking, greasy, fat, and ugly … They are the lowest type of humanity, and after seeing a few for curiosity, you are disgusted with them."[108] As Kate Flint has observed, the squaw in such travelers' observations was often more witch than Pocahontas.[109]

Late nineteenth-century racist and misogynist rhetoric of the unromantic and undignified squaw was also furthered by the retrieval, repeatedly in travel memoirs, of the long-familiar belief that mixed marriages, in the West between Indian women and Anglo-Saxon, Mexican, or French-Canadian men, inevitably led to both physical and moral degeneration. As John Murphy opined of the common marriage of voyageurs with Indian women, half-breed progeny were "much inclined to scrofulous complaints and consumption" and "are also said to be imbued with the vices of both races" (a commonplace of nineteenth-century Anglo-American belief about the half-breed—mestizo, métis, or mulatto).[110] William Henry Barnaby, the trust-fund-enabled younger son of a member of the English landed gentry, parroted the same view a few years later in his book on the *Life and Labour of the Far, Far West* when touring a Flathead Indian reservation: "I am told in every case [of mixed marriages] the man is always certain to be brought down to the lower level, and the woman never rises to his."[111]

In Britain, negative representations of the contemporary native American woman in the West as eugenic threat contrast sharply with the idealized image of the Red Indian drawn from the popular culture of novels and exhibitions. That the two images can coexist is due, in part, to the fact that the Indians on view and in performance in London were mostly warriors from a recent *past*. The Indian squaw was symbolic of the *future*.

When Charles Alston Messiter finally came, in 1890, to write up his recollections of hunting and traveling in the American West in the 1860s and 1870s, he titled the work *Sport and Adventures among the North-American Indians*. Though he had spent much time in the company of Canadian and American Indians, he has, typically, very little to say about "squaws" other than to note their apparent, he claimed, lack of "any idea of cleanliness." Indian "nobility," for Messiter, was entirely a masculine matter. One finds here, already by the last decade of the century, a kind of nostalgia, an element that can also be found in the very popular—on both sides of the Atlantic—Wild West entertainments of the 1880s and 1890s. Messiter allowed, however, that what he had to say about the vanishing native Americans and their world would be recognizable, "even for those who stay at home," "now that 'Buffalo Bill' has made many so familiar with the noble redman and the buffalo."[112]

The Wild West in London and the Popular Theater of Imperialism

The vast exhibition hall at Olympia near Earls Court, completed in 1884, was the "most dramatic metropolitan venture" in the provision of spaces for popular entertainment in late-Victorian London. The extensive grounds (24 acres), sheltered stands, and amphitheater provided viewing area for *c.* 40,000 when, three years later, "Buffalo Bill" Cody's Wild West Exhibition—an extravaganza that would run in one version or another to 1894, and again from 1902 to 1916—opened with 92 Indians, 100 cowboys (and Annie Oakley), 180 horses, a herd of 18 buffalo, and mules, elk, Texas longhorns, donkeys, bears, and deer.[113] It is important to see the runaway popularity of the American Wild West in Britain, not simply as a singular example of the romantic fascination with cowboys and Indians, but as an imperial spectacle akin to the colonial exhibitions that proliferated in the capital from the 1870s. The year 1887 was also the year of Victoria's Golden Jubilee, and empire-wide festivities celebrated the reign of the Empress of India. A reduced version of Cody's extravaganza was presented to the Queen as a command performance. Presumably, as it had on opening day, Cody's 36-member "cowboy band" played "God Save the Queen" along with "The Star Spangled Banner" before a royal box decorated with crossed British and American flags.[114] With some pride, Cody reported the reception he enjoyed in "the Motherland" from royalty—especially his joking conversations with the Prince of Wales[115]—and would, in fact, be taken to task by some for an unrepublican hobnobbing with aristocracy, for prostituting, in a sense, the grand design of his celebration of America in a sweeping panorama of the American frontier epic. By the time Cody died in 1917 however, such criticism was buried in the wartime patriotism of America's entry as an ally (or "associated power") with the British Empire—in the defense, many thought, of Anglo-Saxon brotherhood. As Cody himself claimed, the "fascinating" story of his own life enshrined just those things in the West that "proclaim to a wondering world the march of the Anglo-Saxon race." The "Memorial Edition" of Cody's autobiography that appeared that year bore on its title page the crossed American and British flags and was dedicated to "the American and English Publics."[116]

William Frederick Cody (1846–1917) was born in the Iowa territory and brought up in Canada and Kansas. As a young man he may have been a Pony Express rider for a brief time, and was a civilian scout during the Indian wars before serving as guide for touring British big game hunters like George Watts Garland and Thomas P. Medley (at $1,000 a month).[117] His early theatrical performances with Texas Jack led to his own Western shows, culminating in the creation of his astoundingly successful touring company, Buffalo Bill's Wild West, in 1883. The show was performed by a large cast, musical accompaniment, parades, and reenactments.[118] There were Indian attacks on wagon trains, and a dramatization of Custer's Last Stand. Cody took his "Exhibition" triumphantly throughout the United States, and amassed a considerable fortune before crossing the ocean to tour Britain and the Continent.

Invited by John Robinson Whitley, a British businessman-impresario who organized the first commercial exhibitions at Earls Court and who had met Cody in America, the show Cody brought to London was a profit-making theatrical venture in transatlantic entertainment (a company of investors from both America and Britain had been formed to underwrite and promote the project). It was intended that Cody's show be an "adjunct" (with a percentage of gate receipts) to a more general international "American Exhibition"—a world's fair to be held in London in 1886 but which was delayed a year so as not to compete with the Colonial and Indian Exhibition of that year. In the event, the popularity of Cody's Wild West simply overwhelmed whatever other events may have been planned. After 300 performances in London, it toured Birmingham, Manchester, Hull, and other provincial centers. When it returned to Britain in 1891, Cody took his show—now including seventeen ex-prisoners of war among the fifty or so native American performers—to Glasgow.[119]

Among those who wined and dined with Cody in London were, prominently, the "local literati and theatrical profession," including Oscar Wilde and his wife and Irving's set—Irving, Ellen Terry, the American Mary Anderson, and others. What Cody had to offer was, of course, spectacle rather than legitimate theater, but it was more than a Barnum circus—an extravaganza of skills and reenactments that comprised "gala folklore and military parade," not only within arenas, tents, and amphitheaters, but in the streets. It represented "the ultimate national will," the conclusion of the American West's Indian Wars, while at the same time idealizing the American Indian's proud "defiance in the face of oppression." As Joseph Roach has emphasized, the wild and noble Red Indian becomes here "richly polysemic,"[120] but not only for white Americans. The British who turned out to see the show in their millions[121] could see and hear with familiarity not only the novels of Mayne Reid and the America of their imagination, but also the vanishing races of their own imperial West where the prairie cyclorama and the reservation Indian village find a parallel in the outback, the veldt and the (tamed) kraal.

Red Skins and Zulus As Joy Kasson has argued, Cody's Wild West Show evoked "a world of risk and dominance, of virility and exoticism that also formed the serious business of the *British* Empire,"[122] a view that has been persuasively expanded by Kate Flint, for whom "the Indian is a figure charged with significance when it comes to Britain's interpretation of her whole imperial role" as well as "a touchstone for a whole range of British perceptions concerning America during the long nineteenth century."[123] Imperial exhibitions—with displays of colonial settlers and "natives," military reviews, and reenactments—had been mounted in London by both imperial officialdom and commercial entrepreneurs for some time. These displays can be seen in the wider context of the international trade exhibitions—beginning famously with that of the Crystal Palace in 1851—as well as in the popular entertainments offered by Barnum. On both sides of the ocean, regional, national, and international (or imperial) exhibitions reached out to draw in the global. Celebration of the American centennial at Philadelphia in 1876 or the Columbian Exposition at Chicago in 1893 were themed and promoted to attract, as they successfully did, international visitors. British tourists responded in significant numbers, while imperial or colonial exhibitions in Britain hoped to do the same in reverse by appealing to American tourism. The inclusion of American themes promoted a kind of frontier exoticism that paralleled their own drama of empire and suggested that Anglo-Saxon brotherhood might evolve, not into competition and confrontation, but into a confraternity of global trusteeship.

The ethnological simulation of kraal and reservation presented evidence of the success of domestication and education, if not Christianization. Buffalo Bill was not allowed to bring his Wild West to the Columbian Exposition in 1893 because it was feared that his recreation of the warlike Red Indian of the recent past would jar with the desire of the Indian Bureau to emphasize the "productive citizenship" being inculcated in the reservation schools: "On the fairground, the Indian Office directly challenged the Wild West show for supremacy in a battle over whose image of the Indian would prevail."[124] The same tension between propaganda and dramatic presentation, between the official wish to emphasize the fruits of a civilizing Empire and the eagerness of commercial interests to profit from the violent drama of historical recreation, might be observed in London.

By the end of the century, cosmopolitan, transatlantic impresarios of spectacular mass entertainments such as Imre Kiralfy[125] had achieved a global reach and ambition. In 1895 Kiralfy, who had organized theatrical spectacles in Paris and at the Columbian Exposition in Chicago, crossed to England to produce a commercial exhibition "Empire of India" at Olympia. He followed this success with annual colonial-themed spectacles and, in 1899, in the months before the outbreak of the second Boer War, an even more ambitious mass entertainment, "Greater Britain." This series of tableaux and action pieces played out in the ample grounds at Earls Court included, among the quasi-anthropological displays of pacified natives that had become common in colonial exhibitions, also an "American panorama" with rodeo-like performances.

The dramatic presentation of the American West at the Greater Britain exhibition would have owed much, of course, to Cody's tours between 1887 and 1892. But the fashion for Western spectacle, Red Indian tableaux and performances, and cowboy-and-Indian adventure stories also influenced the manner in which British colonial settlers and natives, especially in southern Africa, were dramatically represented. The recreation of native domesticity in metropolitan exhibitions, dating at least as far back as the 1850 "African Exhibition" that coincided with the outbreak of yet another "Kaffir War" (the eighth Xosha War 1850–3 at Cape Colony), had been followed by a string of similar entertainments importing "real" natives—as in 1853 when thirteen "Zulus" were brought to London to perform "tribal" dances and rituals.[126] The parading of native warriors and the recreation of their huts and kraals for public view would even then, as theater, have resonated with the similar importation of performing native Americans, with their wigwams, weapons, and war paint in the 1840s. Such entertainments evolved together as, to a degree, co-constituted. By the end of the century, Buffalo Bill's Wild West show was billing itself as "an Ethnological, Anthropological and Etymological Congress."[127]

In 1899, Kiralfy's Greater Britain production included a special "Savage South Africa" display and entertainment imported by Frank Fillis, a South African circus owner, memorializing the defeat of Lobengula's Matabele people in a second war of 1896. This involved a living tableau of life in a native kraal, a recreation of the Matabele attack on the Gwelo stage coach, and the "last stand" of Major Allan Wilson[128] against warriors in feathered headdress and war paint, as well as rodeo events such as zebra lassoing. Fillis would take "Savage South Africa" on tour throughout Britain, and reproduce Wilson's Last Stand as a novel cinema attraction the next year.

As it happens, there were tangible connections with the American West in these late-Victorian little wars in Africa and elsewhere, not only in representation but on the ground. There were the obvious tactical parallels in fighting native "rebellion" (the laagering/corralling of wagons, the surprise attack on domestic native encampments, the forced moving of native peoples to more "secure" villages, etc.), and the presence in southern Africa of British officers who had been involved in the Indian/Métis rebellions in western Canada. There were also freebooting American "cowboys," scouts and Indian-fighters, on the scene—seeking out in the wider Anglosphere venturesome roles, as observers or participants, in the similar-seeming embattled rangeland of southern Africa or Australia. Perhaps the best-known of these at the turn of the century was Frederick Russell Burnham (1861–1947), an experienced scout who had been born on an Indian reservation in Minnesota and served as a young man in the Apache wars of the 1880s. He moved to South Africa in 1893, seeking the kind of frontier life that was rapidly vanishing in America, and served as scout in engagements with the Matabele (he was a survivor of Wilson's last stand), and later in the second Boer War. Though he retained his US citizenship, Burnham was given the rank of major in the British Army and received the DSO in 1901, returning to the United States to promote Baden-Powell's Boy Scout movement there.[129]

Western America had a presence in Australia and South Africa beyond the privateering services of unemployed scouts, emigrants looking for rangeland no longer freely available in the American West, self-promoters, and adventure-seekers. The same kind of popular, circus-like Wild West entertainments Buffalo Bill had performed to great applause in Britain[130] found audiences in Cape Town and Sydney, organized often by those who claimed an authentic American provenance. One of these was so-called Texas Jack, Jr. (1860–1905), who said he had been orphaned by Indian marauders and saved by the famous Texas Jack Omohundro. After the original Texas Jack's early death, he dropped the "Jr." to promote his own Wild West show of trick riders and sharpshooters, and took this spectacle, with its "marvelous feats of horsemanship, shooting, lasso throwing," to Australia and then South Africa in 1898 before moving his crew the next year to London and signing on to perform in "Savage South Africa." He himself took the role of poor Major Wilson in both the Earls Court show and the subsequent film. After the conclusion of the Boer War, his "Texas Jack's Wild West Show & Circus" played in South Africa for some years before his death in Kroonstad in 1905.

3 Cowboy Anglo-Saxonism

Amid the racial *olla podrida* of the American West, it is the idealized, blue-eyed "Anglo-Saxon" who signifies, in romantic literature as well as, often, travelers' memoirs, the heroic and the masculine—from Dunraven's blue-eyed Texas Jack ("who might have sat as a model for a typical modern Anglo-Saxon") to Custer's flowing golden locks and fierce blue eyes, from William Black's tanned and blue-eyed Buckskin Charlie to e.e. cummings' "blue-eyed boy," Buffalo Bill. Eyes—bold, flashing, staring, or stern—can signify command and control, as when, in his Western novel of 1877, Walter Besant describes the "clear blue eyes" of cold and reserved Captain Ladds, an Englishman: "servants—the nigger of Jamaica, the guileless Hindoo of his Indian station, and other members of the inferior human brotherhood—trembled exceedingly when they met those eyes."[131]

To the Victorian both in Britain and in the United States, the mélange of Englishness became rather more Teutonicized than history, strictly speaking, could justify. In the heightened race-awareness of the second half of the century, American Anglo-Saxonism—which from the 1840s was commonly extended to include descendants of Pennsylvania Germans and Dutch[132]—usefully served as an *exclusionary ideal*, denying its defining bundle of traits (stoicism, laconic speech and humor, liberty-loving independence of mind and firmness of purpose) not only to (de-romanticized) Red Indians, Mexicans, Chinese, or African Americans, but to non-Teutonic immigrant "whites." It also served, in the face of a British Empire that was increasingly multi-cultural and an America in which the English-heritage part of the population was an ever-smaller minority, to preserve the centrality of a racial/cultural elite with a genius, it was claimed, for honest self-governance and the stoical shouldering of the burden of ruling selflessly other peoples, other races. If, in the American Northeast and South the Yankee Brahmin caste and the old plantation aristocracy appeared to have abandoned or to have been forced out of their natural leadership roles, in the far West of straight-shooting, rough-riding Anglo-Saxondom it might be otherwise.

Just before the Civil War, William Fowler, professor of rhetoric at Amherst College, had presented his students an image of the Saxon, whose language provided the enduring backbone for the English language: they were a fierce, large-boned race, "their eyes blue, their complexion fair, and their hair almost uniformly of a light colour." Ruled by their passion for "piratical gain," they nevertheless "showed a high regard for honor, and a pride of mind that could not endure disgrace."[133] Late nineteenth-century Anglo-Saxonism would craft an historical image that matched a present need. There might come a time, the English historian Edward A. Freeman suggested, for a nation to "go back to its youth." The wilderness of the American frontier had demanded as much, calling for the American Anglo-Saxons to reassert "their Teutonic nature."[134] There was, many thought, a buried Anglo-American affinity, a deeply shared racial character, that allowed some Americans to rise above their customary suspicions about aristocratic British character. And there remained deep within the *common* Englishman something of the passed-on virtue that was winning the West. When the Unitarian minister Moncur Conway traveled to Britain in 1863 to lobby for support for the Union cause, he remained in London for some years, preaching at the South Place Chapel in Finsbury, writing on literature and history, and editing the work of that "common man" shared by the two countries, Tom Paine. In 1872 Conway told the American readers of *Harper's Monthly* that Joseph Arch, the leader of the farm laborers' unionization movement then much in the British news, was "a humble son of the poor," and "a sturdy Saxon man, with blond complexion and light blue eyes, a straight, frank look, and strong features."[135]

Anglo-American Anglo-Saxonism was not of course an invention of the second half of the nineteenth century, though it most flourished, in some circles at least, in the fin de siècle era of "rapprochement." Previously, however, the "Anglo-Saxon race" had been commonly used, like "race" itself, in a loose, unreified sense, implying as much heritage and culture as "blood." It received a more concrete, quasi-biological reading in Britain at the hands of some nationalist historians like Freeman (though he preferred "English" to "Anglo-Saxon"). Similarly, in America a more sharply racialized character was advanced by those nativists who were appalled at the swelling tide of Irish, southern European, Polish, and Jewish immigration and who, in the West, encountered the ambiguities of a racial typology that had to deal with the less certain distinctions of whiteness among a population of Mexicans, native Americans, and their racial mixtures—a phenomenon that seemed to call for a new defensive language where a simple, prejudicial distinction between "white" and "black" might no longer suffice. In this, "Anglo-Saxon" shifted from a kind of uncertain cousinhood, a sometime dysfunctional family relation that could be marked as much by feuding as affinity, to a bonding racial brotherhood at home and globally. This was, for a host of historical and situational reasons, an incomplete and unstable phenomenon, localized among certain classes and regions, and in the everyday world inspired more rhetorical flourish than real commitment. In the end, as overt racialism and racial Darwinism became less acceptable in both Britain and America, the "Anglo-Saxon race" yielded—in the rhetoric of a Theodore Roosevelt or a Winston Churchill—to (or was disguised by) the "English-Speaking peoples."

The philologists of the early Republic were often keen to discover the Old and Middle English roots of American speech as a kind of defense against British charges of cultural vulgarity and linguistic corruption. These antique, preserved characteristics of American speech were generally assumed to be more prevalent among the less cultivated and less urbanized, among the backwoods folk in the trans-Appalachian northwest and west. Admittedly, in the far West local cowboy speech reflected also the language and accent of the Old South, the Spanish of the Mexican settlers and vaqueros, and, to a lesser degree, words picked up from native American peoples. But, among the blue-eyed heroes of the frontier, language retained its Anglo-Saxon core. The rough and notoriously loose cursing of a largely male comradery was, except for borrowings from the French Canadians, unabashedly Anglo-Saxon, if delivered with a uniquely American fluency, with the ease, force, frequency, and aim of a proficient tobacco-spitter. Though Bartlett had carefully excluded from his dictionary "obscene and blasphemous" words, American cursing was widely noted by British visitors like Charles Murray, who thought western (i.e., trans-Appalachian) swearing worse than that heard in Billingsgate or London gin-shops. Some visitors like Burton, who collected examples, were amused rather than offended by voluble, irreverent profanity; others, with the recent histories of, say, Freeman, in mind, might have reflected on the course the English language had taken after the Norman conquest, whereby the untutored common folk preserved the churlish, bawdy, and coarse words of the plain, blunt Anglo-Saxon tradition rather than adopting the Latinisms of their conquerors.

Anglo-Saxon philology[136] itself flourished in the early and mid-century and provided one, albeit antiquarian, source of a growing Anglo-Saxon*ism* on both sides of the Atlantic—often confirming the project of the earlier lexicographers like Webster. A more than antiquarian interest in Anglo-Saxon studies had been well under way by the beginning of the nineteenth century, when Sharon Turner's three-volume *History of the Anglo-Saxons* (1799–1805) stimulated for decades a wide interest in the freedom-loving and honest folk whom Walter Scott would idealize in *Ivanhoe* (1819). In 1831, Sharon's history was supplemented by that of Francis Palgrave, *History of the Anglo-Saxons*, a work that went through a number of London editions. Both were cited by Joseph Bosworth in his well-received Anglo-Saxon dictionary of 1838. An anonymous critic (Henry Rogers), writing in the *Edinburgh Review*, claimed that, according to Bosworth, nearly five-eighths of the English language was "of Anglo-Saxon origin" (an overestimate), and that these words were "generally expressive of the strongest emotions … the most stirring scenes of human life from the cradle to the grave," it ought to be considered disgraceful "to be ignorant of the history and structure of the English tongue."[137]

By mid-century the Anglo-Saxon idea, not earlier an especially racial construct but one which emphasized language, institutions, the ideals of liberty, and early English Christianity, was coming to mean blood and the struggle of a Teutonic folk. John M. Kemble's two-volume *The Saxons in England: A History of the English Commonwealth Till the Period of the Norman Conquest* (1849) cautiously advanced a racial reading of the destiny of the Anglo-Saxon people—a view that was endorsed less cautiously by

Thomas Carlyle and, in 1864, adopted wholesale by Charles Kingsley in *The Roman and the Teuton*. The robust survival of Englishness amid catastrophe was a major theme of Freeman's five-volume history of the Norman conquest (1870–6),[138] and the institutional history and legacy of England's Anglo-Saxon past formed a large part of the first volume of William Stubbs' monumental *The Constitutional History of England* (Oxford, 1874).

The rhetoric of late nineteenth-century Anglo-Saxonism as a close, transatlantic affinity grounded in history, culture, and blood came easiest, no doubt, to those who already enjoyed some tangible connection or loyalty, whether of genealogy, religious affiliation (especially in the global work of Protestant missionary activity), history, or traveled experience. By the end of the century, as Stephen Tuffnell has observed, "U.S. nationals were diffused widely in the British imperial world ... American communities ... performed specialist, sub-imperial functions to the British imperial state in South Africa, the Sudan, and Egypt, or simply extended the footprint of American commerce to colonial markets in Australia and India."[139] And in the media, the widely publicized marriages in the late nineteenth century of British aristocrats and imperial officials with American heiresses served, as Paul Kramer has suggested, to crystallize "a language of Anglo-Saxon blood and cultural 'kinship,'"[140] though they also were the butt of much derision among American Anglophobes. In America, one may find Anglo-Saxonism often among the New England Brahmin caste with their transatlantic social and intellectual connections, even among those who were aggressively opposed to British imperial meddling in the Western hemisphere: Richard Olney, Cleveland's Secretary of State during the bitter Venezuela crisis, can be found only a year later telling Joseph Chamberlain that Americans would "stand shoulder to shoulder with England in support of a great cause," "[b]ecause of our inborn and instinctive English sympathies, proclivities, modes of thought and standards of right and wrong."[141]

Anglo-Saxonism as Anglophilia was marked in those American tourists to Britain who anticipated not the discovery of difference, but the recovery of "lost relations," and especially pronounced among those many middle- and upper-middle-class Americans who sought to confirm and celebrate their transatlantic ancestry—a prominent phenomenon from the 1880s to the end of the century and beyond. One can find the rhetoric of a hopeful Anglo-American Anglo-Saxonism in some British travelers' journals throughout the century—in 1848 Archibald Prentice of Manchester, England, rejoiced in the expectation of a future in which "men in both countries would drop all narrow jealousies" and look "to the great mission of the Anglo-Saxon family ... to christianise and civilize the whole human race!"[142] It appealed, especially however, in the era of the second Boer and Spanish-American Wars, to those who hoped the Americans might be enlisted in a fraternal defense of global order and beneficent rule. For some Americans, this was a matter of learning as well as racial affinity, of being tutored in the arts of colonial governance by a British Empire that was no longer inimical to American ambition. Much was made in these circles of the widespread, if unsubstantiated, belief that, as Dewey steamed into Manila Bay, the British admiral there not only refrained from intervening but actually restrained other European powers from doing so. As Henry Cabot Lodge put it, at Manila "England stood by the United States."[143] The Rev. Josiah Strong, and much

American journalism, leapt to the same conclusion, with characteristic exaggeration: the Pacific was destined to become an "Anglo-Saxon Sea."[144] Drawing yet wider conclusions, a professor of Political Science at Columbia University, Franklin Henry Giddings, was prepared by 1900 to see imperial Britain no longer as a threat to American democracy but as a fraternal ally in the global rule over "semi-civilized, barbarian, and savage communities." Britain, like the newly imperial America, was "not merely a combination of democracy with empire in a fortuitous association. The union is organic; the whole is a democratic empire." The "future of civilization" would lie in the ability of "English-Speaking people" to dominate in an "international struggle for existence."[145]

Of course, even in the flush of America's easy victories in the Caribbean and the Pacific, Anglo-America was not of one mind. There were those in both Britain and America who doubted the virtue of a global condominium of English-speaking people and expected the likely result of the American projection of its power would be fraternal rivalry. Certainly, British strategic realists, whatever they may have thought or said about the idea of an Anglo-Saxon cousinhood, feared the destabilization of Britain's long-held command of the seas that America's entry into global politics, the proposed Panama Canal, and Roosevelt's Great White Fleet portended. And in America, even those who hoped an Anglo-Saxon understanding would lead to a sharing of global policing also were leery of being dragged as a junior partner into commitments the American public were unlikely to understand or approve. Even the enthusiastic Rev. Strong, keen for a Christian, Anglo-Saxon Anglo-American global imperialism, envisioned a future that was less a sharing of trusteeship than an inheritance of Britain's former role. Already in 1893 he had written of a coming "era of transition": "Americans have outgrown the English." The scepter of world power was passing.[146]

It was a much-contested question whether, by century's end, the pacification and settlement of the American far West meant the successful *conclusion and fulfillment* of its "destiny," as the historian Frederick Jackson Turner seemed to suggest, or, as Brahmin American imperialists like Brooks Adams or Henry Cabot Lodge hoped and expected, would signal the next stage of a wider destiny. At the same time, vocal American anti-imperialists worked hard to counter an Anglo-Saxonism that implied an Anglo-American global condominium. Western and mid-western populists, especially, saw a future American empire as likely to serve the same plutocratic interests they attacked for endorsing the gold standard that was closely associated with British (and Jewish) financial interests—in New York, London, or South Africa.[147] In this, they were not necessarily anti-English (as were, undoubtedly, the New York Irish who had organized an Anti-British Alliance Society in February 1898) and associated their resistance with, and sometimes took their cue from, the Radical-Liberal pro-Boers in Britain. A British-style American imperialism pursued in the Caribbean and the Philippines would subvert, they believed, domestic liberties as well as upend rather than advance, as some imperialists claimed, the century-long hope that the United States would become a beacon of democracy worldwide.

And yet, the struggle in the American West had seemed to many Americans and to British visitors as a wished-for prelude rather than conclusion, and not only among those commercial and financial interests who hoped to profit from empire. Martin Sklar has made the compelling argument, endorsed by Walter LaFeber, that fin de siècle America was transitioning, in its associations and identities, from the isolated local to the intersectional, national, and international.[148] Was this true of Westerners reaching beyond their cowboy parochialism for a central role in the new nation/new empire? In the long decades since Appomattox, it was the West that had provided a testing and training ground for a much-reduced military establishment, distinguished in the spreading cultural mythologies of the West by a special racial heroism. Much was made of the raising of volunteers in the West and Southwest for the war with Spain (Roosevelt famously recruited his Rough Riders from the bar at the Menger Hotel in San Antonio). The American Southwest and West had provided a new generation of ambitious young officers with some hope for advancement. Missouri-born John Joseph Pershing (1860–1948) served with the Sixth Cavalry in California, Arizona, and New Mexico in the final campaigns against the Apache, and in South Dakota and Iowa against the Lakota Sioux in the last of the "Ghost Dance" engagements in 1891. As with many officers kicking their heels at the conclusion of the Indian campaigns, Pershing marked time (as an instructor at West Point) before doing well in the Spanish-American War— he participated in the attack on San Juan Hill, received a Silver Citation Medal, was promoted to major, and took part in the occupation and pacification of Cuba, Puerto Rico, the Philippines, and Guam. In the so-called Philippine Insurrection of 1899– 1902, Pershing was famously, or infamously, central to the army's aggressive counter-insurgency tactics that mirrored, some thought, the most brutal British "methods of barbarism" in South Africa and South Asia.

Though there were those, on both sides of the Atlantic, who enthusiastically thought America, in its reach for world status, could learn much from the British, Pershing, at least later, claimed to have been somewhat skeptical of America's "costly" experiment, driven by "a coterie of imperialists" in Washington "obsessed with the idea of maintaining [America's] new position."[149] He was, however, no Anglophobe, and, en route to assume his duties in the Philippines, embarked in New York on a British steamship for Liverpool and an extended holiday in Great Britain and on the Continent before joining a US hospital ship at Suez for the passage to the Orient. Unlike many traveling fin de siècle Americans, he did not, however, boast of a special need to explore his Anglo-American Anglo-Saxon heritage, but rather was interested, he says, in the "practical" and "instructive." Later, in Hong Kong, he claims to have been "glad to get a first-hand impression of … a clean, well-governed city," "having [himself] been face-to-face with the problem of governing an Asiatic people," and contrasted "the British attitude of permanence with ours of uncertainty" and "no fixed policy."[150]

The great outpouring of Anglo-Saxonist rhetoric at the turn of the century was prompted in part by the contemporary sense, at least in some transatlantic circles, that Great Power politics—no longer confined to Europe—would in the future dictate some form of Anglo-American cooperation. Some fantasized (it was an idea that would survive well into the twentieth century in times of international crisis) that this could take the shape of a formally organized, even perhaps a federated, Anglo-America; others, a growing number of British politicians and military planners in the Edwardian age, if more realistic, came to imagine a world of shared rather than competing imperialisms in which there was a growing "understanding" that, as First Lord of the Admiralty Jackie Fisher (whose only son had married an American) acknowledged, the Americans and British could hardly in the future ever be expected actually to go to war with each other.[151] Moreover, American assumption of a Pacific presence would allow Britain to concentrate on its North Atlantic and North Sea defenses. Joseph Chamberlain,[152] Britain's imperialist Colonial Secretary before and during the second Boer War, and ardent promoter of imperial reform thereafter, for a brief period actually envisioned a formal "Teutonic" alliance with America and Germany before turning to the tighter economic and political organization of British overseas dominions that, without America, could give the United Kingdom the equivalent of the kind of vast internal market and contiguous territorial base that America and Russia possessed.

It may be supposed that the fin de siècle yearning for global Anglo-Saxon cooperation would find a significantly larger and more eager audience in an over-stretched Britain that Chamberlain, quoting Matthew Arnold, would refer to as a Weary Titan. And so it was, at least in that turn-of-the-century moment when Cuba, Puerto Rico, and the Philippines fell into the hands of the Americans.[153] Edward Dicey, a well-connected, prolific journalist and author who had visited America during and after the Civil War, waxed enthusiastic over the "New American Imperialism" in the prominent British monthly *Nineteenth Century*, and, drawing the Americans into an imperial "us," lectured that, as "Great Britain and the United States are complements of one another," they now had an obligation to rule what they had conquered. "With us of the Anglo-Saxon race, as with the Romans of old, there is an innate conviction, sometimes suppressed, but never abandoned, that it is our mission, our manifest destiny, to rule the world."[154] But even among, perhaps especially among, the Unionist and Liberal Imperialist political class there was some skepticism and a reluctance to welcome Buffalo Bill's Wild Westerners as equal partners in any future exercise of British global power—however useful the Americans might be in balancing against other expansionist nations. Though many in Britain applauded, in the moment, America's conquest of maritime Spain,[155] savvier heads were more cautious. Even Dicey was unimpressed with the pre-prandial oratory that flourished in London in '98, speeches that "dwelt mainly upon the fact of blood being thicker than water, upon the brotherhood between the two nations to whom Shakespeare and Milton were common possessions, and upon the guarantees afforded by Anglo-American amity for the interests of peace and progress."[156] Prime Minister Salisbury himself, no lover of vulgar, materialistic, and democratic America, resisted the enthusiasm of some of his cabinet, promised a strict neutrality, and worried at the dramatic diminishing of a Spain that had been a useful (if declining) factor in the balance of power in Europe.[157] Others argued in public against the emotional current: in the *Saturday Review*, an anonymous contributor dismissed the American victory in Cuba as "the spectacle of seventy-two millions of people playing the armed highwayman with a nation of seventeen millions; a nation that poses as the champion of freedom … the whole incident is simply a piece of land-grabbing." Writing anonymously as "Diplomaticus" in the *Fortnightly Review*, Lucien Wolf, Anglo-Jewish journalist and historian, argued for a larger realist view in the face of the pro-American stance of much of the British press, and attacked those British statesmen such as Chamberlain, Balfour, and Asquith who claimed to find promise in the dream of a "closer union of Great Britain and America." "The popular idea that an Anglo-American alliance may be based on affinities of race or identity of language … is a delusion. … Prince Bismarck … declared it the other day to be 'nonsense.'" Alliances were best based on "material interests" such as might possibly be found in some limited Anglo-American arrangement in the far East. The same year, the journalist and naval historian Herbert W. Wilson, writing anonymously in a journal not known for pro-American sentiments and recalling the "unprovoked and indefensible menaces of the United States" during the Venezuela affair, was nevertheless less pessimistic, taking, oddly, some encouragement from the fact that, he claimed, nearly "every admiral and captain on the American Navy List has an unmistakably British name."[158]

In neither Britain nor America did Anglo-Saxon, Anglo-American vaporings, though taken up in many journals and newspapers,[159] have anything like universal attraction. As early as 1872 a highly annoyed and exasperated Allayne Legard claimed that it was "impossible" to think that "Americans are destined to carry farther west the stream of civilization which has gone out from England … our ideas of honour, honesty, truth, religion, self-restraint, and moral conduct … the advance of the Anglo-Saxon race and religion."[160] In America, even an Anglo-Saxonist like Roosevelt, though eager to emulate Britain, saw the relationship as one of guarded-if-friendly competition rather than alliance and consolidation. Americans were, in any event, long and deeply invested in a politics of isolation and the Monroe Doctrine, and Irish-Americans were, to say the least, loudly opposed to any Anglo-American reconciliation.

Finally, however much some western Americans may have found themselves soldiers of the Queen in various theaters of the British Empire, or performing for British audiences in London, there hardly seems to be the kind of enthusiasm in the Western United States for the Anglo-American Anglo-Saxonism that one could find in Boston, New York, or London. That may be due to the prevalence of Irish-American newspaper editors from Chicago to San Francisco, to the bad odor of British land-grabbing in the western states and territories, or to the derision in which the British dude was held, or even, in the enthusiasm of the moment, to a reluctance to share pride in the Great Republic's single-handed conquest of a European so-called Power. In the West, Anglo-Saxonism had some traction in the conceit that it suggested a kind of *ur*-democracy—a harkening back to the idealized egalitarianism of the warrior band and the ancient witans and moots praised by Stubbs, Freeman, et al. This interpretation rubbed against the elitist, Brahmin-class Anglophilia of East-coast Anglo-Saxonism. When, in 1902, the Australian author George E. Boxall published his loose and ranging book, *The Anglo-Saxon: A Study in Evolution*, he was concerned to locate real Anglo-Saxonism among the more democratic settler-peoples of Greater Britain, rather than in Britain itself with its hereditary nobility and hereditary poverty. Having lived in both America and Australia, Boxall was convinced that one had to turn to these countries to find societies that were both abolishing privilege and preserving the Anglo-Saxon drive to expand and colonize. It was this ancient drive that propelled the American, having reached the limits of his continental frontier, to seek a role in the world. For Boxall, Anglo-Saxonism implied a "young and growing race" no longer to be found in Britain: "The great barrier to the union of the Anglo-Saxons throughout the world is undoubtedly the tenacity with which the Englishman adheres to the relics of his medievalism."[161]

While we find some British tourists in America and adventure-writers like Henty ready to invoke the Anglo-Saxon ideal in their observations of western American life, can the same be said of westerners themselves? Clearly, the mythology of the West—of a significantly masculine society of gold rushers, hunters, and ranchers—had encouraged an idealization of an unrestrained white manhood on the periphery of empire that resonated with the fin de siècle Anglo-American racialized and gendered understanding of "Anglo-Saxon."[162] But in spite of tracts like Boxall's, and the many titles invoking some aspect of Anglo-Saxondom that were rushed through the London and New York presses at the turn of the century,[163] on the ground in the American West it is hard to demonstrate that Anglo-Saxon*ism* exercised a more than occasional rhetorical appeal. It is certainly true that in California the inflamed local politics of Chinese exclusion signaled an intense racial bigotry, but this targeted a much broader than "Anglo-Saxon" part of the, often Irish-American, working-class population who were unlikely to have been amenable to the idea of Anglo-Saxonism as a "racial-exceptionalist bridge" that "developed a self-conscious bond connecting Britons and Americans."[164] Admitting, with Kramer, that Anglo-Saxonism in America seems to have had more to do with affirming American colonial expansion than building bridges to the British, one suspects this still overstates the case. It is hard to discover, in, say, Pershing's stolid memoirs,[165] that Anglo-Saxonist idealism—flourished with such elan by some politicians and in the press in 1898—actually did much to shape private identities or ambitions in the cowboy West. However much facilitated by a white masculine Western ideology, the initiating, driving force behind America's own turn to empire arguably lay elsewhere—in the boardroom perhaps rather than in the street.

CHAPTER 5
TRANSATLANTIC BIRTHRIGHT: "A PILGRIMAGE OF THE HEART"

> We could fancy that amidst all their self-gratulation on the equality of rank and their pride in an all-pervading democracy, there is still some pining for patrician ancestry; some yearning towards venerable dust ….
>
> [Anon. reviewer, "Indications of Philosophic Progress in the United States," *Foreign Quarterly* 24 (1840), 279]

As an ideology, the Anglo-American Anglo-Saxonism of the late nineteenth century can be presumed to have encouraged some prosperous middle- and upper-class Americans to explore, as tourists, their transatlantic cultural and racial/ethnic "birthright." New England Brahmins and those aspiring to be considered such had been concerned to trace their descent from the "Pilgrim fathers" long before the Mayflower Society (no Irish, Germans, or Italians need apply) was founded in 1897. Something of the same zeal probably lies behind the late nineteenth-century interest generally in genealogies that confirmed not just patriotic but transatlantic connections. Following the enthusiasm in higher circles for Anglo-American cooperation in 1898, reciprocating "Pilgrims Societies" were established in New York and London to celebrate and ritualize, at least among the political and diplomatic elite, the turn-of-the-century Anglo-American rapprochement. Ironically, perhaps, the Sons of the American Revolution (1889) and the Daughters of the American Revolution (1890) tacitly endorsed also an exclusionary British heritage—their members were usually if not exclusively descended from colonial families of English and Scots or Scots-Irish origin. As the title of an article in *Harper's Weekly* had announced during the wildly popular visit of the Prince of Wales in 1860, "Every American Descends from a Redcoat."[1]

In 1863, Sir John Bernard Burke of *Burke's Peerage* claimed that, in the 1840s and 50s, "the most intelligent and zealous of my genealogical clients were on the other side of the Atlantic, all yearning to carry back their ancestry to the fatherland."[2] Francesca Morgan has recently described the nineteenth-century growth, especially from the 1840s, of the *practice* of genealogy—Anglo-American families researching their own ancestry, the proliferation of antiquarian journals publishing readers' genealogical queries, and societies like the New England Historic and Genealogical Society (f. 1845) or the New York Genealogical and Biographical Society (f. 1869) that specialized in family histories. Though interest in tracing family history reaches back into the late eighteenth century, like the analogous interest in Anglo-Saxonism it grew significantly from the late antebellum era when Nativism prompted a concerned effort to distance Anglo-American

Protestants from the surging immigration of Irish and Continental Others. By 1868, some 340 American families had *published* their genealogies. By 1909, at least 3,795 had done so. As a phenomenon, Morgan argues, this growth in genealogical interest (and advertisement) may be closely associated through the century with a defense of white supremacy, as well as with status-seeking in an era of growing middle-class prosperity.[3]

The steady growth in American tourism to Britain and to Europe from about 1840[4] extended, especially after the Civil War, from the old establishment of New York, Philadelphia, and Boston to those of the growing mid-western professional and commercial classes now able to indulge themselves in leisured foreign travel, and to the newly wealthy of, say, California, Colorado, and Nevada. How much of that increase in travel was motivated, at least in part, by a search for cultural and personal heritage is impossible to quantify. It was pushed on by a host of factors—especially the rising per capita incomes that enabled it, the increased availability of berths by a multiplicity of steamship companies, the growing provision of quality hotels abroad, guidebooks and tour-facilitating agencies, and simply the convenience of travel—the availability, speed, and comfort that encouraged *families* to travel abroad.[5]

Taking a steamship to Liverpool need not as a matter of course imply Anglophilism among Americans with the means and leisure to travel. Often, for the very wealthy, this was but the first port of call in an extended grand tour, via London, of the Continent. When the wealthy ex-governor and current senator for California, Leland Stanford, and his wife took their fifteen-year-old only son on a second European tour late in 1883, they crossed first to Britain to visit museums and auction houses, then made their way to Paris and the Louvre before departing for the east, to Turkey and Athens where Leland Stanford, Jr., fell ill with typhoid, dying some weeks later in Florence. In Henry James' *The Wings of the Dove* (1902), the young, rich, and, like Leland Jr., fated heiress Milly Theale, New England companion in tow, moved between Switzerland and Venice, but, like many rich Americans abroad, she also had connections of importance in London, the "crown" destination, James tells us,[6] in Milly's moving circuit. It is also true that many Americans who sailed directly to the Continent (where there were American communities of the leisured wealthy in, especially, Florence, Rome, and Venice) would have often been part of a Protestant English-speaking community, sharing with British visitors they may already have known socially in London religious services, dinner tables, and excursions.

Amid the increasing volume of travel to Britain, American sightseers explored "the mighty muchness" (as Henry James called it[7]) of London, provincial England, and Scotland, seeking out the cultural signposts of a common *literary* heritage, as at Shakespeare's Stratford-on-Avon, Sir Walter Scott's Abbotsford, or Wordsworth's Lake District[8] or special sites of transatlantic historical connection associated with Pilgrim or patriot families. Similarly, tourism that centered on the enjoyment of the *natural beauty* of rural Britain—the Lake District, the Cotswolds, northern Wales, the Scottish Highlands—could reflect a Victorian conservationism that became an Anglo-American phenomenon. Memoirs suggest that a personal reconnection to the Mother Country often played at least a part in these travel plans. Already in 1851, Frederick Law Olmsted had managed to combine his search for what England could tell him about conserving open spaces and building parks and gardens with a bit of personal heritage—he stopped at the "Olmsted Hall farm" in Essex and mentioned the fact because "the incident is so characteristic of an American's visit to England."[9]

In America, the "father of the National Parks," John Muir (1838–1914), was a Scot who, like Andrew Carnegie, emigrated with his family as a child of eleven or twelve. He went West in 1868, settled in San Francisco, and campaigned for the preservation of Yosemite and the sequoias. Like Carnegie, he also claimed an enduring attachment to the Scottish (East Lothian) home of his early childhood.[10] The creation of national parks in America or the American-Canadian effort to preserve Niagara Falls from commercialization was paralleled in Britain by the campaigns of the Commons Preservation Society (founded 1865) and the creation in 1895 of the National Trust for Places of Historical Interest or Natural Beauty, both of which drew upon some American financial support and patronage.[11] The American banker Claudius Patten, an advocate for the ongoing work in Britain of the Commons Preservation Society, took his young son on an 1884 walking tour of rural England, "a perfect paradise." He found the scenery beautiful, the remains of ancient Roman roads fascinating, and the locals "servile, stupid, without hope or ambition"—a fact he ascribes to the aristocratic landowners who have taken the commons for their own.[12] Thirty-three years earlier, Olmsted had said something similar about the "degraded, poor, stupid, brutal, and licentious" laborers of the English countryside, beset by gross inequality, the game laws, and the looming presence in the midst of rough rural poverty of towering piles being built by great wealthy magnates such as the Marquis (later Duke) of Westminster.[13] But Olmsted, who became America's leading designer of urban parks and gardens, also found in Britain positive signs that influenced his own developing sense of how cities might be "improved." There were the new urban amenities of English cities as in Liverpool and Birkenhead which were creating pleasing "public gardens and pleasure grounds," and even the country towns "had a better garden-republic [a 'green' or a public garden] than any town I know of in the United States."[14] For the wealthy, name-dropping, much-traveled Philadelphia journalist Charles Godfrey Leland, who took up residence in London in 1869, the carefully tended green and beautiful garden-like English countryside was evocative of an *American* past when

> that older American population was deeply English, with a thousand rural English traditions religiously preserved; and the chief of these is clean neatness, which, when fully carried out, always results in simple, unaffected beauty.[15]

Woodrow Wilson, whose grandfather Thomas Woodrow was from Paisley and whose mother Janet was born in Carlisle, "proud to the last of her English heritage," would visit the Lake District on a number of bicycle tours from 1896, accompanied at times by his friend the Rev. Canon Hardwicke Rawnsley, a founder of the National Trust. He intended to continue doing so after his presidency as "a pilgrimage of the heart."[16]

1 The American in Britain

Americans had traveled to the Mother Country in growing numbers from the late eighteenth century. Some, following in the wake of the late-eighteenth-century domestic British fashion for the aesthetics of the rural picturesque in literature, painting, and guided touring,[17] were dedicated "tourists." Most however arrived with other purposes and combined these with a little sight-seeing before returning to the United States. The number can only be guessed at. As the transatlantic interests of "traveling salesmen, merchants, and financiers" and "socialites and genteel Americans joining headlong the rush of the London social 'Season'" expanded, the number of Americans abroad in the second half of the century grew substantially. Those who for a variety of reasons chose to remain as long-stayers also grew, if less exponentially. From the post-Civil War era to the 1910s the census for England and Wales, which probably missed many, recorded a doubling from around seven or eight thousand, mostly in Liverpool and London, to over fourteen thousand American residents—possibly as many as twenty thousand.[18] These constituted a "metropolitan class" of merchants, financiers, and lawyers from New York, Philadelphia, and New England, as well as artists and wealthy transatlantic socialites. In mid-century London, the more prominent, such as the financier Joshua Bates or, especially, the wealthy philanthropist George Peabody, had attracted about them a set or circle of Americans and the prominent British friends with whom they socialized.[19] This American "colony" in London grew through the late nineteenth century (peaking perhaps in the 1890s) "as a self-constructed national community consisting of social clubs, journals and economic institutions that provided a venue for social, cultural and economic exchange between Anglo-American elites." The thickening network of resident and touring Americans, "transnational connectors," was influential, it has been claimed, in shaping "the nature of US overseas economic exchange, cultural encounter, social interaction, and diplomatic engagement."[20]

Will B. Mackintosh has recently observed that commercial tourism's origins in America (and by extension, one assumes, in Britain) should be traced to the maturing of capitalism in the early nineteenth century, the formation of bourgeois identity, and the "commodification of travel experiences," a "slow, gradual, and uneven process."[21] Though a fully developed international tourism "industry" is often associated with the vast increase in Americans going abroad after the Second World War, Victorian Britain more or less invented commercially organized excursions as an industrial-age phenomenon— in both the facilitation of travel abroad (to the Continent, the Empire, and America) and the creation of a domestic infrastructure that encouraged Europeans, colonials, and, especially, Americans to visit Britain.

The Great Exhibition in 1851 saw an unprecedented number of Americans travel to London. Though the Crystal Palace in Hyde Park may have been one sight among many, it was a "special wonder" and a "cynosure of industry" that marked a "novel phaze [sic] of our civilization" in what Samuel S. Cox of Ohio called that "annus mirabilis"—a matter of awe "in this age of material progress."[22] It also served to encourage a more general interest in sight-seeing among upper-middle-class Americans. Cox, who visited the

Great Exhibition repeatedly, admired other London sights and experiences like the poets' corner at the Abbey (especially the Garrick monument with its bust of "Shakspeare") and applied to the American minister for a ticket for the House of Commons where he observed that the strangers' gallery was "pretty full, mostly of Americans."[23] Visitors were encouraged by trip-planning firms in both America and Britain, the promotional efforts of competing steam-ship companies, and the rapidly expanding railway network in England and Scotland. There was a literature (guidebooks,[24] travel narratives, periodicals extolling town and country sights, and illustrated books of views of London monuments or the Lake District) to inform and entice visitors.

Competing railways built hotels to receive them. Americans landing, as most did, at Liverpool found the London & North Western Railway Hotel there vying with the Midland Railway's Adelphi for their custom, and fast trains to London where the major termini offered at St. Pancras, King's Cross, Euston, Charing Cross, or Paddington large hotels with convenient access to shopping and sight-seeing. These were relatively luxurious institutions that could service, "at varying rates," the needs not only of single male commercial and professional travelers but of respectable families or unaccompanied women,[25] providing not just over-night lodging but "public rooms for ladies," coffee and tea service, bars, restaurants, and reading, smoking, and billiard rooms. For the more modest tourist there were myriad small hotels and boarding houses, and "housing agents" ready to recommend these or private apartments for long-stayers. Hotels in London and the major provincial cities catered as well to specialized fractions of the tourist trade—temperance advocates or those seeking the respectability and security of women-only establishments. From the era of the Great Exhibition to the end of the century, guided tours of many of the capital's iconic sights and institutions—like the National Gallery—proliferated.

Though one can assume that the significant increase in transatlantic tourism from the 1870s through the Edwardian era had something, at least, to do with the growth and prosperity of an enabled upper middle class and, for some at least, with a search for a status-confirming Anglo-American, Anglo-Saxon identity, in fact the decision to travel was likely to have been various, complex, and layered. It was a matter of fashion, curiosity, the search for "culture" and history, and sometimes professional interest and connections, and grew by—that is fed upon—the increased pace and volume of travel itself, the growth of leisure, and some fading of the previously common American sense of a righteous self-isolation. In previous decades, as we have seen, many American travelers to Britain, such as Fenimore Cooper, had material interests to pursue there but sought to maintain a skeptical attitude, protective of American virtue, toward the land of aristocracy, monarchy, and social arrogance. But other literary figures of the antebellum era such as Irving or Emerson were more comfortable in English Society and were on an easy familiarity with English literary figures. Like any tourist, Emerson enjoyed the National Gallery and dined with both British notables and Americans abroad such as the Bancrofts.

Elizabeth Davis Bancroft, married to the American minister (from 1846) to Britain, the Bostonian historian George Bancroft, came to London unsure of what "a republican

Figure 4 "Visitors to the National Gallery" (c. 1874), by James Jacques Joseph Tissot [Alamy].

woman" such as herself (she was born in Plymouth, Mass., "of Puritan stock") would find there, but discovered that "one soon gets used to all things." Putting aside the difficulty of comprehending the elaborate and strict hierarchy, not of the aristocratic class but of the servants who waited upon them, she claimed to have come to like the English "extremely, even more than I expected." Like Emerson, whom she entertained at dinner, Elizabeth Bancroft enjoyed cultural touring with other Americans in residence at the National Gallery and, on open-to-the-public days, Windsor castle. At Hampton Court, guided by a maid of honor to Victoria, she managed to avoid the parties of "150 or so persons [mostly American tourists] following on" one's heels. Though she told the Marquis of Lansdown that she "was as proud of my pure Anglo-Saxon Pilgrim descent as if it were traced from a line of Norman conquerors," she clearly distanced herself from those awkward American friends who "praise the 'model republic' too loudly," and seems to have rather enjoyed the ritual and ceremony of her husband's position. "The courtesy made to royalty is very like the one I was taught to make when a little girl at Miss Tuft's school in Plymouth. One sinks down instead of stepping back in dancing-school fashion."[26]

Nevertheless, well into the later nineteenth century many Americans who visited for whatever reason and enjoyed the companionship of Britons continued, as earlier, to weave a narrative that combined enjoyment of the cultural, literary, and historical offerings with a careful defensiveness of republican American virtue. Emerson had done so ("inequality of power and property shocks republican nerves"[27]); so did Olmsted ("God keep us evermore free from a 'powerful conservative landed gentry'"[28]), and so to the end of the century. As John Stoddard carefully put it in his popular 1898 lecture on Britain, "we are so much alike that both of us, unfortunately, adopt the privilege of relatives and criticize each other … [w]hether we like the English Government or not, nothing can change the fact that England is our old home."[29] This persistent combination of nostalgia and critique was encouraged, no doubt, by the British themselves, who interrogated their American visitors out of curiosity about and expectation of their angular difference.[30] It may also be true that those American visitors to Britain who made a point of expressing their reservations about the English were sensitive to the public expectation back home that Americans abroad would patriotically fly the flag, so to speak. A touchy boastfulness was long claimed by the British to be typical of the American at home and abroad. As George Borrett wrote in his journal of an American tour in 1864:

> Now if you have ever met an American in England or on the Continent, you will have been informed by him before you have had five minutes' conversation with him, that no street in the world is worth looking at after Broadway; that there is no thoroughfare in London, or Paris, or St. Petersburg, half so wide, or one quarter so long, or one tenth part so handsome, or one hundredth part so full of life, and traffic, and business, and trade. If you are talking of shops he will take the opportunity of telling you that there is nothing like 'our stores down Broadway.[31]

Some Americans, however, who found themselves comfortably among social and political friends in Britain may have looked within and wondered about the oppositional definition of Americanness. Elihu Burrit, who traveled to Britain in 1846 to promote world peace and was later made American consul in Birmingham, wrote in his diary that he feared "ceasing to be an American." Oliver Wendell Holmes teasingly admonished his fellow Bostonian John Lathrop Motley, appointed minister to Great Britain in 1869, not to "stay too long" for fear of his changing his allegiance.[32] Henry James would note that a later American minister, the New England poet James Russell Lowell, made, unsurprisingly for the author of the *Bigelow Papers*, an effort to be "conspicuously American."[33] In what David Wrobel calls "an antitravel novel," *A Tramp Abroad* (1880), Mark Twain parodied those Americans who crossed the ocean in search of cultural treasures or renowned landscapes, and as late as 1897 the American humor magazine,

Puck, admonished well-to-do travelers for making inauthentic fools of themselves by affectation and fancy language not their own in a piece on "The American Millionaire at Home and Abroad; or, Why a Great Many of Our Rich Men Ought to Refrain from 'Crossing the Pond.'"[34] It was mining a familiar theme.

Public men (and some women), including literary and artistic ex-pats who took up residence in Britain, were in fact often subjected to criticism in the American press, and some were doubtless sensitive to appearances that time spent there inevitably meant a certain loss of patriotism and identity. This could lead to a defensive reaction, as when Harriet Stanton Blatch, the outspoken feminist daughter of the women's rights activist Elizabeth Cady Stanton, married an Englishman and moved to Hampshire. She protested that nonetheless she had "deep in my heart ... remained an American" though by marriage she "became automatically an Englishwoman." "It satisfied my self-respect, however, to refuse to take a definite step indicating that I considered myself a subject of Queen Victoria."[35] In others, residence in Britain could lead to expressions of actual Anglophobia, as with Adam Badeau, an aide to General and President Grant who appointed him consul-general in London (1870–88). In 1886, Badeau, recycling long-held American views, would claim that the continuing influence of aristocracy and hierarchy rendered the British "often arrogant, supercilious and rude ... debasing the spirit and degrading the behavior to an extent incomprehensible to an American ... this relic of barbarism."[36]

One can find similar long-familiar complaints in at least some of the late nineteenth-century tourist memoirs, but over time it becomes less of a theme as the relatively brief touring holiday rather than long-stay residence came to typify the transatlantic experience. The spread of tourism to the middle classes meant that most visitors increasingly had little to do with Society and the London Season, with letters of introduction and invitations to stay at country houses. Their memoirs are full, not of wariness of losing their republican virtue but of Baedeker sights[37] and the quaintness of an old, perhaps obsolescent, world. In 1867 Percy Roberts found judges' wigs "droll," and, as with the "pomp and ancient circumstance of coronations," a "faint aroma of long-ago hallows the whole body of their customs."[38] Narratives often still commonly present them-vs-us comparisons but in a less acerbic, less adversarial way, as when John Burroughs, a naturalist and biographer of Whitman who had first traveled to Britain (on business) in 1871, commented somewhat condescendingly in 1876 that "the English people are a mellow people ... By contrast, things here [in America] are loud, sharp, and full of violent changes and contrasts ... There is, indeed, a charm about these ancestral races that goes to the heart."[39] Observations are often presented in a comic-ironic rather than apprehensive vein, as in the Rev. George Monroe Royce's humorous if barbed anecdotes.[40] One of these involves a story of a young American who had been to Eton and Oxford, touring with his elderly uncle, a crusty Yankee of a previous generation. The youth can (and wishes to) "pass" as English and admonishes his uncle not to "give yourself away." The uncle retorts that "you are a fool and *have given yourself away* ... in a real sense."[41]

The ever-more-common heritage tourism of the late nineteenth and early twentieth centuries did, especially in the years surrounding the inflated Anglophobia of the

Venezuela affair, trigger ironic commentary in the press. Much the same treatment stressing the probable inauthenticity of wealthy Americans who looked across the ocean for their culture, their history, and their social relationships may be found in commentary on the highly publicized marriage of American heiresses to British aristocrats. James Fullerton Muirhead, a Scot writer of travel guides, observed in 1898 that

> the daughter of a New York multi-millionaire, who has been brought up to regard a British duke or an Italian prince as her natural partner for life, does not look out on the world through genuinely American spectacles, but is biassed [sic] by a point of view which may be somewhat paradoxically termed the 'cosmopolitan-exclusive.' As Mr. Henry James puts it: 'After all, what one sees on a Newport piazza is not America; it is the back of Europe.'[42]

A sense of (or at least a longing for) a shared history and a personal heritage (linguistic, aesthetic, genealogical, and religious) grew after the Civil War and was sustained, at least among many of the middle and upper classes, well into the following century. It was marked by the proliferation of memorials in Britain to American origins there, and was encouraged, often, by British visitors to the States with an interest in confirming transatlantic ties. Following the 1878 visit to Boston of Westminster Abbey's Dean Stanley, "ancient stones" from English Cathedrals, ruined abbeys, and medieval churches were presented by visitors to namesake towns in the United States.[43] Even among the cosmopolitan wealthy of America who sought out the fashions of Paris and the villas of Rome and Venice in their grand touring, there could be an animated interest in reclaiming a presence in the Mother Country. This could take the form of frequent travel[44] and intimate transatlantic social connections, as with the Boston Forbeses or the New York Astors. Some kept palatial residences in both countries. An eccentric case, the American patrician William Waldorf Astor, abruptly broke with his American relations and moved his family to London in 1889, becoming naturalized there a decade later. He regarded England, his grandson said, "as a haven for people like himself who respected tradition and the rule of law and order, and who wished to enjoy, in an untroubled way, the privileges of wealth." His carriages were painted the same chocolate brown used by the royal family.[45] Or Andrew Carnegie, who, though remaining a determined republican, built a baronial manor in Scotland for his frequent stays in the "Old Land."

Carnegie (1835–1919) was, with his very modest origins in Dunfermline, no patrician, having emigrated age twelve to America with his impoverished handloom weaver father and mother. One of the wealthiest of the self-made Gilded-Age industrialists, he claimed in his *Autobiography* that "my heart was [always] in Scotland."[46] On a tour with his mother back to Fife in 1862, he felt, or so he later tells us, "as if I could throw myself upon the sacred soil and kiss it."[47] There were many other trips back to Britain—in 1867 a walking tour through England and in 1881 a coaching party from Brighton to Inverness. In 1877 the freedom of "my native town" was conferred on him, and in 1887 he and his American wife spent their honeymoon on the Isle of Wight. Though Carnegie's affection for Scotland was, like his lifelong Scots identity, real, it is likely that, like his wealth and his philanthropy, it grew with nostalgia over time.

Carnegie's transatlanticism and sense of heritage, not of British institutions but of the domestic virtues of the common, honest, hard-working, self-denying Scot, was as complex an affair as his own national identity. He spoke often, if loosely and inconsistently, of the ties of "race" ("The pride of race is always there at the bottom"[48]) that bound America to Britain, but, as a Scot, the race he invoked was not exactly white Anglo-Saxonism, but something more akin to the older usage—of blood-as-culture ("one language, one religion, one literature, and one law"[49]). A passionate advocate of Anglo-American peace and the drawing together of the English-speaking peoples, he also, as a Scottish-American republican and patriot, wrote and spoke against the British monarchy as a feudal institution, though he had great regard for Victoria. The future he liked to envision was one where a republican Britain would "grasp the outstretched hand of her children in America, and become again as she was before, the mother member of the English-speaking race."[50] Unlike the Tory-leaning Astors, most of his closest British friends and fellow campaigners, such as James Bryce, were of the Liberal and Radical-Liberal left. At the same time, he encouraged by example the growing nostalgic tourism of the era—the coach trip he planned for his mother and select American and British friends in 1881 pointedly rejected the city-to-city rail travel favored by most visitors.

By the late 1880s, in spite of what some were beginning to speak of as the "American invasion,"[51] Americans were still an unusual presence in non-metropolitan, out-of-the-way places. Nora Stanton Barney recalled that in her childhood in the Hampshire market town of Basingstoke—she was born in 1883—she could not remember seeing a single American.[52] Carnegie's leisurely horse-drawn journey (he subsequently planned others) along highways and byways wound through provincial and rural Britain, also pausing at what were becoming the iconic "sights" for literary, cultural-historical, and architectural tourism—Oxford and "its queer old-fashioned places," "superb, grand" Blenheim Palace, Haddon Hall, and Chatsworth ("here we come upon tourists' ground … and readers are therefore respectfully referred to the guidebooks"), and Grasmere and Wordsworth's grave ("[t]he coaches in the Lake District have now the English and American flags upon their sides, and we often see the Stars and Stripes displayed at hotels"). Most evocative of his own sense of Britishness-and-Americanness was, however, their "pilgrimage" to Shakespeare's birthplace at Stratford-upon-Avon ("I have been there often").[53] His love of Shakespeare dated back to his early days as a telegraph messenger in Pittsburgh where telegraph boys had free admission to the second tier of the old Pittsburgh Theater: "Thenceforth there was nothing for me but Shakespeare."[54]

American pilgrimages to Stratford-upon-Avon were nothing new. In 1805 Benjamin Silliman, in Britain to buy books for Yale University, took time for a little sightseeing at Oxford ("No place ever impressed me with such feelings of admiration and awe") and at Stratford to see Shakespeare's "birthplace house."[55] Through the century the association with the national poet made Stratford a mecca of sorts for those Americans like Washington Irving who were associated with literature or the theater. Indeed, undue

American interest in actually acquiring Shakespeare's birthplace—in 1847 P. T. Barnum offered to buy the house and ship it to New York—sparked a movement to preserve it as a national museum.[56] Fanny Kemble's daughter relocated near Stratford after leaving America in 1876 and entertained Henry James and her mother there. The building of a memorial theatre, library, and picture gallery, completed in 1879 and dedicated the next year, after years of fund-raising on both sides of the Atlantic, inaugurated a continuing era in which the city came to be an inevitable center, connected by rail to London via a change at Oxford, of not just theatrical but general commercially organized tourism. In 1887, Henry Irving, in the company of the American minister Edward John Phelps, unveiled a gothic granite monument (water fountain and clock) to Shakespeare, paid for by subscriptions raised by the American newspaper proprietor W. G. Childs.[57] He read verses written for the occasion by Oliver Wendell Holmes.[58]

The California actress, Mary Anderson, as a matter of course visited Stratford, "lingering as long as possible," and would play Rosalind in the Memorial Theatre. She found the experience of the bard's birthplace, as other Americans apparently did, a romantic, almost a mystical one that inspired deep thoughts of a shared bond and heritage:

> I was allowed to sit alone in the room where the great bard was born … Those bright spring mornings in the hallowed house … threw over each hour a spell of the olden time, when the Bard of Avon lived and sang and loved … and, to finish the evening, a row in the moonlight by the old church, where the master now "sleeps well."[59]

William Winter, the influential American drama critic, visited more than once and found in "Shakespeare's church" an eternal and sanctified shrine: "Nothing here is changed. The same tranquil beauty, as of old, hallows this place."[60]

By the 1880s American accounts of traveling in Britain could be expected to include at least a passing reference, and usually more, to a visit to Stratford-upon-Avon. Richard White gives his 1881 memoir a twenty-one-page chapter on the city, noting that on the train down a companion "informed me, before she suspected my nationality, that all 'Americans' go to Stratford" before going on to Paris. White's own (characteristically elitist, somewhat contrarian) regret was that the Stratford of Shakespeare that he had previously known "has passed away," having now "a smug business look, an air of money-making … I felt wronged and robbed by this thrifty, airy, clean, hard, progressive-looking place." Nor would he recommend "Shakespeare's church," which had been restored "to look like some imitation Gothic thing put up on contract yesterday by a firm of carpenters and builders."[61] But this was an eccentric view; the common, reflective American tourist such as Claudius Patten held Stratford because of its meaningful associations to be "a town without an equal in its attractions for the traveler from the United States."[62] In these accounts the clichéd language used to describe encounters with culture-as-a-form-of-religion—their "pilgrimages," the "hallowed" ground they walked upon, the "shrines" of the past, etc.—speaks of a reverence many must have felt, at least before the onslaught of a truly mass tourism of railway and auto day-trippers and crocodiles of well-marshaled school children.

The Earl of Birkenhead claimed, in an introduction to a guidebook of 1924, that "Stratford-upon-Avon belongs almost as much to America as to England."[63] But while a trip to Stratford may have become de rigeur for the American tourist itinerary, those modern tourists who rushed from place to Baedeker-recommended place, and who thronged Stratford's streets between the down and up scheduled trains in Bradshaw's railway timetable, can hardly be expected to have invested quite the depth of connection that more reflective visitors did. In 1883, Daniel Pidgeon, commenting on the rush of American "innocents going abroad," claimed that he had been asked by one at an Oxford hotel,

> Do you think I might shunt York Minster on my way to the north? I have seen everything here, and the English antiques [antiquities] are so much alike that I will lump them, and save a day, if you so advise.[64]

The ignorance of the common tourist would remain well into the twentieth century a matter of condescending British humor. In 1882 Baillie-Grohman noted that "[w]e laugh at the American tourist who at Holyrood mistakes the butler for the Lord Chamberlain, and in Westminster Abbey addresses a chorister as the Dean."[65] A few years earlier, Sir George Campbell observed that Americans "almost invariably, after spending a few days in the country and seeing Windsor, Stratford-on-Avon, and Abbotsford, … go to the Continent of Europe," something he thought might be improved by Britain doing more actually to welcome and encourage the visitors (who Pidgeon estimated had brought $20,000,000 into Europe 1873–83)—a view that would remain a cogent critique well into the twentieth century of a Britain reluctant to view itself as the mere object, like Italy, of tourist consumption.[66]

Much was made of Stratford-upon-Avon and other urban and rural attractions in the travel literature available to Americans in the late nineteenth and early twentieth centuries.[67] To these was added, especially in the Edwardian era and following, a growing number of illustrated guides to sights especially, it was thought, attractive to American visitors because of some transatlantic, often genealogical, association—M. B. Huish, *The American Pilgrim's Way in England to Homes and Memorials of the Founders of Virginia, the New England States, and Pennsylvania, the Universities of Harvard & Yale, the First President of the United States & Other Illustrious Americans* (London, 1907), Alfred T. Story, *American Shrines in England* (New York, 1908), or Anne Hollingsworth Wharton, *English Ancestral Homes of Noted Americans* (Philadelphia and London, 1915). Travel that centered on "pilgrimages" to "American Shrines on English Soil" (the title of James Muirhead's 1924 guide published by a leading travel agency) was a key part of the "heritage tourism" that accompanies fin de siècle transatlantic Anglo-Saxonism. Plaques went up and sites were museumized—usually with the financial support of American backers. Among the first of these were the Harvard house in Stratford's High Street and

Sulgrave Manor in Northamptonshire, a Tudor house built by a distant relative of George Washington.

The "Ancient House" in Shakespeare's Stratford-upon-Avon was built in 1596 by the maternal grandfather of the eponymous benefactor-founder of Harvard College. At the urging of the popular English novelist "Marie Corelli" (Mary Mackay), it was purchased in 1909 by the very wealthy Jewish American, Edward Morris, owner of a Chicago meat-packing company. Heavily restored, the property was given to Harvard University "as a sign of friendship between the two nations." From early in the nineteenth century, Harvard-educated New Englanders had been among the most frequent of

Figure 5 Harvard House, Stratford-upon-Avon [Alamy].

American visitors to England. The physical memento of the university and its founder in Stratford was as appropriate an acknowledgment of these Anglo-Saxon connections as the restoration, also co-funded by American graduates of the university, of the so-called Harvard chapel in Southwark Cathedral in 1905–7 (John Harvard had been baptized in what was then St. Saviour's Church, in 1607), or the placing of a stained-glass window and memorial tablet to the Harvard-educated poet and American minister to Great Britain, James Russell Lowell in Westminster Abbey, where it joined the memorial (1884) to Longfellow. The Harvard House became prominent in American tourist itineraries; plaques and memorials to others with American connections proliferated, and guidebooks like Muirhead's helped tourists to find them, including the tomb of the founding benefactor of Yale at St. Giles Church, Wrexham, Wales.[68]

Unlike the Harvard House or Chapel, Sulgrave Manor, though drawing its supporters and benefactors from much the same social class of heritage-seeking Americans, was meant to be, like Shakespeare himself, a symbolic possession of the entire nation, memorializing, as it did, the founder of the United States (that is, his ancestors) rather than one of the elite institutions of Anglo-Saxon, Brahmin New England. Of course, founders' genealogies, as we have argued, inevitably forefront, as did the SAR and DAR, the importance of memories and nostalgias that have little to say to Black Americans or European immigrants of a non-English-speaking background. The movement to turn Sulgrave into a museum-shrine may be an artifact of the pre-Great War rapprochement and the surge in fin de siècle heritage tourism, but the house had, like the association of Benjamin Franklin's ancestors with Ecton, also in Northamptonshire,[69] long been of special interest to visiting Americans such as William Everett.[70]

The preservation of Sulgrave as an "English Mount Vernon," like the contemporary movement to erect a statue of George Washington at Westminster and create university chairs in British-American History,[71] may roughly correspond to the era of political and diplomatic rapprochement. But T. G. Otte has argued[72] that the international movement also may signify more, to the British at least, than this context suggests. The National Trust in Britain became interested in preserving the house for the nation (and from American spoliation) when in 1902 a rumor (unfounded) circulated that it had been purchased by a wealthy American with the intention of pulling it down and shipping it "brick by brick and stone by stone" to the 1904 World's Fair at St. Louis. An American committee for the acquisition and preservation of Sulgrave was finally organized in 1911 (with Roosevelt and Carnegie as patrons and Elihu Root as honorary chairman—in 1913 Woodrow Wilson agreed to head the committee) with the object, through the earlier initiative of international lawyers and arbitration activists, to turn the property into a centenary memorial of the 1815 Treaty of Ghent that had ended the War of 1812. In conjunction with the Americans, a British peace centenary committee organized by Earl Grey of Howick reflected, however, Grey's special concerns with racial purity and Anglo-Saxon liberty, and it is in this light that creating "a place of pilgrimage for Americans in England" that celebrated the "kinship" of the two peoples might specifically be seen.[73]

Sulgrave was finally purchased in 1913, and restoration commenced, somewhat impeded by the falling off of American support just before and during the first year of the war as opposition in America to intervention in support of Britain in Europe and to British interdiction of international shipping rose sharply. The congressional appropriation bill was slashed and further funding left to private efforts. The manor was re-opened in June, 1921.

2 American Anglophilia and the Royals

> As the standard bearer passed the royal box with 'Old Glory' her Majesty arose, bowed deeply and impressively to the banner, and the entire court party came up standing … a great event.[74]

The popular travel lecturer and travelogue publisher John Stoddard (1850–1931), born in Brookline, Massachusetts, a graduate of Williams College and teacher at Boston Latin School, was proud of his Puritan ancestors, descended as he was from Solomon Stoddard, the seventeenth-century Northampton Congregationalist, grandfather of Jonathan Edwards, and first librarian of Harvard College. A world traveler (and amateur photographer) from the 1870s, he lectured widely to audiences that were, one assumes, eager to learn of the wider world and perhaps intending themselves to travel. These lectures were turned into a series of well-illustrated volumes at the turn of the century. The ninth, on Scotland, England, and London, was profusely illustrated with photos, some colored. Stoddard, it would seem, had an especially nostalgic interest in vignettes of the quaint, the rural, and the old. "Scotland," "where Heroism and romance go hand in hand," opened with a photo of a Highland cottage, "England" with an "English Lane" and thatched cottage—followed by a portrait of the Queen-Empress Victoria.[75]

Twenty-some years earlier, the Scot journalist, William Fraser Rae, in his travel memoir of his tour of "the Great Republic," told of attending the annual dinner of the Massachusetts Medical Society, seating a thousand in the Music Hall at Boston. The chairman, Dr. John H. Mackie, Harvard graduate and a New Bedford surgeon, rose to tell the company that "they ought not to be unmindful of the loins from which their country sprang." He then proposed a toast to "the Mother Country," to which Rae responded. A band played the British national anthem as the governor of Massachusetts rose to his feet, "The whole company followed his example, remaining standing while the national air of the Motherland was played." Rae subsequently mused that "[i]f a closer tie is to bind the two English-speaking nations, something more durable than a treaty ought to form the nexus between them"—perhaps an act of Parliament and an amendment to the US Constitution providing "common citizenship in the Anglo-American Empire." An oration he had heard delivered by the Rev. Dr. George Edward Ellis, graduate of the Harvard Divinity School and pastor of the Unitarian Church in Charlestown, may suggest another kind of "nexus": "the Queenly Lady" whose coronation Ellis had witnessed in Westminster Abbey, and whose "serene course of dignity and fidelity as a wife, mother, and Queen" prompted him to offer "the expression of our profoundest homage and respect"—"our ally and our friend."[76] One may see some corroboration of a growing Anglophilia in the increase in American interest in and affection for the British monarchy, anathema to the Patriots of the Revolution and early Republic but an object, often, of flattering comment in at least the non-Irish-American press of the late-antebellum era and Gilded Age. Ironically, at a time in the 1860s and 1870s when the British radical Left flirted with American-inspired republicanism, the cult of Victoria Regina grew in *American* popular culture, and would continue to do so into the next century.

Focusing on the years before the Civil War, Elisa Tamarkin, in a complicating argument, has attempted to locate this apparently un-American phenomenon, not, or not solely, as social historians of class have commonly done, in a conservative anti-democratic, perhaps Anglo-Saxonist reaction among the "dandy-gentility" of New York, the new rich and the "newly-middle class," or a lineage-confirming old elite. Rather, she argues that it may be read as a widespread, in fact itself *democratic*, phenomenon. A "fascination with both the sacred rituals of state and the personalized authority of the British monarchy" functioned as a way of rediscovering an emotional commitment to "belonging" in an antebellum Republic drifting into disunion, a redefining of allegiance that was not based solely on "the rational bonds of democratic ideology." According to Tamarkin, this demonstration of "loyalism" (affection for Victoria or her son the Prince of Wales transferred to a renewed commitment to the Union) reflects "a desire for community" and an "impulse of a people towards its symbols."[77]

It may be that Tamarkin overstates the reach of "Monarch-Love" in America, both during the late-antebellum era and following the climacteric of the Civil War. One hesitates to throw out class analysis altogether, of course, or to locate the phenomenon of Anglophilia only in the anxieties of pre-Civil War national dysfunction. In a larger and longer sense, affection for, or nostalgia for, "Old England," like the rise of Anglo-Saxonism generally, must on some level still be associated with class, race, and a nativist response to the surge in non-English immigrants. One may also query the universality of popular responses to British royalism. Though interestingly informed by Tamarkin's speculations, how, exactly, to "read" the crowds that turned out to see the Prince of Wales in 1860 or that bought memorabilia of Queen Victoria's coronation remains an open question. Certainly, one can find violent expressions of antipathy then and throughout the century to British royalism and social hierarchy. In New York the 69th Infantry Regiment, filled with Irish recruits, refused to parade in honor of the visiting Prince of Wales (its colonel Michael Corcoran was commander of the recently-founded Fenian movement's military wing).[78] But Tamarkin's contribution that Anglophilia may be regarded more as a way of feeling, a child's veneration, as in Olmsted's "cultural fantasy" of homecoming,[79] than an endorsement of the British royals per se or the British constitution, is full of insight. The American regard for Victoria, Albert, and the Prince of Wales rose above and was quite other than an endorsement of the Mother Country's political establishment. In 1899, Charles Beresford observed that on his visit to the States he had been "greatly struck" by "the hearty and loyal enthusiasm with which Queen Victoria's name was received on all occasions, and I believe as much affection is felt for Her Majesty in the United States as in this country."[80] That the royals became highly personalized symbols for many Americans seems undeniable—rather as a late twentieth century bedeviled by radical counter-culture, political scandal, stagflation, and post-Vietnam syndrome saw an American middle-class public that came to cherish the social order of "Upstairs-Downstairs" and the soap opera of the Royal Family, and, some think, to become in fact arguably more royalist than the British themselves.

From the beginning of her 64-year reign, regard for Victoria in America seems to have rested on what was imagined to be her personal character rather than, or as well as, on her symbolic, ritualized role as head of state, as suggested in the responses of the many Americans who were "presented" to the Queen over the years. Walter Arnstein suggested five overlapping explanations for the sympathetic image of Victoria in the States: what was regarded as the pro-northern stance of the Queen and Albert during the Civil War, the friendly interest she appeared to take in the lives of individual Americans, her reputation as a philanthropic benefactor and "fountain of honor," the way her public presence in the press allowed ordinary Americans to feel themselves vicariously drawn into the personal life and family of the monarch, and, finally, by the end of the century, the way the labels "Victorian" and "Victorianism" seemed to confirm in art, architecture, and the general ethos of the age her centrality in much beyond her role as a constitutional monarch.[81] Of course, public sentimentality could in fact, if counter-intuitively, also entrench American condemnation of the Mother Country's political and social establishment, to the extent that she, and her assumed to be naturally generous, motherly feelings, came to be regarded by some as trapped by (and separate from) the forces of reaction and social exclusion. The same can be said for the gratitude many Americans paid to Albert's supposed intervention keeping Britain neutral at the beginning of the Civil War. In this view, Palmerston and the anti-American aristocracy, Whig or Tory, not the royal family, were to be regarded as the enemies of the Republic in the time of its greatest crisis. It may be, of course, that later in the century Victoria's growing familiarity, not as bride and mother but as queen-empress, as the public symbol, not of the British Empire alone but of imperial*ism*, that is the beneficent if firm rule of Anglo-Saxondom over others, shifted the way her image played in an America that was itself reaching out for a destiny beyond the bounds of the continent. The sentimental personal became mixed, if not with a specifically British constitutional location, then, along the lines argued by Bagehot, with dignified rule in a more generalized sense and with a racially ordered cosmos.

Victoria's accession in 1837 received much attention in America and was celebrated in some of the press and denigrated by others—rather as was the case in a United Kingdom torn by radical reformism, Chartism, and Irish nationalism. The following year, St. Louis saw a popular burlesque, *Victoria*, written and produced by the American actor Noah Ludlow, who managed theaters in the then West and South, and was an admirer of Edwin Forrest. The sketch featured the young queen, "a timid girl" afraid to commit herself on issues of policy while being (fictively) interviewed by the aggressive, impudent editor of the New York *Herald*, the Anglophobic James Gordon Bennett.[82] In the metropolitan East, however, Victoria's accession and coronation, relayed and reproduced at length in the popular and society press, inaugurated what one skeptic called "this Queen-mania," a surprisingly broad fashion for things royal—cheap portraits, mantel-piece plaster busts, decorated hair-brushes and tins of tooth-powder, Queen Victoria clocks, soap, riding hats and whips, a "Victoria Grand March" and "Victoria quadrilles" in music shops, and, finally, it was (perhaps sarcastically) claimed, "Victoria bean soup" and "Queen Victoria's Family Pills." Or so reported the somewhat baffled editor of the *Democratic Review*, the Irish-American John L. O'Sullivan, no friend of things British ("Our paper money, banking credit, and stock operations, are dependent, even to their minutest ramifications, on the temper of the Bank of England and the change-jobbers of London"):

> We are painfully startled as we write with intelligence that looks very much as if this Victoria feeling had penetrated farther than the columns of a few Tory newspapers.[83]

Tamarkin writes of the "sheer fetishism of the American public of the Queen's person, the 'Reginamania'" with which the papers seized on her toilette, breakfast, shoes, and feet. Commissioned by the St. George's Society of Philadelphia, American painter Thomas Sully took the young Queen's portrait—she sat for him at the palace—and this was exhibited across the United States, in Philadelphia, New York, Boston, and New Orleans, engraved, and made available to the masses in cheap prints.[84] Sympathetic reportage of the royal family through the course of the century was dominated by issues of personal character and experience, Victoria as bride, as mother, as grieving widow, as much as head of state. Newspapers and journals brought the American public the coronation, Victoria's marriage and the birth of her many children, the death of Albert, the Jubilees, and those moments when Victoria addressed America: her message across the new transatlantic cable, her commiseration over the great Chicago fire and her gift of books to libraries there, or her messages of consolation after the assassinations of Lincoln and Garfield.[85] American tourists by mid-century could cherish her as a celebrity *sighting*. When he recounted his visit to the Crystal Palace in May of 1851, Samuel Cox could hardly contain his thrill at actually *seeing* the Queen at the Exhibition, "an ordinarily dressed and tolerable good-looking woman" and *being seen* by her: "the Queen herself turned round, and gave us a good-natured look and a full view."[86] The Victoria of Grace Greenwood [Mrs. Sara Jane Lippincott]'s popular biography, meant for "young Americans," would communicate "the generous, whole-souled sympathy of the English people" at Lincoln's death, "her great power of loving … her sincerity, her downright honesty."[87] Victoria herself came to believe that she was well-loved across the ocean. As she wrote to Gladstone in 1881, "in *America generally* she is a *great favourite*, she knows."[88]

Admittedly, there were many who chose not to celebrate this version of the British monarch, and among whom a crude, patriot-and-school-tutored mistrust and misconception of the mysterious workings of the British constitution persisted throughout the century. British tourists were often presented with what seemed to them examples of risible American ignorance, especially the farther one got from the eastern seaboard. In 1872, for example, Allayne Legard, in Colorado, was addressed, he tells us in some surprise, by "an educated man" of, apparently, "some wealth," who asked "How is the Queen over there; is she pretty lenient or very tyrannical? Have been told she was very tyrannical."[89] Isabella Bird, making her way to Estes Park in Colorado, had a rather more direct encounter when her "frugal, sober, hard-working" Scots-American guide said that he "trusts to live to see the downfall of the British monarchy and the disintegration of the empire." His hatred of England was, she says, of a "bitter, personal" kind and he regarded "any allusions which I make to the progress of Victoria as a personal insult."[90] Some years later, Cecil Roberts, working his way across America, found in Santa Fe, New Mexico, "a very pretty and lady-like woman" who asked him "if I was not very glad to have got away from the power of Queen Victoria" whom she supposed to be a "merciless and powerful tyrant" disliked by her people.[91] Nor were these opinions solely characteristic of a far western provincialism. As late as 1883, William Hardman reported from New York City that the ceremonial opening of the Brooklyn Bridge, by chance being on the birthday of Queen Victoria, "roused feelings of bitterness and jealousy among the more prejudiced Americans," though he himself thought that "our beloved sovereign is … held in highest esteem throughout the States."[92]

High esteem was certainly to be found—most dramatically and unexpectedly in the outpouring of excitement caused by the American tour of eighteen-year-old Albert Edward, Prince of Wales, July to November 1860, just months before the outbreak of the Civil War.[93] Nor was this only the predictable applause of Brahmin Anglophiles and the nostalgic members of metropolitan Sons of St. George societies. Thousands, indeed tens of thousands turned out to catch a glimpse of the royal progress—thirty thousand, it was said, in St. Louis, perhaps a hundred thousand in New York City. The New York diarist George Templeton Strong wrote that "under all this folly" there was "a deep and almost universal feeling of respect and regard," an event "pervading all classes." In Elisa Tamarkin's words, "Albert Edward had become an American icon" with "metonymic status."[94] Whitman celebrated the "Year of Meteors" ("There in the crowd I stood … ") and Harriet Beecher Stowe claimed that the visit "is a deeper and wider thing than it appears to be."[95]

The Prince had been invited to extend his tour of Canada to the United States by President James Buchanan, who had been American Minister to Britain 1853–6 and who as President had exchanged messages with Victoria on the 1858 opening of the first (and abortive) transatlantic cable.[96] The tour—planting a tree at Washington's tomb, attending the opera in Philadelphia (where the audience rose in respect at the playing of "God Save the Queen"), reviewing the cadets at West Point, and attending a ceremony on the Boston Common—saw, to some surprise, open, spontaneous applause that extended celebrity status for royalty well beyond the many balls and other "Society" events. Such massing of thousands of admirers (or at least the gawping curious) could hardly have been replicated in Britain itself—indeed, the Prince's personal morality would come to be regarded there with some dubiety and criticism, as was Victoria's over-extended and extravagant mourning.

Tamarkin is right to search here, deep in antebellum American culture, for large, underlying explanations that go beyond the easy observation (which may, as far as it goes, nonetheless be true) that there is something in all this that anticipates our world of media-created, ephemeral "celebrities." She finds two aspects especially pertinent. First, that the cultish excitement over the Prince (as earlier for Victoria's coronation) seems to spread well beyond the ethnic lines of Anglo-American Anglo-Saxondom, even if one may doubt that it swept, as she claims, "indiscriminately across German and Irish, Catholic and Jew." Her other observation, on perhaps firmer or at least more obvious footing, is that those Americans at home or abroad commonly invoke the metaphor of childhood—that Americans are the children of an English mother, that the infancy of the American nation was lived within the arc of Britishness, that, in the words of Van Wyck Brooks, "America has had no childhood—in America." There is, Tamarkin argues, an inescapable "memory of dependency" and regard for Britain is but "a resumption of filial-piety that is, in no case, un-American."[97] This domestic language of family is easily, casually, and often heard, especially among those Americans who attempted to understand their own emotional responses when traveling back to the old country. Edward Everett wrote in 1843 of the "feelings of a dutiful son" and (like so many others) of a "pilgrimage"; the Maine-born publisher George Palmer Putnam, when in London, "the monarch of cities," in 1838, felt "at home" because "the associations of childhood connect us with it."[98]

The Ancients, and Queen Victoria's Jubilees

The Ancient and Honorable Artillery Company of Boston was chartered as a kind of militia in 1638 by Massachusetts Bay colony and its governor John Winthrop in emulation of the royally chartered Honourable Artillery Company of London (f. 1537). By the mid-and late nineteenth century, it was a largely ceremonial affair headquartered in Faneuil Hall. It drew its members mainly, if not exclusively, from the Anglophilic, Anglo-American middle and upper classes of Massachusetts who enjoyed participating in annual, costumed rituals that emphasized British heritage and "feelings of fellowship and good will between the people of two great nations."[99] The Ancients, who turned out on the Boston Common in 1860 to be reviewed by the visiting Prince of Wales, were especially attractive to those New Englanders, like many of that generation's Protestant Brahmin class, who sponsored historical and antiquarian societies and who celebrated their own British heritage as, on one level at least, a kind of antiphonic response to the sometimes militantly Anglophobic Catholic Irish of Boston.

If the anti-British militancy of mid-century waned somewhat by the 1870s—though aggressively maintained by an activist minority—the Boston Irish as a whole remained defensive of their immigrant origins while ready to confirm their Americanness by loudly opposing any civic manifestations of Anglo-American rapprochement. The decision of the quasi-public institution of the Ancients to celebrate their Englishness and Victoria's Diamond Jubilee by sending a large delegation to London in 1896, as they had sent a delegation in 1887 to celebrate the 350th anniversary of the London Ancients and Victoria's Golden Jubilee, did not go unnoticed. The Ancients' jaunt to England did not come at an especially propitious time—planning began the year after the Venezuela crisis—and could have been expected to at least raise eyebrows not only among the ever-sensitive Boston Irish. In fact, healing the break-down in Anglo-American relations over Venezuela was a proclaimed motive. The trip would, an organizer said, help to restore "fraternal feeling."[100] A delegation of some 272 members, their families, and invited guests, accompanied by the Salem Cadet Band, sailed to Liverpool in July. The Fourth of July at sea was celebrated with British and American flags, the Star Spangled Banner and God Save the Queen, and toasts to Victoria. Welcomed in London by the Captain of the London Ancients, they attended a military review at Aldershot and were entertained, with the American ambassador Bayard, at a Marlborough House banquet hosted by the Prince of Wales. They "presented arms" to Victoria in her carriage at Windsor and sent their officers to be received by the Queen. Official receptions aside, they indulged in general sightseeing in and out of London; at the India Exhibition at Earls Court they were the special guests of Imre Kiralfy.

In his subsequent defense of what was seen by many back home as a somewhat embarrassing kowtowing to the British, William Hichborn, general foreman of the Construction Department of the Boston Naval Yard and a tour organizer, claimed "[w]hile I am an American, and all that implies, I feel proud of my English ancestry." Looking back at the recent diplomatic crisis, he defiantly argued "[w]ith all due respect to the Munroe [sic] Doctrine, I am convinced that … not only Venezuela but the whole of South America would be better off under English rule and flag than they now are," and, anticipating the surge in Anglo-Saxonism in '98 and after, looked to a future when "all the Anglo-Saxon, English-speaking race … would govern the world."[101] This can be seen as an emotional response to the unfriendly attention the trip had surprisingly (to the Ancients) drawn in the press and in the streets in Boston. It was naïve of course for the organizers of the Boston Ancients not to anticipate that their celebration-cum-junket would draw attacks and protests. Some, of course, may have knowingly relished confrontation.

The American Irish had, from the 1830s, grown in confidence and political energy—in 1836 the Ancient Order of Hibernians was founded in New York; four years later the Boston Irish organized the Friends of Ireland to support Daniel O'Connell's campaign in Ireland to repeal the union with England. Repeal organizations spread throughout New England. Immigrant Irish in the following decades, attracted as most were to the already established centers of Irish community rather than dispersing westward, continued to swell the Irish population of Boston.[102] They established their own newspapers and political societies, in part as a defensive response to the Know-Nothing challenge of the 1850s (the nativist Know-Nothings were particularly strong in New England, claiming the offices of Boston mayor and Massachusetts governor as well as the large majority of state representatives in the election of 1854). The politics of the Boston Irish, as in New York, came to be dominated by a rising generation who inherited from the Young Ireland militants of mid-century. These had earlier often fled prosecution and imprisonment in England and Australia and demanded that Irish-American patriotism locally be closely linked to the demands of nationalism across the Atlantic. The 1868 victory of 24-year-old Patrick Collins, born in county Cork, in achieving a seat in the Massachusetts House of Representatives marks the beginning of an Irish ascendency within the Democratic Party in New England. Collins would win a seat in Congress in 1882, and became mayor of Boston in 1901, following Hugh O'Brien who had been the first Irishman to achieve that office (in 1885). Two years later Collins would again win election as mayor, carrying every ward of the city.[103] In the face of the rising fortunes of Irish Americans in New England politics, an apprehensive if tardy Anglo-American resistance took shape around anti-immigration and anti-Catholicism.

There was a history of confrontation at Faneuil Hall itself. The eighteenth-century market and meeting place where the Ancients had their institutional home had long been a contested site in the struggle between the city's "mechanic class" and the governing elite, between radical and Whig, and, latterly, between nativists and Irish nationalists. There had been "monster" meetings there in support of O'Connell and in the year of European revolutions, 1848, a mass meeting was packed into the Hall to express general sympathy for the workers of France and the Chartists of England, as well as the Repealers of Ireland.[104] By the late nineteenth century, the Boston Irish had grown in confidence and organization, and the new militancy in Ireland in the era of boycott, the Irish land war, and renewed demands for Repeal or Home Rule saw a cross-Atlantic intensification of Anglophobia at least in the press and among the more radical organizers. A decade before the Ancients sailed, attempts to celebrate Victoria's *Golden* Jubilee at the Hall had called out mass protests, fanned by an Irish-friendly press and led by, among others, a Catholic priest who was also vice-president of a local association that supported Michael Davitt's Irish Land League.[105]

The day before the 1887 Jubilee banquet,[106] the streets around the Hall and Quincy Market were filled with a crowd that turned angry when denied entry. Confrontation was followed by the forcing of the doors closed to them and the occupation of this patriotic site with "speeches, groans and hisses." As in 1896, this manifestation of anti-British anger in Boston seems to have caught the sponsors of the celebration by surprise and they responded with a strident, nativist defense that targeted "alien agitations" of "foreign born citizens," a "disgrace to the American Republic." In the face of another "mob" and amid cheers for Parnell, the next day the Hall was resecured for respectability by hundreds of police. The banqueting 400 celebrated Victoria's fifty-year reign—though the governor of the state was prudently "out of town," the mayor of Boston was sick and unable to attend, and several of the civic officials who had accepted invitations "were conspicuous by their absence."[107]

Though the organizers of the Golden Jubilee celebration, themselves representing as they thought "the average British-American … a better class of citizens," fell back on the familiar clichés of the violent, drunken, shillelagh-wielding Irish Other, full of "ignorant prejudices and passionate resentments," their indictment especially targeted a pandering press and the growing, organized electoral power of those who were easily led by "the meanest class of politicians." Boston politics, they suggested, was tipping toward Tammany-Hall corruption, toward a system of fraud, spoils of office, and misappropriation of public money, and the foreign-grounded, ambiguous "patriotism" of those who rallied for the American tours of Charles Stewart Parnell, John Dillon, and

Transatlantic Birthright: "A Pilgrimage of the Heart"

Michael Davitt as they had earlier celebrated the Anglophobic militancy of the radical Irish ex-pats Thomas Meagher and John Mitchel. This was, in their view, undergirded by a press that had become "a catspaw of Irish schemes."[108] Of course, at the end of the day the banquet had gone ahead with some success, toasts were publicly pledged to Anglo-American amity and to Queen Victoria, and, as the young British diplomat Cecil Spring Rice, who had come up from Washington to attend, thought, the ambitions of the organizers had been met with "wild enthusiasm," unharmed by "[g]reat cursing among the Irish."[109] A decade later the Queen's Diamond Jubilee celebration in Boston would be attended by both the governor and the mayor.[110]

The much-publicized confrontation at Faneuil Hall had the immediate effect of encouraging the further organization of Anglo-Saxonists in New England and beyond who claimed some direct connection with Britain—whether by heritage or recent immigration—within a general fin de siècle revival of nativism, to counter-organize against the political influence of non-Protestant, non-English immigration. Within three weeks they established a British-American Association with the ambition of influencing elections by encouraging recent migrants from England, Scotland, or Canada[111] to take out citizenship papers and organize. Branches sprang up throughout New England and New York,[112] and a newspaper endorsing their views, the *British-American Citizen*, was begun. But most British-Americans had over the century easily assimilated into the native-born majority and had long proved resistant to hyphenated self-identification. In the face of the still-growing (until the 1890s) population of immigrant Irish, the movement proved, even in the encouraging atmosphere of fin de siècle rapprochement, of little consequence.[113]

The Death of a Queen

Victoria's passing in January of 1901 was an "event," long anticipated and, like the fulsome obituaries, black-bordered public expressions of condolence, and various forms of civic mourning, prepared for throughout the British Empire and beyond. Winston Churchill, in Canada on a lecture tour, wrote to his American mother how the Empire stopped to mourn, even there in the western reaches of Manitoba.[114] South of the border, in the America of Dilke's "Greater Britain," the press (always excepting the nationalist Irish organs) was fuller of extravagant eulogies than it had been in 1838 of coronation congratulations. *Harper's Weekly* brought out an illustrated special issue to report her death and another on her funeral. The American flag was lowered over the White House and other government buildings, and President McKinley, with his cabinet, attended a memorial service at St. John's Episcopal Church. Both houses of Congress adjourned and the stock market closed.[115] Many private and public organizations sent condolences—such as, of course, the many British Associations that had been founded, as in Richmond during the post-Civil War land rush there, by mostly immigrant English and Scots.[116] But the need to express sympathy ran wider and deeper than this—the Masonic Veterans' Association of Washington, DC, sent the British ambassador messages of condolence. So did the National Afro-American Council and the students of Sedalia High School,

Missouri, while the Victoria Club of St. Joseph, Missouri, claimed that the Queen's life had been "an example for all ages of a pure Christian woman, noble wife, loving mother and gracious sovereign."[117]

There had, no doubt, been significant changes in the image of the Queen over the years—from that of the young bride of 1840 to the queen-empress of the Silver and Diamond Jubilees,[118] just as the popular culture of the empire she symbolized had matured into late nineteenth-century naval reviews, durbars, music-hall chauvinism, and the stiff-upper-lip stoicism of novels and the illustrated press. Admittedly, for some Americans, schooled in textbook nationalism, any British monarch remained the "tyrant" of the Declaration of Independence. For many (if not all) Irish-Americans she continued, in spite of her presumed personal virtues, to symbolize injustice and bloody suppression and, for some in an age of political assassination, fair game for a bomb or bullet. With his eye on the Irish vote, the Mayor of New York, Robert Anderson Van Wyck, declined to lower the city's flags.[119] But it would seem that most Americans of whatever class were able to weave regard for the person of the Queen in some way into their own lives, if only as the most celebrated widow of the age. She and the other royals became a species of theatrical celebrity, known only, or mainly, through gossip, portraiture, cheap material artifacts, and an illustrated press—and, as Marianne Finch reported in 1853, through the wax figure ("in a dress she had actually worn") that one could view at Barnum's Museum for 25 cents.[120] Popular culture absorbed, as with the American productions of Gilbert and Sullivan operettas, an awareness of England, though whether this may have contributed to Anglophilia or not is an open question. At the same time, the fashion for heritage tourism back to the Mother Country jumbled together the dignified sites of royal residence and governance—Windsor, Kensington, or Buckingham Palace, Parliament with its outsized Victoria Tower—with the more modest ancestral homes of the American nation's founders and the more intimate, nostalgia-enhanced, loci of one's own imagined heritage in the lanes, villages, and manor houses of Old England.

> Far away, they still remember the green lanes of Norfolk, the wolds of Yorkshire, the heather hills of Scotia, the verdant fields of the Emerald isle, the sweet country villages.[121]

3 The Boston Forbeses

Edith Emerson Forbes (1841–1929), a daughter of Ralph Waldo Emerson who had married William Hathaway Forbes, son of the prominent, influential, and very wealthy John Murray Forbes, had many English friends and correspondents and a strong interest in English history and culture. She had, apparently, a particular interest in the rituals of British royalty. In the summer of 1893, while the family were on tour in Britain, she and William had taken rooms at the Berkeley Hotel, Piccadilly, in order to view the bridal procession of Princess Mary of Teck and George, Duke of York (the future

George V), the Prince of Wales, and in her carriage with liveried outriders the aged Queen herself.[122] In the library of her own house[123] in Milton, south of Boston (Milton Hill and surroundings became a kind of compound for the extended Forbes clan), Edith would leave a scrapbook that must have filled hours with careful labor at the turn of the century. It contained hundreds of clippings from journals and newspapers about the death of Queen Victoria in January 1901, rituals of mourning in Britain and in the Dominions, the new king and other members of the British royal family, and tributes from "leading men in Boston," carefully glued into sixty-one folio-sized pages.[124]

When Edith was only seven, "Pappa," on his second tour of Britain, wrote her from London that he would have a great many stories to tell her about England and France. Ralph Waldo Emerson, though dedicated to charting a new course for American literature and character, made three visits to Britain (in 1833, 1847–8, and 1872) and found himself there comfortably among the literati of what he regarded as the "best of actual nations"—there was, he affirmed, a sense of coming home: "The shop signs spoke our language; our country names were on the door-plates."[125] He became, especially, a warm friend of Thomas Carlyle, whom he had first met in 1833 and with whom he visited Stonehenge in 1847. When in 1872 Edith and William H. traveled to London with their four young children, they saw much of Carlyle who "received Edith like a daughter."[126] Photographs were taken of Edith and her eldest son, Ralph Emerson, with the great Sage, while Edith's brother, Edward Waldo Emerson, in London to study medicine at St. Thomas's Hospital, had also come to know Carlyle—and other literary and artistic friends of his father, including Tom Hughes, Edward Burne-Jones, and Matthew Arnold.[127]

Fifteen years after Carlyle's death in 1881 (Emerson would follow the next year), Edith contributed—as did Andrew Carnegie, Henry Cabot Lodge, Pierpont Morgan, and Cornelius Vanderbilt—a modest sum to the project to preserve Carlyle's London house in Cheyne Row, Chelsea. Her husband was one of the Carlyle House Memorial board of trustees.[128]

One might claim, easily enough, that the extremes of Anglophilia and Anglophobia can be found together in late nineteenth-century Boston. On the one side there was the Protestant Brahmin class—flatteringly described by a visiting Briton as "combining the virtues of democracy with the manners of aristocracy";[129] on the other, the myriad poor Catholic Irish and their Irish-American sons and daughters. There is obvious truth in such a blanket observation, though one must be careful to distinguish the warm social, cultural, and intellectual transatlantic relations of the wealthy and professional classes from their political opinions and their often-expressed patriotic support for American ambitions versus the British Empire. One thinks, for instance, of Henry Cabot Lodge's vehemently anti-British defense of the Monroe Doctrine at the turn of the century, though Lodge was personally an Anglo-Saxonist who believed that American society was "essentially English in its standards and fashions."[130]

At the same time, the almost universal contemporary assumption, reiterated in many of the travel memoirs throughout the century and in British and American journalism, that Irish Americans were necessarily and violently anti-British—one of the enduring

Figure 6 Thomas Carlyle and R. E. Forbes, photo 1872 [National Portrait Gallery, London].

clichés of the era—may mislead as well. Hatred of the British, long memories of famine and evictions and failed national rebellion, and determination to advance "the cause" back in the old country were certainly common in nineteenth-century America, preserved at the grassroots level in the oral culture of local communities, if perhaps over-determined by opportunistic Irish-American newspaper editors and metropolitan ward-politicians. For Irish-American nationalists, to be "American" meant to be radically republican rather than aristocratic and monarchical, that is, by definition, to be anti-British. But, as David Wilson has argued, to assume that militant Irish nationalism was a defining characteristic of Americans of Irish ethnicity is to over-generalize from those who lived in the eastern seaboard cities and from the peak of militancy at mid-century to the rest of the country and the long nineteenth century: "Most Irish in the United States," he provocatively claims, "were probably not particularly interested in Irish-American nationalism."[131]

Certainly, not everyone with an Irish pedigree could, after a generation or two of self-advancement and acculturation into the white American middle class, be said to pay more than a little lip service to physical force extremism.[132] By the end of the century, second- and third-generation Irish in America who had achieved some standing and wealth were as susceptible as those of British origin to the lure of heritage tourism and a romanticized view of the Old Country that was not the suppressed, poverty-ravaged image favored by the militant Feenian. In Chicago, with its substantial Irish-American population, many thronged to the folkish "Irish Village" offered on the Midway at the Columbian Exposition, sponsored in part by the wife of the governor-general of Canada.[133] Irish-America had not been unanimous in its opposition to celebrations of Victoria's Golden Jubilee. A number of "lace-curtain" Irish Catholic publications praised the Queen and noted that Catholicism in Britain enjoyed greater toleration than in Protestant America.[134] And among the respectable Irish community leaders of note in an 1889 compilation of the Catholic Irish of Boston there is the Harvard-trained lawyer Timothy Dacey, son of an immigrant father and graduate of the College of the Holy Cross, Worcester. A Democrat, elected to the Massachusetts General Court, and a president of the Charitable Irish Society—he was also a member of the Ancient and Honorable Artillery Company and traveled to London in 1887 with the delegation to celebrate the 350th anniversary of the London Ancients and to salute the Queen.[135]

Representation of the romanticized rural Irish village, with a recreated Blarney Castle, at the Chicago world's fair offers a sharp contrast to the "regular Irish village" recorded by British novelist Iza Dufus Hardy when she visited an Irish "squatters' town" outside New York City in 1883 with its "tribe of immigrants," its mud, its straggling "hovels," and ragged laundry flapping in the breeze.[136] Her observations resonated with the common views of both Anglo-Saxon Americans and British visitors that the Irish in America were like the Irish of the United Kingdom—ignorant, priest-ridden, drunken, violent, and mired in poverty. One must bear in mind that, for many American and British observers who wished for warmer transatlantic relations, anti-Irish prejudice and anti-Catholicism had long and conveniently served to bind many middle and upper-class Americans and Britons together at multiple levels, international and national, local and personal. On October 2, 1883, Edith Emerson Forbes wrote to her sister Ellen in Concord to defend her decision to send her children to a local private school rather than, as was common among the New England Emersons, placing them in the public school system. She made her reasoning, in line with the shift in demographics and a tightening of Brahmin cohesion and apprehension, explicit: "I cannot appreciate your regret that I do not send my children to school with the Irish population which make one half at least of every school." Moreover, the public schools were "principally carried on by committees selected by the Irish vote—or are likely to be," while "the children in the public schools are not many of them going to college in our part of the world."[137]

This section will examine the extended family of the wealthy Forbeses, their history and milieus in Boston, on Milton Hill, and at the family retreat at Naushon Island off Cape Cod, their social, cultural, and intellectual transatlantic connections, and the wider

Milton Hill and London

The complicated genealogy of the American Forbeses reaches back to an eighteenth-century Scotland of merchants and travelers, a prolific family intertwined in Britain, Asia, and the new world with the commerce and entrepreneurial opportunities of empire as well as with the networks of low church, nonconformity, abolitionism, and moderate, free-trade liberalism.[138] A later generation of Sir Walter Scott-reading Forbeses would somewhat romanticize the family's origins: "Thus Highland hardiness and valour, romantic imagination and love of nature were added to the Lowland industry and logic, while Lowland shrewdness and dourness were corrected by Highland generosity and fire." A grandson claimed that John Murray Forbes "reminded one of the best of the old cavaliers or highland chiefs in Scott's novels which he loved so well."[139] The first of the Forbes family of note to migrate to mid-eighteenth-century America was an Anglican clergyman who married into the Murrays of Boston (themselves of lowland Scottish heritage). The Murrays had put down roots in the colony and were connected by marriage with the Winthrops and other Puritan founders of the Massachusetts Bay Colony. When the Revolution came, however, James Murray, a loyalist, left Boston for Halifax. His London-born daughter Dorothy (Dolly) had married the Rev. John Forbes in 1769. John Forbes died in Britain in 1783, leaving his wife Dolly and two children in a substantial house she had inherited in Milton, south of Boston. Their sons followed the opportunities provided by further marriages into New England families that were engaged in overseas commerce to Europe and Asia.

Commercial life in late-colonial New England, marked by relative small enterprises and the absence of banks, had depended to a significant degree on family capitalism, on "kinship networks and economic alliances"[140] to provide both capital and personnel. After the Revolution, and especially after the conclusion of the War of 1812, participation in an expanding, more global trade required ever more capital and involved more risk. The China trade called for resources that intra-family networks alone—siblings and cousins—strained to find. The most ambitious of the trading families like the Perkinses reached out, not only to London financial institutions like Barings bank, which in this era rapidly developed a significant interest in financing American enterprise,[141] but also, via intermarriage and commercial partnerships, to other New England families.[142] These interlocking genealogies would produce the Brahmin class that came to dominate for a century the economic, social, civic, and cultural life of Boston. The youngest son of John Forbes, Ralph Bennet (1773–1824), entered this world of enterprise when he married Margaret Perkins, whose brother, beginning as a trader in slaves and opium, became one of Boston's most successful China merchants. Ralph B.'s own ventures did not prosper—as when he and his wife took up residence in Bordeaux, *c.* 1811–14, to try to get a footing in the profitable claret export trade. In due course, however, his sons, helped into the

China trade by their uncles and whose marriages deepened and strengthened the ties to New England nonconformity, wealth, and influence, were much more successful.

The most prominent of the nineteenth-century New England Forbeses, John Murray (1813–98), named for an uncle, was born in Bordeaux.[143] His older brother Robert Bennet (1804–89) had entered the China trade at an early age, thanks to Perkins & Co., and became a renowned sea captain and ship builder, trading as far afield as Manilla, China, Buenos Aires, Smyrna, Europe, and California. Like others of his extended family, he and his brother J.M. established themselves in Milton where they built a Greek revival house at 215 Adams Street for their widowed mother Margaret Perkins Forbes in 1833. Robert B. furnished it with "the muted splendor of blues, greens, golds and red of Canton pottery and of lacquer work" acquired from his travels in Asia.[144] Some years later, in 1847, as he expanded his interests into railroad building and other financial investments, he built

Figure 7 John Murray Forbes [Alamy].[145]

another house for himself nearby. In later life, wealth provided the leisure to travel, less for business than, increasingly, pleasure—fox-hunting in France, touring in England. His brother, J.M., however, would, though younger, become the family patriarch.

John Murray Forbes was connected by his own marriage to New England Quaker families, the Hathaways and the Swains, and, in spite of the slave-trading past of some of his Perkins relatives, embraced emancipation after hearing Wendell Phillips speak in 1837. Though never himself a radical abolitionist (as late as 1863 he pressed Sumner to support compensation for slave-holders in Missouri), he was on friendly terms with Sumner and Garrison, and, before the rising at Harper's Ferry crossed a line, interested enough in John Brown's militancy to have him down to Milton. He helped provide resources (rifles) for the anti-slavery struggle in Kansas, and included English abolitionist nonconformists like John Bright among his friends and correspondents. Sarah Swain Hathaway, who married J.M. in 1834, and would accompany him to London on the trips he made in the 1850s, provided on both her father's and mother's side, some access to the wider Quaker circles of business, finance, and liberal free trade politics in Britain.[146]

For her part, Sarah seems to have enjoyed playing "a gentle and charming hostess"[147] in Milton to British visitors, though she had wider interests and sharper views than this may suggest—being apparently well-read in contemporary science and having a keen interest in women's issues. In 1868 she called on Fanny Kemble, about to depart for England. They spoke of English and American "differences," Fanny emphasizing what she took to be the immorality (from the perspective of her own theatrical profession no doubt) of English men who commonly, she said, took mistresses. Sarah demurred, claiming in a letter to Kate Stanley that the New Englanders she knew, descended from the English, "must have inherited from them a respect for the relations of life & a belief in their sacredness ... I hope she [Fanny] generalizes quite too much ... ".[148]

After a year or so working in his Perkins uncles' Boston counting house, J.M. went out to Canton where, in addition to the advice and connections he had received from the Perkinses, he profited from a close association with an important Hong merchant Houqua—a "special friend" of Barings Bank who shipped merchandise to the United States on his own account.[149] When J.M. returned to Boston in 1837 (Robert B. took his place in Canton), he maintained a close correspondence and, though still a young man yet in his twenties, was entrusted by Houqua during the turmoil of the first Opium War to place, shield, and manage in America a very large part of Houqua's assets. These hundreds of thousands of dollars remained under J.M.'s personal direction for decades after Houqua died in 1843. Much apparently went into railway companies in which he had an interest, as well as (later during the Civil War) government bonds.[150]

John Murray Forbes became very wealthy, not only through the China trade but increasingly, with the convenient, continuing confidence of Barings, as a merchant banker and financial investor (he founded the investment firm into which Houqua's fortune was placed, J.M. Forbes & Co., in 1838). He was especially successful in the spreading business of building regional networks of American railways, becoming by the 1850s president of both the Michigan Central Railroad and the Chicago, Burlington, and

Quincy Railroad, and had an important interest in the Joliet & Northern Indiana and the Hannibal & St. Joseph railroad companies. Barings bank significantly underwrote many of these projects by taking up their bonds for resale in the United States and Britain.[151]

Wealth and prominence led to an expanded presence beyond commerce and industry; J.M. endorsed Lincoln and the Republicans, served as chairman of the Republican National Committee, and attended the party conferences as a delegate in 1876, 1880, and 1884. During the war, his earlier personal contacts with Barings bank in London (he traveled to Britain in 1857 to secure an emergency loan during the Panic of that year to save the Michigan Central Railroad) promised to make him useful in London. Late in 1862, J.M. proposed that he return to Britain on a secret mission to "preclusively purchase" warships being built there in all likelihood for the Confederacy, and in March, 1863, Secretary of the Treasury Salmon P. Chase and Secretary of the Navy Gideon Wells sent Forbes and a long-time business associate of his, the New York merchant and ship-owner William. H. Aspinwall, to London as, ostensibly, private citizens but with 10 million dollars' worth of US bonds to serve as collateral for a Barings bank loan to buy ships out from under Confederate agents. The scheme fell through—in part because the secret mission was revealed in April by the *Times*, in part because Confederate agents had been able to secure "cotton loans" that would give them larger resources than the Forbes-Aspinwall mission could command, and, ultimately, because the US purchase of the warships, had it been successful, would have undermined the American argument that a neutral Britain was by international law constrained not to arm belligerents. In the event, though the mission failed in its immediate objective, it may have influenced the British government's decision to detain in September the two iron-clad Laird rams that had been the chief concern in Washington. After the war, during the drawn-out negotiations over the *CSS Alabama* claims, J.M. would argue that France, which had armed Confederate raiders, had been at least as culpable as the British who had built them.[152]

By the mid-1880s J.M. ceased to take an active role in the Republican Party, alienated, it seems likely, as were other merchants and financiers in the Northeast, by the rising Anglophobic, anti-Cobdenite populism of Blaine and the party's endorsement of protective tariffs. Though he withdrew nationally (just as many of the New England Brahmin class would do locally) from an active political role, his increasing wealth—which would spread like a nourishing tide through the following generations[153]—ensured that his children and grandchildren would have easy access to the emerging national and transatlantic social, intellectual, and cultural milieus of the later-nineteenth-century coalescing elite. This raises the issue of shifting class locations and identities. There was a generational movement, not least in their own self-regard, toward a more homogeneous national upper class of wealth and privilege, a phenomenon that can be seen, if with significant differences, in both Gilded-Age America and late-Victorian Britain. In private and elite institutions of education, in society marriages, and in rituals of consumption and display, industrial, commercial, financial, and traditional patrician wealth tended to merge or mingle.

This was not, especially at the local level, a sudden or new phenomenon of course. In New England there had been, from early in the century, a drawing together of families of commercial and financial enterprise into the nascent Brahmin class, bound by marriage, religion, civic and philanthropic activity, partnerships and investments, and, above all, a shared prosperity (by 1860 the top 1 percent of Boston's population owned two-fifths of its taxable wealth).[154] The Brahmin class was in the antebellum era generationally attached to its regional location, closer to the counting house than would come to be true in the decades following the Civil War. In an era of economic panics, bank failures, and bankruptcy, business required the kind of confidence and trust that close family connections or religious association—the Quaker meeting or the Unitarian congregation—might provide. The Boston business elite was "a complex tangle of human relationships" where "virtues and vices could be closely observed."[155] In the postbellum world, however, a Harvard-educated, increasingly leisured, transatlantically traveled, and often culturally Anglophilic generation moved away from its specifically local, civic, religious, and philanthropic location toward that of a nation-wide board-room aristocracy of (often inherited) wealth.

In Britain, there was a similar transition among a business class whose great wealth lifted it beyond its domestic, local (often northern, nonconformist) origins into the national establishment. On the one hand, this raised (sometimes anti-Semitic and often anti-American) fears of the suspect morality (the hidden immorality) of a new class of global, or at least transatlantic, stockjobbers, manipulators, and promoters who could be judged only by the wealth they appeared to possess.[156] On the other, critics would latterly claim that the capture of great industrial, commercial, and financial wealth-creators by the world of the traditional landed elite—in the House of Lords, in the shared huntin' and shootin' rituals of upper-class display, in gentlemen's clubs, and, ultimately, onto the Tory backbenches in Parliament—carried a threat of a different kind. It presaged, it has been argued, the loss of industrial-revolution-era drive, with deep cultural and economic consequences for Britain. The drawing of self-made wealth into a traditional (or traditional-seeming) culture that valued manners, proper speaking, a degree of noblesse oblige, and investment in the social capital of fine country estates meant the long-term attrition of the entrepreneurial push that had made Britain the global economic and imperial hegemon.

However true that might have been for Britain—and it is an easily-exaggerated and much debated thesis[157]—for America, the coalescing class of the super-wealthy, though it might be pilloried for its display, vulgarity, affectation, and lack of social or, sometimes, economic morality, could never in the sprawling nation be as central to the identity and ethos of the country as was, at least before the Great War and for some time afterward, the British upper class. The Gilded-Age Republic lacked, after the destruction of the Southern plantation system, anything like England's national landed aristocracy and its grounding in primogeniture, hierarchy, and deference. In New England Brahmin assumptions that wealth carried with it civic responsibility and authority weakened in the face of politically mobilized immigrants. American wealth-holders generally by the fin de siècle were arguably less interested in their social-cum-civic and political leadership, in their character as an overt "ruling class." Retreating from a public sphere to the boardroom and golf course, they came to share, not a Gospel of wealth, but the private consumption and the social exclusivity wealth afforded. Leisure itself served to define a social world that embraced it—the transatlantic ocean-liner- and jet-set to be.

John Murray Forbes and his immediate family, his sons and daughters, grandsons and granddaughters, might be said to bridge these worlds. This is, of course, an oversimplification. Fin de siècle Forbeses did not exactly cease to be entrepreneurial, nor had the founders themselves been unacquainted with leisured enjoyment. J.M. was a cultured man, at home among the literati of New England. The family connection with the Emersons (J.M.'s Harvard-educated[158] son William Hathaway married, as we have seen, a daughter of Ralph Waldo Emerson) suggested and encouraged an interest in literature and the arts. Ralph Waldo Emerson was a warm friend of J.M. and praised him in his *Letters and Social Aims* for his "force, good meaning, good sense, good action" and his philanthropic benevolence. His "grace and power of expression" were, he suggests, as impressive as those of an earlier generation "bred after English types."[159]

Rather like Emerson, however, J.M., though he admired and enjoyed much that he found in England, did not admire its aristocratic governing classes or self-consciously seek to emulate their de-haute-en-bas style. When, during the Civil War, he traveled to London to attempt to buy warships away from Confederate agents, he reported back to Washington that—it was a common American view—the "upper classes" (elsewhere he says "the British ruling class" and "vicious elements in the upper classes") were "entirely against" the North but "the people are with us and are moving in their strength." Moreover, many within the traditional ruling class, he thought, looked to war with the United States as a means of crushing democratic tendencies in their own country. The aristocracy, like "rich slaveholders," "feared the uprising of their own people to a share of power." The mass of the people, the inarticulate and those without the vote, was on the side of the Union.[160] And yet, J.M.'s connections within certain, often liberal, upper-class financial and mercantile circles in Britain were close and mutual—including the prosperous nonconformists of his (and his wife's family's) acquaintance. He addressed the Quakers at their Yearly Meeting while in London in 1863, and was in close correspondence with prominent, often wealthy, liberal businessmen and M.P.s such as Cobden, Bright, and Forster.[161]

J.M.'s distrust of the English aristocratic establishment, like his liberalism, mirrored of course that of many *British* men of commerce, industry, and finance of his own generation. Succeeding generations were, however, inevitably less censorious as social contexts shifted. As with other such wealthy Americans, the Forbeses came to enjoy a style of living (though more sober than some of the Newport super-rich) that drew on the social rituals (riding, yachting, hunting) of British models, just as Emerson and his transatlantic circle offered and encouraged connections to the world of British arts and letters. J.M.'s older brother Robert B. both during and after a successful commercial career found himself often in London and on the Continent. He managed to pursue his pleasure in riding to the hounds there, as well as frequent deer hunting at Naushon. In 1868 he interrupted fox-hunting in Pau to look for horses in Ireland for himself and his son Murray (James Murray Forbes, 1845–1937). "Several hunters" were bought and sent to France (and presumably on to the United States for their stud back home).[162] Francis

Blackwell Forbes (1839–1908), a cousin in the New York line of Forbeses, would turn from the opium trade and the Shanghai Steam Navigation Company to become, at the urging of a director of Kew Gardens, a writer of books about poppies and Chinese plants, and in 1882 would move to England. Among the successor generation of Boston Forbeses, a son of William H., Edward Waldo Forbes (1873–1969), would study art history at Harvard and spend two years at Oxford. He later served as director of the Fogg Museum from 1909, and aided in securing land for Harvard down to the Charles River to preserve this stretch from commercial development and to give the university an Oxford college-like riverside presence.[163]

With the growth of J.M.s' prominence and his transatlantic circle of friends and correspondents,[164] the connective, reciprocating courtesies of social visiting grew as well—both on Milton Hill and, especially, at Naushon, a seven square mile island bought by J.M. and his uncle-in-law William Swain in 1843. In 1856 J.M. became the principal host there and the island was set up as a family trust on his death in 1898. Situated between Cape Cod and Martha's Vineyard, it became during the later nineteenth century a favored site, not only for family rest and recreation, but for the increasing number of summer visitors from Britain invited to join them there in comfortable, companionable seclusion to enjoy lobster, marmalade teas, and poetry readings.[165]

It may be that such entertainments at Milton Hill and Naushon grew in size and opulence with successor generations, suggested by the grandness of William H.'s new houses on Adams Street (1874) and at Naushon.[166] The guest lists included special friends such as James Bryce, A. V. Dicey, and Goldwin Smith, but there came also to be "a steady stream"[167] of almost any touring Britons of some note. As Sarah Forbes Hughes would later recall, there was "an endless succession" of men of business, science, and politics.[168] At Naushon there was deer-hunting for those who enjoyed that sort of thing (J.M. did not), sailing in Buzzards Bay, and long conversations. Polo (there is no evidence that J.M. had an interest) became increasingly popular. William H. at least tried his hand at it, and his son Cameron became seriously dedicated to the sport. Though Naushon might not have offered suitable terrain for formal games there, at his mainland house he created a polo ground and stables.

In Boston, social, cultural, and philanthropic institutions served to confirm the elite status of the upper commercial class, to give them a place among an older patriarchy, and to socialize with the non-commercial literary and artistic community. Many of the successor generation of Forbeses took an interest in historical and antiquarian societies, and in the "Saturday Club," a loosely organized dinner society for, originally, New England literati that was formed in the 1850s and met at the Parker House hotel. Proposed as a member by Emerson, J.M. was an eager attender, and brought stories of the "best wits" of the town home to the family circle at Milton Hill—Emerson, Oliver Wendell Holmes, Sr., Whittier, Longfellow, Lowell, and others, though it is likely that some of the Boston intelligentsia were already personally known to him through his wife's mother's family, the Swains. In 1864 he helped Emerson organize a Saturday Club dinner celebrating the three-hundredth anniversary of Shakespeare's birth.[169] There was a special dinner there on his eightieth birthday in 1893. By the late nineteenth century a "club" originally for the New England cultural elite had become commonly available for almost anyone of political, commercial, or social prominence. Since a member could bring along a guest, J.M. would have been able to (and did) introduce visitors from Britain to meet famous cultural icons. In the early twentieth century, his grandchildren would help write the multi-volume history of this Boston institution.[170]

Reciprocal transatlantic social visiting among the wealthy and well-connected commercial, professional, and traditional elites had gathered pace after the Civil War, reflecting the growing obligations collected by those like the Forbeses during their own trips to Britain. Business interests had taken Robert B., J.M.'s older brother, to Britain well before the war and encouraged him to explore family ties there. In 1841, for instance, he crossed the Atlantic with his uncle T. H. Perkins. They met important members of the major banking houses, Baringses and Rothschilds, and made the acquaintance of Sir Charles Forbes of Forbes, Forbes, & Co., "who claimed consanguinity with our family, and with whom we had extensive business relations."[171] Visiting continued after the war, when Robert B. had more leisure. A tour with his son Murray 1868–9 saw them traveling to Leamington, Kenilworth, Warwick Castle, Stanleigh Park, Mattock, Bath, and Windermere before following their Scottish heritage interests above the border in Glasgow, Dumbarton, Greenock, Perth, Ballater, "and so on to the burial place of my ancestor" at Sir Charles Forbes' estate at Strathdon. Here he got the local clergyman to "erect a tablet in the church commemorative of my ancestor." They carried on to Aberdeen, Edinburgh, Abbotsford, and Dryburgh Abbey, and sailed back to the States from Liverpool with "an oak tree which I brought from Sir Charles Forbes' place" to be planted at his house in Milton.[172]

J.M. first visited Britain "for business and pleasure" in 1855 (traveling to Liverpool, Birmingham, London, but also Warwick Castle). In London to deal with Barings bank, he was taken by Edward Baring to the Derby races "with a hamper." He found the capital's "wealth and magnificence" "incalculable," and returned—accompanied by two of his daughters—to negotiate a further "emergency" loan from Barings during the Panic of 1857.[173] In 1867 the Viscount Amberleys (John Russell—the son of the then, briefly, Prime Minister Earl Russell—and his wife Katherine [Kate] Stanley) stayed at the Milton house and at Naushon *en route* to a further round of visiting at Newport. Kate and J.M.'s wife Sarah, who was godmother to Amberley's daughter, were intimate, gossipy correspondents—a tie no doubt established in London and strengthened by their mutual admiration for Ralph Waldo Emerson, to whom the Amberleys carried an introduction from John Stuart Mill. Such visits led to connections that produced further introductions and invitations—as when Kate suggested Sarah receive the Leslie Stephenses who were due to tour America the following year.[174]

In the libraries at the Forbes houses in Milton, such as that created for their new residence at 304 Adams Street by William H. and Edith, were, as one would expect, shelves of English letters and antiquarian publications that often emphasized the historical ties that bound the local histories of New England with those of the Mother Country. Such mid- and late-Victorian collections gathered not only Milton and Shakespeare and contemporary British literature—Scott, Hazlitt, Dickens, Thackeray, Kinglake, Eliot,

Arnold, Ruskin, Carlyle—but maps and illustrated guides to "picturesque England," reflecting not only the sober seriousness of an educated businessman that Emerson praised in J.M., but the developing habit of transatlantic travel and the intellectual, artistic interests of a later, somewhat less commercial generation. As a young man recently returned from the war,[175] William H. dabbled in the arts while serving in his father's firm—composing an operetta "Marion Lee" in 1865 (the year of his marriage to Edith) and in 1867 published a volume of poetry.

Edith Emerson Forbes' correspondence with her sister Ellen, who remained unmarried living with their mother at Concord, records the connections they maintained with intimate and casual British friends. Some of these had been, no doubt, guests at Naushon and Milton. Others were added during the several family excursions William H. and Emily made to Europe.[176] The first of these, in 1872, was a journey, in part at least, of tourist discovery. William and Edith, accompanied by four of their children (including a toddler and a baby in arms) plus nurse and governess, left London, and its round of social visiting, for the Isle of Wight, Torquay, Stratford-on-Avon, and the Lake district. William wrote his father that the English countryside was "new to me and beautiful to see and pleasant to remember. Edith too likes it." The tour was rounded off by a trip to ancestral Scotland and to Castle Urquart, "the [medieval] castle of Alexander Forbes."[177] Another family excursion with four children and nanny in February of 1888 involved a trip to the West country and the city of Chester where they were guests at Thomas Bate's estate. William had met him in British Columbia.[178] These later tours seem less a matter of simple tourism and more an educative routine to introduce maturing children to the wider world as well as an excuse for reciprocal social visiting—and for shopping for pictures, decorative household objects, and thoroughbred horses. In autumn of 1892 William H. sailed to Britain with his two eldest sons Cameron ("Cam") and Ralph who had just graduated from Harvard. Like Robert B. before him, William and Cam took the opportunity the trip to Britain offered to buy horses (for William H.'s stud but also perhaps to further Cam's growing interest in polo), while Ralph studied French in Paris. There his father and brother joined him, paintings were bought, and a three-month tour of the Continent followed. Edith came over to Britain early the following year with two of her younger children in tow—Alexander and Violet (Waldo and Edward joined them later)—and her sister Ellen Emerson followed.[179] At the turn of the century, Edward would return to attend Oxford University for two years.

Some of the attendant transatlantic social connections sprang no doubt from continuing commercial and financial interests, as when a W. Campbell wrote Edith thanking her for a gift of her father's works, inviting her son Edward to Scotland, and recommending that her son Cameron receive a friend of his in Boston: "I think they might be mutually helpful to one another in business … My American ventures have done so well this winter." Others reflect a shared interest in the arts (a children's pony at Naushon was oddly named "Pre-Raphael," another, "Iolanthe"). One of J.M.'s four daughters, Sarah (1853–1917), studied watercolor in England in 1874-5 and, having become a good friend of the English author Thomas Hughes' sister Jane Elizabeth, later (1887) married her brother William Hastings Hughes. The mother of the arts and crafts movement architect and designer Charles Robert Ashbee wrote from Cheyne Walk that she hoped Edith's son Edward would come to London from Oxford: "I shall be so pleased to see him & show him something of London which he may possibly not have seen yet." And still other connections are recorded in the quotidian, gossipy back and forth of mere transatlantic acquaintanceship, as when Perenna Bate, wife of the Thomas Bate whom Edith and William had visited in 1872, in 1884, and, again during the 1893 tour, wrote to apologize for a footman who had privately written asking for a job at Naushon.[180]

Fin de siècle

By the end of the century, some of the New England Forbeses, now commonly university-educated and intimately connected with other wealthy New England families like the Cabots by marriage and social intercourse,[181] had come to share with them an interest in transatlantic genealogies,[182] antiquarian local histories, and a confirming sense of the national significance of a rootedness (if not exactly their own) in the Pilgrim past. In 1896 they celebrated, as did many of the Brahmin elite, the return to Massachusetts (and the nation) of William Bradford's "History of Plymouth Plantation."[183]

John Murray Forbes' generation had regarded Britain as much for the business that could be done there as for the thickening social and cultural connections it represented. His own railroad enterprises looked westward. The year of his death (1898) saw his twenty-year-old grandson Waldo Emerson Forbes (1879–1917), helped no doubt by the settling of his father's estate (William H. died in 1897) and urged to go West after college to better cope with what was feared to be the onset of tuberculosis, negotiate the purchase of a ranch near Sheridan, in the foothills of the Big Horn mountains. He and his brother Edward spent a winter homesteading. This Wyoming property had previously been owned by Oliver Wallop, the third son of the Earl of Portsmouth, who would later renounce his US citizenship in order to succeed as the 8th Earl. Many of the surrounding ranches that had been bought up by other land-hungry British aristos had, by the turn of the century, been sold and turned into "dude ranches" for the eastern tourist trade. Though Waldo was deputed by his brothers to find a property, the Sheridan ranch did not exactly become a kind of Naushon West. It was a working ranch rather than strictly a recreational affair and subsequently stayed in Waldo's family though remaining hospitable to visiting relations. Much later, in the 1930s, Cameron would find a ranch nearby where he could breed polo ponies.

Some other Forbeses of Waldo's generation, especially those with cultural as well as the commercial interests they pursued increasingly from a distance as trustees and legatees, were more likely perhaps to look eastward, to enjoy heritage tourism and amateur antiquarianism. Robert B.'s grandson Allan Forbes (1874–1955), son of (James) Murray and a polo-loving hunt-club enthusiast who had been educated at Harvard, became a Boston banker but with a particular interest in "the historical implications of the surroundings in which he did business [the center of old Boston]."[184] He became a prolific author of antiquarian books and pamphlets (thirty-nine in all) dealing with a myriad of subjects from the history of banking to maritime history, including a series of essays on New England towns. These interests were often informed by an appreciation of their English contexts and derivations. In 1920–1 he published two booklets on *Towns of New England and Old England, Ireland and Scotland* that focused on the "connecting links" of their names and on memorials "on both sides of the ocean" to founders and settlers. He praised Ambassador Bayard for dedicating such sites and presiding over the return of the Bradford *History*. His own motive, he tells us, was to educate Americans who might not appreciate the history of "close relationships" with the Mother Country, to encourage "pilgrimages" to the "shrines" in England of the Pilgrim Fathers, and "to further interchanges of friendship, gifts and correspondence, either official or unofficial, between cities and towns in America and … [those] in Great Britain." The first chapter of *Towns of New England* dealt with Plymouth and Southampton in England and was fronted by a full-page photograph of the "Pilgrim Fathers Memorial" in Southampton that had been unveiled August 14, 1913.[185]

Of course for many of this turn-of-the-century class of well-off New Englanders, travel to Britain was not so heavily freighted with meaning—less of a pilgrimage than a recreational summer escape or an education in the arts, antiquities, and architecture of the old world. Alicia Keyes, who as a child had lived with Ellen Emerson in Concord and whose sister would marry Edith's brother Edward Waldo Emerson, traveled to Britain in 1884 to see, among other sights, Salisbury Cathedral.[186] Like her brother-in-law, she too would make a profession of Arts lecturing. Edward Waldo Emerson himself, who had spent two years 1871–2 training at St. Thomas's Hospital in London, turned from his medical career to the arts in the early 1890s, and in 1893 traveled to Hull in England and on to the Continent to study and paint. But for many, perhaps most of this class, travel had a more immediate and material purpose—the collection of objects to decorate new houses and present to friends. Edith would complain on return from Britain in December 1893 of the high duty she was forced to pay on the precious or curious things she had brought back to Milton and Naushon. A few years later, her cousin, Haven Emerson, whose tour through Europe ended with a month in London, boasted of his appropriation of the "beauties of this rare rich old world": "And then the fun of getting home and finding all the treasures of books, pictures, lamps and clocks to be woven into our home."[187]

SUMMATION AND EPILOGUE

The five parts of this study treat separable themes, each of which—on language, theater, race, the far West, and Anglophilia—offers a more or less self-contained exploration of, for the most part, respectable middle- and upper-class transatlantic, transnational culture. They share an approach grounded in a substantial body of contemporary travel literature, of Britons in America and latterly of Americans in Britain. The "reading" of this genre offered here has emphasized throughout, not so much the minutiae of description, but how what is seen, experienced, and written about may be shaped by preconceptions and by the genre itself and how, over the decades, imagined and rehearsed identities are sustained by performance and projection.

Chapter 1 began by drawing attention to speech itself, and the ways in which a common language was made to express both cultural similarity and difference—how Britons and Americans sought to express their understanding of themselves and their not-so-foreign Other. Born out of an early era of disputation over the speech of a supposed American provincialism versus that of polite British culture, dictionaries and etymologies of the English language came, however, to express by their transnational inclusiveness a kind of cultural unity rather than separation. Even the long-contested issue of Americanisms, driven along by the birth of modern philology and entrenched and extended by the publication of ever-larger lexicons, in the end could not be made to sustain the early American idealists' expectations of an evolving, separate national language. In the travel memoirs, as in popular culture, the caricatured reiteration of a *few* signifiers of American speech, pronounced with a New England "twang," served ultimately and paradoxically to narrow rather than extend the field of difference. For the British, by the end of the century shrinking transatlantic distance and with it a dawning of American industrial and geopolitical hegemony came to flip the issue of language from one of assumed cultural superiority to that of threatened vulnerability, a kind of reverse cultural colonization that highlighted closeness rather than distance.

Chapter 2 explores a cohering theme of this study—that performance and self-presentation are of importance in understanding how national and transnational cultures operate—by taking theater in its literal sense as an institutionalized dramatic art. The history of the nineteenth-century British and American stage reveals close Anglo-American connections, of British-born actors and managers and of dramatic matter, especially Shakespeare. On the one hand, popular contemporary plays, especially comedies, served through language and caricature to entrench a binary of national stereotypes of Britishness and Americanness. Some British actors were, before mid-century, attacked by patriotic mobs in American cities. On the other, there persisted a close underlying connectedness that, with the popularity of touring actors and troupes in both directions later in the century, appears to strengthen rather than diminish transnational ties. The dynasties of actor-managers, in their own cross-ocean, back-and-forth nomadism, followed careers that challenged national boundaries and national identities. This close transoceanic thespian relationship of mutuality and exchange persisted to the end of the period, though it also displayed a certain dynamic. As with discourse over language, by the end of the long era transatlantic theater saw a shift from American dependency and provinciality to, if not the threat of outright Americanization of British theatrical culture, then the successful export across the ocean of American plays, actors, commercial impresarios, and financiers.

Taking its cue from the previous chapters, Chapter 3 offers a route into the complexities of Anglo-American racial attitudes and identities via language and performance. Beginning with the ways in which London audiences and critics "heard" the Black American actor Ira Aldrich, it proceeds to examine how Black speech was treated by lexicographers and in the travel memoir. In the travel literature, minstrelsy's blackface performance in both America and Britain not only evoked issues of performed identity but influenced the language used subsequently to color understandings of American race relations and Black culture. Drawing in both the antebellum slave narratives and the slave auction as species of theater and spectacle, Chapter 3 also explores the proliferation of "Uncle Tom" roles on the Anglo-American stage and how these drew on previous comedic routines and minstrelsy. There was a drift over time away from abolitionist sympathy toward a popular genre of mere transatlantic entertainment. Viewing post-bellum America through the eyes of British travelers, and the shifting language of racial difference they employed, the chapter concludes that there was a significant movement in racial representation away from an earlier condemnation of American slavery toward a transatlantic consolidation of pejorative upper-class white opinion. Where the slavery debate before the American Civil War had highlighted Anglo-American differences, white elites in the late nineteenth-century British Empire and in Jim Crow America co-elaborated strategies of racial definition, separation, and subordination in an era in which the parallel problematic of white governance of non-whites drew the Anglo-world together.

Chapter 4 follows the British traveler westward in the second half of the century, emphasizing ways in which the Briton as observer-participant in the far West, a developing world of American empire but also an imagined "Greater Britain," acted out often temporary roles as flaneur, hunter, cowboy, and rancher while investors and "land-grabbers" established significant British outposts of settlement and financial investment. As with the popular romances of adventure fiction and western-themed plays performed in New York or London, travel memoirs helped make the colorful argot of the West familiar across the Atlantic, just as encounters with the plains Indian, the Mexican half-breed, or the Chinese coolie contributed to a literature of racial difference that complicated the simple Black-versus-white themes of earlier memoirs. In the later part of the century, the American West was transported to Britain itself, most notably in the Wild West extravaganza imported by Buffalo Bill Cody. Such very popular American spectacles both echoed and influenced the ethnological displays already on offer there by imperial exhibitions and entertainments. The fin de siècle performance of the taming of Zulu and Redskin that was displayed in the metropolis of Empire served to amplify the great outpouring of Anglo-Saxonist rhetoric that briefly at least characterizes the era following the Spanish-American War. Though Anglo-Saxonism was especially attractive to some of the East Coast Brahmin class and among those Americans who sought to rediscover and celebrate their British ancestry, and though it left a legacy in the rhetorical trope of "English speaking peoples," it was by no means a universal or uncontested phenomenon on either side of the ocean.

The concluding Chapter 5 turns from British tourists in America to their American counterparts who traveled to Britain. It focuses especially on the latter part of the nineteenth and early twentieth centuries, and on an Anglophilia that was marked by tourism as a "pilgrimage" and a sense of transatlantic birthright that employed often the domestic language of "family." At some level a nostalgia for Mother England also must reflect for white Anglo-Americans a nativist response to the surge in poor, non-English immigration—as well as the increased comfort and speed of travel, the growth of leisure among the upper middle classes, and the fading of the earlier idealist sense of a righteous self-isolation. It led to a thickening of reciprocal transatlantic social relations as travel for business, profession, and family holidays grew ever more routine and frequent. On the other hand, there was also the dawning of mass tourism in a more modern sense among the more modest middle classes that threatened to relegate the sense of a special, familial cross-Atlantic relationship to mere Baedeker-guided holidaying. Signs of an enduring Anglophilia below the social elite can, however, also be traced, as British diarists were happy to report, in the surprising popularity of British royalty and of Victoria especially, or in the reverence Americans on tour in Britain had for the shared national poet at Stratford-upon-Avon and in the museumization of the sites of the British origin of American founding fathers.

Bringing nineteenth-century transatlantic relations down to the narrative of a single family, the book ends with a portrait of the Boston Forbeses of Milton Hill, a prosperous trading family of Scottish origin that, as prosperity grew, multiplied its ties not only to the local Brahmin elite and intelligentsia, but to larger financial and social worlds. The growth of their transatlantic commercial and social connections marked their shifting class location and identity within a more homogeneous national class of wealth and privilege that characterizes the end of the Gilded Age. The well-traveled, well-endowed successor generation with wider, often trans-America and trans-Atlantic interests were as a matter of course more familiar and more comfortable with their British counterparts (who were frequent guests at Milton Hill and their private island of Naushon) than with the rising Boston Irish. The third generation came, often, to enjoy antiquarian, Anglophilic interests in a transnational world of first-class steamship berths and, for some, the recreational rituals of fox-hunting and polo.

Language and performance run as threads through much of this study, whether on the actual stage or in the metaphorical theater of daily lives. They served to anticipate— that is, to imagine, shape, confirm, and maintain—cultural topographies. Britons traveling to America enacted and perpetuated in the memoirs of their experiences expectations already scripted in the genre. Throughout the long century they (a few outliers aside) tended to exhibit a considerable degree of representational inertia. Descriptions, understandings, and realizations of personal, group, and national identity can, that is, hardly be said to have simply evolved along with ever-shrinking distances and ever-closer communication. Rather than articulating, except among a cosmopolitan elite and not completely there, a more shared, transatlantic sense of commonality the travel memoir as a genre often continued to offer a familiar, iterative endorsement of distance and difference. And yet, the Anglo-American representational field was not entirely static nor was it grounded always in a merely antagonistic binary. Over time, British observers came to accept, or at least acknowledge, the legitimacy of American sensitivity to criticism. The tone of mid-century and later travel memoirs softened. Growing convenience of travel within the States, the spread of urban amenities beyond the eastern seaboard, and the moderating over time of the testy defensiveness of the early Republic—signified perhaps by the enthusiastic reception given to the Prince of Wales in 1860—made for a less judgmental representation of national character. The disappearance of abolitionism and slavery as signifiers of national difference and the transatlantic consolidation of post-Civil War, post-Indian Mutiny attitudes toward racial governance also worked to defuse the earlier antagonisms while leaving differences in place that were often humorized rather than demonized.

As in our concluding chapters, one may observe among some a significant commitment to transatlantic cultural, social, and, less convincingly, political kinship, marked by fin de siècle Anglo-Saxonism, American heritage tourism, and the rhetoric of the unity of "English-speaking peoples." But this *transatlantic* affinity can be said ironically to have worked *domestically* to further and confirm the segregation of other classes, ethnicities, and races outside a national sodality that was grounded in heritage nostalgia. The American Anglophilia that was advanced within the social networks of traditional and aspiring elites offered a collective consciousness that was by definition not easily accessible by those outside these circles, those who were unlikely or unable to assimilate to a white, Anglo-Saxon, Protestant understanding of the nation. In America, the simple demographics of non-Anglo-Saxon immigration threatened to overwhelm any attempt to maintain a national identity grounded in historical, racial, and linguistic Britishness. In Britain, Anglo-American affinities were subordinate within the larger Anglosphere of Empire, and transatlanticism struggled to overcome the widespread conviction that the relationship had long been and remained an unequal one of metropole to province—at least until twentieth-century economic and political hegemonies shifted and forced a reluctant coming to terms with global and transatlantic strategic realities. And even then, a retained sense of *cultural* superiority, a legacy of the long nineteenth century and before, remained for many a kind of *pis aller*.

And yet, under the skin, as it were, of the enduring discourses of national difference there was the dense reality of a heightened, decade by decade, transatlantic intercourse that is revealed in each chapter of this book—in the obsessions of philologists, the reverence for the works of Shakespeare, the theatrical cross-traffic of plays, managers, and actors, the understanding and performance of "race," the popular, romanticized mythology of the far West, or the "heritage" preoccupations of American tourists. This intercourse was played out within an ecology of a common literary culture and the shared social practices of polite society—especially among the growing urban middle classes on both sides of the Atlantic. Richard Bushman has observed, as have others, that the growth of "civility" among smaller merchants and shopkeepers, professionals, well-off farmers, and industrial managers was marked on both sides of the Atlantic from the late eighteenth and early nineteenth century by the popularity of etiquette books, dictionaries of proper pronunciation, and other guides to genteel behavior, and by concern for more elegant houses and "new modes of speech, dress, body carriage, and manners."[1] This was a transformation that was dependent to a significant degree, as with etiquette manuals and dictionaries, on a literate awareness of transatlantic cultural standards. And perhaps not only among the well-off and urban.

John Joseph Long was born in Tennessee in 1810, married a woman from Virginia and moved to Arkansas, where their son Frank was born in 1849. Trekking farther west they settled among the Rough Creek farming and cattle-ranching community near San Saba, Texas. Lives lived in such far-flung rural places were, one imagines, highly domestic and local, though when the war came John Joseph, now in his fifties, enlisted in the 1st Regiment of the Texas Infantry (CSA). There is no record that he had much formal education or possessed many books, but it would be wrong to assume that his cultural horizon or ambition was thereby strictly limited or uninformed. A few years after he returned from the war, he took the opportunity that a trip to Austin provided to buy a 1,000-page leather-bound compendium of all of Shakespeare in a single volume:[2] a (literally) heavy investment in transatlantic literary culture. It was much used, it appears, in the following decades by John Joseph (who firmly wrote in his own name on the frontispiece) and his children and grandchildren—the binding at some point was carefully repaired with an awl and heavy twine.

As the British editor rather optimistically claimed in her preface to both the London and New York editions of this collection,

> Shakespeare's works are a library in themselves. A poor lad, possessing no other book, might, on this single one, make himself a gentleman and a scholar. A poor girl, studying no other volume, might become a lady in heart and soul. Knowledge, refinement, experience in men and manners, are to be gathered from his pages in plenary abundance.

And the Bard might provide more than manners:

> Shakespeare may be taken as a standard for language; it is manly, expressive, and purely English … it would be a wholesome return to indigenous form of speech, were we to abide by Shakespeare's integrity. Instead of framing new-fangled and alien nomenclature, let us maintain the use of Shakespeare's right and true words, and we shall preserve our language ["the British mother-tongue"] in its purity. His is genuine Saxon English ….[3]

The book much resembles, in fact, a family Bible, and must have sat with a few other volumes in a place of honor in that Rough Creek ranch-house, next perhaps to the violin John Joseph's grandson and my great-grandfather, George William Long (b. 1869), played in the evenings. Like a family Bible, it contained bits and pieces of family life pressed between the pages—a scrap of mourning cloth, dried flowers. Passages were well-thumbed, and on a few pages a child has practiced his or her calligraphy. What was made of the quasi-pornographic poems of, say, Venus and Adonis (945–56) or The Passionate Pilgrim (999–1002) one can only imagine. It was more than an object of ownership and display as in some Milton Hill library; it gave a hold-in-one's-hand tangible (and perhaps talismanic) access to a transatlantic culture that nineteenth-century Bostonians could enjoy at the theater and club, but which two thousand miles to the west in the very rural, sparsely populated Texas hill country was available only in the domestic privacy of family—passages perhaps read aloud of an evening in a broad Texan drawl before a mesquite and oak wood fire.

NOTES

Introduction

1. For a brief, early treatment of some of the issues imbedded in any consideration of Anglo-American transatlantic culture in the nineteenth century, see Daniel Walker Howe, "Victorian Culture in America," in *Victorian America*, ed. D. W. Howe (Philadelphia: University Pennsylvania Press, 1976), 3–24.
2. For an influential general treatment of transnationalism in American historiography, see Ian Tyrrell, *Transnational Nation: United States History in Global Perspective since 1789*, 2nd edn (New York: Palgrave, 2015).
3. Linda Colley, "How British Is It?" *New York Review of Books*, September 23, 2021.
4. Bradford Perkins, *The First Rapprochement: England and the United States 1795–1805* (Philadelphia: U. Pennsylvania Press, 1955); *Prologue to War: England and the United States 1805–1812* (Berkeley: University California Press, 1961); *Castlereagh and Adams: England and the United States 1812–1823* (Berkeley: U California Press, 1964); and *The Great Rapprochement: England and the United States 1895–1914* (New York: Scribner, 1968).
5. See Audrey Fisch, *American Slaves in Victorian England: Abolitionist Politics in Popular Literature and Culture* (Cambridge: Cambridge University Press, 2000) or Fionnghuala Sweeney, *Frederick Douglass and the Atlantic World* (Liverpool: Liverpool University Press, 2007), and Tracy C. Davis (ed., with S. Mihaylova), *Uncle Tom's Cabins: The Transnational Histories of America's Most Mutable Book* (Ann Arbor: University of Michigan Press, 2018).
6. Elisa Tamarkin, *Anglophilia: Deference, Devotion, and Antebellum America* (Chicago: University of Chicago Press, 2008).
7. Kariann Akemi Yokota, *Unbecoming British: How Revolutionary America Became a Postcolonial Nation* (Oxford: Oxford University Press, 2011), 9.
8. E. Catherine Bates, *A Year in the Great Republic* (London: Ward and Downey, 1887), I, x–xi.
9. See, for instance, Max Berger's treatment of the antebellum era in *The British Traveller in America* (New York: Columbia University Press, 1943), or Robert G. Athearn's work on visitors to the American West in *Westward the Briton* (New York: Scribner's, 1953).
10. For some of the postmodern-informed scholarship on how to read tourism, see for instance, James Buzard, *The Beaten Track: European Tourism, Literature, and the Ways to Culture, 1800–1918* (Oxford: Oxford University Press, 1993); Simon Coleman and Mike Crang (eds.), *Tourism: Between Place and Performance* (New York: Berghahn, 2002); Kevin Meethan, *Tourism in Global Society: Place, Culture, Consumption* (Basingstoke: Palgrave Macmillan, 2001); and especially, John Urry, *The Tourist Gaze* (London: Sage, 1990). For a recent general history, see Eric G. E. Zuelow, *A History of Modern Tourism* (London: Red Globe Press, 2015); also the *Journal of Tourism History*.
11. See Christopher Mulvey's two studies, *Anglo-American Landscapes: A Study of Nineteenth-Century Anglo-American Travel Literature* (Cambridge: Cambridge University Press, 1983) and *Transatlantic Manners: Social Patterns in Nineteenth-Century Travel Literature* (Cambridge: Cambridge University Press, 1990).

Notes

12. See Tamson Pietsch, "Rethinking the British World," *Journal of British Studies* 52, 2 (2013), 441–63.
13. James Belich, *Replenishing the Earth: The Settler Revolution and the Rise of the Anglo-World 1783–1939* (New York: Oxford University Press, 2009).

Chapter 1

1. For this topic, see especially Joseph Eaton, *The Anglo-American Paper War: Debate about the New Republic, 1800–1825* (New York: Palgrave Macmillan, 2012).
2. See Keith Thomas, *In Pursuit of Civility: Manners and Civilisation in Early Modern England* (New Haven: Yale University Press, 2018), *passim*.
3. William B. Cairns, *British Criticisms of American Writings, 1783–1815. A Contribution to the Study of Anglo-American Literary Relationships* (Madison: University of Wisconsin Press, 1918). The second volume, covering the years 1815–1833, appeared four years later, in 1922.
4. Robert Walsh, Jr., *An Appeal from the Judgments of Great Britain Regarding the United States of America* (Philadelphia: Mitchell, Ames, and White, 1819), iv. Walsh, born in Baltimore, had visited London as a young man and founded, in Philadelphia, the *American Review of History and Politics*, modeled on the British monthlies, in 1811.
5. "In the four quarters of the globe, who reads an American book? Or goes to an American play? Or looks at an American picture or statue?" (*Edinburgh Review*, May, 1820).
6. James Kirke Paulding, *John Bull in America; Or, the New Munchausen* (London: John Miller, 1825), ix–x, 120, 137, 153–4, etc.
7. Cairns, *British Criticisms … 1783–1815*, 93; *British Criticisms … 1815–1833*, 21, 296.
8. From the preface of his popular general textbook, *A History of American Literature* (New York and London: Oxford University Press, 1912), v, also 158, based he says on the courses he taught at Madison.
9. Quoted by Lane Cooper, "Travellers and Observers, 1763–1846," in *The Cambridge History of American Literature*, vol. 1, ed. William Peterfield Trent, John Erskine, Stuart Pratt Sherman, and Carl Van Doren (New York: Cambridge University Press, 1917), 207.
10. Benjamin Silliman, *A Journal of Travels in England, Holland and Scotland*, 2nd edn (Boston: T. B. Ait & Co., 1812), I, 227; III, 63–4.
11. [Anon.], "The Life of Washington …," *The British Critic* 31 (April, 1808), 386.
12. On British and American readings of similarity and difference in historical texts, see Mark Towsey, *Reading History in Britain and America, c.1750–c.1840* (Cambridge: Cambridge University Press, 2019).
13. Of the 245 British travelers' accounts consulted for this study, 11 were published in the 1830s, 18 in the 1840s, and 27 in the 1850s. After a Civil War hiatus, the numbers surged in the 1870s (34) and, especially, the 1880s (59), encouraged by the easier access to the American West. Over 10 percent (rising to more than 15 percent in the 1880s) were written by women.
14. Will B. Mackintosh, *Selling the Sites: The Invention of the Tourist in American Culture* (New York: New York University Press, 2019), 15, 38, and *passim*.
15. John Delaware Lewis, *Across the Atlantic* (London: George Earle, 1851), vi–vii.
16. On the British tourist in America as ethnographer, see Christopher Flynn, *Americans in British Literature, 1779–1832: A Breed Apart* (Farnham: Routledge, 2008), chapter 4.

17. Anon. [James Aitken], *From the Clyde to California, with Jottings by the Way* (Greenock: Greenock Herald, 1882), 152.
18. Johnson, from the Preface to his *Dictionary*, as quoted in Dennis Freeborn, *From Old English to Standard English*, 3rd edn (New York: Red Globe Press, 1984), 389.
19. Captain Francis Grose, et al., *Lexicon Balatronicum. A Dictionary of Buckish Slang, University Wit, and Pickpocket Eloquence* (London: C. Chappel, 1811 [originally published in 1785 as *A Classical Dictionary of the Vulgar Tongue*, with a further edition in 1788]).
20. Noah Webster, *Dissertations on the English Language* (Boston: Isaiah Thomas and Co., 1789), quoted by Sterling Andrus Leonard, *The Doctrine of Correctness in English Usage 1700–1800* (Milwaukee: University of Wisconsin Press, 1929), 163.
21. Robert Keith Leavitt, *Noah's Ark. New England Yankees and the Endless Quest: A Short History of the Original Webster Dictionaries, with Particular Reference to Their First Hundred Years* (Springfield: G. C. Merriam and Co., 1947), 14. For a general treatment of "American English" see Joey Lee Dillard, *Toward a Social History of American English* (Berlin: Walter de Gruyter and Co., 1985), and *A History of American English* (London: Routledge, 1992); also, Henry Kahane, "American English: From a Colonial Substandard to a Prestige Language," in *The Other Tongue: English across Cultures*, ed. Braj B. Kachru (Urbana-Champaign: University of Illinois Press, 1982), 229–36. For language and spelling reform in the early republic, see Dennis E. Baron, *Grammar and Good Taste: Reforming the American Language* (New Haven: Yale University Press, 1982), chs. 2–5.
22. Noah Webster, "Remarks on the Manners, Government, and Debt of the United States [1787]," published in *A Collection of Essays and Fugitiv Writings, on Moral, Historical, Political, and Literary Subjects*, ed. Noah Webster (Boston: I. Thomas and E. T. Andrews, 1790), 96.
23. Noah Webster, *Sketches of American Policy* (Hartford: Hudson and Goodwin, 1785), Part IV; Noah Webster, *Dissertations on the English Language: With Notes Historical and Critical* (Boston: Isaiah Thomas and Co., 1789), 406.
24. From an 1807 letter to Joel Barlow, quoted by Earl L. Bradsher, "Book Publishers and Publishing," in *The Cambridge History of American Literature*, vol. III, ed. Trent, Erskine, Sherman, and Van Doren (New York: Cambridge University Press, 1921), 541.
25. See Olivia Smith, *The Politics of Language 1791–1819* (Oxford: Oxford University Press, 1984), esp. ch. 1: "The Problem," 1–34.
26. Webster, *Dissertations*, 38. Dennis Baron ("Going Native: The Regeneration of Saxon English," *American Dialect Society* 69, 1 [1981], 23–4) briefly treats Webster's view of the Anglo-Saxon basis of contemporary English.
27. See Stephen Prickett, "Radicalism and Linguistic Theory: Horne Tooke on Samuel Pegge," *Yearbook of English Studies* 19 (1989), 1. Also Olivia Smith, "Winged Words: Language and Liberty in John Horne Tooke's *Diversions of Purley*," in *The Politics of Language 1791–1819*, 110–53.
28. Webster, *Dissertations*, vii, ix.
29. Noah Webster, *A Grammatical Institute* (Hartford: Hudson and Goodwin, 1790), v.
30. Noah Webster, *A Compendious Dictionary of the English Language* (Hartford: Hudson and Goodwin, 1806), Preface, v, xv.
31. *Ibid.*, xxiii.
32. Vincent P. Bynack, "Noah Webster's Linguistic Thought and the Idea of American National Culture," *Journal of the History of Ideas* 45, 1 (1984), 108.
33. *Gazette of the United States*, June 12, 1800, cited by Vincent Bynack, "Noah Webster's Linguistic Thought," 249; also see Jill Lepore, "Noah's Mark: Webster and the original dictionary wars," *New Yorker* (November 6, 2006), 78–87.

Notes

34. On such connections generally, see for instance, Frank Thistlethwaite, *The Anglo-American Connection in the Early Nineteenth Century* (Philadelphia: University of Pennsylvania Press, 1959), Chs. 3–4.
35. Webster, quoted by Bynack, "Noah Webster's Linguistic Thought," 111.
36. Barker to his banker Dawson Turner, August 2, 1829, as quoted by Harlow Giles Unger, *Noah Webster: The Life and Times of an American Patriot* (New York: John Wiley and Sons, 1998), 310.
37. Barker to Turner, September 30, 1829, as quoted in *Ibid.*, 312.
38. Richard M. Rollins, "Words as Social Control: Noah Webster and the Creation of the *American Dictionary*," *American Quarterly* 28, 4 (1976), 421.
39. Quoted by Unger, *Noah Webster*, 337.
40. Quoted by *Ibid.*
41. Quoted by *Ibid.*, 299.
42. Quoted by Basil Hall, *Travels in North America, in the Years 1827 and 1828* (Philadelphia: Carey, Lea and Carey, 1829), I, 319–20. Captain Hall's memoir is not to be confused with the earlier, and also critical, observations of Lt. Francis Hall's *Travels in Canada and the United States* (London: Longman, 1818).
43. Leavitt, *Noah's Ark*, 34–5; David Mickelthwaite, *Noah Webster and the American Dictionary* (Jefferson, No. Car: McFarland, 2004), 69, 276–8, 285–6.
44. H[enry] L[ouis] Mencken, *The American Language* (New York: Knopf, 1923 [1st edn, 1919]), 7.
45. Flynn, *Americans in British Literature, 177–1832*, 6.
46. *Ibid.*, 3–4, 114.
47. Trollope, Dickens (especially), and other British visitors often commented (it becomes a familiar subject in the genre) on the seriousness with which Americans in boarding houses and restaurants devoted themselves to eating, without polite conversation of any kind.
48. Frederick Marryat, *A Diary in America* (London: Longman, 1839), II, 30.
49. Though Frances Wright's *Views of Society and Manners in America* (New York: Bliss and E. White, 1821) offers a more sympathetic view ("They all spoke good English, with a good voice and accent" [8]), her positive reportage of American culture was something of an outlier among the early nineteenth-century memoirs.
50. John Witherspoon, "Lectures on Eloquence," *Collected Works* 4 (1802), 281 (cited by John Russell Bartlett, *Dictionary of Americanisms. A Glossary of Words and Phrases Usually Regarded as Peculiar to the United States* [New York: Bartlett and Welford, 1848], xxxi).
51. Witherspoon, *The Druid*, 5 (1781), in *Collected Works*, 4 (quoted by Mencken, *The American Language*, 49).
52. Jonathan Boucher, *Boucher's Glossary of Archaic and Provincial Words*, ed. Joseph Hunter, Joseph Stevenson, and James Odell (London: Black, Young, and Young, 1832–33), xx, xxiii, 15.
53. *Ibid.*, xxiii n.
54. Theodric Romeyn Beck, "Notes on Mr. Pickering's *Vocabulary of Words and Phrases Which Have Been Supposed to be Peculiar to the United States*, with preliminary observations," *Transactions of the Albany Institute* 1(1830), 25–31.
55. See Octavius Pickering and Charles W. Upham, *Life of Timothy Pickering* (Boston: Little, Brown, and Co., 1867–73); Gerard H. Clarfield, *Timothy Pickering and the American Republic* (Pittsburgh: University of Pittsburgh Press, 1980).

56. For the toast, see Perkins, *Prologue to War*, 57–8.
57. Thomas R. Lounsbury, "Americanisms, Real or Reputed," *Harper's Magazine* 127 (September, 1913), 591.
58. Pickering, *A Vocabulary*, iii–vi, 9, 11–12, 17, 19–20, and 20n.
59. Hall, *Travels in North America*, I, 321.
60. James Fenimore Cooper, *The Last of the Mohicans, or a Narrative of 1757* (London: John Miller, 1826, 3), ch. 26.
61. Harry Morgan Ayres, "The English Language in America," *The Cambridge History of American Literature* 4 (1921), 563–4.
62. Anon. review of *The Water-Witch* in the *Literary Gazette* 14 (October 23, 1830), 686.
63. James Fenimore Cooper, *Gleanings in Europe. England: By an American* (Philadelphia: Carey, Lea, and Blanchard, 1837), I, iii, v, 43, 47–9, 81–2, 116–17, 207; II, 88–9, 207, 260.
64. *Ibid.*, II, 92, 129–30.
65. James Fenimore Cooper, *Notions of the Americans: Picked Up by a Travelling Bachelor* (London: Henry Colburn, 1828), I, ix.
66. Wright, *Views of Society and Manners in America*: "they [Americans in New York City] all spoke good English, with a good voice and accent … my experience would dispose me to dissent from those travellers in the United States who complain, in our newspapers and journals …" (8, 16).
67. Charles William Janson, *The Stranger in America, 1793–1806* (London: Albion Press, 1807), vi; John Robert Godley, *Letters from America* (London: John Murray, 1844), I, xiv.
68. Marryat, in the *Metropolitan Magazine*, 1833, cited by Mackintosh, *Selling the Sights*, 131–3 (Marryat's article caricatures memoirs of European Continental travel); Hall, *Travels in North America*, I, iii; Amanda Claybaugh, "Towards a New Transatlanticism: Dickens in the United States," *Victorian Studies* 48, 3 (Spring, 2006), 445–6.
69. Charles Dickens, *American Notes* (New York: Penguin, 2004 [1st pub. 1842]), 163. Marryat, in *A Diary in America* of 1839, with which presumably Dickens was quite familiar, makes much of the Americanism "to fix," (it is "universal" and "means to do any thing" [II, 35]), as well as "to guess," "to reckon," and "to calculate."
70. Bartlett, *Dictionary of Americanisms*, first edition preface, vii, viii, and viii n, x, xii; second edition preface (1859), iv–v.
71. *Ibid.*, 2nd edn, Introduction, xxxi–ii.
72. *Ibid.*, xxi.
73. M. Schele De Vere, *Americanisms, or the English of the New World* (New York: Scribner and Co., 1872), 3.
74. Richard Grant White, *Shakespeare's Scholar* (New York: D. Appleton and Co., 1854), 343–4 (and cited in Bartlett's 2nd edn, 1859).
75. Geikie, "Americanisms," *Canadian Journal* (1857), cited by Bartlett, 1859; also see Richard Grant White, "Americanisms, I," *Atlantic Monthly* 41 (April, 1878), 495–502.
76. Charles Mackay, *Life and Liberty in America: Or, Sketches of a Tour in the United States and Canada in 1857–8*, 2nd edn (London: Smith, Elder and Co., 1859 [1st edn., also 1859]), I, 154–74.
77. Henry Bradshaw Fearon, *Sketches of America: A Narrative of a Journey of Five Thousand Miles through the Eastern and Western States of America* (London: Longman, 1818), 59–60; J[ohn]Benwell, *An Englishman's Travels in America: His Observations of Life and Manners in The Free and Slave States* (London: Binns and Goodwin, n.d. [1853]), 38.

Notes

78. Alfred Elwyn, *Glossary of Supposed Americanisms* (Philadelphia: J. B. Lippincott, 1859), iii.
79. Isabella Bird, *My First Travels in North America* (Mineola: Dover Publications, 2010 [first pub. as *The Englishwoman in America* in 1856]), 286.
80. Censor [Oliver Bell Bunce], *Don't: A Manual of Mistakes & Improprieties More or Less Prevalent in Conduct and Speech*, 2nd edn (London: Field and Tuer, 1888? [1st edn, 1884]), 5–6, 10, 61–73.
81. Richard Grant White, *Every-Day English* (Boston: Houghton, Mifflin and Co., 1880), 91, 496.
82. Quoted by Thomas R. Lounsbury, "The Standard of Pronunciation," *Harper's Magazine* 107 (May 2, 1903), 264. Emphasis added.
83. Marryat, *A Diary in America*, II, 31; George Perkins Marsh, *Lectures on the English Language. First Series*, 4th edn (New York: Charles Scribner's Sons, 1864 [1st pub. 1859]), Lecture XXX, the English Language in America, 666–7, 670; White, *Every-Day English*, 98–100, 243.
84. Marsh, *Lectures on the English Language*, 684; Edward Money, *The Truth about America* (London: Sampson Low, 1886), 52; Edward A. Freeman, "Some Points in American Speech and Customs, I," *Longman's Magazine* 1, 1 (November, 1882), 95–6; Rudyard Kipling, *American Notes* (Middletown, Delaware: Bravo Books, 2016 [1st pub. 1891, reissued 1899]), 6–7.
85. De Vere, *Americanisms*, 3–5.
86. Iza Duffus Hardy, *Between Two Oceans: Or, Sketches of American Travel* (London: Hurst and Blackett, 1884), 229.
87. John S. Farmer, *Americanisms—Old and New* (London: Thomas Poulter & Sons, 1889), vi–vii, xi–xii. This was the last, but one, substantial dictionary of Americanisms to be published before the First World War. Richard Harwood Thornton's *An American Glossary, Being an Attempt to Illustrate Certain Americanisms upon Historical Principles* (Philadelphia: J. B. Lippincott, 1912) was a work of fewer words but more extensive etymological descriptions.
88. His memoir of a visit to England in 1876–7, *England Without and Within*, was published in Boston and London (Sampson Low) in 1881; the novel, *Mr. Washington Adams in England*, was published in Edinburgh (David Douglas) in 1883.
89. White, *Every-Day English*, xi; also *Words and Their Uses* (Boston: Houghton, Mifflin, 1870), ii–iii.
90. For Hall's later work on James Murray's New English Dictionary (the OED), see Katherine Maud Elisabeth Murray, *Caught in the Web of Words: James A. H. Murray and the Oxford English Dictionary* (New Haven: Yale University Press, 1977), 305.
91. Fitzedward Hall, *Recent Exemplifications of False Philology* (New York: Scribner, Armstrong and Co., 1872), 40–1, 53, 59, 63, 66.
92. "Americanisms II," *Atlantic Monthly* 41 (May, 1878), 658; "Americanisms III," *Atlantic Monthly* 42 (July, 1878), 103–4, and the 5th edition of *Words and Their Uses* (Boston, 1882), i.
93. Fitzedward Hall, "English Rational and Irrational," *Nineteenth Century* 8, 43 (September, 1880), 424–5, 444.
94. "Americanisms I," *Atlantic Monthly* 41 (April, 1878), 495–9, 502; "Americanisms V," *Atlantic Monthly* 42 (November, 1878), 628.
95. Quoted in White's *Words*, 44, from Henry Alford, *A Plea for the Queen's English: Stray Notes on Speaking and Spelling* (London: Strahan, 1864), 6.

Notes

96. Marquis of Lorne, *A Trip to the Tropics, and Home through America* (London: Hurst and Blackett, 1867), 205–6.
97. Gilbert M. Tucker, "American English," *North American Review* 136, 314 (January, 1883), 55. Also Gilbert M. Tucker, *Our Common Speech* (New York, 1895), 152–3.
98. Hall, "English Rational and Irrational," 443.
99. Tucker, "American English," 55.
100. White, *Every-Day English*, 88–9; White, *Words*, 365–8.
101. For the story of Hall and Minor as contributors to the OED, see Simon Winchester, *The Meaning of Everything* (Oxford: Oxford University Press, 2003), 190-201, and for Minor's bizarre story, *The Surgeon of Crowthorne: A Tale of Murder, Madness and the Love of Words* (New York: Viking Press, 1998); also Murray, *Caught in the Web of Words*, 304–7.
102. James Murray, as quoted by Murray, *Caught in the Web of Words*, 184.
103. Murray, *Caught in the Web of Words*, 102, 169, 184, 366n.
104. Charles Mackay, *Through the Long Day: Or, Memorials of a Literary Life during Half a Century* (London: W. H. Allen and Co., 1887), II, 333.
105. Joseph Sturge, *A Visit to the United States in 1841* (London: Hamilton, Adams and Co., 1842 [also pub. in Boston]), 3, 16, 28.
106. George Lewis, *Impressions of America and the American Churches* (Edinburgh: W. P. Kennedy, 1845), iv.
107. Robert Everest, *A Journey through the United States and Part of Canada* (London: John Chapman, 1855), 33–4., 160.
108. Frederick James Jobson, *America and American Methodism* (New York: Virtue, Emmins, 1857), 27–8.
109. Newman Hall, *From Liverpool to St. Louis* (London: George Routledge and Sons, 1870), 27.
110. Frances Trollope, *Domestic Manners of the Americans* (London: Whittaker, Treacher and Co., 1832), chapters 11 and 15.
111. Lewis, *Across the Atlantic*, 192–208.
112. Richard Parkinson, *Tour in America in 1789, 1799, and 1800* (London: J. Harding, 1805), II, 460–1.
113. Edward William Watkin, *A Trip to the United States: In a Series of Letters* (London: W. H. Smith and Son, 1852), vii, viii, xii, 88.
114. George Combe, *Notes on the United States of North America* (Edinburgh: Maclachlan, Stewart and Co., 1841), I, 65.
115. Boyd Hilton, *The Age of Atonement: The Influence of Evangelicalism on Social and Economic Thought, 1795–1865* (Oxford: Oxford University Press, 1988).
116. Adam Hodgson, *Letters from North America* (London: Hurst, Robinson and Co., 1824), I, 399. A few years earlier the traveling actor and theatre manager John Bernard had similarly commented on an obscure Vermont farmer's "three books ... the Bible, the almanac, and the dictionary" (*Retrospections of America, 1798–1811* [New York: Harper and Bros., 1887], 325).
117. Richard Cobden, *England, Ireland, and America, by a Manchester Manufacturer* (London: James Ridgway and Sons, 1835), i, 103–5, 108, 112, 114, 120–1, 137.
118. Combe, *Notes on the United States of North America*, I, xiv–xvii, 28.
119. Newman Hall, *From Liverpool to St. Louis*, 248.

Notes

120. A. Thomason [pseud. for Andrew Bell, "a businessman"], *Men and Things in America* (London: William Smith, 1838), 2, 205, 272–3, 281, 286.
121. Foster Barham Zincke, *The Plough and the Dollar, Or the Englishry of a Century Hence* (London: Kegan Paul, Trench & Co., 1883 [pamphlet orig. written 1881]), 14–15, 24, 31.
122. De Vere, *Americanisms*, 295, 575; he devoted a chapter to "cant and slang" (295, 575); Bartlett simply cited the "Almighty dollar" as an American phrase "applied to money as 'the root of all evil'" in his *Dictionary of Americanisms* (1859).
123. James Stirling, *Letters from the Slave States* (London: John W. Parker and Son, 1857), 360–1.
124. Frank William Green, *Notes on New York, San Francisco, and Old Mexico* (Wakefield: E. Carr, 1886), 85–6.
125. Bartlett, *Dictionary of Americanisms*, xii.
126. Geoffrey Russell Searle, *Entrepreneurial Politics in Mid-Victorian Britain* (Oxford: Oxford University Press, 1993), 187n.
127. Quoted in Howard Temperley, *Britain and America since Independence* (New York: Palgrave, 2002), 67.
128. Charles Whibley, *American Sketches* (Edinburgh: William Blackwood & Sons, 1908), 216–17.
129. Lounsbury, "The Standard of Pronunciation," 261.
130. *Ibid.*, 262, and Lounsbury, "The Standard of Pronunciation. Second Paper," 578–9.
131. Lounsbury, "Differences in English and American Usage," *Harper's Magazine* 127 (July, 1913), 274, 277; and "What Americanisms Are Not," *Harper's Magazine* 126 (May, 1913), 619.
132. William Edwin Adams, *Our American Cousins: Being Personal Impressions of the People and Institutions of the United States*, 2nd edn (London: Walter Scott, 1887 [1st edn., pub. 1883]), 3–4.
133. Richard Grant White claimed, in *Words and Their Uses*, (1870 edn) iii, that "in language, as in morals, there is a higher law than mere usage."
134. Henry Watson and Francis George Fowler, *The King's English*, 2nd edn (Oxford: Clarendon Press, 1908), 24, cited by Lynne Murphy, *The Prodigal Tongue: The Love-Hate Relationship between British and American English* (New York: Penguin, 2018), 8, 98–9.
135. William Fraser Rae, *Westward by Rail: A Journey to San Francisco and Back and a Visit to the Mormons*, 3rd edn (London: W. Isbister & Co., 1874 [1st pub. 1871]), 320.
136. By which he appears to mean words derived from the Latinate languages of the Continent, especially French. In 1882 George Augustus Sala dwelt on this choice of French words over words of Anglo-Saxon origin like "elevator" for "lift," "bureau" for "office," or "depot" for "station" (*America Revisited: From the Bay of New York to the Gulf of Mexico and from Lake Michigan to the Pacific*, 3rd edn (London: Vizetelly and Co., 1883 [1st edn., 1882]), I, 25n.
137. Whibley, *American Sketches*, 206, also 207–9, 214–17, 222–3.
138. Brander Matthews, "A Campaign for Pure English," *New York Times*, September 26, 1920. Matthews "was a diligent collector of Americanisms."
139. Henry Watson and Francis George Fowler, *The King's English*, 25.
140. Thomas William Hodgson Crosland, *The Abounding American* (London: A. F. Thompson & Co., 1907), 18, 114. Crosland wrote a series of such provocative, humorous sketches such as *The Unspeakable Scot* (1902).

Notes

141. Henry Yule and Arthur Coke Burnell, *Hobson-Jobson: A Glossary of Colloquial Anglo-Indian Words and Phrases, and of Kindred Terms, Etymological, Historical, Geographical, and Discursive* (London: John Murray, 1886, and subsequent editions).
142. Farmer, *Americanisms—Old and New*, vii.
143. Stead, an Americanophile, "kept a large 'Anglo-American' flag in his office, which merged the colors of both countries and which he described as 'the flag of the future'" (Joel H. Wiener, *The Americanization of the British Press, 1830s–1914: Speed in the Age of Transatlantic Journalism* [London and New York: Palgrave Macmillan, 2011], 171).
144. James Burnley, *Two Sides of the Atlantic* (Bradford: T. Brear [1880]), 184–5.
145. In the *Nineteenth Century*, quoted by Wiener, 11.
146. Matthew Arnold, *Civilization in the United States: First and Last Impressions of America* (Boston: Cupples and Hurd, 1888), 79–80, 85, 88–9, 177–8.
147. Wiener, *The Americanization of the British Press*, 4, 10–11.
148. Mencken, *The American Language*, vii.
149. Mark Twain, *Following the Equator: A Journey Around the World* (Hartford: Harper Bros., 1897 [pub. in Britain as *More Tramps Abroad*]), 230.
150. Christopher Orlando Sylvester Mawson (ed.), *Roget's Thesaurus* (New York: Thomas Y. Crowell, 1911), v.
151. Arnold Bennett called it a "masterpiece ... for which I would sacrifice the entire works of Thackeray and George Eliot" (*Your United States: Impressions of a First Visit* [New York and London: Harper & Bros., 1912], 108).
152. Mark Twain, "Concerning the American Language," in *The Stolen White Elephant, etc* (Boston: James R. Osgood and Co., 1882), 265, 269.
153. Quoted by Gilbert Milligan Tucker, *American English*, 12.
154. Twain, "Concerning the American Language," 265.
155. Hamilton Aide, "Social Aspects of American Life," *Nineteenth Century* 29, 172 (June, 1891), 892. The term, according to Kipling, had become a favorite topic in "the comic papers" (*American Notes*, 53).
156. William Archer, *America To-Day: Observations & Reflections* (London: William Heinemann, 1900), 76.
157. John Kasson, *Rudeness and Civility: Manners in Nineteenth-Century Urban America* (New York: Macmillan, 1990), 47.
158. Harold Spender, *A Briton in America* (London: William Heinemann, 1921), 21.
159. Kipling, *American Notes*, 53.
160. Lepel Henry Griffin, *The Great Republic*, 2nd edn (London: Chapman and Hall, 1884), 11.
161. William Howard Russell, *Hesperothen; Notes from the West: A Record of a Ramble in the United States and Canada in the Spring and Summer of 1881* (London: Sampson Low, 1882), I, 26–8.
162. Lodge, "Colonialism in the United States," *Atlantic Monthly* (1883), as quoted by Murphy, *The Prodigal Tongue*, 19.
163. Van Wyck Brooks, *America's Coming of Age* (New York: B. W. Huebsch, 1915), 15.
164. Lounsbury, "Americanisms, Real or Reputed," 592.
165. Mencken, *The American Language*, viii.
166. Act III, 26.

Notes

Chapter 2

1. Johnston Forbes-Robertson briefly treats this, his third visit to America, in his memoir *A Player under Three Reigns* (London: Little Brown and Co., 1925), 227-35.
2. See Margot Peters, *Mrs. Pat: The Life of Mrs. Patrick Campbell* (London: Bodley Head, 1984), 341-7.
3. William Cobbett, *A Year's Residence in the United States of America* (Boston, n.d. [1819]), 125, commenting on an American pamphlet claiming that "the People of America sigh *with delight* to see the plays of Shakespeare."
4. Alexis de Tocqueville, *Democracy in America* (New York: Knopf, 1956 [1st pub. 1840]), II, 55.
5. James Robertson Anderson, *An Actor's Life* (London: Walter Scott, 1902 [written 1887-8]), 146-7.
6. Lawrence W. Levine, *Highbrow/Lowbrow: The Emergence of Cultural Hierarchy in America* (Cambridge, MA: Harvard University Press, 1990), 30.
7. Webster, *A Collection of Essays*, 86-7, 400-1; Joshua Kendall, *The Forgotten Founding Father: Noah Webster's Obsession and the Creation of an American Culture* (New York: G. P. Putnam's Sons, 2011), 30 and 125.
8. Don B. Wilmeth, and Christopher Bigsby, "Introduction," in *American Theater*, ed. Wilmeth and Bigsby (Cambridge: Cambridge University Press, 1998), I, 5; also see Stephen Elliot Wilmer, *Theatre, Society and the Nation: Staging American Identities* (Cambridge: Cambridge University Press, 2002), ch. 1, "From British Colony to Independent Nation: Refashioning Identity," 16-52.
9. Janson, *The Stranger in America*, 28-9.
10. Joseph N. Ireland, *Records of the New York Stage from 1750 to 1860* (New York: Burt Franklin, 1866-7) I, 1, cited Hallam's company, though "others had preceded him," as first appearing in New York in the early 1750s.
11. Wilmer, *Theatre, Society and the Nation*, 17-18; Odai Johnson, *London in a Box: Englishness and Theatre in Revolutionary America* (Iowa City: University of Iowa Press, 2017), *passim*; Douglas McDermott, "Structure and Management in the American Theatre," in *American Theater*, ed. Don B. Wilmeth and Christopher Bigsby (Cambridge: Cambridge University Press, 1998), I, 186-90.
12. See Ireland, *Records of the New York Stage*, I, 63-72.
13. Lewis, *Impressions of America*, 181.
14. Frances Trollope, *Domestic Manners*, 218; Elizabeth Hoon Cawley (ed.), *The American Diaries of Richard Cobden* (New York: Greenwood Press, 1952), 195.
15. Charles H. Shattuck, *Shakespeare on the American Stage: From the Hallams to Edwin Booth* (Washington, DC: Associated University Presses, 1976), 1, 25-6.
16. See Rosemarie K. Bank, *Theatre Culture in America, 1825-1860* (Cambridge: Cambridge University Press, 1997), who makes use of a wider sense of theater culture that includes parades, public ceremonies, exhibits, lectures, circuses, magic shows, and medicine shows (4, 8-9, 140-1, 186, 189, etc.).
17. Jacky Bratton, *The Making of the West End Stage: Marriage, Management and the Mapping of Gender in London, 1830-1870* (Cambridge: Cambridge University Press, 2011), 1-2. Also see Tracy C. Davis, *Economics of the British Stage 1800-1914* (Cambridge: Cambridge University Press, 2000).

Notes

18. See Susan Harris Smith, *American Drama: The Bastard Art* (Cambridge: Cambridge University Press, 1997), chapter 2.
19. *Ibid.*, 36; John Frick, "A Changing Theatre: New York and Beyond," in *American Theater*, ed. Don B. Wilmeth and Christopher Bigsby (Cambridge: Cambridge University Press, 1998), II, 216.
20. Quoted in Jürgen C. Wolter, *The Dawning of American Drama: American Dramatic Criticism, 1746-1915* (Westport: Praeger, 1993), 209.
21. See Simon Williams, "European Actors and the Star System in the American Theatre, 1752-1870," in *American Theater*, ed. Don B. Wilmeth and Christopher Bigsby (Cambridge: Cambridge University Press, 1998), I, 303-37. Also McConachie, "American Theatre in Context, from the Beginnings to 1870," and McDermott, "Structure and Management," 147-8, 175, 191-210.
22. George Rose, *The Great Country: Or, Impressions of America* (London: Tinsley Bros., 1868), 17.
23. Emmeline Stuart Wortley, *Travels in the United States, Etc.: During 1849 and 1850* (London: Richard Bentley, 1851), I, 45, 185, 285.
24. Godley, *Letters from America*, I, ix, 144.
25. Charles Augustus Murray, *Travels in North America During the Years 1833, 1835, and 1836* (London: Richard Bentley, 1839), II, 180-1.
26. Frances Anne Butler, *Journal* (London: John Murray, 1835), II, 136.
27. Charles Lyell, *A Second Visit to the United States of North America* (London: John Murray, 1849), I, 89, 197; II, 117-18; Frederick De Roos, *Personal Narrative of Travels in the United States and Canada in 1826* (London: William Harrison Ainsworth, 1827), 4-5, 37, 48.
28. John Bernard, *Retrospections of the Stage* (London: Henry Colburn and Richard Bentley, 1830), II, 335.
29. For a memoir of the Drury Lane theatre in the nineteenth century, including a few pages (vol. I, 238-40) on Price's tenure there, see Edward Stirling, *Old Drury Lane: Fifty Years' Recollections of Author, Actor, and Manager* (London: Chatto and Windus, 1881).
30. Francis Courtney Wemyss, *Twenty-Six Years of the Life of an Actor and Manager* (New York: Burgess, Stringer & Co., 1847), I, 85-6.
31. Frederick Pollock (ed.), *Macready's Reminiscences, and a Selection from His Diaries and Letters* (London: Macmillan & Co., 1876), 233-4. Macready performed (1826-7) in New York, Boston, Philadelphia, Baltimore, and Albany (William Archer, *William Charles Macready* (London: Kegan Paul, 1890), 76-7). For a short life from an American point of view, see William Thompson Price, *A Life of William Charles Macready* (New York: Brentano, 1894).
32. Wemyss, *Twenty-Six Years*, I, 215-7. Though Wemyss resided in the States for decades, he claimed that "the language spoken by all around me, the nasal twang with which it was pronounced" made him feel himself to be a "stranger," "the foreigner" (I, 72).
33. *Ibid.*, I, 94-5.
34. Bernard, *Retrospections of the Stage*, II, 281-2.
35. Wemyss, *Twenty-Six Years*, I, 125, 135.
36. An English tenor, Joshua Anderson, who had caused outrage when it was reported that he had called someone "an impudent Yankee," was driven from the stage by protesters (Nigel Cliff, *The Shakespeare Riots: Revenge, Drama, and Death in Nineteenth-Century America* (New York: Random House, 2007), 126).

Notes

37. Ireland, *Records of the New York Stage*, I, 459–62. Hamblin was reputed to have left more than $100,000.
38. Jeffrey H. Richards, "Theatre, Drama, Performance," in *Transatlantic Literary Studies, 1660-1830*, ed. Eve Tavor Banat and Susan Manning (Cambridge: Cambridge University Press, 2012), 91–105.
39. Ireland, *Records of the New York Stage*, I: 341–44, 375–7, 396, 493, 615, 683; II: 193, 323, 386, 406, 493–4, 642, 659.
40. See John Lester Wallack, *Memories of Fifty Years* (New York: Charles Scribner's Sons, 1889). Also, Montrose J. Moses, *Famous Actor-Families in America* (New York: Thomas Y. Crowell, 1906), 195–224; and Brander Matthews, and Laurence Hutton (eds.), *Actors and Actresses of Great Britain and the United States* (Boston: L. C. Page & Co., 1900), 5, 283–300.
41. There is a quite substantial literature on Boucicault. See Townsend Walsh, *The Career of Dion Boucicault* (New York: The Dunlap Society, 1915); Richard Fawkes, *Dion Boucicault: A Biography* (London: Quartet Books, 1979), and Robert Hogan, *Dion Boucicault* (New York: Twaine Publishers, 1969).
42. Fawkes, *Dion Boucicault*, 77.
43. Quoted by William H. A. Williams, *Twas Only an Irishman's Dream: The Image of Ireland and the Irish in American Popular Song Lyrics, 1800-1920* (Urbana: University of Illinois Press, 1996), 70.
44. Ireland, *Records of the New York Stage*, II, 464–5.
45. *Ibid.*, II, 331–2.
46. Fawkes, *Dion Boucicault*, 82–3.
47. From Boucicault's "Leaves from a Dramatist's Diary," *North American Review* 149, 393 (August, 1889), 230; also see Fawkes, *Dion Boucicault*, 77–8.
48. Dierdre McFeely, *Dion Boucicault: Irish Identity on Stage* (Cambridge: Cambridge University Press, 2012), 13; and Christopher Morash, *A History of Irish Theatre 1601-2000* (Cambridge: Cambridge University Press, 2002), 92–3.
49. John Russell Stephens, *The Profession of the Playwright: British Theatre, 1800-1900* (Cambridge: Cambridge University Press, 1992), 25, 58.
50. See Fawkes, *Dion Boucicault*, 114–50, for a narrative of these years.
51. McFeely, *Dion Boucicault*, 80, 85, 195.
52. On this debated subject, see for instance, Sarah Meer, "Foreign Constellations in a National Drama: Becoming American in Boucicault's *Belle Lamar*," *Nineteenth-Century Theatre and Film* 39, 2 (December, 2012), 19–38.
53. *Ibid.*, 20.
54. Emphasis added.
55. Rick Bowers, "Shakespearean Celebrity in America: The Strange Performative Afterlife of George Frederick Cooke," *Theatre History Studies* 31 (2011), 44 and *passim*, 27–50. Also see Don B. Wilmeth, *George Frederick Cooke: Machiavel of the Stage* (New York: Praeger, 1980), and William Dunlap, *Memoirs of George Frederick Cooke* (New York: D. Longworth, 1813).
56. Ireland, *Records of the New York Stage*, I, 288–90.
57. *Ibid.*, I, 370–1.
58. *Ibid.*, I, 371–2; Wemyss, *Twenty-Six Years*, I, 43, 97–9, 114.
59. Samuel Haynes, *Unfinished Revolution: The Early American Republic in a British World* (Charlottesville: University of Virginia Press, 2010), 80.

60. De Roos, *Personal Narrative*, 46–8.
61. Wemyss, *Twenty-Six Years*, I, 98–9.
62. Quoted in Robert L. Klepac, *Mr Mathews at Home* (London: Society for Theatre Research, 1979), 20.
63. Anon., *Tallis's Acting Edition of Shakspeare* [sic] (London: John Tallis & Co., n.d. [1851]), 68–9.
64. Gariff B. Wilson, "The Acting of Edwin Forrest," *Quarterly Journal of Speech* 36, 4 (December, 1950), 484–5.
65. Frances Trollope, *Domestic Manners of the Americans* [1st edn., 1832, ed. Donald Smalley] (New York, 1949), 132 and 340.
66. Thomas Hamilton, *Men and Manners in America* (Edinburgh: William Blackwood & Sons, 1833), I, 51–3.
67. William Toynbee (ed.), *The Diaries of William Charles Macready* (London: Chapman and Hall, 1912), I, 349, 352–3.
68. *Ibid.*, II, 231.
69. Quoted in Archer, *Macready*, 162.
70. Shattuck, *Shakespeare on the American Stage*, vol. 1, 71.
71. Pollock, *Macready's Reminiscences*, 613.
72. See Cliff, *The Shakespeare Riots*, ch. 11, for a full description of the riot; also H. M. Ranney, *Account of the Terrific and Fatal Riot at the New-York Astor Place Opera House* (New York: H. M. Ranney, 1849).
73. Levine, *Highbrow/Lowbrow*, 68.
74. See Marc David Baer, *Theatre and Disorder in Late Georgian London* (Oxford: Clarendon Press, 1992), chs. 2 and 7; St. Vincent Troubridge, "Theatre Riots in London," in *Studies in English Theatre History in Memory of Gabrielle Enthoven*, ed. Muriel St. Clare Byrne (London: Society for Theatre Research, 1952), 84–97; and Heather McPherson, "'Theatrical Riots' and Cultural Politics in Eighteenth-Century London," *The Eighteenth Century* 43, 3 (2002), 236–52.
75. McConachie, "American Theatre in Context," 132.
76. Cliff, *The Shakespeare Riots*, 126–7; McConachie, "American Theatre in Context," 127, 132, 152. Also see Bruce McConachie, "'The Theatre of the Mob': Apocalyptic Melodrama and Preindustrial Riots in Antebellum New York," in *Theatre for Working-Class Audiences in the United States, 1830–1980*, ed. Bruce McConachie and Daniel Friedman (Westport: Praeger, 1985), 17–46.
77. McPherson, "Theatrical Riots," 236, 339–40.
78. Cliff, *The Shakespeare Riots*, 220.
79. McConachie, "American Theatre in Context," 152.
80. Anderson, *An Actor's Life*, xxii, 130–1.
81. See Thomas Edgar Pemberton, *Edward Askew Sothern, with a Brief Sketch of the Career of E. H. Sothern* (New York: Knickerbocker Press, 1910 [1st pub. 1890]), 135–6; and Clara E. Laughlin, "'Our America Cousin,'" *McClure's Magazine* 32, 2 (December, 1908), 186.
82. Tom Taylor, *Our American Cousin* (San Bernardino: CreateSpace, 2017), 6–7, 22. Brandy or whiskey "cobblers," with "smashes," "juleps," "corpse revivers," "gum-ticklers," and a variety of other "cock-tails," were reported by censorious or admiring British travelers to be often copiously on offer from their American hosts.

Notes

83. *Ibid.*, 36.
84. For Jefferson's career, see his *Autobiography* (New York: The Century Co., 1890), as well as Wilson Winter, *Life and Art of Joseph Jefferson, Together with Some Account of His Ancestry and of the Jefferson Family of Actors* (New York: Macmillan & Co., 1894). There is a modern biography by Arthur Bloom, *Joseph Jefferson, Dean of the American Theatre* (Savannah: Frederick C. Bell, 2000).
85. Laughlin, "'Our American Cousin,'" 188; Pemberton, *Edward Askew Sothern*, 20–1.
86. Quoted in Pemberton, *Edward Askew Sothern*, 30.
87. Henry Barton Baker, *History of the London Stage and Its Famous Players* (London: Benjamin Blom, 1904 [revised edn, 1st pub. 1889]), 236–8.
88. For this subject, see Francis Hodge, *Yankee Theatre: The Image of America on the Stage, 1825–1850* (Austin: University of Texas Press, 1964).
89. Jeffrey Mason, "American Stages," in *Performing America: Cultural Nationalism in American Theater*, ed. Jeffry Mason and J. Ellen Gainor (Ann Arbor: University of Michigan Press, 1999), 1–2.
90. J. Ellen Gainor, "Introduction," in *Ibid.*, 9 (citing Rosemarie K. Bank, "Meditations Upon Opening and Crossing Over," in *Of Borders and Thresholds*, ed. Michal Kobiaka [Minneapolis: University of Minnesota Press, 1999]).
91. Bartlett, in the first, 1848, edition of his *Dictionary of Americanisms*, reserves the term "Yankee" for only "a portion" of America, while, he claims, "Brother Jonathan" has come to designate "the whole country," as "John Bull" does for England (50).
92. X., Y., Z. [John Neal], "Speculations of a Traveller Concerning the People of the United States," *Blackwood's* 16 (July, 1824), 95. An American writer, art critic, abolitionist, and feminist from Maine, Neal (1793–1876) was a frequent contributor to Blackwood's and other journals on American affairs. He was a defender of American colloquialisms and of American literature.
93. See Hodge, *Yankee Theatre*, 45–53.
94. For Hackett, see *Ibid.*, chs. 5–8; also, his entry in the *Encyclopedia Britannica*, 11th edn.
95. Quoted from the *Times* by Hodge, *Yankee Theatre*, 131–2.
96. Hodge, *Yankee Theatre*, chs. 9–11; for Hill generally, see Gaylan Collier, "George Handel Hill: Yankee of Them All," *Southern Speech Journal* 24, 2 (1958), 91–3; George Handel Hill, *Scenes from the Life of an Actor; Compiled from the Journals, Letters, and Memoranda of the Late Yankee Hill* (New York: Garrett and Co., 1853); and William Knight Northall, *Life and Recollections of Yankee Hill Together with Anecdotes and Incidents of His Travels* (New York: W. F. Burgess, 1850).
97. Hodge, *Yankee Theatre*, 222, 238–9.
98. When Joseph Hatton saw the play in London he observed that the "native American" (Asa Trenchard) was no longer depicted as the "loud, noisy, irrepressible person" he had previously seen "on the stage and in humorous literature" (Joseph Hatton, *To-Day in America. Studies for the Old World and the New* [London: Chapman and Hall, 1881], I, vi–viii).
99. Hatton, *To-Day in America*, I, vii–viii.
100. See Tice L. Miller, "Plays and Playwrights: Civil War to 1896," in *American Theater*, ed. Wilmeth and Bigsby, vol. II (Cambridge: Cambridge University Press, 1999), 240–1.
101. Taylor, *Our American Cousin*, 6–7.
102. From the title of a humorous fictionalized memoir of a transatlantic crossing by British theater critic Alfred J. Cohen ("Allen Dale," in *The Great Wet Way* [New York: Dodd, Mead and Company, 1910]), playing of course on "The Great White Way" (Broadway).

103. Ireland, *Records of the New York Stage*, I, 255-7.
104. Quoted from the *Weekly Dispatch* by Brian N. Morton, *Americans in London* (New York: William Morrow, 1986), 49.
105. Boucicault, "Leaves from a Dramatist's Diary," 133.
106. Griffin, *The Great Republic*, 95.
107. Quoted by Joseph Hatton in "Henry Irving at Home," *Harper's Magazine* (February, 1882), 386-7.
108. Joseph Hatton, *Henry Irving's Impressions of America, Narrated in a Series of Sketches, Chronicles, and Conversations* (Boston: James R. Osgood and Co., 1884), 2.
109. See Lisa Merrill, *When Romeo Was a Woman: Charlotte Cushman and Her Circle of Female Spectators* (Ann Arbor: University of Michigan Press, 1999).
110. Emily Faithful, *Three Visits to America* (Edinburgh: David Douglas, 1884), 364; Ellen Terry, *The Story of My Life: Recollections and Reflections* (New York: Doubleday, 1909 [1st pub. 1908]), 184.
111. Faithful, *Three Visits*, 364.
112. On this subject, see Laurence Senelick, "Sexuality and Gender," in *A Cultural History of the Theatre*, vol. 5: *In the Age of Empire*, ed. Peter Marx (London: Bloomsbury, 2019), 77-96.
113. Elizabeth Robins, *Way Stations* (New York: Dodd, Meade & Co., 1913), 308-9. For Robins' life and work, see Angela V. John, *Elizabeth Robins: Staging a Life* (Brimscombe Port: Tempus, 2007 [1st pub. 1995]).
114. Thomas Postlewait, "The Hieroglyphic Stage," in *American Theatre*, II, eds. Don B. Wilmeth and Christopher Bigsby (Cambridge: Cambridge University Press, 1999), 159-60; also see Jack Poggi, *Theater in America: The Impact of Economic Forces, 1870-1967* (Ithaca: Cornell University Press, 1968), chs. 1-3; and Alfred L. Bernheim, *The Business of the Theatre: An Economic History of the American Theatre 1750-1932* (New York: Actors' Equity Assn., 1932), ch. 6 on the star system in America and chs. 8-15 on the late nineteenth, early twentieth century "centralization" of the theater business.
115. See Stephens, *The Profession of the Playwright*, 107-9. For the US touring of *Pirates of Penzance* in 1879 and *Patience* in 1881, see Paul Seeley, *Richard D'Oyly Carte* (London: Routledge, 2019), 264-84.
116. Henry Irving, "Preface, to the American Public," in Hatton, *Henry Irving's Impressions of America*, 1.
117. Austin Brereton, *The Life of Henry Irving* (New York: B. Blom, 1969 [1st pub. 1908]), II, 10; Laurence Irving, *Henry Irving: The Actor and His World* (London: Columbus Books, 1989 [1st pub. 1951]), 418.
118. Brereton, *Life of Henry Irving*, II, 45, 58.
119. The company toured America in 1883-4, 1884-5, 1888, 1893-4, 1895-6, 1899-1900 (the most profitable), 1901-02, and 1903-04.
120. Brereton, *Life of Henry Irving*, I, 1.
121. *Ibid.*, II, 296; Laurence Irving, *Henry Irving*, 109.
122. Peters, *Mrs. Pat*, 206. For Tyler and Liebler & Co., see, for example, the *New York Times* for August 4, 1910.
123. For Daly, see Joseph Francis Daly, *The Life of Augustin Daly* (New York: Macmillan, 1917), and the 1911 *Encyclopedia Britannica*.
124. Postlewait, "The Hieroglyphic Stage," 107.

Notes

125. Laurence Irving, *Henry Irving*, 419; Laura Beatty, *Lillie Langtry* (London: Vintage, 2000 [1st pub. 1999]), 226–7.
126. Obituary in Anon., *The Sun*, March 15, 1907, 9: "Impresario Grau Is Dead. The Man Who Made the Metropolitan Famous."
127. Mary Anderson, *A Few Memories* (New York: Harper and Brothers, 1896), 128–9.
128. George Arliss, *Up the Years from Bloomsbury: An Autobiography* (New York: Blue Ribbon Books, 1927), 193–5.
129. William Winter, *The Wallet of Time* (New York: Moffat, Yard and Co., 1913), II, 143–4.
130. Postlewait, "The Hieroglyphic Stage," 144.
131. Marlis Schweitzer, *Transatlantic Broadway: The Infrastructural Politics of Global Performance* (Basingstoke: Palgrave Macmillan, 2015), 2, 5, 77, 86, and "Networking the Waves: Ocean Liners, Impresarios, and Broadway's Atlantic Expansion," *Theatre Survey* 53, 2 (September, 2012), 241–67.
132. For Belasco and the Frohman brothers, see Wilmeth and Bigsby (eds.), *American Theater*, II, *passim*. Also, Isaac F. Marcossan, and Daniel Frohman, *Charles Frohman: Manager and Man* (New York: Harper & Bros., 1916), and David Belasco, *The Theatre through Its Stage Door* (New York: Harper & Bros., 1919).
133. Morton, *Americans in London*, 138–9.
134. Schweitzer, "Networking the Waves," 251–2.

Chapter 3

1. Matthews to James Smith, quoted by Hazel Waters, *Racism on the Victorian Stage: Representation of Slavery and Black Character* (Cambridge: Cambridge University Press, 2007), 511.
2. Anon., *Sketches of Mr. Mathews' Celebrated Trip to America* (London: J. Limbird, 1823), cited by Joyce Green MacDonald, "Acting Black: *Othello*, *Othello* Burlesques, and the Performance of Blackness," in *Ira Aldridge: The African Roscius*, ed. Bernth Lindfors (Rochester: University of Rochester Press, 2007), 138.
3. From a New York press account, quoted by MacDonald, "Acting Black," 137–8.
4. Quoted by Sean Wilentz, *Chants Democratic: New York City and the Rise of the American Working Class, 1788–1850* (New York: Oxford University Press, 1984), 259.
5. See Waters, *Racism on the Victorian Stage*, for a treatment of how black characters, including Aldridge's Othello, developed on the British stage through the 1850s, with a focus especially on American influence, from the vengeful moor to the comical Jim Crow and sympathetic Uncle Tom.
6. Until 1843, some theatres without a patent license to perform legitimate drama would simply add some musical, humor, or dance business to a serious play to get around the prohibition (Nicholas M. Evans, "Ira Aldridge: Shakespeare and Minstrelsy," in *Ira Aldridge: The African Roscius*, ed. Bernth Lindfors (Rochester: Rochester University Press, 2007), 162).
7. Bernth Lindfors, "'Mislike Me Not for My Complexion … ': Ira Aldridge in Whiteface," *African American Review* 33, 2 (Summer, 1999), 348.
8. Bernth Lindfors, "'No End of Dramatic Novelty': Ira Aldridge at the Royal Coburg Theatre," *Nineteenth-Century Theatre and Film* 34, 1 (July, 2007), 30.

Notes

9. MacDonald, "Acting Black," 136. For a general treatment of whites blacking up in legitimate theatre, see William Torbet Leonard, *Masquerade in Black* (London: Scarecrow Press, 1986).
10. See the October, 1825, *Times* review cited by Hazel Waters, "Ira Aldridge's Fight for Equality," in *Ira Aldridge: The African Roscius*, ed. Lindfors, 98–9.
11. MacDonald, "Acting Black," 136.
12. John Lambert, *Travels through Lower Canada, and the United States of North America in the Years 1806, 1807, and 1808* (London: Richard Phillips, 1810), II, 374.
13. Anderson, *An Actor's Life*, 129.
14. Quotations from *Figaro in London* (April 6, 1833), *John Bull* (April 14, 1833, a journal funded by West India merchants), the *Atheneum* (April 13, 1833), and the *Times* (April 11, 1833) cited by Waters, "Ira Aldridge's Fight for Equality," 107–8. Also see Herbert Marshall and Mildred Stock, *Ira Aldridge: The Negro Tragedian* (London: Rockliff, 1958), 121–7.
15. Waters, *Racism on the Victorian Stage*, 2.
16. Evans, "Ira Aldridge," 163, referencing Gilroy's *Black Atlantic*.
17. Ibid., 175; also Errol Hill, *Shakespeare in Sable: A History of Black Shakespearean Actors* (Amherst: University of Massachusetts Press, 1984), 44–5; Jack Shalom, "The Ira Aldridge Troupe: Black Minstrelsy in Philadelphia," *African American Review* 28, 4 (1994), 653–8.
18. See Marshall and Stock, *Ira Aldridge*, *passim*, for these citations.
19. Hodgson, *Letters from North America*, I, 153; William Faux, *Memorable Days in America*, I (London: W. Simpkin and R. Marshall, 1823), 9; Hamilton, *Men and Manners in America*, I, 210; Mrs. John Felton, *American Life: A Narrative of Two Years' City and Country Residence in the United States* (Hull: John Hutchinson, 1838), 58.
20. Bartlett, *Dictionary of Americanisms*, xi.
21. George William Featherstonhaugh, *Excursion through the Slave States from Washington on the Potomac to the Frontier of Mexico* (London: John Murray, 1844), a memoir of a tour of 1834–5; Dickens, commenting on the Southern accent, remarked that "all the women who have been bred in the slave-states speak more or less like negroes, from having been constantly in their childhood with black nurses" (cited in Edgar Johnson, *Charles Dickens: His Tragedy and Triumph* [New York: Simon and Schuster, 1952], I, 413), echoing a similar observation by Fanny Kemble, *Journal of a Residence on a Georgia Plantation in 1838–1839* (New York: Harper & Bros., 1863), 211–12.
22. Bartlett, *Dictionary of Americanisms*, viii, and throughout.
23. William C. Fowler, *The English Language in Its Elements and Forms* (New York: Harper & Bros., 1855 [1st edn., 1850]), xi, 120.
24. De Vere, *Americanisms*, 148–54.
25. White, "Americanisms, I," 496–7.
26. Farmer, *Americanisms—Old and New*, vii–viii.
27. Twain struggled to get the rhythms and diction of negro dialect "right" (see Deborah Freidell's review of Percival Everett's *James*, "Put on your clown suit," *London Review of Books* May 23, 2024, 39).
28. Farmer, *Americanisms—Old and New*, vii, and throughout.
29. Mawson, *Roget's Thesaurus*, v, 121 (under "Blackness"), and elsewhere.
30. Felton, *American Life*, 58.

Notes

31. Stirling, *Letters from the Slave States*, 56.
32. Ibid., 56.
33. Kenneth D. Rose, *Unspeakable Awfulness: America through the Eyes of European Travelers, 1865-1900* (London: Taylor and Francis, 2014), 15-16.
34. P. W. Hamer, *From Ocean to Ocean, Being a Diary of Three Months' Expedition from Liverpool to California and Back* (London: William Clowes and Son, 1871), 19.
35. Wortley, *Travels in the United States*, 126.
36. Quoted by Davis, "Acting Black, 1824," 182-3.
37. Mrs. Edward Hamer Carbutt [Lady Mary Rhodes], *Five Months' Fine Weather in Canada, Western U.S., and Mexico* (London: Sampson, Low, 1889), 9; Winefred, Lady Howard of Glossop, Baroness, *Journal of a Tour in the United States, Canada and Mexico* (London: Sampson, Low, Marston, 1897), 3-4.
38. Walter Gore Marshall, *Through America: Or, Nine Months in the United States* (London: Sampson, Low, 1882 [1st pub. 1881]), 40-1.
39. Montague Davenport, *Under the Gridiron: A Summer in the United States and the Far West, Including a Run Through Canada* (London: Tinsley Bros., 1876), 27. For Wilde's comment, printed in the New Orleans *Daily Picayune*, see Mary W. Blanchard, "Boundaries and the Victorian Body: Aesthetic Fashion in Gilded Age America," *American Historical Review* 100, 1 (February, 1995), 43.
40. Arthur George Guillemard, *Over Land and Sea: A Log of Travel Round the World in 1873-74* (London: Tinsley Bros., 1875), 304; Burnley, *Two Sides of the Atlantic*, 30-1; Robert Anderton Naylor, *Across the Atlantic* (London: Roxburghe Press, n.d. [1893]), 257-8.
41. Samuel Reynolds Hole, *A Little Tour in America* (London: Edward Arnold, 1895), 37; Hare Booth, *Glimpses of Our American Kith and Kin* (London: Charles H. Kelly, 1896), 13.
42. John Francis Campbell, *My Circular Notes: Extracts from Journals, Letters Sent Home, Geological and Other Notes, Written While Travelling Westwards Round the World from July 6, 1874, to July 6, 1875* (London: Macmillan & Co., 1876), I, 26-7.
43. Frederick Trench Townshend, *Ten Thousand Miles of Travel, Sport, and Adventure* (London: Hurst and Blackett, 1869), 6.
44. Emily Jane Pfeiffer, *Flying Leaves from East to West* (London: Field and Tuer, 1885), 84.
45. Rose Pender, *A Lady's Experience in the Wild West in 1883* (London: George Tucker, n.d. [1888]), 3.
46. Rudyard Kipling, *American Notes*, 17.
47. Burnley, *Two Sides of the Atlantic*, 30-1; Guillemard, *Over Land and Sea*, 304; Richard Tangye, *Reminiscences of Travel in Australia, America, and Egypt* (London: Sampson, Low, Marston, 1883), 136-7.
48. James Wentworth Leigh, *Other Days* (London: T. Fisher Unwin, 1921), 178. A clergyman, he married Fanny Kemble's daughter Frances Butler, and lived with her for some time at the family plantation in Georgia.
49. Bird, *My First Travels*, 132, 134.
50. Barbara Leigh Smith Bodichon, *An American Diary 1857-8* (London: Routledge & Kegan Paul, 1972), 56, 128 [ed. Joseph W. Reed, Jr.]. For the most recent full biography of Bodichon, see Jane Robinson, *Trailblazer: Barbara Leigh Smith Bodichon, the First Feminist to Change Our World* (New York: Penguin, 2024).
51. Burnley, *Two Sides of the Atlantic*, 41.

52. Bodichon, *An American Diary*, 83.
53. Combe, *Notes on the United States of North America*, I, 252.
54. Mathews was not the first to bring "negro impressions" to the London stage. The popular actor and song-writer, Charles Dibdin, had done so for his "Table entertainments" at the turn of the century (Davis, "Acting Black," 163n).
55. Rice (1808–60) was a New York-born itinerant actor who had also performed "Yankee" roles before making blackface acts his special claim to fame.
56. Waters, *Racism on the Victorian Stage*, 4.
57. Dave Russell, "Popular Entertainment, 1776–1895," in *The Cambridge History of British Theatre*, vol. 2, ed. Joseph Donohue (Cambridge: Cambridge University Press, 2004): 1660–1785, 372.
58. Dale Cockrell, *Demons of Disorder: Early Blackface Minstrels and Their World* (Cambridge: Cambridge University Press, 1997), 57, 68.
59. The *Times*, October 26, 1836.
60. Mackay, *Through the Long Day*, I, 132–3.
61. Richard Heathcote Heindel, *The American Impact on Great Britain 1898–1914: A Study of the United States in World History* (Philadelphia: University of Pennsylvania Press, 1940), 330; Derek B. Scott, "Blackface Minstrels, Black Minstrels, and their Reception in England," in *Europe, Empire, and Spectacle in Nineteenth-Century British Music*, ed. Rachel Cowgill and Julian Rushton (Aldershot: Ashgate, 2006), 270.
62. Elizabeth Mavor (ed.), *Fanny Kemble: The American Journals* (London: Weidenfeld and Nicolson, 1990), 140 [January, 1839].
63. See William Taylor Lhamon Jr., *Raising Cain: Blackface Performances from Jim Crow to Hip Hop* (Boston: Harvard University Press, 1998) and *Jump Jim Crow: Lost Plays, Lyrics, and Street Prose of the First Atlantic Popular Culture* (Boston: Harvard University Press, 2003).
64. Henry Mayhew, *London Labour and the London Poor* (London: Griffin and Bohn, 1861 [1st pub. 1851]), 3, 190–1.
65. *Ibid.*, 190–4.
66. Daphne A. Brooks, *Bodies in Dissent: Spectacular Performances of Race and Freedom, 1850–1910* (Durham: Duke University Press, 2007), 8, with reference especially to black women negotiating such borders; here more widely applied.
67. Michael Pickering, *Blackface Minstrelsy in Britain* (London: Routledge, 2008), 134, and "'A Jet Ornament to Society,'" 88–9.
68. Eric Lott, *Love and Theft: Blackface Minstrelsy and the American Working Class* (New York: Oxford University Press, 1993), 4.
69. *Ibid.*, 4–6; also Douglas A. Lorimer, "Bibles, Banjoes and Bones: Images of the Negro in the Popular Culture of Victorian England," in *In Search of the Visible Past*, ed. Barry Morton Gough (Toronto: Wilfrid Laurier University Press, 1975), 39.
70. Pickering, *Blackface Minstrelsy in Britain*, 1, and *passim*, ch. 1.
71. Bank, *Theatre Culture in America*, 163.
72. See Howard LeRoy Malchow, *Gothic Images of Race* (Palo Alto: Stanford University Press, 1996), 117–23.
73. Bratton, *The Making of the West End Stage*, 58–9.
74. Quoted by Douglas C. Riach, "Blacks and Blackface on the Irish Stage, 1830–60," *Journal of American Studies* 7, 3 (1973), 1830–60," 233.

Notes

75. In the sense often deployed in Marxian cultural theory, as a reified (and commodified) experience that substitutes for and shapes the perception of reality.
76. Brooks, *Bodies in Dissent*, 4–6.
77. Brown (1815–1897) fled to Britain as a fugitive in 1850, lectured there, presided over a "panorama of slavery," and married an English woman.
78. Pickering, in "'A Jet Ornament to Society,'" considers audience reception and the signification of black performance in Britain.
79. Peter Fryer, *Staying Power: The History of Black People in Britain* (London: Pluto Press, 1984), 442–3. Also, Postlewait, "The Hieroglyphic Stage," 181–2.
80. Robert Nowatzki, *Representing African Americans in Transatlantic Abolitionism and Blackface Minstrelsy* (Baton Rouge: Louisiana State University Press, 2010), 64–5.
81. See J. B. T. March, *The Story of the Jubilee Singers* (Cleveland: Cleveland Printing and Publishing Co., 1892 [1st edn, 1875]). At least two of the original chorus stayed on in Britain at the end of the 1873 trip.
82. William Chambers, "The Jubilee Singers," *Chambers's Journal* 733 (January 12, 1878), 19.
83. Richard J. M. Blackett, *Building an Antislavery Wall: Black Americans in the Atlantic Abolitionist Movement, 1830–1860* (Baton Rouge: Louisiana State University Press, 1983), 26.
84. Fisch, *American Slaves in Victorian England*, 50.
85. Van Gosse, "'As a Nation, the English Are Our Friends': The Emergence of African American Politics in the British Atlantic World, 1772–1861," *American Historical Review* 113, 4(2008), 1016.
86. Nowatzki, *Representing African Americans*, 24–5.
87. Ibid., 68.
88. George Shepperson, "The Free Church and American Slavery," *Scottish Historical Review* 30, 110 Part 2 (October, 1951), 128.
89. Lewis, *Across the Atlantic*, 214–5.
90. Cited by Catherine Hall, *Civilising Subjects: Metropole and Colony in the English Imagination, 1830–1867* (Oxford: Oxford University Press, 2001), 393.
91. Anon, "The Negro, His Friends, and His Prospects," *Saturday Review*, December 9, 1865.
92. For a recent biography of Brown, see Martha J. Cutter, *The Many Resurrections of Henry Box Brown* (Philadelphia: University of Pennsylvania Press, 2022).
93. Blackett, *Building an Antislavery Wall*, 145. Blackett provides vignettes of some twenty-two black Americans who came to Britain 1830–60.
94. William Farmer, "Memoir of the Author," in Wells, *Three Years in Europe*, xxii, xxv.
95. Gosse, "As a Nation, the English Are Our Friends,'" 1005.
96. Ibid., 1023.
97. Perhaps the most prominent of these was James McCune Smith (1813–65), a free black man from New York who, having been denied admission to Columbia, went to Glasgow University where he took a B.A., an M.A., and, in 1837, a medical degree. See John Stauffer (ed.), *The Works of James McCune Smith: Black Intellectual and Abolitionist* (Oxford: Oxford University Press, 2006).
98. Harriet Jacobs, *Incidents in the Life of a Slave Girl* (Boston: Thayer & Eldridge, 1861), 275, 278.
99. Thomas Allston Brown, *Three Years in Europe* (London: Charles Gilpin, 1852), 251–2, 310–11.

Notes

100. For the slave auction as a theatrical event, see Joseph R. Roach, "Slave Spectacles and Tragic Octoroons: A Cultural Genealogy of Antebellum Performance," *Theatre Survey* 33, 2 (November 1992), 167–87. Henry Ward Beecher staged slave auctions in his Brooklyn church as rituals in which a white abolitionist would buy a slave in order to emancipate him or her (Heather S. Nathans, *Slavery and Sentiment on the American Stage, 1787–1861: Lifting the Veil of Black* [Cambridge: Cambridge University Press, 2009], 193).
101. Ebenezer Davies, *American Scenes and Christian Slavery: A Recent Tour of Four Thousand Miles in the United States* (London: John Snow, 1849), 22–3.
102. Henry Ashworth, *A Tour in the United States, Cuba, and Canada* (London: A. W. Bennett, 1861), 43–6, 81.
103. Anderson, *An Actor's Life*, 129.
104. Bodichon, *An American Diary*, 103.
105. James Grant Wilson, *Thackeray in the United States, 1852–3, 1855–6* (London: Smith, Elder & Co., 1904), I, 131. Crowe was an accomplished painter, and exhibited his "Slaves Waiting for Sale, Richmond, Virginia" in 1861.
106. Roach, "Slave Spectacles," 171.
107. Marianne Finch, *An Englishwoman's Experience in America* (New York: Negro Universities Press, 1969 [1st pub. 1853]), 294–5, 301, 304.
108. Benwell, *An Englishman's Travels in America*, 99–100.
109. Cited by Jamie L. Bronstein, "From the Land of Liberty to Land Monopoly: The United States in a Chartist Context," in *The Chartist Legacy*, ed. O. Ashton, R. Fyson, and S. Roberts (Rendlesham: Merlin Press, 1999), 151.
110. Mackay, *Life and Liberty in America*, I, 317.
111. Joseph W. Reed, "The English Visitors, from Dickens to Trollope 1841–1861," in Bodichon, *An American Diary*, ed. Joseph W. Reed, 10.
112. Nowatzki, *Representing African Americans*, 69.
113. *The Nonconformist*, September 8, 1852, 708, cited by Lorimer, "Bibles, Banjoes and Bones," 36–7.
114. Waters, *Racism on the Victorian Stage*, 159.
115. Laurence Senelick, *The Age and Stage of George L. Fox, 1825–1877* (Iowa City: University of Iowa Press, 1999 [1st pub. 1988]), 65, 67, 70.
116. Gary Richardson, "Plays and Playwrights: 1800–1865," in *Cambridge History of American Theatre*, I, eds. Don B. Wilmeth and Christopher Bigsby (Cambridge: Cambridge University Press, 1998), 163, 290–2. Also, T. Allston Brown, *A History of the New York Stage* (New York: Benjamin Blom, 1903), I, 312–19.
117. See John W. Frick, *"Uncle Tom's Cabin" on the American Stage and Screen* (New York: Palgrave Macmillan, 2012), 96, 116–17, and Richardson, "Plays and Playwrights," 466. According to Waters, *Racism on the Victorian Stage*, 161, nearly all the plays, including Taylor's, had difficulty with Tom's piety.
118. As with Eliza's dash across the Ohio river ice floes (Richardson, "Plays and Playwrights," 262).
119. Ireland, *Records of the New York Stage*, II, 608.
120. See *Ibid.*, 596, 608, 619, and Brown, *A History*, I, 312–19, who lists more than a dozen pre-war versions, some running simultaneously in New York City.
121. Scott, "Blackface Minstrels," 278.

Notes

122. See Audrey Fisch, "'Exhibiting Uncle Tom in Some Shape or Other': The Commodification and Reception of *Uncle Tom's Cabin* in England," *Nineteenth-Century Contexts* 17, 2 (1993), 145-6, 148.
123. Quoted by Waters, *Racism on the Victorian Stage*, 175.
124. Lorimer, "Bibles, Banjos and Bones," 39.
125. Burnley, *Two Sides of the Atlantic*, 43.
126. Davis, *Uncle Tom's Cabins*, 4.
127. Nassau W. Senior, "Slavery in the United States," *Edinburgh Review* 101, 206 (April, 1855), 293, 311, 316.
128. Quoted by Sidney Kaplan, "*The Octoroon*: Early History of the Drama of Miscegenation," *Journal of Negro Education* 20, 4 (1951), 552, 554.
129. Ibid., 549, 551, 556.
130. See Sarah Meer, "Boucicault's Misdirections: Race, Transatlantic Theatre and Social Position in *The Octoroon*," *Atlantic Studies* 6, 1 (2009), 82; also John Degan, "How to End *The Octoroon*," *Educational Theatre Journal* 27, 2 (1975), 170-8.
131. Brooks, *Bodies in Dissent*, 31.
132. Bernth Lindfors (ed.), *Africans on Stage: Studies in Ethnological Show Business* (Bloomington: Indiana University Press, 1999), i, ix.
133. John James Aubertin, *A Fight with Distances: The States, the Hawaiian Islands, Canada, British Columbia, Cuba, the Bahamas* (London: Kegan Paul, Trench & Co., 1888), 301.
134. Everest, *A Journey*, 95, 101-2.
135. Ibid., 92-3, 106.
136. Charles Lyell, *Travels in North America in the Years 1841 and 1842* (New York: Wiley and Putnam, 1845), I, 44.
137. Everest, *A Journey*, 76, 80, 87-8, 126, 146.
138. Ibid., 124, 126, 161.
139. Ibid., 146.
140. Nowatzky, *Representing African Americans*, 93-4.
141. Lewis, *Across the Atlantic*, 194.
142. James Grant Wilson, "Thackeray in the United States: I, The First Visit (November 1852-April 1853)," *Cornhill Magazine* 11, 66 (December, 1901), 740.
143. Lewis, *Across the Atlantic*, 214-5.
144. Amelia Matilda Murray, *Letters from the United States, Cuba and Canada* (London: John W. Parker & Son, 1856), I, 47-8.
145. Letter to Lady Elliot and Miss Perry, March 3, 1853, quoted by Wilson, *Thackeray in the United States*, I, 135. Thackeray was wined and dined in Charlottesville by Schele de Vere, probably the occasion where he knocked off a comic sketch of a corpulent Negro waiter (Wilson, 136).
146. James Fergusson, *Notes of a Tour in North America in 1861* ([London?: for private circulation], 1861), 36-7, 66; "Some Account of Both Sides of the American War," *Blackwood's* 90 (December, 1861), 770, 777-9.
147. For a very full recent treatment, see Amanda Foreman, *A World on Fire: Britain's Crucial Role in the American Civil War* (London: Allen Lane, 2010). Much of the historiography is outside our chief interest in exploring transatlantic popular culture, but see, for example,

Peter O'Connor, *American Sectionalism in the British Mind, 1832—1863* (Baton Rouge: State University of Louisiana Press, 2017).

148. See also for example, [Lt.-Col. Henry Charles], "A Run through the Southern States," *Cornhill Magazine* 7, 40 (April, 1863), 495–515; or John Francis Campbell, *A Short American Tramp in the Fall of 1864* (Edinburgh: Edmonston and Douglas, 1865).

149. See William Howard Russell, *My Diary North and South* (London: Bradbury and Evans, 1863).

150. Goldwin Smith, Regius Professor of History at Oxford and a vigorous supporter of the Union cause, traveled to the United States in 1864 for a lecture tour. See his *The Civil War in America* (London: Simpkin, Marshall and Co., 1866) and *England and America* (Manchester: A Ireland & Co., 1865).

151. Wolsely, "A Month's Visit to the Confederate Headquarters," *Blackwood's* 93 (January, 1863), 1–29; Hartington to the 7th Duke of Devonshire, as quoted by Hugh Dubrulle, "'We Are threatened with … Anarchy and Ruin': Fear of Americanization and the Emergence of an Anglo-Saxon Confederacy in England during the American Civil War," *Albion* 33 (2001), 596.

152. Barham Zincke, *Last Winter in the United States, Being Table Talk Collected through a Tour through the Late Southern Confederacy, the Far West, the Rocky Mountains, &c.* (London: John Murray, 1868).

153. Charles, "A Run through the Southern States," 498–9, 508.

154. William Glasgow Bruce Carson (ed.), *Letters of Mr. and Mrs. Charles Kean Relating to Their American Tours* (St. Louis: Washington University, 1945), 166–7.

155. Rose, *The Great Country*, 162–3, 177.

156. William Hepworth Dixon, *New America* (London: Hurst & Blackett, 1867), II, 325.

157. Percy Gregg, *History of the United States from the Foundation of Virginia to the Reconstruction of the Union* (London: W. H. Allen, 1887), II, 93–4.

158. Campbell, *A Short American Tramp*, 285–6, 330–1, 336–7.

159. The Rev. James Wentworth Leigh (1838—1923), a son of Chandos Leigh, 1st Baron Leigh of Stoneleigh Abbey. A southern sympathizer, he met her when traveling through the United States (Margaret Armstrong, *Fanny Kemble: A Passionate Victorian* [New York: Macmillan, 1938], 352); they married in 1871. See his memoir, *Other Days*, where he freely uses, in a crude pejorative sense, the word "nigger."

160. In her widely-reviewed *Journal of a Residence on a Georgian Plantation*, not published until 1863.

161. Frances Butler Leigh, *Ten Years on a Georgia Plantation since the War* (London: Richard Bentley and Son, 1883), 1–3, 14, 19, 21–2, 25 and 25 ft.nt. 1, 27–8, 36–7, 59, 70, 75–6, 124, 130, 137–8, 179–81.

162. See, for instance, Gen. William Henry Adelbert Fielden's plea, "What Shall I Do with My Son?" the *Nineteenth Century* 13, 74 (1883); or James Aspdin, *"Our Boys": What Shall We Do with Them?* (Manchester: John Heywood, 1890).

163. David Macrae, *The Americans at Home: Pen and Ink Sketches of American Men, Manners, and Institutions* (Edinburgh: Edmonston and Douglas, 1870), I, 152–4.

164. William Stamer, *The Gentleman Emigrant: His Daily Life, Sports, and Pastimes in Canada, Australia, and the United States* (London: Tinsley Bros., 1874), II, 63.

165. William Saunders, *Through the Light Continent; Or, the United States in 1877—8*, 2nd edn (London: Cassell, Petter and Galpin, 1879), preface and 74.

Notes

166. John Clay, Jn., *New World Notes: Being an Account of Journeyings and Sojournings in America and Canada* (Kelso: J and J. H. Rutherford, 1875), 5, 7–8. 12–13.

167. Arthur Granville Bradley, *Other Days* (London: Constable and Co., 1913), 254–270, and "A Social Study of Our Oldest Colony," *Macmillan's Magazine* 49, 294 (April, 1884), 430–1.

168. Arthur Granville Bradley, "A Peep at the Southern Negro," *Macmillan's Magazine* 39, 229 (November, 1878), 61–7.

169. Theresa Yelverton [Viscountess Avonmore], *Teresina in America* (London: Richard Bentley & Son, 1875), I, 154.

170. *Ibid.*, I, 47, 60, 66, 70, 147–51.

171. Mrs. Emily Jane (Davis) Pfeiffer, *Flying Leaves*, 193, 278–9.

172. [Mary Anne] Lady Duffus Hardy, *Down South* (London: Chapman and Hall, 1883), 22–3, 84–5; Hardy, *Between Two Oceans*, 235–6, 298–300.

173. For Freedmen's Aid in Britain, see Christine Bolt, *The Anti-Slavery Movement and Reconstruction: A Study in Anglo-American Co-operation in 1833—77* (Oxford: Oxford University Press, 1969), Chs. 3–5.

174. See *Ibid.*, 154; George Campbell, *White and Black, the Outcome of a Visit to the United States* (London: Chatto & Windus, 1879), 140, 195–6; Edward A. Freeman, *Some Impressions of the United States* (New York: Henry Holt and Co., 1883), 139, 144–5.

175. Benwell, *An Englishman's Travels in America*, 98–9, 109, 218. For a general treatment of lynching see Philip Dray, *At the Hands of Persons Unknown: The Lynching of Black America* (New York: Modern Library, 2002).

176. Campbell, *White and Black*, 171.

177. William Ballantine, *The Old World and the New* (London: Richard Bentley & Son, 1884), 40–1.

178. Hole, *A Little Tour in America*, 63–5.

179. Edith M. Nicholl, *Observations of a Ranchwoman in New Mexico* (London: Macmillan & Co., 1898), 226–7.

180. William H. Davies, *The Autobiography of a Super-Tramp* (London: A. C. Fifield, 1908 [2nd edn]), 112–3, 120–1.

181. Griffin, *The Great Republic*, 136, 138–40.

182. D. J. Bannatyne, "Civilisation, Social Order, and Morality in the United States of America," *Blackwood's* 151, 919 (May, 1892), 632–3, 735–6.

183. Roger Pocock, *Rottenness: A Study of America and England* (London: Neville Beeman, 1896), 104.

184. George Warrington Steevens, *Land of the Dollar* (Edinburgh: William Blackwood & Sons, 1897), 103–4.

185. George Alfred Henty, *With Lee in Virginia: A Story of the American Civil War* (New York: A. L. Burt Company, n.d. [1890]), iii.

186. *Ibid.*, 379–80.

187. Anon. [Leslie Stephen], "Some Remarks on Travelling in America," *Cornhill Magazine* 19, 111 (March, 1869), 323.

188. Anon. [Charles Mackay], "The Antagonism of Race and Colour; or, White, Red, Black, and Yellow in America," *Blackwood's* 107 (March, 1870), 314.

189. Frank McLynn, *Stanley: Sorcerer's Apprentice* (London: Constable, 1991), 137.

Chapter 4

1. By 1852, there were over 10,000 UK-*born* residents in rapidly mushrooming San Francisco, or about 30 percent of its total population; by 1870, over 36,000, or about 53 percent. An increasing percentage of the later arrivals were Irish.
2. See Earl Pomeroy, *In Search of the Golden West: The Tourist in Western America* (Lincoln: University Nebraska Press, 1957).
3. David Wrobel, "Global West, American Frontier," *Pacific Historical Review* 78, 1 (February, 2009), 1, 4–5.
4. William Adolf Baillie-Grohman, *Camps in the Rockies* (London: Sampson Low, 1882), 368.
5. See Sebastian Lecourt, "The Mormons, the Victorians, and the Idea of Greater Britain," *Victorian Studies* 56, 1 (Autumn, 2013), 85–111.
6. Horace Greeley, *An Overland Journey from New York to San Francisco in the Year 1859* (New York: C. M. Saxon, Barker & Co., 1860).
7. Richard Burton, *The City of the Saints, and across the Rocky Mountains to California*, 2nd edn (London: Longman, Green, 1862), 603.
8. In the book he lists some sixty titles on Mormonism, the majority strongly negative (*Ibid.*, 250n and ff).
9. Burton, *The City of the Saints*, xi; Edward Rice, *Captain Sir Richard Francis Burton* (New York: Charles Scriber's Sons, 1990), 333.
10. Burton, *The City of the Saints*, 249, 257–8, 305; also see Daniel Bivona, "Richard F. Burton, Polygamy, and the Worlding of the American West," *Yearbook of English Studies* 41, 2 (2011), 73–93.
11. Fawn M. Brodie, *The Devil Drives: A Life of Sir Richard Burton* (New York: W. W. Norton and Co., 1967), 182.
12. Robert Michael Ballantyne, *The Prairie Chief* (London: James Nisbet and Co., 1886), 1.
13. On the cult of the Western novel see Ray Allen Billington, *Land of Savagery, Land of Promise: The European Image of the American Frontier* (New York: W. W. Norton and Co., 1981), 37–51, 74–6.
14. Hardy, *Between Two Oceans*, 229.
15. By 1882, San Francisco had at least twelve theaters and an opera house that could seat 2,000—Denver's could seat 800 (Lloyd Lewis and Henry Justin Smith, *Oscar Wilde Discovers America [1882]* (New York: Harcourt, Brace and Co., 1936), 246, 313).
16. The texts of *The Amateur Emigrant*, the four essays of *The Old and New Pacific Capitals*, and *The Silverado Squatters* may conveniently be found together in James D. Hart's amended edition, with restored deletions, of Stevenson's travel writings, *From Scotland to Silverado* (Cambridge, MA: Harvard University Press, 1966).
17. Stevenson, "A Humble Remonstrance," 1884, printed in *Memories and Portraits*, vol. 279 (New York: Charles Scribner's Sons, 1895 [1st pub. London, 1887]), 283–5.
18. Quoted by Hart, *From Scotland to Silverado*, Introduction, xx–xxi.
19. Stevenson, *The Amateur Emigrant*, in *From Scotland to Silverado* ed. Hart, 90.
20. Stevenson, "The Old Pacific Capital," in *Ibid.*, 167.
21. Stevenson, "San Francisco," from "Old and New Pacific Capitals," in *Ibid.*, 182–3.
22. *Ibid.*, 184–5.

Notes

23. Crofutt's was originally published, in 1869, as the *Great Trans-Continental Tourist's Guide*.
24. Quoted in Beatty, *Lillie Langtry*, 248.
25. Cited by Rose, *Unspeakable Awfulness*, 68–9.
26. Edward A. Freeman, "Some Points in American Speech and Customs. II," *Longman's Magazine* 1, 3 (January, 1883), 331.
27. Oscar Wilde, *Impressions of America*, ed. Stuart Mason (Sunderland: Keystone Press, 1906), 21, 25.
28. Quoted by Kevin O'Brien, "'The House Beautiful': A Reconstruction of Wilde's American Lecture," *Victorian Studies* 17, 4 (June, 1974), 416: "the only well-dressed men I have seen in America were the miners of the Rocky Mountains …"
29. On masculinity, see Monica Rico, *Nature's Noblemen: Transatlantic Masculinities and the Nineteenth-Century American West* (New Haven: Yale University Press, 2013). Miller, self-described "squaw-man," gold-miner, Indian fighter, and worshipper of Lillie Langtry, was invited to Britain by Rossetti's brother William (Lewis and Smith, *Oscar Wilde Discovers America*, 49).
30. The phrase is from Peter Pagnamenta, *Prairie Fever: British Aristocrats in the American West, 1830–1890* (New York: W. W. Norton and Co., 2012), xvi, who provides the best introduction to the American West as playground for upper-class Britons.
31. Charles Wentworth Dilke, *Greater Britain* (London: Macmillan & Co., 1868), I, 34, 188–9.
32. Dunraven, 4th Earl of, "A Colorado Sketch," *Nineteenth Century* 8, 43 (September, 1880), 448.
33. Francis Francis, Jr., *Saddle and Moccasin* (London: Chapman and Hall, 1887), 320.
34. Dunraven, "Wapiti Running on the Plains," *Nineteenth Century* 8, 44 (October, 1880), 595.
35. Pagnamenta, *Prairie Fever*, 93–106.
36. Anon., "Colorado, Home of the Farmer," *Fraser's Magazine* 18, 107 (November, 1878), 623; Rose, *Unspeakable Awfulness*, 242.
37. Allayne Beaumont Legard, *Colorado* (London: Chapman and Hall, 1872), 28–9, 31, 33–4, 40, 56, 66.
38. George Crofutt, *Overland Tourist* (Chicago: the Overland Publishing Co., 1878–9 edn), front.
39. For his own account of these expeditions, see *The Great Divide: Travels in the Upper Yellowstone in the Summer of 1874* (London: Chatto and Windus, 1876); *Canadian Nights: Being Sketches and Reminiscences of Life and Sport in the Rockies, the Prairies, and the Canadian Woods* (London: Smith, Elder & Co., 1914); and *Past Times and Pastimes* (London: Hodder and Stoughton, 1922). Also "A Colorado Sketch," *Nineteenth Century* 8, 43 (September, 1880), 445–57; and "Wapiti Running on the Plains," *Nineteenth Century* 8, 44 (October, 1880), 593–611. Also see Pagnamenta, Prairie Fever, 148–74.
40. Dunraven, "Wapiti Running on the Plains," 597.
41. Dunraven, *Past Times and Pastimes*, I, 65.
42. Dunraven, "Wapiti Running on the Plains," 595–6; Pagnamenta, *Prairie Fever*, 156–7.
43. For Texas Jack, see Herschel C. Logan, *Buckskin and Satin: The Life of Texas Jack … and His Wife Mlle. Morlacchi* (Harrisburg: The Stackpole Co., 1954); also, Dunraven, *The Great Divide*, 30–4, 254–5; and Roger A. Hall, *Performing the American Frontier, 1870–1906* (Cambridge: Cambridge University Press, 2002), 54–64.
44. Subsequently published in Isabella L. Bird, *A Lady's Life in the Rocky Mountains*, 4th edn (London: John Murray, 1881 [1st pub. 1878?]), 206.

45. Dunraven, *The Great Divide*, xi.
46. Dunraven, "A Colorado Sketch," 445.
47. Pagnamenta, *Prairie Fever*, 167–74.
48. Total British investment in the United States may have amounted to $2 billion in 1890, much of which went to the American West (according to Edward P. Crapol, *America for Americans: Economic Nationalism and Anglophobia in the Late Nineteenth Century* [Westport: Greenwood Press, 1973], 223), though this must be put into the context of the significant rise of the east coast, especially New York, banking houses and their own westward investments. Also see Roger V. Clements, "British Investments and American Legislative Restrictions in the trans-Mississippi West, 1880–1900," *Mississippi Valley Historical Review* 42 (1955).
49. March, 1885, quoted by Pagnamenta, *Prairie Fever*, 271.
50. For Frewen, see his memoir, *Melton Mowbray and Other Memories* (London: Herbert Jenkins Ltd, 1924). Also Rico, *Nature's Noblemen*, ch. 2, "'What Shall I Do with My Son?' Moreton Frewen and Aristocratic Masculinity on the Ranching Frontier."
51. See Maurice Frink, W. Turrentine Jackson, and Agnes Wright Spring, *When Grass Was King: Contributions to the Western Range Cattle Industry* (Boulder: University of Colorado Press, 1956), cited by Rico, *Nature's Noblemen*, 51.
52. John Baumann, "The Cow-Boy at Home," *Cornhill* 54 (September, 1886), 294, 301.
53. John Baumann, "On a Western Ranche," *Fortnightly Review* 41, 244 (April, 1887), 516.
54. William Black, *Green Pastures and Piccadilly*, revised edn (London: Sampson Low, Marston & Co., 1892 [1st pub. London, 1878]).
55. For an account of Scully's evasions of the Missouri state law limiting foreign holdings to 10,000 acres, see the *Cambridge Tribune* 22, 28 (September 9, 1899), quoting from the *St. Louis Republic*.
56. Crapol, *America for Americans*, 102. Also see Paul W. Gates, "Frontier Landlords and Pioneer Tenants," *Journal of the Illinois State Historical Society* 38, 2 (June, 1945).
57. William Adolf Baillie-Grohman (1851–1921) was an Anglo-Austrian travel writer, mountaineer, and big game hunter who traveled to the Rockies in the late 1870s and early 1880s and published accounts of his experiences in journal articles and in two books, *Camps in the Rockies* (London: Sampson Low, 1880); and *Fifteen Years of Sport and Life in the Hunting Grounds of Western America and British Columbia* (London: Horace Cox, 1900).
58. See, for instance, his "Cattle Ranches of the Far West," *Fortnightly Review* 28, 166 (October, 1880), 438–57.
59. Baillie-Grohman, *Camps in the Rockies*, 322.
60. Baillie-Grohman, "Cattle Ranches of the Far West," 441, 457.
61. Samuel Nugent Townshend, *Colorado: Its Agricultural, Stock-Feeding, Scenery, and Shooting* (London: The Field Office, 1879), v–vi, 50–1, 63–4.
62. James Macdonald, *Food from the Far West* (Edinburgh and London: William P. Nimmo, 1878), 4, 34, 258–9, 291–2.
63. James B. Close, and William B. Close, *Stock Raising and Sheep Farming* (Manchester, Iowa: J. B. Cornish, 1879), 18–19.
64. William French, *Some Recollections of a Western Ranchman, New Mexico, 1833–1899* (London: Methuen and Co., 1927), 1–2.

Notes

65. *Ibid.*, 282.
66. Mrs. Algernon St. Maur [Susan Margaret McKinnon, Duchess of Somerset], *Impressions of a Tenderfoot, During a Journey in Search of Sport in the Far West* (London: John Murray, 1890), viii; and Georgina M. Synge, *A Ride Through Wonderland* (London: Sampson Low, Marston & Co., 1892).
67. Born Edith Marion Bradley in England in 1852, she presumably emigrated with her first husband, Frederick Nicholl (1851–84) to New Mexico territory about 1872.
68. Nicholl, *Observations of a Ranchwoman*.
69. Wilde, "American Women," as cited by Rose, *Unspeakable Awfulness*, 151.
70. Nicholl, *Observations of a Ranchwoman*, 4–3, 14–5, 26–7, 192, 213.
71. Reginald Aldridge, *Life on a Ranch; Ranch Notes in Kansas, Colorado, the Indian Territory, and Northern Texas* (London: Longmans, Green and Co., 1884), 159.
72. Money, *The Truth about America*, 1–3, 8–9, 29, 42–5, 52, 148, 172.
73. See Pagnamenta, *Prairie Fever*, 177–94, 205–229, for some of these.
74. Baillie-Grohman, *Camps in the Rockies*, 322.
75. The *Standard*, April 3, 1889–June 17, 1890.
76. Thomas Carson, *Ranching, Sport, and Travel* (London: T. Fisher Unwin, 1911), *passim*. Also see Lowell H. Harrison, "Thomas Simpson Carson, New Mexico Rancher," *New Mexico Historical Review* 42, 2 (April, 1967), 127–43.
77. Baillie-Grohman, *Camps in the Rockies*, 1–2.
78. John J. Fox, "The Far West in the '80s," *Annals of Wyoming* 21, 1 (January, 1949), as cited by Athearn, *Westward the Briton*, 72. And not only men. In 1892 Georgina Synge recalled the "critical eyes" and "disdainful glances" of cowboys watching as she waited for her sidesaddle (Synge, *A Ride Through Wonderland*, 6).
79. Harry Leon Wilson, *Ruggles of Red Gap* (Garden City: Doubleday, Page and Co., 1922 [1st pub. 1915]), 368–7.
80. Hall, *Performing the American Frontier*, 3–4; for Western melodrama, also see Jeffrey D. Mason, *Melodrama and the Myth of America* (Bloomington: University of Indiana Press, 1993); and Rosemary K. Bank, "Frontier Melodrama," in *Theatre West: Image and Impact*, ed. Dunbar H. Ogden (Amsterdam: Brill, 1990), 151–60.
81. Hall, *Performing the American Frontier*, 7–8, 11–12, 227.
82. *Ibid.*, 37, 74, 98, 170.
83. Maurice O'Connor Morris, *Rambles in the Rocky Mountains: With a Visit to the Gold Fields of Colorado* (London: Smith, Elder & Co., 1864), 101–2; Nicholl, *Observations of a Ranchwoman*, 32, 38.
84. Townshend, *Colorado*, 56.
85. Or so British/Canadian administrators and commentators commonly asserted in attempting to contrast inhumane American treatment with a supposedly more generous approach to tribal relations that characterized British North America. See Kate Flint, *The Transatlantic Indian, 1776–1930* (Princeton: Princeton University Press, 2009), 13–15.
86. Flint, *The Transatlantic Indian*, 5–6; on the role of the noble Red Man in the foundation myths of American nationalism, see Joseph Roach, *Cities of the Dead* (New York: Columbia University Press, 1996), 187–8.
87. On Catlin in London, see his *Notes of Eight Years Travels and Residence in Europe, with the North American Indian Collection* (London, 1848); also Flint, *The Transatlantic Indian*,

ch. 3, "'Brought to the Zenith of Civilization': Indians in England in the 1840s," 53–85; and Pagnamenta, *Prairie Fever*, ch. 3, "Red Men and Blue Bloods," 71–9.

88. George Catlin, *Letters and Notes on the Manners, Customs, and Condition of the North American Indians*, 7th edn (London: Henry G. Bohn, 1841), II, 10, cited by Flint, *The Transatlantic Indian*, 56.
89. John Mortimer Murphy, *Rambles in North-Western America from the Pacific Ocean to the Rocky Mountains* (London: Chapman and Hall, 1879), title-page, 208, 233.
90. Thomas Gladstone, *The Englishman in Kansas: Or, Squatter Life and Border Warfare* (New York: Miller and Co., 1857) [Introduction by Frederick Law Olmsted]), 197–8, 200. His letters from Kansas were first published in the London *Times*.
91. William Abraham Bell, *New Tracks in North America: A Journal of Travel and Adventure Whilst Engaged in the Survey for a Southern Railroad to the Pacific Ocean during 1867–8*, 2nd edn (London: Chapman and Hall, 1870), viii, 157–9.
92. Stevenson, *From Scotland to Silverado*, 141.
93. Dilke, *Greater Britain*, I, 93.
94. Townshend, *Ten Thousand Miles*, 211–12.
95. Henry Latham, *Black and White: A Journal of a Three Months' Tour in the United States* (London: Macmillan, 1867), 281, 294.
96. Greeley, *Overland Journey*, 151–3.
97. Mackay, "The Negro and the Negrophilists," *Blackwood's Edinburgh Review* 99, 607 (1866), 590.
98. Mrs. Frances D. Bridges, *Journal of a Lady's Travels Round the World* (London: John Murray, 1883), 351.
99. Pender, *A Lady's Experience in the Wild West in 1883*, 8–9.
100. [Mary Anne] Lady Duffus Hardy, *Through Cities and Prairie Lands: Sketches of an American Tour* (Chicago: Belford, Clarke and Co., 1882 [1st pub. 1881]), 27–8.
101. Rico, *Nature's Noblemen*, 37, citing the observations of Sir William Drummond Stewart in the 1830s. Also, Flint, *The Transatlantic Indian*, 175.
102. Hall, *Performing the American Frontier*, 200–6.
103. John S. Campion, *On the Frontier: Reminiscences of Wild Sports, Personal Adventures, and Strange Scenes*, 2nd edn (London: Chapman and Hall, 1878), 225, 227.
104. Gladstone, *The Englishman in Kansas*, 200.
105. Robert Michael Ballantyne, *Hudson Bay; or, Everyday Life in the Wilds of North America*, 4th edn (London: Thomas Nelson and Sons, 1875), 68–9.
106. Henry Hussey Vivian, *Notes of a Tour in America from August 7th to November 17th, 1877* (London: Edward Stanford, 1878), 121–2.
107. Wallis Nash, *Oregon: There and Back in 1877* (London: Macmillan, 1878), 30.
108. Green, *Notes on New York, San Francisco, and Old Mexico*, 50–1.
109. Flint, *The Transatlantic Indian*, 173.
110. Murphy, *Rambles in North-Western America*, 109–10; Malchow, *Gothic Images*, ch. 4, "The Half-Breed as Gothic Unnatural," 167–237.
111. W[illiam] Henry Barneby, *Life and Labour in the Far, Far West* (London and New York: Cassell and Co., 1884), 167.
112. Charles Alston Messiter, *Sport and Adventures among the North-American Indians* (London: R. H. Porter, 1890), v, 304.

Notes

113. William F. Cody and William Lightfoot Visscher, *Buffalo Bill's Own Story of His Life and Deeds* (Chicago: Stanton and Van Vliet, 1917), 324; Russell, "Popular Entertainment, 1776–1895," in *The Cambridge History of British Theatre, vol. 2*, 372–3. Morton, *Americans in London*, 205.
114. Cody would make much of Victoria's bowing to the American flag held aloft by the riders at the beginning of the program (Cody and Visscher, *Buffalo Bill's Own Story*, 331–2).
115. Cody and Visscher, *Buffalo Bill's Own Story*, 316, 326–33.
116. Ibid., i, iii, v.
117. Ibid., 217, 268–9.
118. See Louis Warren, *Buffalo Bill's America: William Cody and the Wild West Show* (New York: Knopf Doubleday, 2005).
119. Tom F. Cunningham, "Buffalo Bill's Wild West in Scotland: Buffalo Bill's Wild West Came to Scotland Twice in 1891–1892 and Again in 1904," *Whispering Wind* 42, 4 (March–April, 2014), 21.
120. Roach, *Cities of the Dead*, 203–5.
121. More than 2,500,000 tickets were sold for the 300 performances of the show in 1887 alone, though some of these would have been repeats.
122. Joy S. Kasson, *Buffalo Bill's Wild West: Celebrity, Memory, and Popular History* (New York: Hill and Wang, 2000), 79.
123. Flint, *The Transatlantic Indian*, 2.
124. L. G. Moses, "Indians on the Midway: Wild West Shows and the Indian Bureau at World's Fairs, 1893–1904," *South Dakota History* 21, 3 (September, 1991), 205.
125. The Kiralfy brothers Imry (1845–1919) and Bolossy (1848–1932) were Hungarian Jews who made a strikingly successful career, first as dancers, then as impresarios who mounted theatrical spectacles in Europe, Britain, and the United States.
126. Lindfors, *Aldridge*, II, 181–2.
127. Moses, "Indians on the Midway," 221.
128. This engagement, in which Wilson and most of his small patrol were overwhelmed and killed, was then and later compared by white South Africans to the death of Gen. Custer at the hands of the Sioux.
129. See Frederick Russell Burnham, *Scouting on Two Continents* (Garden City: Doubleday, Doran and Co., 1926).
130. The 1904 Wild West tour was captured on ten reels by the British Bioscope Company and shown throughout Britain (cited by Flint, *The Transatlantic Indian*, 255).
131. Walter Besant, *The Golden Butterfly: A Novel* (London: Chatto and Windus, 1887 [1st pub. 1877]), I, 23, 27.
132. Francesca Morgan, *A Nation of Descendants: Politics and the Practice of Genealogy in U.S. History* (Chapel Hill: University of North Carolina Press, 2021), 22.
133. Fowler, *The English Language*, 81.
134. Freeman, quoted by H. A. Tulloch, "Changing British Attitudes," 827, and Duncan Andrew Campbell, *Unlikely Allies: Britain, America, and the Victorian Origins of the Special Relationship* (London: Hambledon Continuum, 2007), 218.
135. Conway, quoted in Henry Steele Commager (ed.), *Britain through American Eyes* (London: Bodley Head, 1974), 443.

136. See, for instance, Joseph Bosworth's *Dictionary of the Anglo-Saxon Language* (London: Longman, 1838), or the German-American Louis F. Klipstein's *A Grammar of the Anglo-Saxon Language* (New York: George P. Putnam, 1849). Inspired by the local dialect of Dorsetshire, the Rev. William Barnes labored to promote Saxonisms in his *Elements of English Grammar* (London: Longman and Co., 1842).

137. Anon. [Henry Rogers], *Edinburgh Review* 70, 141 (October, 1839), 221–44.

138. See Reginald Horsman, "Origins of Racial Anglo-Saxonism in Great Britain before 1850," *Journal of the History of Ideas* 37, 3 (July/September, 1976), 387–410, and *Race and Manifest Destiny*, Pt. I.

139. Tuffnell, "Expatriate Foreign Relations," 663.

140. Paul A. Kramer, "Empires, Exceptions, and Anglo-Saxons: Race and Rule between the British and United States Empires, 1880–1910," *Journal of American History* 88, 4 (2002), 1327.

141. Olney to Chamberlain, in response to Chamberlain's proposal of Anglo-American cooperation over the Armenian atrocities (cited by Ernest R. May, *Imperial Democracy: The Emergence of America as a Great Power* [New York: Harper and Row, 1973 (1st pub. 1961)], 60–1).

142. Archibald Prentice, *A Tour in the United States* (London: Charles Gilpin, 1848), 105.

143. Henry Cabot Lodge, *One Hundred Years of Peace* (New York: Macmillan, 1913), 130. For the legend that grew up around Admiral Chichester's actions at Manilla, see Perkins, *The Great Rapprochement*, 47.

144. Josiah Strong, *Expansion under New World Conditions* (New York: Baker and Taylor Co., 1900), ch. 7.

145. Franklin Henry Giddings, *Democracy and Empire, with Studies of Their Psychological, Economic, and Moral Foundations* (New York and London: Macmillan, 1901 [1st pub. 1900]), v, 3.

146. Josiah Strong, *The New Era or the Coming Kingdom* (New York: Baker and Taylor Co., 1893), 3, 78.

147. See Nathan Jessen, *Populism and Imperialism: Politics, Culture, and Foreign Policy in the American West, 1890–1900* (Lawrence: University of Kansas Press, 2017).

148. Martin J. Sklar, *The United States as a Developing Country* (Cambridge: Cambridge University Press, 1992), cited by LaFeber, *The New Empire* (Ithaca: Cornell University Press, 1998 edn), xxvii.

149. John J. Pershing, *My Life before the World War, 1860–1917* (Lexington: University Press of Kentucky, 2013 [ed. by John T. Greenwood from an unpublished MS written *c.* 1936–7]), 122–3, 207.

150. *Ibid.*, 129–31, 207.

151. John Arbothnot Fisher, 1st Baron, *Memories and Records* (New York: George H. Doran Co., 1920), I, 220; Perkins, *The Great Rapprochement*, 158.

152. His third wife (m. 1888) was Mary Endicott, daughter of the US Secretary of War, William Crowninshield Endicot.

153. See Geoffrey Seed, "British Reactions to American Imperialism Reflected in Journals of Opinion," *Political Science Quarterly* 73, 2 (June, 1958), 254–72.

154. Edward Dicey, "The New American Imperialism," *Nineteenth Century* 44, 259 (September, 1898), 489.

155. Not, however, Queen Victoria, who confided to her journal April 21, 1898 that "War [between Spain and the U.S.] seems hopelessly declared … It is monstrous of America"

(*Letters of Queen Victoria*, ed. George Earle Buckle [London: John Murray, 1932], 244) 3rd Series, vol. III, 1856–1901.

156. Dicey, "The New American Imperialism," 496.
157. For the consequences for British diplomacy raised by America's new imperialism, see R. G. Neale, *Britain and American Imperialism 1898–1900* (Brisbane: University of Queensland Press, 1965).
158. Anon., "The Cuban Crisis," *Saturday Review* 86, 2215 (April 9, 1898), 479–80; Diplomaticus [Lucien Wolf], "Is There an Anglo-American Understanding?" *Fortnightly Review* 64, 379 (1898), 163–74; Anon. [Herbert W. Wilson], "The United States and Spain," *Quarterly Review* 188, 375 [July, 1898], 218, 241.
159. William Thomas Stead, editor of the "new journalism" *Pall Mall Gazette* and a British advocate of what he called *The Americanization of the World* (New York and London: Horace Markley, 1901), posed the question "Has the time not come when we should make a resolute effort to realize the unity of the English-speaking race?" (6).
160. Legard, *Colorado*, 162–3.
161. George E. Boxall, *The Anglo-Saxon: A Study in Evolution* (London: Grant Richards, 1902), 298–9.
162. On this subject, see Christopher Herbert, *Gold Rush Manliness: Race and Gender on the Pacific Slope* (Seattle: University of Washington Press, 2018).
163. Such as Aline Gorren's white supremacist *Anglo-Saxons and Others* (New York: Scribner's Sons, 1900).
164. Kramer, "Empires, Exceptions, and Anglo-Saxons," 1318–19, 1326.
165. In the volume treating the Great War, Pershing derides the Anglo-Saxon rhetoric of those Britons who urged American involvement and a closer cooperation between American and British forces (*My Experience in the War* [New York: Frederick A. Stokes Co., 1931], 47–8, 52).

Chapter 5

1. October 13, 1860, 647.
2. Quoted in Morgan, *A Nation of Descendants*, 24.
3. Ibid., 1–2, 9–10, 13, 20, 32.
4. Significant growth in the numbers of Americans traveling abroad is evident from the 1840s, when the 7,400 or so who left in 1840 rose to 14,000 in 1850 and 27,000 in 1860; by 1913 some 237,000 traveled abroad. For a careful attempt to gauge the volume of American travel to Europe and to assess the factors behind its steady increase, see Brandon Dupont, Alka Ghandi, and Thomas Weiss, "The Long-Term rise in Overseas Travel by Americans, 1820–2000," *Economic History Review* 65, 1 (February, 2012), 144–67.
5. Dupont, Gandhi, and Weiss, "The long-Term Rise in Overseas Travel," 149–53, 165.
6. Henry James, *The Wings of the Dove* (New York: Charles Scribner's Sons, 1902), Bk. III, ch. 2.
7. Henry James, *The Middle Years* (New York: Charles Scribner's Sons, 1917), 48.
8. For the attractions of the Lake District and "literary tourism," see Melanie Hall, "American Tourists in Wordsworthshire: From 'National Property' to 'National Park,'" in *The Making of*

Notes

       a Cultural Landscape: The English Lake District as Tourist Destination, 1750–2012, ed. John K. Walton and Jason Woods (Aldershot: Ashgate, 2013), 87–109.

9. Frederick Law Olmsted, *Walks and Talks of an American Farmer in England* (New York: George Putnam, 1852), 350–1.

10. See John Muir, *The Story of My Boyhood and Youth* (Boston: Houghton Mifflin, 1913); also, *John Muir: His Life and Letters and Other Writings*, ed. Terry Gifford (London: Baton Wicks, 1996).

11. In 1900, Charles Robert Ashbee, architect and arts and crafts designer, at the urging of Canon Rawnsley, toured the United States to speak on the work of the National Trust and raise contributions. See [Ashbee], *American Sheaves & English Seed Corn: Being a Series of Addresses Mainly Delivered in the United States, 1900–1901* (London: Edward Arnold, n.d. [1901]). For transatlantic preservationism, see Melanie Hall, "Niagara Falls: Preservation and the Spectacle of Anglo-American Accord," and Thomas G. Otte, "'The Shrine at Sulgrave': The Preservation of the Washington Ancestral Home as an 'English Mount Vernon' and Transatlantic Relations," in *Towards World Heritage: International Origins of the Preservation Movement, 1870–1930*, ed. Hall (Farnham: Ashgate, 2011), 23–44; 109–35.

12. Claudius Patten, *England as Seen by an American Banker: Notes of a Pedestrian Tour* (Boston: D. Lothrop & Co, 1885), 3, 41, 84–5.

13. Henry Adams would later (*The Education of Henry Adams* [New York: Modern Library, 1931 (privately printed 1906)], 72) recollect the "overwhelming" experience of the duke of Westminster's Eaton Hall: "The long suite of lofty, gilded rooms with their golden furniture; the portraits; the terraces; the gardens, the landscape; the sense of superiority in the England of the fifties … Aristocracy was real."

14. Olmsted, *Walks and Talks*, 54–5, 96, 259, 275.

15. Charles Godfrey Leland, *Memoirs* (New York: D. Appleton & Co., 1893), 388.

16. Andrew Wilson, *A President's Love Affair with the Lake District: Woodrow Wilson's "Second Home"* (Windemere: Lakeland Press Agency, 1996), 1–2, 5, 20–1.

17. See Malcolm Andrews, *The Search for the Picturesque: Landscape Aesthetics and Tourism in Britain, 1760–1800* (Palo Alto: Stanford University Press, 1989), esp. chs. 1–2.

18. Stephen Tuffnell, *Made in Britain: Nation and Emigration in Nineteenth-Century America* (Oakland: University of California Press, 2020), 2, 10; Stephen Tuffnell, "Anglo-American Inter-Imperialism: US Expansion and the British World, c.1865–1914," *Britain and the World* 7, 2 (2014), 178–80. Also Stephen Tuffnell, "Expatriate Foreign Relations: Britain's American Community and Transnational Approaches to the U.S. Civil War," *Diplomatic History* 40, 4 (2016), 637–40.

19. Peabody advanced a loan for the American exhibit at the Crystal Palace in 1851 and also hosted a dinner for 800 British and American guests (cited by Tuffnell, *Made in Britain*, 69–70).

20. Tuffnell, "Anglo-American Inter-Imperialism"; Tuffnell, *Made in Britain*, 23.

21. Mackintosh, *Selling the Sights*, 15.

22. Samuel S. Cox, *A Buckeye Abroad: Or, Wanderings in Europe, and in the Orient* (Cincinnati: Moore, Anderson & Co., 1854 [1st pub. New York, 1852]), 6, 28–9.

23. *Ibid.*, 51.

24. Guidebooks after 1820 were, according to Daniel Kilbride, "a new genre … which told [American travelers] where to go, what to do, and—increasingly—what they should think" (Daniel Kilbride, *Being American in Europe, 1750–1860* [Baltimore: Johns Hopkins Press, 2013]), 83).

Notes

25. Touring American women increasingly drew comment toward the end of the century. William Archer observed that there was a distinctively good-natured type of American woman: "When one meets her in Bloomsbury (where she abounds in tourist season) one readily distinguishes the American lady" (*America To-Day*, 47).
26. Elizabeth Davis Bancroft, *Letters from England 1846–1849* (New York: Charles Scribner's Sons, 1904), 22, 24, 42–3, 45, 110–1, 144, 187.
27. Ralph Waldo Emerson, *English Traits* (Boston: Phillips, Sampson & Co., 1857), 183 [on his 1847–8 tour of Britain].
28. Olmsted, *Walks and Talks*, 287.
29. John L. Stoddard, *Scotland, England, London* (Boston: Balch Bros. Co., 1909), 116, 119.
30. As early as 1824, John Neal, an American who published in both the United States and Britain, complained in an anonymous piece in *Blackwood's*, that the American abroad was "talkative, noisy, imperious; often excessively impertinent, capricious, troublesome, either in his familiarity, or in his untimely reserve" (X., Y., Z. "Speculations of a Traveller Concerning the People of the United States," *Blackwood's* 16 [July, 1824], 95). In 1849 Alexander Mackay claimed that Americans who travel did so "with as thick a coat of prejudice about them, as Englishmen generally wear in visiting America" (Alexander Mackay, *The Western World; or Travels in the United States in 1846–47*, 2nd edn (London: Richard Bentley, 1849), III, 322).
31. George Tuthill Borrett, *Letters from Canada and the United States* (London: J. E. Adlard, 1865), 272–3. Many of Borret's views, originally expressed in letters to his father, have, like his extended attack on the American habit of spitting tobacco (80) or their love of pistols and bowie-knives (116, 148), a somewhat dated feeling, replicating as they do the themes of the antebellum genre of travel-writing.
32. Cited by Tuffnell, *Made in Britain*, 75.
33. Wilson Sullivan, *New England Men of Letters* (New York: Atheneum, 1972), 219.
34. David M. Wrobel, *Global West: Travel, Empire, and Exceptionalism from Manifest Destiny to The Great Depression* (Albuquerque: University of New Mexico Press, 2013), 74; *Puck*, May 12, 1897.
35. Harriet Stanton Blatch, and Alma Lutz, *Challenging Years: The Memoirs of Harriet Stanton Blatch* (New York: G. P. Putnam's Sons, 1940), 76–7.
36. Adam Badeau, *Aristocracy in England* (New York: Harper and Bros., 1886), 155, 164 [in a chapter on "Caste"].
37. Already in 1841, George Combe had commented on the "trite and commonplace" reportage in the travel journals of American tourists (Combe, *Notes on the United States of North America*, I, xvi–xvii).
38. "Carte Blanche" [Percy Roberts], "England and the English," *De Bow's Review* 3 (1867), 235–43 [cited by Commager, 400–1].
39. John Burroughs, *Winter Sunshine* (Boston: Houghton Mifflin, 1887 [1st pub. 1876]), 205.
40. George Monroe Royce, *Americans in Europe by One of Them* (New York: J. Selwyn Tait & Sons, 1893); and *The Note Book of an American Parson in England* (New York: G. Putnam's Sons, 1918).
41. Royce, *Americans in Europe*, 8–9.
42. James Fullerton Muirhead, *The Land of Contrasts: A Briton's View of His American Kin* (Boston, New York, and London: Lamson, Wolffe and Co., 1898), 24–5.

43. Melanie Hall and Erik Goldstein, "Writers, the Clergy, and the 'Diplomaticization' of Culture: Sub-Structures of Anglo-American Diplomacy, 1820–1914," in *On the Fringes of Diplomacy*, eds. Fisher and Best (Farnham: Ashgate, 2011), 140–2.
44. Carnegie commented in 1883 that "[w]hen one has crossed the Atlantic twenty odd times" there was as little sense in boring his readers with an account of the passage "as if the journey were by rail from New York to Chicago" (*An American Four-in-Hand in Britain* [New York: Doubleday & Co., 1933 (1st pub. 1883)]), 12.
45. Michael Astor, *Tribal Feeling* (London: John Murray, 1964), 8–9, 18.
46. Andrew Carnegie, *Autobiography* (Boston: Houghton Mifflin, 1920), 45.
47. *Ibid.*, 150.
48. Andrew Carnegie, "Does America Hate England?" *Contemporary Review* 72 (November, 1897), 661. Also *The Reunion of Britain and America: A Look Ahead* (Edinburgh: Andrew Elliot, n.d. [reprinted from the North American Review, June 1893]), where he writes of "race confederation" binding a Britain that includes the English, Scots, Irish, and Welsh together with America and Canada.
49. Carnegie, "Does America Hate England?" 661.
50. Andrew Carnegie, *Drifting Together: Will the United States and Canada Unite?* (New York: The World's Work Press, 1904), 11.
51. In 1886, for instance, Capt. Jackie Fisher, then Director of Naval Ordnance, complained of "the flood of Americans ... so nauseous and disagreeable" on the Continent; the Americans "swarm so everywhere" (cited by Massie, *Dreadnought*, 426).
52. Ellen Carol DuBois, "'Spanning Two Centuries': The Autobiography of Nora Stanton Barney," *History Workshop* 22, Special American Issue (1986), 136.
53. Andrew Carnegie, *An American Four-in-Hand in Britain*, 103, 106, 130–1, 195–6, 230.
54. Carnegie, *Autobiography*, 85.
55. Silliman, *A Journal of Travels*, I, 120, 123.
56. Melanie Hall, "Plunder or Preservation? Negotiating an Anglo-American Heritage in the Later Nineteenth Century in the Old and the New: Shakespeare's Birthplace, Niagara Falls, and Carlyle's House," in *From Plunder to Preservation: Britain and the Heritage of Empire*, ed. Peter Mandler and Astrid Swenson (Oxford: Oxford University Press, 2013), 241–65. The birthplace became a deeded museum and library in 1866.
57. See *The Story of the Memorial Fountain to Shakespeare at Stratford-upon-Avon*, ed. Lemuel Clarke Davis (Cambridge: Riverside Press, 1890).
58. Irving, *Henry Irving*, 487.
59. Anderson, *A Few Memories*, 129–30.
60. William Winter, *English Rambles: And Other Fugitive Pieces in Prose and Verse* (Boston: James R. Osgood and Co., 1884 [1st pub. 1883]), 68. Also, Winter, *The Trip to England* (Boston: James R. Osgood and Co., 1881), 166.
61. Richard White, *England Without and Within* (London: Sampson Low, 1881), 509–30.
62. Patten, *England as Seen by an American Banker*, 313.
63. Frederick Edwin Smith, 1st Earl of Birkenhead, "Introduction," in James Fullarton Muirhead, *American Shrines on English Soil* (London: The Dorland Agency, 1924), ix.
64. Daniel Pidgeon, *An Engineer's Holiday: Or, Notes of a Round Trip from Long. 0 to 0*, 2nd edn (London: Kegan, Paul, Trench & Co., 1883 [1st pub. 1882]), 206.

Notes

65. Baillie-Grohman, *Camps in the Rockies*, 25. Grohman was making the point that British tourists in America were also often misinformed in their expectation of desperadoes and violence there.
66. Campbell, *White and Black*, 4. Pidgeon, *An Engineer's Holiday*, 206. Pidgeon's guess about what Americans brought to Europe is likely to have been a significant underestimate. Henry Allen estimates that in the years before 1914 American visitors were bringing 15-20 million dollars into Britain annually (Harry Cranbrook Allen, *Great Britain and the United States: A History of Anglo-American Relations (1783-1952)* [New York: St. Martin's Press, 1952], 109).
67. See for instance William Deane Howells, *Certain Delightful English Towns* (New York: Harper and Bros., 1906).
68. Muirhead, *American Shrines*, gives Elihu Yale's last resting place a chapter of its own, after Stratford, Sulgrave, and Harvard House.
69. Visiting Americans came to stare at the tombs of Franklin's relations in the Ecton churchyard and in 1910 donated a bronze memorial plaque to the Ecton parish church.
70. William Everett, *On the Cam: Lectures on the University of Cambridge in England* (Cambridge, MA: Sever and Francis, 1865), 13; Muirhead, *American Shrines*, 83.
71. Oliver Bainbridge, *The Lesson of the Anglo-American Centenary* (London: Heath Cranton and Ouseley, n.d. [1914]), 23.
72. Otte, "'The Shrine at Sulgrave,'" 111. Also see Harold Clifford Smith, *Sulgrave Manor and the Washingtons: A History and Guide to the Home of George Washington's Ancestors* (London: J. Cape, 1933).
73. Otte, "'The Shrine at Sulgrave,'" 121.
74. Cody and Visscher, *Buffalo Bill's Own Story of His Life and Deeds*, 331-2.
75. Stoddard, *Scotland, England, London*: "Scotland," frontispiece, 1, 7; "England," frontispiece, 1.
76. William Fraser Rae, *Columbia and Canada: Notes on the Great Republic and the New Dominion* (London: Daldy, Isbister & Co., 1877), 167, 183, 315-16.
77. Tamarkin, *Anglophilia*, xxvii-viii.
78. Foreman, *A World on Fire*, 117.
79. "We feel indeed like children that have come back to visit the paternal house ... these relics of our old England" (Olmsted, quoted by Tamarkin, *Anglophilia*, 71-2).
80. Charles Beresford, "The Anglo-American Entente," *Pall Mall Magazine* 18, 75 (July, 1899), 383.
81. Walter L. Arnstein, "The Americanization of Queen Victoria," *The Historian* 72, 4 (2010), 834.
82. Noah Miller Ludlow, *Dramatic Life as I Found It* (St. Louis: G. I. Jones & Co., 1880), 507-8.
83. Anon. [probably O'Sullivan], "The Victoria Fever," *Democratic Review* 6 (July, 1839), 74-6.
84. Tamarkin, *Anglophilia*, 30-47.
85. She ordered a wreath placed on Garfield's casket when the president's body lay in state in Washington, DC, and ordered the British court into mourning for a week (Arnstein, "The Americanization of Queen Victoria," 839-40).
86. Cox, *A Buckeye Abroad*, 41.
87. Grace Greenwood, *Victoria Queen of England, Her Girlhood and Womanhood* (London: Sampson Low, 1884 [1st pub. New York, 1883]), 1, 383-6.
88. Victoria to Gladstone, June 15, 1881, in *The Letters of Queen Victoria*, 2nd series, III, 222.
89. Legard, *Colorado*, 124-5.

90. Bird, *A Lady's Life in the Rocky Mountains*, 51–2.
91. Cecil Robert, *Adrift in America, or Work and Adventure in the States* (London: Lawrence and Bullen, 1891), 101.
92. William Hardman, *A Trip to America* (London: T. Vickers Wood, 1884), 37.
93. The most substantial scholarly treatment of the Prince's visit can be found in Tamarkin, "Monarch-Love; or, How the Prince of Wales Saved the Union," the first chapter of *Anglophobia*, 1–86. For a contemporary account, see the British-born travel writer and journalist Kinahan Cornwallis, *Royalty in the New World: Or, the Prince of Wales in America* (New York: M. Doolady, 1860), a "panorama" of "the most auspicious event of the age."
94. Strong, *Diary*, vol. 3, 51–2; Tamarkin, *Anglophilia*, 7. The metonyms she means are those of loyalty and the impulse to collective order—a "displaced patriotism."
95. Walt Whitman, "Year of Meteors" (1860), *Leaves of Grass*; Harriet Beecher Stowe, "The Prince," *Liberator* (November 24, 1860) [both cited by Tamarkin].
96. In 1845 Buchanan had proclaimed (just before the war with Mexico) that "Anglo-Saxon blood could never be subdued" (quoted by Reginald Horsman, *Race and Manifest Destiny: The Origins of American Racial Anglo-Saxonism* [Cambridge, MA: Harvard Press, 1981], 208).
97. Van Wyck Brooks, *The Wine of the Puritans: A Study of Present-Day America* (London: Sisley's, 1908), 22 (cited by Tamarkin, *Anglophilia*, 70).
98. Edward Everett, *Orations and Speeches* (Boston: Little and Brown, 1853), II, 472; George Palmer Putnam, *The Tourist in Europe* (New York: Wiley and Putnam, 1838), 107.
99. William Hichborn, *The Trip of the Ancients: A Memoir of Events, Personal Experiences, and Impressions* (Malden: George E. Dunbar, 1897), ii.
100. *Ibid.*, iii.
101. *Ibid.*, 35, 45, 47, 49–50, 133–4.
102. By 1850 80 percent of foreign-born Irish lived in New England and the middle states, though in the following decades the Irish population grew significantly in Chicago, St. Louis, and San Francisco (Jay P. Dolan, *The Irish Americans: A History* [London: Bloomsbury, 2008], 82).
103. Dolan, *The Irish Americans*, 147–8. San Francisco had elected its first Irish mayor as early as 1867. William R. Grace, elected in 1880, was the first Catholic Irish mayor of New York City and an articulate supporter of Davitt's Land League.
104. Clifton K. Yearley Jr., *Britons in American Labor: A History of the Influence of United Kingdom Immigrants on American Labor, 1820–1914* (Baltimore: Johns Hopkins Press, 1957), 27. As late as 1902, a single meeting at Faneuil Hall could raise $200,000 in support of Irish Home Rule (Perkins, *The Great Rapprochement*, 142).
105. For the Irish Land League in America, see Ely M. Janis, *A Greater Ireland: The Land League and Transatlantic Nationalism in Gilded Age America* (Madison: University of Wisconsin Press, 2015). Also, James J. Green, "American Catholics and the Irish Land League, 1879–1882," *Catholic Historical Review* 35, 1 (April, 1949), 19–42.
106. There would also, as in 1896, be a delegation that traveled to London, in this case to help celebrate the 350th anniversary of the London Ancients.
107. [British-American Association], Faneuil Hall, *Who Are Its Conservators?* (Boston: British-American Assn., n.d. [1887]), 3, 19, 25, 47–50.
108. *Ibid.*, 5, 9.

Notes

109. *The Letters and Friendships of Sir Cecil Spring Rice: A Record*, ed. Stephen Gwynn (Boston: Houghton Mifflin, 1929), I, 67.
110. Michael J. Sewell, "Queen of Our Hearts," in, *Victorianism in the United States: Its Era and Its Legacy*, ed. Steve Ickingrill and Stephen F. Mills (Amsterdam: VU University Press, 1992), 217.
111. Interestingly, the bulk of Irish Catholics in Canada—more scattered and rural than in the United States—appear not to have been as susceptible to the politics of Irish nationalism as the American Irish. And in the United States, Irish-America was not unanimous in opposition; a number of "lace-curtain" Irish Catholic publications praised the Queen and noted that Catholicism in Britain enjoyed greater toleration than in Protestant America (Sewell, "Queen of Our Hearts," 210).
112. In New York City, in spite of the large and politically active Irish-American population there, the Queen's Jubilee was celebrated with a minimum of opposition at the Metropolitan Opera House (Pagnamenta, *Prairie Fever*, 285).
113. Four years after the 1887 affair at Faneuil Hall both of the national party platforms had championed Irish Home Rule (Rowland Tappan Berthoff, *British Immigrants in Industrial America, 1790-1950* [Cambridge, MA: Harvard University Press, 1953], 198-9).
114. "So the Queen is dead. The news reached us at Winnipeg and this city far away among the snows—fourteen hundred miles from any British town of importance—began to hang its head and hoist half-masted flags," January 22, 1901, in *My Darling Winston: Forty Years of Letters between Winston Churchill and His Mother*, ed. David Lough (London: Pegasus, 2018), 382.
115. Arnstein, "The Americanization of Queen Victoria," 845.
116. The annual Richmond British Association banquets were attended, John Clay reported in 1875, by about 350, concluded with cheers for Queen Victoria, and sent a telegram to the Queen on her birthday (Clay, *New World Notes*, 17).
117. Sewell, "Queen of Our Hearts," 206, 214.
118. The *New York Times* declared on the occasion of Victoria's Diamond Jubilee in 1897 that "we are a part, and a great part, of the Greater Britain which seems so plainly destined to dominate this planet" (cited by Temperley, *Britain and America*, 86-7).
119. Perkins, *The Great Rapprochement*, 116.
120. Finch, *An Englishwoman's Experience in America*, 256.
121. Clay, *New World Notes*, 17-18.
122. Arthur S. Pier, *Forbes: Telephone Pioneer* (New York: Dodd, Mead & Co., 1953), 208-10.
123. The architect, commissioned by J. M. Forbes, was a cousin, William Ralph Emerson.
124. My thanks to my colleague Beatrice Forbes Manz for saving this album for me when the house was sold in 2019.
125. Quoted by Yokota, *Unbecoming British*, 241. See Ralph Waldo Emerson, *English Traits* (London: G. Routledge & Co, 1856), passim. For Emerson as Anglo-Saxonist, as "the philosopher king of American white race theory," see Nell Irvin Painter, *The History of White People* (New York: W. W. Norton and Co., 2010), chs. 10-12 (151-89).
126. William H. to his mother Sarah, quoted by Pier, *Forbes*, 86.
127. *Saturday Club: A Century Completed*, ed. Edward Waldo Forbes (Boston: Houghton Mifflin, 1958), 32.
128. For the transatlantic movement in the 1890s to preserve Carlyle's house in Chelsea, see Melanie Hall, "Museums and the Display of International Friendship: Diplomatic Interests,

American Philanthropy, and Preserving Thomas Carlyle's London House, c. 1894," *Diplomacy & Statecraft* 32, 2 (2021), 241–62; also Hall, "Plunder or Preservation," 241–65.

129. The Boston gentleman was, he continued, "liberal in religion," "enlightened," and "finely mannered ... distributing his leisure between art, literature, and outdoor occupations" (Muirhead, *The Land of Contrasts*, 204).

130. Henry Cabot Lodge, *Early Memories* (New York: Charles Scribner's Sons, 1913), 203–4.

131. David A. Wilson, "Whiteness and Irish Experience in North America," *Journal of British Studies* 44, 1 (January, 2005), 156, 158. Also see Dale T. Knobel, *Paddy and the Republic: Ethnicity and Nationality in Antebellum America* (Middletown: Wesleyan University Press, 1986).

132. Kevin Kenny, "American-Irish Nationalism," in *Making the Irish American: History and Heritage of the Irish in the United States*, ed. Joseph Lee and Marion Casey (New York: New York University Press, 2006), 291.

133. Along with other—German, Japanese, and Egyptian—living ethnic exhibitions that the Warrington poet and travel-writer Robert Anderton Naylor found charming (*Across the Atlantic*, 152). Also see George Washburn Smalley, *Anglo-American Memories* (New York: G. P. Putnam's Sons, 1911), 280, and George Adam Smith, *The Life of Henry Drummond*, 2nd edn (London: Hodder and Stoughton, 1899), 420.

134. Sewell, "Queen of Our Hearts," 210.

135. *The Story of the Irish in Boston*, ed. and comp. James Bernard Cullen (Boston: James B. Cullen, 1889), 288–9.

136. Hardy, *Between Two Oceans*, 99–100.

137. Edith Emerson Forbes to Ellen Emerson, October 2, 1883 (Emerson Family Correspondence, 1883–1903, Carton 3, Mass. Hist. Soc.).

138. In the long nineteenth-century debate between American protectionists and Cobdenite free-traders, John Murray Forbes embraced the latter, and, in 1889, delivered and published a speech attacking tariffs that was praised in England by William Rathbone and others (Sarah Forbes Hughes [ed.], *Letters and Recollections of John Murray Forbes* [Boston: Houghton Mifflin, 1899], II, 221–3).

139. Edward Waldo Forbes, "John Murray Forbes," in *The Early Years of the Saturday Club*, ed. Edward Waldo Emerson (Boston: Houghton Mifflin, 1918), 228, 232.

140. See Betty G. Farrell, *Elite Families: Class and Power in Nineteenth-Century Boston* (Albany: State University of New York Press, 1993), chs. 3–5.

141. Barings provided the Perkinses with market reports and special advices as well as credit for the China trade. Between 1832 and 1834 Perkins & Co. remitted almost $1,000,000 to Barings (Ralph Willard Hidy, *The House of Baring in American Trade and Finance: English Merchant Bankers at Work, 1763–1861* [Cambridge, MA: Harvard University Press, 1949], 191). On ways in which the American China trade was "entangled" with the British Empire, see Dael A. Norwood's recent study, *Trading Freedom: How Trade with China Defined Early America* (Chicago: University of Chicago Press, 2022). This subject is also touched upon by Dane A. Morrison, *Eastward of Good Hope: Early America in a Dangerous World* (Baltimore: Johns Hopkins University Press, 2021), ch. 3.

142. See Peter Dobkin Hall, "Marital Selection and Business in Massachusetts Families 1700–1900," in *The American Family in Socio-Historical Perspective*, ed. Michael Gordon, 2nd edn (New York: St. Martin's Press, 1978), 101–14; also Hidy, *The House of Baring*, 107, 166–7.

143. For John Murray Forbes, see Hughes (ed.), *Letters and Recollections, passim*, as well as Henry Greenleaf Pearson, *An American Railroad Builder: John Murray Forbes*

Notes

(Boston: Houghton Mifflin, 1911); Forbes, "John Murray Forbes," 227–33; and John Lauritz Larson, *Bonds of Enterprise: John Murray Forbes and Western Development in America's Railway Age* (Iowa City: University of Iowa Press, 2001). There is an extensive MSS collection of letters, etc., of the extended family at the Massachusetts Historical Society.

144. Recalled by a grandson, Allan Forbes (cited by Walter Muir Whitehill, "Allan Forbes," *Proceedings of the Massachusetts Historical Society*, 3rd Ser., 71 [October 1953–May 1957], 413). Also see Robert B. Forbes, *Personal Reminiscences*, 2nd edn (Cambridge, MA: privately printed by John Wilson and Son, 1882), 136, 169, 223, 255, and Forbes House Museum at www.forbeshousemuseum.org/.

145. From a crayon drawing by Seth Wells Cheney (Pearson, *An American Railroad-Builder*, frontispiece, ii).

146. On Cobdenism in America and Anglo-American relations, see Marc-William Palen, "Foreign Relations in the Gilded Age: A British Free-Trade Conspiracy?" *Diplomatic History* 37, 2 (2013), 217–47.

147. Edmund S. Ions, *James Bryce and American Democracy 1870–1922* (New York: Humanities Press, 1970 [1st pub. London, 1968]), 76.

148. Hughes (ed.), *Letters and Recollections*, II, 105–6.

149. Hidy, *House of Baring*, 192, 353.

150. See John D. Wong, *Global Trade in the Nineteenth Century: The House of Houqua and the Canton System* (Cambridge: Cambridge University Press, 2016), 88, 107–9, 148, 177–8, 189–202, and *passim*. Also, Wang Shua, *Negotiating Friendships: A Canton Merchant between East and West in the Early Nineteenth Century* (Munich and Vienna: De Gruyter Oldenbourg, 2020).

151. Hidy, *House of Baring*, 107.

152. In a letter to Sumner, October 31, 1869, cited by Adrian Cook, *The Alabama Claims* (Ithaca: Cornell University Press, 1975), 22.

153. William Hathaway Forbes (1840–97), would become the first president of the American Telephone and Telegraph Company. See Pier, *Forbes, passim*. Also, Farrell, *Elite Families*, 154.

154. Ronald Story, *The Forging of an Aristocracy: Harvard & the Boston Upper Class, 1800–1970* (Middletown: Wesleyan University Press, 1980), 3; and xii–xiii, ch. 1. Paul Goodman, "Ethics and Enterprise: The Values of a Boston Elite, 1800–1860," *American Quarterly* 18, 3 (Fall, 1966) 437–51, makes some useful observations but is, overall, an uncritical panegyric. Also see Hall, "Marital Selection and Business in Massachusetts Merchants' Families 1700–1900," 101–14.

155. Goodman, "Ethics and Enterprise," 441.

156. See, for instance, Anthony Trollope's novel *The Way We Live Now* (London: Chapman and Hall, 1875). The deviously conniving railway shares speculator Auguste Melmotte who buys a country house and takes a seat in parliament was originally conceived of as American.

157. Martin J. Wiener's *English Culture and the Decline of the Industrial Spirit 1850–1980* (Cambridge: Cambridge University Press, 1981) sparked a long-running debate over "declinism" and culture.

158. William Hathaway Forbes attended Harvard from 1857 until he was expelled in 1860 for assaulting a night watchman in the college chapel during an undergraduate prank gone awry. Harvard, however, awarded him a BA degree in 1871.

159. Ralph Waldo Emerson, *Letters and Social Aims*, 2nd edn (Boston: James R. Osgood and Co., 1876), 84–5, though Emerson does not name J. M. Forbes in the text.

160. Cited in Douglas H. Maynard, "The Forbes-Aspinall Mission," *Mississippi Valley Historical Review* 45, 1 (June, 1958), 73, 78–9.
161. *Ibid.*, 80, 84.
162. Forbes, *Personal Reminiscences*, 283–4. For deer-hunting at Naushon, see for example pp. 166 and 310.
163. See the collection of essays in *Edward Waldo Forbes, Yankee Visionary* (Cambridge, MA: Fogg Art Museum, 1971).
164. These included among many John Bright, Thomas Hughes, William Rathbone, Jr., Goldwin Smith, and Nassau Senior (Hughes, *Letters and Recollections*, *passim*).
165. See, for instance, Edith Emerson Forbes to Ellen Emerson, 23 [or 25] July 1883 (Emerson Family Correspondence, 1883-1903, Carton 3, Mass. Hist. Soc.).
166. Receptions at Milton could be large affairs, as when in 1884 William H. and Edith invited "very near five hundred, perhaps more" to their house—with a caterer and "five or six musicians playing before the hall fire-place" (Edith Emerson Forbes to Ellen Emerson, July 1, 1884 [Emerson Family Correspondence, 1883-1903, Carton 3, Massachusetts Historical Society]).
167. Ions, *James Bryce and American Democracy*, 76–7.
168. Hughes (ed.), *Letters and Recollections*, I, 8.
169. *Ibid.*, I, 33–4, and II, 87.
170. For the history of the Saturday Club, see *Early Years of the Saturday Club* and *Later Years of the Saturday Club, 1870-1920*, ed. De Wolfe Howe (Boston: Houghton Mifflin, 1927), to which E. W. Emerson contributed several bios, Edward Waldo Forbes one on the painter Sargent, and Cameron Forbes one on S. W. McColl. Edward Waldo Forbes (and J. H. Finley, Jr.) continued this series with *Saturday Club: A Century Completed, 1920-1956*, including an essay, by E. W. Forbes, on his uncle E. W. Emerson.
171. Forbes, *Personal Reminiscences*, 165.
172. *Ibid.*, 290–1.
173. Hughes (ed.), *Letters and Recollections*, I, 141, 168–9; also Jay Sexton, *Debtor Diplomacy: Foreign Relations in the Civil War Era* (Oxford: Oxford University Press, 2005), 109. In 1851, Barings had brought an American, the Bostonian China merchant Richard Sturgis, into the partnership, where he joined another Boston merchant (and friend of J. M. Forbes), Joshua Bates. Each, in succession, would come to head the firm. See Hidy, *House of Baring*.
174. *The Amberley Papers*, II, 51, 64, 69–70, 105–7.
175. He served in the Massachusetts Volunteer Cavalry and was a prisoner of war in South Carolina for some months in 1864 before being exchanged.
176. For the transatlantic family trips of 1872, 1888, and 1892–3, see Pier, *Forbes*, 81–90, 183–4, 206–10.
177. *Ibid.*, 90.
178. *Ibid.*, 183–4.
179. See the Edith Emerson Forbes and William Hathaway Forbes Papers at the Massachusetts Historical Society (esp. Emerson Family Correspondence 1883-1903, and Forbes' Family Correspondence, 1833-1901), *passim*. Also Pier, *Forbes*, 205–10.
180. W. Campbell to Mrs. Forbes, February 27, 1901; Perenna Bate of Kelsterton Hall to Mrs. Forbes, 1901; Elizabeth Ashbee to Mrs. Forbes, April 11, 1901 (Forbes Family Papers, Carton 11).

Notes

181. In January 1901, William Hathaway and Edith Emerson's eldest son Ralph Emerson Forbes married Elise Cabot.
182. A newspaper favored by the Boston upper classes, the *Transcript*, regularly offered genealogical information from 1876, weekly by 1894, and twice weekly by 1891 (Morgan, *A Nation of Descendants*, 20).
183. Bradford's early seventeenth-century manuscript had been taken by the British as they left Boston and subsequently deposited at the Bishop of London's Lambeth Palace library. For the full story, see Erik Goldstein, "Diplomacy in the Service of History: Anglo-American Relations and the Return of the Bradford History of Plymouth Colony, 1898," *Diplomacy & Statecraft* 25, 1 (2014), 26–40.
184. Whitehill, "Allan Forbes," 415.
185. The volumes were illustrated throughout by photos taken by Ian Forbes-Robertson, brother of the actor-manager Forbes-Robertson—perhaps there was some family connection. See Allan Forbes, *Towns of New England and Old England I* (Boston: State Street Trust, 1920), 9–11, 17–18. Forbes was president of the State Street Trust Company which published many of his antiquarian pieces. In the Great War and after Forbes was active in raising money for the allies, in the work of the English Speaking Union, and in the restoration of St. Botolph's church tower in Boston, Lincolnshire (Whitehill, "Allan Forbes," 420).
186. Alicia Keyes to Ellen Emerson, September 7, 1884 (Emerson Family Correspondence, 1883–1903, Carton 3).
187. Haven Emerson to Edith Emerson Forbes, August 23, 1901 (Emerson Family Correspondence, Carton 4). Haven's sister Ruth would the same year be married to an Englishman.

Summation and Epilogue

1. Richard Bushman, *The Refinement of America: Persons, Houses, Cities* (New York: Alfred A. Knopf, 1992), xii.
2. *Shakespeare's Works, with a Scrupulous Revision of the Text*, ed. Mary Cowden Clarke (New York: D. Appleton & Co., and London, Trübner & Co., 1869 [orig. pub. 1859]). Cowden Clarke, née Novello (1809–98) was an English author who had published in 1846 a Shakespeare concordance. In the 1840s she herself performed in private theatricals in aid of the preservation of Shakespeare's birthplace at Stratford-upon-Avon. In 1856, she published a "companion" piece to Longfellow's "Hiawatha," adopting the humorous pseudonym Harry Wandsworth Shortfellow.
3. Ibid., v.

SELECT BIBLIOGRAPHY

The following is a selection of some primary and secondary sources. Note that the travel memoirs upon which much of this book was based are too numerous to be listed here. Only a few of the better-known are cited below; the rest may be found in the chapter notes.

Primary Sources

Bartlett, John Russell. *Dictionary of Americanisms*. New York: Bartlett and Welford, 1848.
Bird, Isabella L. *A Lady's Life in the Rocky Mountains*, 4th edn. London: John Murray, 1881.
Bird, Isabella L. *My First Travels in North America*. Mineola: Dover Publications, 2010.
Bodichon, Barbara Leigh Smith. *An American Diary 1857-8*, ed. Joseph W. Reed, Jr. London: Routledge & Kegan Paul, 1972.
Burton, Richard. *The City of the Saints, and across the Rocky Mountains to California*, 2nd edn. London: Longman, Green, 1862.
Cawley, Elizabeth Hoon (ed.) *The American Diaries of Richard Cobden*. New York: Greenwood Press, 1952.
Combe, George. *Notes on the United States of North America*. Edinburgh: Maclachlan, Stewart and Co., 1841.
Cooper, James Fenimore. *Gleanings in Europe. England*. Philadelphia: Carey, Lea, and Blanchard, 1837.
De Vere, M. Schele. *Americanisms, or the English of the New World*. New York: Scribner and Co., 1872.
Dickens, Charles. *American Notes*. New York: Penguin, 2004.
Dilke, Charles Wentworth. *Greater Britain*. London: Macmillan & Co., 1868.
Dixon, William Hepworth. *New America*. London: Hurst & Blackett, 1867.
Elwyn, Alfred. *Glossary of Supposed Americanisms*. Philadelphia: J. B. Lippincott, 1859.
Emerson, Ralph Waldo. *English Traits*. Boston: Phillips, Sampson & Co., 1857.
Farmer, John Stephen. *Americanisms Old and New*. London: Thomas Poulter & Sons, 1889.
Fearon, Henry Bradshaw. *Sketches of America*. London: Longman, 1818.
Finch, Marianne. *An Englishwoman's Experience in America*. New York: Negro Universities Press, 1969.
Freeman, Edward A. *Some Impressions of the United States*. New York: Henry Holt & Co., 1883.
Griffin, Lepel Henry. *The Great Republic*, 2nd edn. London: Chapman and Hall, 1884.
Hall, Basil. *Travels in North America*. Philadelphia: Carey, Lea and Carey, 1829.
Hamilton, Thomas. *Men and Manners in America*. Edinburgh: William Blackwood & Sons, 1833.
Hatton, Joseph. *Henry Irving's Impressions of America*. Boston: James R. Osgood and Co., 1884.
Hughes, Sarah Forbes (ed.) *Letters and Recollections of John Murray Forbes*. Boston: Houghton Mifflin, 1899.
Hunter, Joseph, Joseph Stevenson, and James Odell (eds.) *Boucher's Glossary of Archaic and Provincial Words*. London, Black, Young, and Young, 1832-33.
Ireland, Joseph N. *Records of the New York Stage from 1750 to 1860*. New York: Burt Franklin, 1866-7.

Select Bibliography

Kemble, Fanny. *Journal of a Residence on a Georgia Plantation in 1838–1839*. New York: Harper & Bros., 1863.
Latham, Henry. *Black and White: A Journal of a Three Months' Tour in the United States*. London: Macmillan, 1867.
Legard, Allayne Beaumont. *Colorado*. London: Chapman and Hall, 1872.
Mackay, Charles. *Life and Liberty in America*, 2nd edn. London: Smith, Elder and Co., 1859.
Marryat, Frederick. *A Diary in America*. London: Longman, 1839.
Olmsted, Frederick Law. *Walks and Talks of an American Farmer in England*. New York: George Putnam, 1852.
Ranney, H. M. *Account of the Terrific and Fatal Riot at the New-York Astor Place Opera House*. New York: H. M. Ranney, 1849.
Royce, George Monroe. *Americans in Europe by One of Them*. New York: J. Selwyn Tait & Sons, 1893.
Russell, William Howard. *Hesperothen; Notes from the West*. London: Sampson Low, 1882.
Sala, George Augustus. *America Revisited*, 3rd edn. London: Vizetelly and Co., 1883.
Silliman, Benjamin. *A Journal of Travels in England, Holland and Scotland*, 2nd edn. Boston: T. B. Ait & Co., 1812.
Stirling, James. *Letters from the Slave States*. London: John W. Parker and Son, 1857.
Sturge, Joseph. *A Visit to the United States in 1841*. London: Hamilton, Adams and Co., 1842.
Thornton, Richard Harwood. *An American Glossary*. Philadelphia: J. B. Lippincott, 1912.
Trollope, Frances. *Domestic Manners of the Americans*. London: Whittaker, Treacher and Co., 1832.
Wright, Frances. *Views of Society and Manners in America*. New York: Bliss and E. White, 1821.

Secondary Sources

Bank, Rosemarie K. *Theatre Culture in America, 1825–1860*. Cambridge: Cambridge University Press, 1997.
Billington, Ray Allen. *Land of Savagery, Land of Promise*. New York: W. W. Norton and Co., 1981.
Brothers, Barbara, and Julia Gergits (eds.) *British Travel Writers, 1837–1939*. Detroit: Gale Research, 1997.
Brown, T. Allston. *A History of the New York Stage*. New York: Benjamin Blom, 1903.
Bushman, Richard. *The Refinement of America*. New York: Alfred A. Knopf, 1992.
Cairns, William B. *British Criticisms of American Writings, 1783–1815*. Madison: University of Wisconsin Press, 1918.
Cairns, William B. *British Criticisms of American Writings, 1815–1833*. Madison: University of Wisconsin Press, 1922.
Campbell, Duncan Andrew. *Unlikely Allies: Britain, America, and the Victorian Origins of the Special Relationship*. London: Hambledon Continuum, 2007.
Cliff, Nigel. *The Shakespeare Riots*. New York: Random House, 2007.
Commager, Henry Steele (ed.) *Britain through American Eyes*. London: Bodley Head, 1974.
Crapol, Edward P. *America for Americans: Economic Nationalism and Anglophobia in the Late Nineteenth Century*. Westport: Greenwood Press, 1973.
Davis, Tracy C. (ed., with S. Mihaylova) *Uncle Tom's Cabins: The Transnational Histories of America's Most Mutable Book*. Ann Arbor: University of Michigan Press, 2018.
Eaton, Joseph. *The Anglo-American Paper War*. New York: Palgrave Macmillan, 2012.
Fisch, Audrey. *American Slaves in Victorian England*. Cambridge: Cambridge University Press, 2000.
Flint, Kate. *The Transatlantic Indian, 1776–1930*. Princeton: Princeton University Press, 2009.

Select Bibliography

Flynn, Christopher. *Americans in British Literature, 1779–1832*. Farnham: Routledge, 2008.
Foreman, Amanda. *A World on Fire*. London: Allen Lane, 2010.
Frankel, Robert. *Observing America*. Madison: University of Wisconsin Press, 2006.
Gibbs, Jenna M. *Performing the Temple of Liberty*. Baltimore: Johns Hopkins Press, 2014.
Gruen, J. Philip. *Manifest Destinies: Cities and Tourists in the Nineteenth-Century American West*. Norman: University of Oklahoma Press, 2014.
Hall, Roger A. Hall. *Performing the American Frontier, 1870–1906*. Cambridge: Cambridge University Press, 2002.
Haynes, Samuel. *Unfinished Revolution: The Early American Republic in a British World*. Charlottesville: University of Virginia Press, 2010.
Ickingrill, Steve, and Stephen F. Mills. *Victorianism in the United States*. Amsterdam: VU University Press, 1992.
Jessen, Nathan. *Populism and Imperialism: Politics, Culture, and Foreign Policy in the American West, 1890–1900*. Lawrence: University of Kansas Press, 2017.
Johnson, Odai. *London in a Box: Englishness and Theatre in Revolutionary America*. Iowa City: University of Iowa Press, 2017.
Kasson, John. *Rudeness and Civility*. New York: Macmillan, 1990.
Kendall, Joshua. *The Forgotten Founding Father: Noah Webster's Obsession and the Creation of an American Culture*. New York: G. P. Putnam's Sons, 2011.
Kilbride, Daniel. *Being American in Europe, 1750–1860*. Baltimore: Johns Hopkins Press, 2013.
Leavitt, Robert Keith. *Noah's Ark. New England Yankees and the Endless Quest: A Short History of the Original Webster Dictionaries*. Springfield, MA: G. C. Merriam and Co., 1947.
Levine, Lawrence W. *Highbrow/Lowbrow: The Emergence of Cultural Hierarchy in America*. Cambridge, MA: Harvard University Press, 1990.
Mackintosh, Will B. *Selling the Sites: The Invention of the Tourist in American Culture*. New York: New York University Press, 2019.
Marx, Peter (ed.) *A Cultural History of the Theatre, vol. 5: In the Age of Empire*. London: Bloomsbury, 2019.
Mason, Jeffrey, and J. Ellen Gainor (eds.) *Performing America: Cultural Nationalism in American Theater*. Ann Arbor: University of Michigan Press, 1999.
Mulvey, Christopher. *Anglo-American Landscapes: A Study of Nineteenth-Century Anglo-American Travel Literature*. Cambridge: Cambridge University Press, 1983.
Mulvey, Christopher. *Transatlantic Manners: Social Patterns in Nineteenth-Century Travel Literature*. Cambridge: Cambridge University Press, 1990.
Murphy, Lynne. *The Prodigal Tongue: The Love-Hate Relationship between British and American English*. New York: Penguin, 2018.
Nowatzki, Robert. *Representing African Americans in Transatlantic Abolitionism and Blackface Minstrelsy*. Baton Rouge: Louisiana State University Press, 2010.
Pagnamenta, Peter. *Prairie Fever: British Aristocrats in the American West, 1830–1890*. New York: W. W. Norton and Co., 2012.
Pickering, Michael. *Blackface Minstrelsy in Britain*. London: Routledge, 2008.
Pomeroy, Earl. *In Search of the Golden West: The Tourist in Western America*. Lincoln: University Nebraska Press, 1957.
Rico, Monica. *Nature's Noblemen: Transatlantic Masculinities and the Nineteenth-Century American West*. New Haven: Yale University Press, 2013.
Rose, Kenneth D. *Unspeakable Awfulness: America through the Eyes of European Travelers, 1865–1900*. London: Taylor and Francis, 2014.
Schweitzer, Marlis. *Transatlantic Broadway: The Infrastructural Politics of Global Performance*. Basingstoke: Palgrave Macmillan, 2015.
Shattuck, Charles H. *Shakespeare on the American Stage*. Washington, DC: Associated University Presses, 1976.

Select Bibliography

Stowe, William W. *Going Abroad: European Travel in Nineteenth-Century American Culture.* Princeton: Princeton University Press, 1994.
Tamarkin, Elisa. *Anglophilia.* Chicago: University of Chicago Press, 2008.
Tuffnell, Stephen. *Made in Britain: Nation and Emigration in Nineteenth-Century America.* Oakland: University of California Press, 2020.
Tyrrell, Ian. *Transnational Nation: United States History in Global Perspective since 1789*, 2nd edn. New York: Palgrave, 2015.
Urry, John. *The Tourist Gaze.* London: Sage, 1990.
Waters, Hazel. *Racism on the Victorian Stage.* Cambridge: Cambridge University Press, 2007.
Watson, Nicola J. *The Literary Tourist.* New York: Palgrave Macmillan, 2006.
Wilmer, Stephen Elliot. *Theatre, Society, and the Nation: Staging American Identities.* Cambridge: Cambridge University Press, 2002.
Wrobel, David M. *Global West.* Albuquerque: University of New Mexico Press, 2013.
Yokota, Kariann Akemi. *Unbecoming British: How Revolutionary America Became a Postcolonial Nation.* Oxford: Oxford University Press, 2011.

INDEX

Abbey, Henry Eugene 90
Adams, Henry 47
Adams, William Edwin 48
African Americans 93–106, 108–9, 111–12, 114, 118, 124, 126–8, 130, 143, 156
African Theater 93–4
Aiken, George 77, 115–16
Aimard, Gustave 140
Aitken, James 14
Alabama claims 4, 82, 205
Aldrich, Ira 214
Aldridge, Ira Frederick 93–7, 105
Aldridge, Reginald 152–3
Alexander, Caleb, *Columbian Dictionary of the English Language* 26
Alford, Henry, *The Queen's English* 40
Allen, Henry 254 n.66
Allen, William Francis, *Slave Songs of the United States* 100
Almighty dollar 44, 46
Amer-English 49
American actors 59, 61, 66, 71, 84–8, 91–3, 97, 133, 191, 214
American Anglophilia 189–98, 216
American Civil War 3–4, 24, 30, 33, 38, 42, 59, 63, 70, 75–6, 80–2, 85, 96–7, 99, 103–4, 109–10, 115, 118–19, 121, 123, 127, 130–2, 135, 139, 146, 151, 155, 167, 172, 176, 178, 183, 190–1, 193, 197, 206–7, 209, 214, 216
American English 14, 17–19, 24, 40, 48–9, 52, 100
American identity 4–5, 19, 33, 68
American in Britain 50, 178–89
American Irish 195, 256 n.111
Americanisms 9, 14, 21–8, 30–41, 46, 48–51, 77, 97–101, 213
Americanization 2, 45, 51, 214
American language 10, 14, 16–18, 22, 24, 31–2, 37, 40, 49, 98–9
American linguistic difference 2, 26, 28
American manager 62–5
American Philological Association 34
American Revolution 111, 175
American Roscius 84
American theater 55–6, 59–65, 68, 92, 95
American tourism 3, 5, 14, 35, 43, 50, 59, 66, 71, 77, 87–91, 133, 164, 169, 176, 180–1, 185–6, 188, 192–3, 196, 217

American West 3, 38, 84, 86, 133, 135–8, 143, 145, 147, 150–1, 153, 155–66, 170–1, 174, 214
American writing and speech 10–13, 31, 38, 47
Ancient and Honorable Artillery Company of Boston 194–8
Anderson, James Robertson 76, 95, 113
Anderson, Joshua 229 n.36
Anderson, Mary 86, 185
Anglo-American
    Anglo-Saxonism 167, 169, 173, 175
    English 14–22
    racial representation 119–33
    War of 1812–15 11
    World 41–7
Anglomania/Anglomaniac 52–4
Anglophilia 3–4, 11, 40, 54, 169, 173, 176, 189–94, 198–9, 213, 215–16
Anglo-Saxonism 3, 6, 34, 156
    cowboy 166–74
    supremacy 130
Anglosphere 6, 66, 92, 118, 120, 133, 135, 165, 216
Anglo-world 2, 6, 41, 45, 50, 60, 101, 118, 133, 135, 154, 214
Archer, William 52
Arnold, Matthew 51
Arnstein, Walter L. 191
Ashbee, Charles Robert 211, 251 n.11
Aspinwall, William. H. 205
Astor Place Riot 75–6
Astor, William Waldorf 183
Atlantic Monthly 39
Ayres, Harry Morgan, *The Cambridge History of American Literature* 28

Badeau, Adam 182
Baillie-Grohman, William 136, 150, 153–5, 186, 245 n.57, 254 n.65
Ballantine, William 131
Ballantyne, Robert M.,
    Fort Desolation; Or, Solitude in the Wilderness 139
    Hudson Bay 161
    The Prairie Chief 139
    The Red Man's Revenge 139
Bancroft, Elizabeth Davis 179–80
Bancroft, George, *History of the United States* 140, 179
Bannatyne, D. J., *Blackwood* 131
Barker, Edmund Henry 20

Index

Barker, James Nelson, *Marmion* 60
Barnaby, William Henry, *Life and Labour of the Far, Far West* 161
Barney, Nora Stanton 184
Barnum, P. T. 59, 66, 70, 115
Barrett, Lawrence 85, 87–8
Barrie, James Matthew, *Peter Pan* 92, 160
Bartlett, John Russell, *Dictionary of Americanisms* 27, 31–3, 37, 41, 46, 98–101, 138, 140, 168, 232 n.91
Bates, Emily Catherine 5
Belasc, David 91
Belich, James 6
Bell, Andrew 45
Bell, William 158
Bennet, Ralph 202
Bennet, Robert 203
Bennett, James Gordon 191
Benwell, John 33, 113, 131
Beresford, Charles 190
Bernard, John 62
Besant, Walter 166
Bird, Isabella 35, 38, 104–5, 133, 146–7, 151, 193
Black, William 149
Blaine, James G. 82
Blatch, Harriet Stanton 182
Bodichon, Barbara Leigh Smith 105, 113
Book of Mormon 138
Booth, Edwin 85–7, 89
Booth, Hare 103
Bopp, Franz 34
Borrett, George Tuthill 181, 252 n.31
Boston Forbeses 198–212
Boucher, Jonathan 25–6
Boucicault, Dion 3, 60, 66–70, 77–8, 84, 87, 91, 96
    Arrah-Na-Pogue ("Arrah of the kiss") 69–70
    Belle Lamar 70
    The Colleen Bawn 68–9, 85
    The Octoroon 68, 77, 96, 112, 114–19
    The Poor of New York 68–70
    The Shaughraun ("the wanderer") 69–70
Bowers, Rick 71
Boxall, George E., *The Anglo-Saxon: A Study in Evolution* 173–4
Bradford Observer 50
Bradley, Granville 128
Brahmin class 169–70, 173, 175, 194, 199, 202, 206, 215
Brereton, Austin 88–9
Bridger, Jim 145
Bridges, F. D. 160
Bridges, Robert 49
British actors 15, 55, 59–60, 62–3, 66, 71–3, 79–80, 91, 95, 160, 213
British English 15–17, 32, 35–6, 51–2

British imperialism 6, 130, 158
Britishness 52, 71, 81–3, 152, 154, 184, 194, 213, 216
British royals 189–98
British theatre 55–6, 59–62, 69
British theatrical touring 87–9
British tourists 3, 9, 35, 38, 61, 85, 98, 104, 112, 141, 159, 164, 174, 192, 215
Britons 7, 10, 15, 22, 25, 37, 42, 47, 56, 74, 78, 81–4, 102, 104, 122–4, 128, 132, 135–6, 141, 145, 147, 149–50, 152–3, 174, 181, 199, 201, 208, 213–15
Brooks, Daphne 108
Brooks, Van Wyck 54, 194
Brother Jonathan (character) 9, 79, 81, 112
Brown, T. Allston 115
Buchanan, James 36, 193, 255 n.96
Bunce, Oliver Bell, *Don't: A Manual of Mistakes & Improprieties More or Less Prevalent in Conduct and Speech* 35–6
Bunyan, John, *Pilgrim's Progress* 41, 109
Burke, John Bernard, *Burke's Peerage* 175
Burnell, Arthur Coke, *Hobson-Jobson* 50
Burnham, Frederick Russell 165
Burnley, James 50, 103, 105
Burrit, Elihu 181
Burroughs, John 182
Burton, Richard Francis, *The City of the Saints, and Across the Rocky Mountains to California* 137–40, 142, 168
Bushman, Richard 217
Butler, Frances 126
Bynack, Vincent 18

Cairns, William Bateman 11–13
Cambridge 19–20, 151, 153
Campbell, George 130–1, 186
Campbell, John Francis 104, 125–6
Campion, J. S. 161
Carlyle, Thomas 82, 169, 199–200
Carnegie, Andrew 177, 183–4, 253 n.44
    Autobiography 183
Carson, Thomas 154
Catlin, George, *The Manners, Customs and Condition of the North American Indians* 157–8
Chamberlain, Joseph 172
Charles, Henry 124–6
Chestnut Street Theatre 58, 62–3, 76
Childs, W. G. 185
Christy Minstrels 105–6, 108
Churchill, Winston 197
Clay, John 128
Cobbett, William 56
Cobden, Richard 43–5, 58
    England, Ireland, and America, by a Manchester Manufacturer 44

Index

Cody, William Frederick (Buffalo Bill) 3, 59, 84, 133, 143, 146, 162–6, 172, 214, 248 n.114
Coke, Henry 144
Colley, Linda 3
Collins, John 67
Combe, George 43, 45
Commons Preservation Society 177
Conolly, Thomas 124
Conway, Henry J. 115
Conway, Moncur 167
Cooke, George Frederick 71–2, 87
Cooper, James Fenimore 13–14, 36, 47, 159–60, 179
  antipathies 29
  The Last of the Mohicans 28
  Notions of the Americans 29
  Precaution 28–9
  regional differences in pronunciation 31–2
Cooper, Lane 12
Corelli, Marie 187
corruption 10, 18, 26–7, 48–51, 99–100, 131, 168, 196
cowboy 3, 84, 137, 139, 148–50, 152, 154–7, 162, 165–74
Cox, Samuel S. 178–9, 192
Crosland, T. W. H. 50
Crowe, Eyre 113, 122, 239 n.105
cultural conservatism 16
cultural imperialism 11
Cushman, Charlotte 86

Daily Mail 50, 132
Daly, John Augustin 90
Davies, William Henry 131
Davis, Emily Jane 130
Davis, Tracy C. 116
Dennie, Joseph 18
De Vere, Maximilian Schele 37, 46, 99–100, 136
Dibdin, Charles, *The Padlock* 94
Dicey, Edward 172
Dickens, Charles 31, 50, 68, 99, 111, 114, 137, 223 n.69, 235 n.21
  American Notes 30
  Martin Chuzzlewit 30
diglossic language 52
Dilke, Charles Wentworth 2, 133, 138, 143, 159, 197
Dixon, William Hepworth 125
domestic tourism industry 13
Douglass, David 57
Douglass, Frederick 3, 109–11
D'Oyly Carte, Richard 87–8, 142
Drury Lane Theatre 62, 74–5, 80, 84, 229 n.29
Dunraven, Lord 143–50, 166

Edward, Albert 193
Ellis, George Edward 189

Elwyn, Alfred, *Glossary of Supposed Americanisms* 34
Emerson, Ralph Waldo 82, 179–81, 198–9, 207, 209
Encyclopedia Britannica 48–9
English Mount Vernon 188
Evans, Nicholas 96
Everest, Robert, *A Journey Through the United States* 42, 120–1

Faithful, Emily 86
Fallows, Samuel 37
Farmer, John Stephen, *Americanisms* 37–8, 50, 100–1
Faux, William 97
Fearon, Henry Bradshaw, *Sketches of America* 33, 101–2
Featherstonhaugh, George William 99, 235 n.21
Felton, Mrs. John, *American Life* 97–8, 102
Fergusson, James 123
Fillis, Frank 165
Finch, Marianne 198
fin de siècle 3, 85, 125, 132–3, 158, 167, 171–2, 174, 186, 188, 197, 206–7, 211–12, 215–16
  impresarios 89–92
  philology 47–54
First World War 34, 53, 81, 84, 91
Fisher, John Arbuthnot (Jackie) 172, 253 n.51
Flagg, James Montgomery, Side-by-Side—Britannia 83
Flynn, Christopher 22–3
Forbes, Allan, *Towns of New England and Old England, Ireland and Scotland* 211–12
Forbes, Edith Emerson (Ralph Waldo Emerson's daughter) 198–201, 210
Forbes, Edward Waldo 208
Forbes, Francis Blackwell 207–8
Forbes, John Murray 198, 202–11
Forbes, Margaret Perkins 203
Forbes, Ralph Emerson 200, 260 n.181
Forbes, Waldo Emerson 211
Forbes, William Hathaway 198, 258 n.153, 258 n.158
Forbes-Robertson, Johnston 55, 228 n.1
Forrest, Edwin 63, 73–6, 85, 191
Fowler, H. W., and Fowler, F. G., *The King's English* 48–9
Fowler, William C., *The English Language in Its Elements and Forms* 99, 167
Fox, John 155
Francis, Francis Jr. 144
Franklin, Benjamin 15–16, 188
Freeman, Edward A. 130, 142–3, 167
The Freeman's Journal 108
Frewen, Moreton 148, 153
Frohman, Charles 91–2
Fugitive Slave Act 109, 111

267

Index

Garland, George Watts 163
Geikie, Archibald C. 32
Giddings, Franklin Henry 170
Gilbert, William Schwenck 78, 83, 153, 198
    Patience 88
    The Pirates of Penzance 88
The Girl I Left Behind Me 156
The Gladiator 75
Gladstone, Thomas 161
Godley, John Robert 30, 61
Godwin, William 29
Grant, George 153
Grant, Ulysses S. 182
Greater Britain 133, 143, 164–5, 173, 197, 214
Great Exhibition (1851) 178–9
great rapprochement 1
Great War 47, 132, 188, 206, 260 n.185. *See also* First World War
The Great Wet Way 84–92
Great White Way 59
Green, Frank William 46
Greenock Herald 14
Gregg, Percy 125
Grey, Earl 188
Griffin, Lepel Henry 53, 85–6, 131
Grimm, Jacob 34
Grose, Francis, dictionary 14, 32, 35

Hallam, Lewis 57
Hall, Basil, *Travels in North America* 29–30
Hall, Fitzedward, false philology 39–41
Hall, Newman 42, 45
Hall, Roger 155
Hamblin, Thomas Sowerby 64
Hamilton Aide, Charles 52
Hamilton, Thomas 74
Hardman, William 193
Hardy, Iza Duffus 38, 130, 139, 201
Harmsworth, Alfred 50
Harper's Magazine 47
Harper's Weekly 175, 197
Harris, Joel Chandler 100–1
Harvard House 186–8
Hatton, Joseph 81, 88, 232 n.98
Henty, G. A. 132
heritage tourism 182–3, 186, 188, 198, 201, 211, 216
Hichborn, William 195
Hilton, Boyd 43–4
Hodgson, Adam 44, 97
Hole, Samuel Reynolds 131
Holman, Joseph George 72
Holmes, Oliver Wendell 181, 185
Homestead Act of 1862 147, 152
Hotten, John Camden, *A Dictionary of Modern Slang, Cant, and Vulgar Words* 35

Howard, Bronson, *The Henrietta* 81
Hughes, Sarah Forbes 208
hunt/hunting 143–7, 150, 155, 162, 207

Ibsen, Henrik, *Hedda Gabler* 87
Irish 66–70, 104, 111–13, 135, 195–201
Irish American newspaper 67
The Irish Artist 68
Irving, Henry 59, 70, 85–9, 185
Irving, Washington 12–13, 28, 84, 184

Jacobs, Harriet 112
James, Henry 140, 181, 183, 185
    The Wings of the Dove 176
Janson, Charles William 30
Jefferson, Joseph 77–8, 80–1, 85, 115, 133
Jim Crow laws 102, 105–7, 115, 125, 129, 132, 156, 214
John Murray (publishing house) 13, 20
Johnson, Samuel, *Dictionary* 14, 16–17, 19–20, 25
Jonathan in England 73, 79–80

Kasson, Joy 164
Kean, Edmund 56, 62, 71–4, 85, 95
    Othello 74, 95
Kemble, Frances Anne (Fanny) 61, 65, 86, 99, 106, 126–7, 129, 185, 204
Kemble, John M. 168
Keyes, Alicia 212
Kingsley, Charles, *The Roman and the Teuton* 169
Kipling, Rudyard 37, 51, 53, 104, 132–3, 141
Kramer, Paul 169, 174
Ku Klux Klan 130–1

LaFeber, Walter 171
Lambert, John 95
Langtry, Lillie 82, 88, 90
late-Victorian philology 34–8
Lee, Samuel 19
Legard, Allayne Beaumont 144–5, 173, 192–3
Leigh, Frances Butler, *Ten Years on a Georgia Plantation Since the War* 126–7
Leigh, James Wentworth 104
Leland, Charles Godfrey 177
Lewis, George 42, 58
Lewis, John Delaware 110, 122
Liebler Company 91
Lindfors, Bernth 95
literary war 12
Livingstone, David 124
Livingstone, Robert 124
Lodge, Henry Cabot 54, 169–70, 199
Longfellow, Henry Wadsworth, *The Song of Hiawatha* 160

Index

Long, George William 218
Long, John Joseph 217
Lorimer, Douglas 114
Lott, Eric 107
Lounsbury, Thomas R. 47–8, 54
Lowell, James Russell, *The Bigelow Papers* 28, 181, 188
Lyell, Charles 61–2
lynchings and lynch-law 131–2

MacDonald, Joyce 95
Mackay, Charles, *Life and Liberty in America* 32–3, 42, 46, 106, 113, 133, 159
Mackie, John H. 189
Mackintosh, Will B. 178
Macrae, David 127
Macready, William Charles 62, 73–6, 86, 112, 229 n.31
Maitland, Frederic William, *The Constitutional History of England* 169
March, Francis A. 41
Marcy, Randolph Barnes, *The Prairie Traveler, A Hand-Book for Overland Expeditions* 138
Marryat, Frederick, *A Diary in America* 24, 30, 36
Marsh, George Perkins 36
Mathews, Charles 72–4, 78–80, 93, 95, 102–3, 105, 237 n.54
    A Trip to America 73–5
Mawson, Christopher Orlando Sylvester, *Roget's Thesaurus* 51, 101
Mayhew, Henry 106–7
Mayo, Frank 156
McCloskey, James J., *Across the Continent* 156
McDowell, Mary Anne 130
McKinley, William 197
Medley, Julius George 129
Medley, Thomas P. 163
Mencken, H. L., *The American Language* 22, 51, 54
Messiter, Charles Alston, *Sport and Adventures among the North-American Indians* 162
Miller, Joaquin 143, 156
Milton Hill 3, 199, 201–11, 215, 218
Money, Edward, *The Truth About America* 153
Moody, Dwight L. 42
Morgan, Francesca 175–6
Morris, Maurice O'Connor, *Rambles in the Rocky Mountains* 156
mother country 5–6, 11, 15, 24–5, 34, 41, 55, 58, 78, 82, 155, 176, 178, 183, 189–91, 198, 209, 212
Motley, John Lathrop 181
Muirhead, James Fullerton 183, 188
Muir, John 177
Mundella, A. J. 47
Murphy, John Mortimer 158, 161
Murray, Amelia Matilda 122
Murray, Charles 61, 168
Murray, James 41, 202

Nash, Wallis 161
National Theater 65
National Trust, in Britain 177, 188
native American 26–7, 31, 34, 98–9, 139, 151, 157–8, 160–3, 165, 167–8, 232 n.98
Naushon Island 201
Naylor, Robert Anderton 103
Neal, John 79, 252 n.30
"Negroisms" 31, 51, 99, 101
Newcastle Weekly Chronicle 48
New English Dictionary 31, 36, 40–1
New Mexico 131, 148, 151–2, 154, 171
Nicholl, Edith 131, 152
The Nonconformist 114
Nordhoff, Charles, *California: For Health, Pleasure, and Residence* 142

O'Brien, Hugh 196
O'Connell, Daniel 195–6
Ogilvie, John, *Imperial Dictionary* 22, 41
Olmsted, Frederick Law 176–7, 181, 190
Olney, Richard 169
O'Sullivan, John L. 192
Otte, T. G. 188
Oxford 19–20, 39, 184–6, 208, 210

Parkinson, Richard 43
Park Street Theater 55, 58, 62, 64, 80, 93–4, 106
Patten, Claudius 177, 185
Payne, John Howard 84
Peabody, George 178, 251 n.19
Pender, Rose 104, 160
Pershing, John Joseph 171, 174, 250 n.165
Philippine Insurrection of 1899–1902 171
Philological Society in London 34
philology 14, 16–17, 26–7, 32
    Anglo-Saxon 168
    fin de siècle 47–54
    late-Victorian 34–8
    transatlantic 33–4
Pickering, John 26–7
    A Vocabulary, or Collection of Words and Phrases Which Have Been Supposed to Be Peculiar to the United States 27
Pidgeon, Daniel 186
Pierpont, Francis Harrison 127
Pilgrims Societies 175
Pocock, Roger 131
Power, Tyrone 67
Price, Stephen 62, 94
pronunciation 12, 14, 16–18, 20, 24, 31–3, 35–6, 47–8, 52, 57, 80, 84, 217
Puck 155, 182
pure English 11, 17

Index

Puritans 25, 57, 72, 189, 202
Putnam, George Palmer 194

Quarterly 11–12

race and racism 96–8, 101, 119, 126, 129, 136, 149
   American language 98–101
   American West 156–62
   blackface minstrel 105–9
   blackness 93–5, 107–9
   British travelers and black Americans 101–5
   "negro/negroisms" 31, 51, 97–108, 110–11, 114–17, 120–31, 157–8
   racial difference 95, 115, 119, 214
   radical Reconstruction, failure of 98, 100
   slave auction 112–14
Rae, William Fraser 49, 189
ranch/ranching 145, 148–54, 211
Rawnsley, Canon Hardwicke 177
Red Indian 139, 145, 156–7, 159, 161–5
Reform Acts 58
Reid, Mayne, *The Quadroon* 3, 117, 139, 145, 163
Rennel, James 12
Rice, Thomas Dartmouth 102–3, 105–7, 109, 115
Richardson, Charles, *A New Dictionary of the English Language* 21
Roach, Joseph 163
Roberts, Cecil 193
Roberts, Percy 182
Robins, Elizabeth 87
Rose, George 61
Royal Geographical Society 158
Royce, George Monroe 182
Royle, Edwin Milton, *The Squaw Man* 160–1
Rush, Benjamin, "Plan of a Federal University" 17
Russell, William Howard 53, 123

Salisbury, Lord 172
San Francisco 49, 53, 55, 70, 89, 135–42, 160, 173, 177, 243 n.15
Sankey, Ira D. 42
Saturday Club 208
Saunders, William 127–8
Scully, William 149
Second Great Awakening in America 18
Second Reform Act 82
Second World War 52, 178
Senior, Nassau W. 116–17
Shakespeare, William 32, 56, 58, 60, 87, 90, 92–3, 172, 176, 184–5, 188, 208–9, 213, 216–17
   Hamlet 56, 75, 93
   Othello 85, 95
   Richard III 71
Shaw, George Bernard
   Caesar and Cleopatra 55
   Pygmalion 54–5

Shay's rebellion 16
Sheridan, Richard B., *Pizarro* 94
Sheridan, Thomas 17–19, 36
Silliman, Benjamin 12, 184
Simpson, Edward 62
Smith, Goldwin 130, 241 n.150
Smith, James McCune 238 n.97
Smith, W. H. 50
Society for Pure English 49, 54
Sothern, Edward Askew 78
Southerne, Thomas 93
Southern provincialisms 31, 98
Spanish-American War 47, 169, 171, 215
Spender, Harold 53
stage-Yankee 73, 77–82, 84–5
Stamer, William 127
Stamp Act 75
Stanford, Leland 176
Stanley, Henry Morton, *How I Found Livingstone* 133
Stanton, Elizabeth Cady 182
star system 60–1, 73
Stead, W. T., *Pall Mall Gazette* 50
Steevens, George Warrington 132
Stephen, Leslie 133
Stevenson, Andrew 21
Stevenson, Robert Louis 133, 139–42, 159
   Across the Plains 140
   The Amateur Emigrant 140, 159
   The Silverado Squatters 140
Stirling, James, "Wall Street 'mammonism'" 46, 102
Stoddard, John L. 181, 189
Stone, John Augustus, *Metamora: or, The Last of the Wampanoags* 75
Stowe, Harriet Beecher, *Uncle Tom's Cabin* 3–4, 68, 77, 104–5, 107, 109, 111–17, 124–5, 132, 193
Strong, George Templeton 193
Strong, Josiah 169–70
Sturge, Joseph 42, 44
Sulgrave Manor 187–9
Sullivan, Arthur 78, 83, 88, 153, 198
   H.M.S. Pinafore 88
   The Mikado 88
   Patience 88
   The Pirates of Penzance 88
Swain, William 208

Tamarkin, Elisa 4, 190, 192–4
Tarkington, Booth 155
Taylor, Tom, *Our American Cousin* 77–8
Thackeray, Richmond 122
Thackeray, William Makepeace 113, 121–2, 128
   The Virginians 128
Theatrical Syndicate, Frohman 92
Tocqueville, Alexis de 56

Index

Tooke, Horne, *The Diversions of Purley* 16–17
tourist itineraries 136–55
Townshend, Frederick 159
Townshend, Samuel Nugent 150, 152, 157
transatlantic business 89–92
Trollope, Anthony, *The Way We Live Now* 45, 123
Trollope, Frances, *Domestic Manners of the Americans* 30, 42–3, 61, 74, 80, 105, 137
Tucker, Albert M. 40
Turner, Lorenzo Dow 99
Turner, Sharon, *History of the Anglo-Saxons* 168
Twain, Mark 51–2, 133, 139
    Life on the Mississippi 51–2
    A Tramp Abroad 181
Tyler, George Crouse 89–91

Vanbrugh, John, *The Provoked Husband* 57
Van Wyck, Robert Anderson 198
Victoria, Queen 3, 21, 40, 67, 69, 108, 153, 180, 182, 184, 190–4, 199, 215
    death of 197–8
    Diamond Jubilee 194
    Golden Jubilee 162, 194, 196, 201
    late-Victorian Britain 155–66
    mid- and late-Victorian era 119–33
Vivian, Henry Hussey 161

Wakefield Herald 46, 161
Walker, David, *An Appeal to the Coloured Citizens of the World* 112
Wallack, Henry John 64–5, 93–4, 96
Wallack, James William 64–5, 93–4
Wallack's Theater 65–6
Walsh, Robert 11, 220 n.4
Waters, Hazel, *Racism on the Victorian Stage* 96, 114, 234 n.5
"The Wearing of the Green" 69–70
Webster, Noah 14–22, 24–5, 27–9, 34, 36, 40–1, 46, 48, 52, 56–7, 71, 98, 168
    American Dictionary of the English Language 18, 21–2, 27–9
    A Compendious Dictionary of the American Language 17–18

Dissertations on the English Language 16
A Grammatical Institute of the English Language 15–16
Sketches of American Policy 15
Wemyss, Francis 62–3, 73
Wentworth-Fitzwilliam, Charles 144
Western America 165–6, 174
Westminster Review 52
Whibley, Charles, *American Sketches* 47, 49
White, Richard Grant 32, 36, 38–40, 52–3, 100, 185
    Every-Day English 39
    Words and Their Uses 39
Whitley, John Robinson 163
Whitman, Walt 94, 141, 182, 193
    Leaves of Grass 141
Whitney, William Dwight 34
Wignell, Thomas 62, 79
Wilde, Oscar 88, 103, 141–3
    The Importance of Being Earnest 92
Wild West 59, 84, 138, 146, 157, 162–6, 214
Williams, Barney 67
Wilson, David 200
Wilson, Harry Leon, *Ruggles of Red Gap* 155
Wilson, Herbert W. 173
Wilson, Woodrow 177, 188
Winter, William 91, 185
Winthrop, John 194, 202
Witherspoon, John Knox 24–5
Wolf Club 73
Wolf, Lucien 173
Wolseley, Garnet 124
Worcester, Joseph E., *Dictionary* 47–8
Wortley, Lady Emmeline Stuart 61, 103
Wright, Frances 29
Wrobel, David 135, 181
Wyndham-Quinn, Windham Thomas 145

Yelverton, Theresa 129–30
Yokota, Kariann 4
Yule, Henry, *Hobson-Jobson* 50

Zincke, Foster Barham 45, 124